Corridors of Pain

Cecilia V. Gomez Andersen

Eloquent Books
New York, New York

Eloquent Books
An imprint of AEG Publishing Group
845 Third Avenue, 6th Floor—6016
New York, NY 10022
http://www.eloquentbooks.com

ISBN: 978-1-60693-311-4, 1-60693-311-6
Printed in the United States of America
Book Design: Bruce Salender

Dedication

FOR ROGER

WITH ALL MY LOVE
—THE LITTLE ONE

In Memory of my parents,
Victor Gomez Sr. and Isidra Villalva Gomez.

My oldest brother, Alvaro Gomez, Sr.,
and my youngest brother, Victor Gomez, Jr.

My cousin, Almanzur Gomez Villalva,
whose lives have touched mine deeply in
War and in Peace.

Author's Note

This book is dedicated to my husband, Roger R. Andersen, who believes in my individuality enough to insist that I use my maiden name along with my married name so I could keep my own identity. Roger always believed I could write with power and authority and encouraged me to publish no matter what the odds were.

The truth is often stranger than fiction. When I told Roger that we lived in the swamps for four long years during the Japanese occupation in southern Negros Occidental in the Philippines in World War 1I, I thought that sometimes he, as did the other friends I often told the stories to, was somewhat stunned or overwhelmed. At some point, I decided to write about my experience to make them come alive and be more convincingly real. I remember the bombing of *Ilog* that I wrote about in the prologue and the subsequent life in the swamps. Although I was a young girl then, the experience of roaming in the heart of the swamps with my brother, Victor, searching for *barasbaras* saplings to use for building the huts we lived in as we moved from one place to another in the swamps, the difficulty of staying alive, and the deprivations we suffered are seared in my memory. Before I wrote about what we went through in this book, I used to entertain my American friends and neighbors about the fun and the horrors of living in the swamps. Who can ever really believe life can be lived under such conditions? We did live like water gypsies. We had to move many times, sometimes once in three weeks, to avoid capture by the Japanese. We worked hard to make our homes as comfortable as we could. We enjoyed fishing with safety pins as hooks; we used our toes to root seashells from the riverbanks. We went barefoot most of the time. My brother built a fish trap; fish and seashells were our main diet and we traded salt and shrimp paste for rice in unoccupied territory. *Ilog* never surrendered to the Japanese and was razed to the ground. The ancestral home my grandfather built, the one I knew when I was a child, burned with the town.

After the war, when I graduated from Silliman University, I was fortunate to meet a Fulbright exchange professor from Cedar Rapids, Iowa. He heard me speak in a conference of English teachers and asked if I was interested in graduate studies in the U.S. Of course I was interested, but who could afford it at teachers' salary in the Philippines? He said there were other ways and he told me how to apply for the

Fulbright Exchange Scholarship. I competed for it, and that opportunity changed my life forever.

My husband is one of those "black and white" people who look ahead and stick to their guns as though nothing can ever change what they have planned. With my background in the war on the other hand, I see change in every bend in my life. I believe one has to gracefully accept that to change one's mind is often imperative. To alter plans is not being wishy-washy but being strong-minded and determined to chart success. For people like me, accepting change as a challenge is a philosophical climate of mind. It is a gatepost for altering a pointless course. This need for change has especially worked well for my publishing problems. If I didn't change course, this book might never have seen publication. But to return to the swamps . . . .

Because my family chose not to surrender to the Japanese, we had to live in hiding in the swamps. Indeed we had to move farther and farther into the swamps after a narrow escape from a Japanese raid. Fortunately, they dared not follow us deep into the mangrove jungle because getting in and out was a dangerous maneuver. However, *Corridors of Pain* is not autobiography. It isn't a historical novel either. I researched the facts about the B-29 at the Pima Air Museum in Tucson, Arizona. I brought our houseguests to the air museum because it is a tourist attraction. I got curious when I talked to war veterans who volunteered to welcome guests to the museum so I bought booklets about the planes used in World War II. Historically, the Philippines was not the route for the B-29 during the war so I invented the reason why there was this particular B-29 crash. I was set in having nine survivors so I could chart three different routes that would incorporate the horrors of rape, torture, narrow escape, and also the amazing chance to fall in love with women who helped in their rescue.

In 2004, Roger and I thought we would retire in the Philippines. We lived in Dumaguete, Negros Oriental in a subdivision called Monte Mar (literal translation from Spanish is mountain/sea). Our front yard faced the mountains and our back porch looked down on the sea. I simply had to look down on Tannon Strait, the body of water that separates the tip of the island of Cebu from Negros, and imagine the sea encounters in the book.

Roger got sick and had to return to the U.S. for treatment. I stayed for two more months to take care of household matters and had the opportunity to travel with friends to the foothills of Canlaon Volcano in the heart of the island of Negros. I roamed through beautiful mountain forests and valleys. I walked under the oldest tree in the Philippines. Science Departments of both University of the Philippines and Silliman University determine it is 1,237 years old. Then I went to *Bacolod* to meet my niece, Carla P. Gomez, who is managing editor of the *Visayan Daily Star*, a daily newspaper published in *Bacolod* City, capital of Negros Occidental. She took me to a special museum that houses endangered species preserved by donations from wealthy patrons. They bought the land housing these birds and animals in the heart of the city of *Bacolod*. I interviewed the curator of the museum and took notes about deforestation in Negros. The next day, my niece was covering an interesting local event and while we were in the courthouse she showed me notes on Papa Isio, a revolutionary leader, and his exploits during the war with Spain in the 19th century. I took the notes to Dumaguete and had some fun weaving the setting that I visited in Canla-on, the details describing the endangered species in *Bacolod,* and the exploits of a revolutionary leader into the chapter titled "Covenant with the Mountain." I could not use Papa Isio in the time frame of my story so I invented *Toto* Isio, a grandson. *Toto* is a word in the Visayan language used to indicate diminutive stature, so someone either very small or very young. I also invented Lt. Matsuki, the B.S. Biology graduate from Tokyo University, so I could use the facts about the birds and the animals from the museum of endangered species into the book. I could not quite dismiss the facts I learned from the curator of that museum.

Though I used real names of some members of my family, I used them for fictional characters and a plot that is pure fiction. I hope those who recognize their names will not feel offended by the fictional characters they represent. Often, they are glorified, but they are made human by some faults. I like to say that this book is pure fiction based on probable fact.

Japanese cruelty in World War II in the Philippines is undeniable. The historical fact is that the Japanese killed more than 100,000 non-combatant Filipinos in the Philippines in World War II. The resistance in Bata-an lasted six months longer that the Japanese anticipated. Perhaps this is basis for the unforgivable cruelty of the Bata-an Death March? The *Kempetai*, Filipino collaborators, are as real as the Quislings in Europe. I also had to imagine their role in the action. I created the top Japanese officers, vicious characters who craved power over life and death, and minor Japanese officers whose potential for compassion had to be cancelled because the cruel ones blotted their power to exercise it.

The American airmen are also a fictional creation. I heard there was an American pilot who came back after the war to marry a Filipina sweetheart. That is a probable fact, but the Luzuriagas (although there is such a name in southern Negros) are purely fictional. So are the Gatuslaos. Some names may be real but the characters are purely fictional. I had to illustrate the fact of Filipino hospitality with a fictional account. One day in Tucson a real estate salesperson came to our house to discuss business with my husband. He introduced himself as Joe West and almost apologetically said, "with this name how American could I be?" I told him I was writing a book about American airmen and immediately asked him if I could use his name for one of the airmen in my novel. "I would he honored," was the instant reply.

The Villalva-Gomez clan is as close as I could get to autobiography, but then again, it is fact woven into fiction, not fiction rooted on fact.

The Associated Press, Friday, June 6, 2008 reported that J.K. Rowlings, creator of Harry Potter, delivered a commencement address at Harvard University. My niece-in-law, Maina Gomez, is one of the graduates addressed in this commencement. She finished an M.A in Information Technology, Software Engineering concentration, at Harvard. Respect for the value of education in human life extends far in the Gomez clan. In her commencement speech, J. K. Rowlings paid tribute to the power of the imagination as a "uniquely human capacity to envision that which is not." She says it is "the fount of all invention" and is "arguably the most transformative and revelatory capacity." It is "the power that enables us to empathize with humans whose experience we have never shared." So it is that I pay tribute to my readers' imagination to share the experience in the swamps with those who had to endure living there for four long years, and with those who were taken there for temporary refuge until they could rendezvous with a submarine that would take them to greater safety, and even with those who sought to destroy this refuge because of their inhuman need to exercise unlimited power over life and death.

This is a story that needed to be told.

Cecilia V. Gomez Andersen

Table of Contents

Prologue—The Swamps and Beyond

Whenever pain and disappointment struck, Delia's mind did somersaults. It flashed backward and forward, sometimes with vivid pictures in muddied memories wrapped in a blur of feeling. Her mind moved fluidly through remembered, though dissociated events tracing back to her teenage years in the swamps and her years in school after the war.

In the kitchen nook where she dumped her junk mail everyday, the telephone cord coiled like the shallow, narrow waterways, running haywire from the main trunk of the *Ilog* River into the swamps. The town of *Ilog* sits on a promontory where the *Ilog* River forks into two branches that flow into the sea.

In the swamps where Delia and her family were forced to flee, corridors of water choked with swamp growth curved into muddy coves. Giant mangroves stretched their branches overhead, enormous roots splitting in several sections though supporting a single trunk. When Delia and her brother, Victor, hacked away the undergrowth and planed the roots at the base into a smooth surface with sharp *bolos,* long sharp machetes, they created a makeshift landing platform jutting into the water canal. This made unloading their belongings, leftovers in the last get-away flight, more manageable. Small outrigger *bancas* floated snuggly on this platform at high tide; it dropped a meter when the tide was low. Everyone, even Delia's two small nephews, Alvaro Jr. and Arturo, can jump from the *banca* onto the landing and deftly avoid the mud at high tide.

Brackish water covered the low-lying swampy areas at high tide. The roots of the giant mangrove trees protruded through the earth like fingers clutching the salt-soaked clay, mashing it like hands that knead dough into bread; then the smell of the moldy mud drove Delia crazy. Once, she unhooked the outriggers of the *banca,* lay quietly in the beveled bottom, and drifted down to the open river before Victor could pull her back into the dark cove.

"Are you out of your mind?" he chided. "Did we pick this place to hide, so you could be out in the open for those Jap planes to spot?" He took the rope on Delia's *banca* and pulled it past his. "Haven't we moved enough to suit you? How many times this month? Count, dumbhead; if you don't care for yourself, maybe you would for the rest of the family. Can't you see how exhausted we are?"

"Oh, please stop scolding," Delia pleaded, paddling back with him to the cove. "I know the rules as well as you do, but I can't stand the smell. Where else could I go without getting crazy with the nasty smell?"

Understanding her problem, Victor took her and their nephews to the sea where at low tide miles of white sand sparkled in the moonlight. With small wooden buckets, they scooped sand into a *banca* and filled it to the brim. Working back to the cove with the rising tide, they swung their paddles in unison, singing lustily to a rhythm, unafraid, for at evening time the sound could not warn a spying ear. They avoided going in daylight and made only three trips daily. The daily trips took care of the mud and the smell in two weeks. The sun baked the sand dry and the smell of mud faded into the surrounding distance. The task exhausted them, but it was the best thing for fun between early dusk and dark evenings. *Banca* after *banca* load of white sand dumped on the ground in the hideout turned it firm enough to walk on.

Sometimes, Delia and Victor removed outriggers, pushed a *banca* into narrow waterways and wandered deep into the swamps. Razor sharp roots of mangrove trees cut into their bare feet, but Victor's experienced eye saw where roots parted wide enough for the *banca* to slide through. Days of aimless paddling led them to a spot where giant mangrove trees shaded straight, slender *barasbaras* saplings. They had managed entry into a *barasbaras* grove! These trees, only two inches in diameter, grew three meters high. Where they were thickest, they clung together and formed a wall of bark without branches. Reaching no higher than the mangrove arches that sheltered them from sunlight, their round trunks shut straight and had leaves only at the top. They cut and scraped this priceless find. Tied with rattan vines and secured on bamboo supports, these trees made ideal flooring and walls for the small huts in the hideout. They would come back to this spot again and again.

This day, Delia piled the slender stalks to the brim of the *banca*. She crouched at one end and Victor sat at the other end to maintain perfect balance, careful not to tip the precious cargo into the shallow waterway. Barely ten, she nevertheless expertly handled the *bolo,* picked the two-inch diameter trunk, and made a quick estimate it was long enough to lie in the hull of the *banca*. With a sure eye, she struck the base of the *barasbaras* trunk with a single blow. The blade cut at a sharp angle, severed the trunk, but sliced the mud a foot in depth. Blotches of oozy liquid splattered on her blouse. The dark black stain made her scream a piercing resonance coming from deep inside, splintering the silence of the trees. Terror lingered in the sound, floated in the air, and traveled in the brain, painting, in an instant, the same picture she had seen but thought she only dreamt.

* * *

The scorching sun was blinding. Her tears flowed unchecked. She could see only the boot, polished, shiny, moving a step at a time as though marching to a military command. She couldn't turn far enough to see the whole figure. Her head, tied tightly to something, made movement excruciating and impossible. Her hands were pinned behind; she stood on a mound of dirt, freshly dug. Red ants crawled on her already weak legs. The enormous welts throbbed. She had been standing in the same position for nearly half a day. From the height of the afternoon sun, she figured it must be 2:00 o'clock. They were made to stand here at nine in the morning; she had heard a clock chime the time from the building closest to her. Good God! Had it been that long already? She could no longer feel her arms and her lips were dry and cracked. She could taste the salt from the tears; when she licked her lips, the cracks burned and seared.

The boot stopped moving. In broken English, a raspy voice sharply ordered.

"Bow head over hole. Bow low. No look up."

A bayonet was dropped in an empty hole next to her foot; it sank almost to the hilt. Then a hand retrieved it and a voice said something in rapid Japanese. The boot moved three paces at a time. Each time it paused in front of a hole, the same swift blow that felled her *barasbaras* sapling severed a head. It dropped directly into the hole below. Deep black liquid blew into the air like a geyser, and as it flowed down, the color changed from black, to purple, and soaked the dirt red at her feet.

Women and children standing behind the men with bowed heads screamed in unison. Farther down the row, a man managed to get loose. He ran straight for the eight feet wire fence. A spurt of machine gun fire broke the sound of the screams. Then she saw the body hanging inert. The blood flowed black, purple, and red as it emptied from the perforated body, toe to up-side-down head, the way their cook would hang a chicken and let the blood drain into an empty pan. Gunfire close to the feet of the anguished melee cut the screams neatly. A painful silence blanketed all sound. That was always the way the dream ended.

* * *

Victor held Delia's limp body shaking from uncontrolled sobs subsiding into a low moan. He knew what she was seeing again because he was there in the end. He loosened the rigid fingers around the handle of the *bolo* and sat her on top of the logs they had piled. He poured her a drink of warm water that quieted the sobs and the moaning. Automatically, they started scraping the leaves from cut trees scattered around the clearing.

What Delia vividly saw at this instant periodically recurred as a dream. She would wake up in a sweat, screaming. She frightened the matron in the university dormitory with these piercing screams. She loved this fat, kindly, middle-aged woman with a wart on her nose. She came down from her room, a floor above Delia's. Delia looked at the thermos bottle for relief. The hot tea the matron always carried and made Delia drink settled her nerves. In the early morning hours, she roused the row of eight beds of young girls in Delia's room, made them kneel, join hands in a circle and pray. Superstitious, she believed the spirit of dead war victims killed in the building before it was converted into a girls' dormitory at Silliman University haunted Delia. The victims died violent deaths at the hands of Japanese soldiers. They were doomed to visit the place of their tragic death. The haunting, the matron figured, came to Delia because she was highly sensitive, a gift that singled her from the rest of the girls. She admired this gift, but she feared for Delia.

At Silliman University in Dumaguete, Negros Oriental, Philippines after the war, Delia laced her academic program with participation in sports. She joined the swimming team, was elected captain of both the volleyball team and track and field unit. Enjoying all the pleasurable activities, Delia thought she had slipped into another corridor of time, skirting around and beyond the terror of the war years; but the tangle of events that scarred her younger years, clogged, as the lush swamp growth did, even this pleasant extension of time. Four long years of a senseless war lay at the murky base of the unconscious. This base served as a lens through which she saw what lay underneath the interplay of time from which she could draw, at will, the substance at the core of her life at any given age.

After long school hours in Dumaguete, Victor often took Delia out of the dormitory to eateries in town for afternoon snacks. When his monthly allowance ran out, Delia paid for movies they both enjoyed. The musicals and the romances sometimes ran out and there were only war movies that disturbed Delia. Once, she saw the beginning of a movie about Pearl Harbor. She walked out of the movie house before she knew what she was doing. The sound of bombs dropping dredged out so many war memories she thought she had forgotten.

* * *

She dragged her nephews, Alvaro and Arturo, two and four years old, away from the fire as fast as their little legs can manage. The town burned from incendiary bombs dropped by planes flying so low they almost touched the roofs of two-story houses. The blaze traveled swiftly and rumor was that the Japanese were already at the north edge of town for a complete takeover. Delia was playing with the kids when the bombing started. No one knew where anybody was, nor did they know what to do except to run away from the burning inferno. People were dodging debris flying above their heads as bombs hit their targets. Some were desperate enough to stay and take away what hadn't burned. Truth of the matter was, six months after World War II started in the Philippines, Bata-an, in the large island of Luzon, had just surrendered to the invading Japanese troops. The Philippine army defended Bata-an for a long six months but the Japanese, with superior forces, thought they'd overwhelm the defenders within a matter of weeks, days even. It maddened them that it took so long before a complete surrender. But after six months, General Jonathan Wainwright, in charge of the Philippine army after General Douglas McArthur fled to Australia, was forced to give up. They incarcerated him in Santo Thomas University in Manila. Then they came down from island to inhabited island of over seven thousand islands in the entire Philippine archipelago to physically enforce the policies of the East Asia Co-Prosperity Sphere.

"If you resist," they announced, "we'll bomb your towns, create chaos, and demand complete surrender."

The bombing and the chaos had just started in *Ilog*. Civilians fled the town. They had no idea what to do to get away from the planes, the fire, and the incoming Japanese. Instinct dictated to run and hide, where else but to the swamps! To get to the swamps, they needed to cross a bridge.

Delia was several meters shy of it when the Japanese planes circled and used their machine guns on people filling it.

At the sound of the guns, Delia fell flat in a ditch, a nephew on each side of her. She tried to gather them under her own body, putting her hands over their eyes. With her face on the ground she didn't see but only felt the rain of warm, thick blood falling on her body, drenching her and soaking the boys underneath.

Children crying, adults yelling and dodging bullets pushed to get across. Every foot of the long bridge was covered with bodies. Frenzied survivors climbed on fallen people and soaked in the blood of the dying. Delia heard the constant splash of victims falling into the water below. The river turned red from the blood of the wounded and the dying. The event seemed like target practice for the pilots of two unopposed Japanese planes. In ten minutes of fun for the gunners, terror reigned below. She tried vainly to protect her nephews from the horrible sight. For her, for them, for all who survived, what took place was an unparalleled experience in terror. The carnage rocked the entire town. Nothing like this had ever happened in *Ilog* before, but it would happen again and again after this first baptism in horror.

After the planes left, grieving relatives combed the bridge for their own wounded, dying, or dead. The stench of death permeated. From this first experience in terror, Delia would pass from anguish to paralyzing anger. She would come to terms with hunger and violence. Yet, despite their helpless plight and the certainty of Japanese domination, it was for Delia and her entire clan a period of fierce nationalism, the more intense because it couldn't find effective expression.

The Japanese used force to hold the countryside in an iron grip. They exacted servitude and forced obedience on bended knee. Using the butt of the gun, they demeaned the spirit. They rammed butts of guns against a jaw, pressed it at the nape of the neck, or broke a nose at a mere twitch. They pulled the head down to the level of a permanent bow as though to straighten it were to allow it to strike instantaneously like a deadly cobra. For the Japanese, the bow was the sign of submission and respect. Actually, bending made it impossible for victims to see where the butt of the gun would land: on the head, forehead, shoulders, face, nose, jaw, neck, back, chest or arms, aching to lash back at the oppressor. Held back, the fury redoubled in intensity but it was rendered powerless by a force greater than it was able to resist.

* * *

After the war when Delia succeeded in obtaining a Fulbright scholarship to the U.S., the scars from the war still remained. Attending the Friendship Day celebration between the U.S. and Canada with one of her professors, she ducked and fell flat on the ground at the sound of fire works that exploded in the air and floated down harmlessly. Humiliated, she couldn't find tongue for adequate explanation. How could anyone understand the terror it brought back?

In the swamps, Delia and the boys, her cousins, sisters, aunts, and parents, were schooled to run for cover at the sound of a distant airplane engine. Primary rule: if possible, get inside the hollow trunk of the nearest giant mangrove. When she couldn't cover the distance between the strip of coconut clearing and the swamps, she had to fall flat on her face immediately and lie as still as death. Once, at the sound of an airplane, she dragged the same little boys, her nephews, toward the mangrove giants but the airplanes were of a sudden overhead. In an instant, she lay flat on the ground under a coconut tree, pressing both boys close to her own body, lying still, paralyzed with terror for the duration of the raid. The dropping bombs sounded like the fireworks at the Friendship Day celebration, but not as harmless.

The scraps that whizzed by, sharp metal fragments with rugged edges, came out of Japanese bombs that exploded. Shrapnel got stuck on the coconut tree just half a foot above their heads. Had they not been flat on the ground, they would've been perforated. During the war, death was often just a few feet away; in this instance, a few inches above. After the raid, everyone tried to locate each other. Mama Sid, Esperanza, Delia's sister, her cousins, Melcha, Sondra, and Socorro were still in the kitchen, huddled behind upturned tables. The older boys had crossed the clearing and were inside mangrove trunks. Papa was missing. Later, Victor found him. Hiding in the dense *nipa* palm grove at the edge of the river, he fell asleep. He cheated death with a nonchalance known only to those who had no fear of it. He died quietly in 1958, fourteen years after the war, days before Delia left for the U.S.

Delia seldom directly confronted what lay behind her terrors. To open the doors of understanding and protection, she always shifted back to those she loved, those who played a part in her life, be it Papa, *Manong* Alvaro or *Manong* Almanzur.

She loved *Manong* Almanzur fiercely. At the onset of the war, he was in his late twenties. A lieutenant in the guerilla forces, he led men whose families had been tortured or executed by the Japanese. His band had nothing but sawed off shotguns, *bolos*, bow and arrows, and an occasional automatic rifle taken from a dead Japanese soldier during a guerilla ambush. Known for his perfect timing, his knack to strike at the Japanese by surprise and cut them off from their main contingent, and, above all, his uncanny luck to avoid capture, he drew loyalty from men in his command. He had wavy, not black but sandy hair (no doubt inherited from a grandparent of Spanish blood) kept in check by a headband, a large, flowered, folded, kerchief that his loving wife, *Manang* Pilar, sewed so she could identify him at a distance whenever he chanced to return to the swamps. It became his trademark. His men knew it was more than a band to keep the hair from the eyes. It covered an ugly scar from a deep bayonet wound in a hand-to-hand combat in one of his earliest ambushes. He had thin lips that curved into an attractive smile; a naughty spark in his eyes held women and men captive. He told lusty stories he embellished with hand gestures and with a hearty laugh.

Delia was little more than eight, and her nephews were barely two and four when they first lived on the riverbank at the edge of the swamps. *Manong* Almanzur would grab the boys by the arms, toss them in the air, one at a time, catch them and throw them into the river. He knew they hadn't learned to swim yet, but with a hearty bellow he yelled.

"Hey, boys, use your legs and kick for dear life. If you feel like sinking, hold your head under water and paddle with your hands and feet as hard as you can. Get to the river bank fast, or you'll be in trouble."

The boys swallowed a lot of water and their heads bobbed in and out of the river current. Their arms and legs flailing desperately, they managed to get to the riverbank, exhausted. They would both lie there for several minutes, and *Manong* Almanzur would shout.

"That should put hair on your chest before it is time, eh, boys?"

The boys rubbed water from their eyes, spew out mouthfuls, got on their feet unsteadily, and yelled back.

"*Oy, tioy* (uncle) Manzur, don't go away; throw us in again."

Their father, *Manong* Alvaro, tried not to show his anxiety Although his chest filled with pride at their feat, he was ready to dive in and rescue. He never had to teach them how to swim; they learned to survive.

Delia worshipped *Manong* Almanzur's courage and his stubborn streak that suppressed any damper on his will to live. He made Delia feel that to live through the war was to endure, but one either did so with courage and resourcefulness or gave up living. He made her feel there was a lot to life worth the pain of surviving, but to survive she had to constantly push back the threshold of pain. There was that time, for instance, when he rescued her from certain death.

* * *

Her neck tied tightly to a fence, she looked on with unbearable agony from one side of her head. Heads fell into holes at the swift blow of a samurai that snapped lives at an accurate angle. The bodies lay wriggling like headless chickens ready for the pot. A few women wrenched themselves free of the rope that tied them to the fence. They knelt down, put their arms around a headless torso and wailed their grief. A few Japanese soldiers walked away from the scene. Delia speculated these may be ones not entirely without compassion, but as she looked at those who remained, she stared at a wall of deadened humanity, without a tinge of guilt for the savage act just done.

How can harmless civilians deserve such punishment? Here were people just like her who helped themselves to a few sacks of sugar. How can human lives be worth less than ant-infested sacks of sugar stored in a damp warehouse? She had a hard time scraping ferocious ants out of a small bag she filled with sugar to take away before Japanese motorcycles and trucks loaded with armed troops roared in.

Now the Japanese were faced with the problem of disposing of the headless corpses. They dragged, pushed and kicked the wailing women out of their way. An argument ensued among officers looking on the bloody mess with disgust. Some untied the women from the fence and ordered them to dig a mass grave. They were in the process of untying the children as well. The bow-legged boot with the samurai walked straight for Delia. He lifted his sword to cut the rope tying her to the fence. Delia closed her eyes, anticipating the weight of the sword about to end her life. An instant wave of final farewell dimmed her consciousness.

The samurai fell from the officer's hand; a bullet hit him dead center on the forehead. All at once, lighted arrows tipped with rags dipped in coconut oil flew into the rafters of the warehouse. More arrows flew straight to the row of gasoline tanks below the officers' quarters. The explosion sent soldiers scrambling to douse the flames. Sounds of single fire rifles silenced screaming women.

Delia dimly knew what happened. She felt the tug at her swollen neck as the rope that chained her with the rest of the children snapped. Gunfire hit some of the fleeing women and children. The screaming dazed Delia; she didn't know what to do. Groping to help some women crawling and bleeding from bullet wounds, she felt a hand grab her arms and heard desperation in Victor's voice.

"There's no time to lose; run with me as fast as you can.

They ran into what was once a sugar cane field now fallow except for tall, wild *kogon* grass covering it in thick clumps everywhere. Where the grass was sparse and short, they crawled on their bellies. Machine gun fire trailed their progress through the grass. Guerrilla soldiers ran behind and beside them. Hearing the agonized groan of one falling close to them, Victor turned, grabbed the man's arm and whispered for Delia to take the other. They pulled him where the grass was thickest. She had no way of knowing how long they lay there playing dead, without moving a muscle, hearing at close range the tramping of heavy boots and the urgency of guttural Japanese commands.

"Here. There. Over there. Comb the area," the voice seemed to say.

She lay still underneath the *kogon* grass. Though a thick-soled boot stomped on the fingers of one hand, she gritted her teeth and never uttered a sound. Then she heard the call of a swamp dove.

"Here?" She wondered. "No. This is too far away from the swamps for that," she thought; but she trembled with anticipation.

Then an answering call came, ten, maybe fifteen meters away. Victor rose to his knees and crawled toward the sound. *Manong* Almanzur was there, inching out of thick *kogon* grass, a *bolo* on one hand, the other clutching an automatic rifle slung on his shoulder.

The swamp dove called a few more times and the grass rustled as one by one guerrilla soldiers reported their presence. What remained of the guerrilla unit lifted their injured as the group split once more and in pairs made their way toward the river's edge. Victor and Delia were separated from *Manong* Almanzur and his band. Bullets whizzed behind them, not from Japanese soldiers who had already holed back into the garrison, but from *kempetai*, Filipino collaborators, as determined as the Japanese to capture enemy guerrilla They chased the guerrilla band clear to the river and caught Delia and Victor scrambling down the riverbank.

"So, you did not run far enough, did you," a tall, shirtless *kempetai*, obviously the leader, smirked.

"Run, Sir?" Delia looked him straight in the eye and answered. "My brother and I heard the gunfire on our way home. We want to cross the river; we're desperate to stay away from danger."

"Liar," the man rasped. "Get over here where I can see you better."

Delia started to move to his side when she saw the glint of a *bolo* from the corner of her eye. She pulled Victor down with a hard jerk as *Manong* Almanzur's *bolo* swished in the air and hit the shirtless man on the small of his back. Four other *kempetai* ran in fear, guerrilla soldiers chasing them.

Manong Almanzur could not believe the steel in Delia's voice when she lied to the *kempetai* leader.

"Delia you sure can lie with a straight face," he said with a twinkle in his eye. "This is a long way from the swamps. What the heck is your reason for being here?" He asked her sternly.

"We ran with many others this morning when *Tia* Caring paddled a *banca* by, shouting the Japanese were leaving Central Palma for good. We haven't had sugar close to three years. I wanted to get some. We've used only honey to sweeten things. Honey is too expensive to trade with and almost impossible to get."

She was brimming with tears now so Victor finished what she wanted to say.

"I guess no one ever thought the Japanese would come back. I got here late because I was looking for a suitable container but couldn't find anything big enough. When I got near the trees, Japanese motorcycles roared in and trucks followed behind. *Tia* Caring and her husband, *Tio* Pedong, engrossed with pulling sacks of sugar, never heard the roar of the vehicles. "

Delia could not wait to add what happened after. Her tears falling freely, she interrupted Victor.

"Their motorcycles circled around. Soldiers jumped off the trucks and prodded adults and us children into a tight circle with the butts of their guns. Then they lined us by a fence. I was afraid they'd gun us down right then, but they separated children and women from the men.

Softly, she started to sob, but she continued.

"They struck men with the butts of their guns whenever they made a move. Then they gave them each a spade or a hoe to dig with and watched them while they dug holes. If a man quit digging, they hit him hard with a rifle butt. When they thought the holes were deep enough, they made them kneel behind and. . . ."

She was unable to finish.

"We know the rest." Badong had darkened his face with mud and had tied *kogon* grass on his arms and legs. More grass stuck out of his hat.

"I crawled as far in as possible. *Peste (hell)," he swore and spat out his anger.* "I wanted to shoot that bow-legged bastard with the samurai, but they would've wiped us out with their machine guns."

"So, is this trip worth the near death experience?" *Manong* Almanzur glowered at Delia.

"I don't know," she answered, "but I still have a small bag of sugar tied around my waist," She flipped the loose bodice of the now bedraggled dress and tapped at the bag hanging underneath.

Manong Almanzur's laughter broke loose and the chorus of guerrilla guffaws brought tears to Delia's eyes once more.

"I have to hand it to you, Delia. Life in the swamps without sugar certainly isn't easy to endure." *Manong* Almanzur tried to soften his disapproval. "You had that bag on you when you were tied to the fence and even when you crawled through the *kogon* grass? You're as stubborn as I am. You're my cousin all right!"

* * *

Many years later, when Delia came home from a Fulbright stint in Michigan, her nephews were grown men raising their own families. *Manong* Almanzur still had the glint in his eye and a full head of hair. The headband, now faded, kept the hair, a white pepper mesh, in place. The laughter was now a hoarse grunt. He fought against a drinking habit, but his friends always came to his defense.

"Ah, he holds his alcohol problem well," they'd say.

He still managed the farm his father left him and his three sisters. The annual yield could barely keep the farm from being repossessed by the bank. The loans, instead of funding farm equipment, paid for gambling debts, the usual losses from cock fighting, and boozing.

He bought a house in a city subdivision one hundred kilometers away from the farm. He boozed with his tenants who often visited and toasted him. With the same intense protectiveness he exhibited for men who fought with him during the war, *Manong* Almanzur catered to his tenants after the war. He sold or pawned his wife's jewelry to cover the bank debts. Living the way they did put up a false front. His most redeeming gesture was sending his kids to the best schools. After graduating from college, they collectively worked to buy the farm back from the bank. He tried always to hold his head high and bullied his sons to cut the same macho figure he held. *Manang* Pilar drew a convincing picture of submission; actually, she was a strong woman working hard behind his back to maintain financial stability. An excellent cook, she catered for the lavish parties thrown by rich *hacienderos,* extensive farm holders who pampered their wives. A solid pillar of support, she held her head high with pride and dignity.

His eldest son bore the brunt of *Nong* Manzur's emotional burden. Life played a joke on him because this son excelled in Home Economics. As excellent a cook as his mother, he baked cakes "to die for," the women said. He preserved blue ribbon jars of jelly, and knitted sweaters from complicated sweater patterns even Home Economics teachers could not follow. He turned out more feminine than his beautiful sisters, and though his father often caned him to keep him from being soft, he could only toughen himself enough to endure his father's embarrassment.

In the swamps, when *Manong* Almanzur came in and out while serving with the guerrillas, he gathered all his cousins, including young Delia and Victor and organized them into a winning rowing team. Victor was the captain, but instead of directing the course of the *banca* by sitting at the helm, he was stationed at the middle, a position requiring the strongest paddler. Delia was schooled as anchor. Though exceptionally skilled as a paddler, she was not as strong as the older ones, so she trained to put the outrigger *banca* on as straight a course as the river bends allowed. With practice, she developed a good eye to anticipate changes in the current and in the contour of the riverbed. She learned to put the paddle tightly at the side of the *banca* to move it either left or right. She could quickly shift the paddle from side to side with precision to move in either direction. Where the current was strongest, she banged on the side of the *banca* to alert the other paddlers. Holding their paddles straight instead of on a horizontal slant, they had to strike the water in unison and push the paddles straight down, almost clear to the handle, to give the *banca* the swiftest forward motion.

Delia learned how to use the paddle as a drum baton to beat perfect time, leading the team to work as one. On the team were Delia, Victor, Melcha, and Sondra, *Nong* Manzur's sisters, and Rodney, a cousin who later interned at John Hopkins hospital in Maryland while Delia was in graduate school in Detroit, Michigan, Ruperto Jr., *Inday* Choling's

(Soledad) son, and Armingol Tibus, a neighbor and the only non-family member on the team. Later, Ruperto Jr. went to Santo Thomas Medical School to become a doctor also. This rowing team was dubbed the "undefeated seven." Crews from other parts of the swamps challenged them but inevitably lost. Delia enjoyed exhilaration in victory, excitement of performance and confidence in belonging to a group of intelligent, fun-loving kin. She grew straight and slim, was flat chested and could paddle as expertly as any of the boys. In control as anchor, she paddled a straighter course than others even when the river curled, churned, and turned at unexpected bends.

When the downpour of heavy rains in the monsoon season came, water loaded with tons of topsoil from the mountains roared downriver. The river churned with mud and debris. Uprooted trees from the steep banks floated fast and upturned *bancas* that did not flow skillfully with the current.

Delia's life would take as many changes as the swampy riverbed. The unexpected turns challenged all her faculties. At the *banca* races, she anticipated all sharp bends and put to memory where they were, yet she was never assured of ease in any of the races and nothing could prepare her for the pain-filled turns that darkened the coming years.

Chapter 1—The Emergency Landing

The B-29 lost altitude fast. Both Japanese and guerrilla troops raced to see where it would crash. The Japanese were determined to find the kind of plane it was, the size of the crew, and the number, if any, that would survive the crash. The guerrillas were desperate to save the survivors from Japanese capture, torture, and certain death.

The B-29 was 99 feet in length, 27 feet 9 inches to the top of the vertical tail. It had a wingspan of 141 feet 2 inches with a combat ready weight of 135,000 pounds. The first bomber aircraft to be fully pressurized, the first with remote control turrets connected to a fuselage system, and the first to be powered by the new Wright R-3350 engine, it was the heaviest American airplane manufactured in 1942. Powered by the newly developed 2200 hp, 28cylinder Wright R 3350-13 Cyclone, the B-29 had a top speed of 375 mph, a service ceiling of 31,850 feet and a range in excess of 3,250 miles. It had a crew of eleven.

This steel fortress dragged its belly through kilometers of green fields, river mud and stones before it ripped into a wall of mango giants in an abandoned orchard between the towns of *Binalbagan* and *Isabela* in southern Negros Occidental in the Philippines. On the borders of the orchard, tall bamboo trees lined the banks of a creek flowing close to the broken down ancestral dwelling in a once proud *hacienda*. George Miller, the pilot, struggled fiercely to reduce the speed of the aircraft, trying to stay in the air without landing in water surrounding the island of Negros. He took great care not to overshoot its width. The engine had been burning for quite a while; the entire crew tried to put out the fire. Both pilots knew they had to make a crash landing.

"For God's sake, George, fly a little higher. Don't put it down on the water," Frank Defacio, the navigator, gasped. "If we drop in the water, we have no chance to get out of this steel trap."

Co-pilot Bill Bradley, who the crew called BB for short, grabbed every lever he could pull to raise the aircraft above water. "Hallelujah," he yelled, "we've just about cleared the water; everything is getting green below."

"I've dropped almost all of the fuel tanks in the water," Robert Coleman, the tail gunner was puffing heavily, "but guys, you have to drop that 20mm cannon and all the machine guns you can loosen," he yelled to the other gunners.

"Right now," BB asked urgently, "or this death trap will blow sky high with all that."

"Get back in here, BB," Valdez bellowed. "You're the only one tall enough to reach this trap door."

BB was straining. "Robert, come here and use those strong arms to hold this lever up to get us out of water," BB demanded. "George needs help here if I have to get back there."

Valdez cheered, still waving his arms wildly. With Joe West's help, he was able to dislodge the 20 mm cannon at the tail and as it fell off, it careened into a dense *nipa* palm grove at the edge of the river. A huge hole gaped as the vertical tail broke off and the control turrets on the upper fuselage blew off from extreme pressure. All the manned positions were fully pressurized. The bomb bay was not, nor was the aft fuselage between the aft turret's station and the tail gunner's compartment. Air pressure kept the tail flying, though it was cut off from the body of the aircraft. When the air pressure dissipated, the tail fell. On impact, it shredded into hundreds of metal parts scattered over the area it covered. Steve Strasner, the gunner on the upper fuselage, fell off and hit his head on a huge metal plate. His head hung on the side, his neck broken, and his body badly torn.

Debris littered the riverside. Filipino fishermen in the area picked up Marco Yablowski, the tail gunner floating in the river, and dug up Joe West, the gunner from the lower fuselage, pinned inside what remained of the vertical tail. They took the dead body of the gunner from the upper fuselage and covered it with a jute sack, laid all the bodies carefully in the bottom of a *banca* without outriggers, and covered them with *nipa* fronds. Without show of rushing, the fishermen paddled determinedly towards the swampy area at the edge of the river.

Before the tail broke off, every member of the crew heard George's warning.

"I'm trying to skirt a mountain range in the middle of this island; if I turn to the right, I'll overshoot the island and we'll be back in water on the other side. Can't go straight either or we'll nose dive into the mountain. I'm turning to the left a bit," George said evenly. The aircraft listed to the left but the green earth was coming fast.

"This is it guys," was the last thing George said before losing control.

The cockpit, like the vertical tail, broke from the body of the aircraft. The same air pressure that pushed the tail off forced the cockpit to zoom straight ahead, kept it going for about twenty kilometers before it blew up and nose-dived into the dikes of a rice paddy filled with water and soft mud. The B-29, fitted with an ERCO ball turret in the nose, spiraled onto the tallest dikes of the rice paddy just below the foothills of *Isabela*.

Two women were transplanting seedlings in the adjoining rice paddy when flames from the burning engines lighted the sky. The bodies of George and Frank blew out of the cockpit and splashed beside them. Both were unconscious. George's hair was singed; his pants were torn off from the swollen knee, the skin around red and raw. Bleeding scratches covered his arms and face. Frank had a deep gash below his left shoulder and was bleeding profusely.

"Jesus, Maria, tabangi kami," (Jesus and Mary, help us) the women prayed as they ran to the unconscious bodies.

"What can we do, *Manang* Simang," Consuelo, Simang's younger sister, stuttered.

Blood shimmered in the rice field. Shaking with fright, Simang managed an answer.

"Take off the shirt from the badly injured one and tie it tight around his shoulders to stop the bleeding," she told her sister.

They had never seen bodies as long as these before. Without hesitation, they took off their *patadiongs* (loose cotton woven skirts), tied them together and wrapped them around the airmen and, hammock-like, used them to lift the bodies from the water and mud. They dragged and half lifted their burden to their hut at the edge of the rice field adjacent the banana grove by the hillside. A ways down from the hut was a deep well hidden in the darkness of a wooded slope.

Robert's head had a big lump. He landed on soft mud about half a kilometer away from the burning cockpit. An old man found him half-conscious. Miraculously, he suffered only minor burns; his arms were singed clear to his fingers and, though he walked like a drunken sailor, his guide pushed him into an abandoned church half a kilometer away and turned him over to the local priest.

The heaviest part of the 135,000 lb. Super Fortress drifted on its own weight and moved sidewise until the monstrous steel belly lay motionless, like a huge gecko that crawled into a crack on a wall. Huge trunks of mango trees ripped the wings off the 65 feet structure before the thick clump of bamboos stopped it from moving any farther. Wild and unattended, the bamboo trees had grown high. As the aircraft plowed into its thick roots, the trunks, like long arms dropped and wrapped around it as if to cradle and hold it from harm. Like a gigantic spade the open end, where the cockpit broke off from the body, heaved soil and stones on the bank of the creek and piled it high against the mango trunks. The narrower end of this long body tipped and, like the long handle of a spade, lifted itself up and rested on the leafy branches above. A wide gash opened on each side where the wings ripped off. The forty feet tunnel running through the upper part of the bomb bays and connected the forward cabin to the aft gunner's compartment opened upward on one side. It kept the center of gravity balanced and held the long body intact.

Three airmen still in ejection gear came out of the openings on the side. All three, scrambling and yelling, tried to jump out of the burning steel trap. BB, a six feet two broad shouldered but slender athlete, desperately kicked the glass top of the manned ball turret, trying to pull a body out. A .50 caliber machine gun jammed in the ball turret pinned the body in. When BB finally kicked it loose, a flattened body was exposed. The chest had caved in from the pressure. Pounds of broken steel had crushed the skull and the blood that filled the ball turret sizzled in the fire engulfing the hole where the ball turret had loosened free. BB turned around abruptly, his teeth clenched and his eyes filled with tears.

"Son of a gun," he spat in helpless anger. "Why the hell did he have to die? Why couldn't it have been me?" He cradled the remains of his best buddy and cried unashamedly.

"Quit your bellyaching and help me get Spencer out," Romero Valdez, the Mexican-American gunner yelled at him." I don't know about you, but I think we have to get out of here pronto."

BB turned around and helped Valdez pull Spencer from the space next to the ball turret. Jagged sides on the opening scraped Spencer's burned belly. Spencer screamed in agony.

"Take it easy boys. My guts are burning; find a first aid kit. There must be one lying around." He was writhing in pain, hardly able to breathe.

"Mark's dead, you hear me?" BB said.

"Leave him be. Let's get out of here, fast," Valdez hissed.

"Can't we bury Mark first?" BB lifted the limp body from the shattered remains of the ball turret.

"Are you nuts?" Scott Rankin yelled from inside the tunnel. He was scrounging around for a first aid kit but couldn't find any. "We have no time to waste. This wreck is leaking fuel; the fuses are popping in here.

In less than twenty minutes, this blaze will spread to the lower fuselage. She's going to blow."

BB grabbed Mark's body. He still didn't want to leave it behind.

"Put that body down, or hide it behind those dense palm leaves. Grab a hold of Spencer instead. He needs more help," Scott yelled, still opening heavy doors and banging on the closet walls searching for a first aid medicine kit.

"I give up," he yelled as he dashed through the tunnel. "I can't go back any farther. I'm sure she's going to blow soon."

"Jump down. Now! Jump down, Scott," Valdez shouted, wild with fear.

* * *

The water in the creek was shallow. Cool and clear, it flowed steadily and felt good on his feet.

"Gosh, I could stay here for a while," Spencer said, wading out to the bank.

Nearer the bank, the side of the B-29 cut a two feet wide gash where the water now ran deeper than in any other part of the creek. Spencer splashed clear, cool water on his burning belly before he let out a scream. The water stung and he grabbed for support at the stones the aircraft heaved on the side of the creek. He knew he lost his balance. Much later, he realized he must have passed out because he was lying on the bank of the creek though he thought he had fallen in the water.

There were helping hands everywhere. He was certain he was pulled up the bank and he realized he was sitting behind someone on a horse. Mark's body was lying behind him, wrapped in a cotton blanket.

"Could you hold on to me tightly? We have to get out of here fast. We need to pick up another one of your crew a little farther from here," a firm, clear voice told him.

"Hey, that's Marco behind the other rider," Spencer said wondering where the heck they'd come from. "But where are the rest of the horses, and where did you find Marco?"

"This is all there is. The rest of your crew who can walk and aren't too badly wounded had to run with some of us," the voice answered urgently.

"I don't understand. Where are the rest of the guys? Where are BB, and Scott, and Valdez? Was there an explosion? Scott told us she was going to blow in twenty minutes and Scott should know," Spencer wondered, very much confused.

"We got here as fast as we could. We helped put out the popping fuses and most of the fire with cool water from the creek. The one you call Scott showed us how to get into the tunnel and cut all the burning wires," the voice said again. "Thank God for his know how." He turned and looked at Spencer.

"He couldn't cut all the wires by himself and was ready to jump, but two of your other companions, BB and Valdez, I think they were, and a few more of us, with sharp *bolos*, went back inside the tunnel with him and he showed us what wires to cut and how to cut them."

"There has been no explosion yet so we hope the Japanese won't be able to locate the plane quickly. Scott said it might take a half hour more before the whole thing will blow. We need to get out of here fast," another voice warned.

The other rider trotted beside them.

"The rest of your friends have already started running with our men. They know where to go," he assured Spencer. It was clear he was the leader.

"Let's talk as we travel," he said. "We can't go fast or we risk being heard; in fact, we can't go any faster than a steady trot. Fortunately, the sky is getting darker. We'll be lucky if it rains."

The horses trotted at a steady pace but the sky got pitch black. The leader jumped down from his horse and pulled the reins. Spencer could no longer see where they were going. The outline of the horizon moved in fast. A black wall loomed in front of them so quickly it made him lose all sense of direction. He felt they were sliding down a hillside. Darkness engulfed both horse and rider beside him; loud rumblings broke loose. Lightning flashed and cracked all around and in minutes a heavy downpour fell on their heads, hitting their backs, and shoulders. The driving rain fell hard. Spencer couldn't see, but he felt the horses' hooves slide downhill and then go up again. His burns were soaked in rainwater and he was in agony. He just let himself be taken away.

The creek now swollen with rushing muddy water made crossing almost impossible. The horses bolted and neighed so loud Spencer cringed when he saw the men tie the ropes around their mouths to keep their noise down. He turned to see the leader huddle with his men. Two men immediately sprung on the horses and rode upriver while the rest of them crept through the *nipa* palms to try to get where they were thickest before all hell broke loose.

Gunfire was bursting everywhere. BB asked for a gun; a guerrilla soldier thrust a *bolo* into his hand before he slid through the mud and disappeared. All three of them were knee-deep in mud and half buried in *nipa* fronds. Mark's dead body was rotting somewhere near; Spencer couldn't tell if the stink came from the mud or the dead body. He was sure they had been abandoned. Mud caked on his burns and it quit burning. Instead, he felt a dull, gnawing pain; he didn't know but he had passed out again.

When he came to, he thought he was being pushed into a concrete dump; the walls were narrow and straight, and he sniffed the same smell that came from Mark's rotting body; or, maybe it was the smell of the mud from the *nipa* grove by the creek. The square opening above his head was closed in with dead leaves.

"Don't try to come out; sleep or keep absolutely quiet."

He heard the same voice again. He wondered what had happened to BB and Marco; they could be dead for all he knew. He got used to the pain on his belly but now he was aware of another kind of pain. He knew he hadn't eaten in a while and his stomach started to grind. He had a splitting headache and after some time he fell into troubled sleep.

He woke up to the smell of ripe bananas; he was so hungry, he almost fainted from the smell. He was lying beside the dump he had been stuffed into. Had he been pulled out of it? He wondered. He sat up to grab the bananas, ignoring the men who obviously brought them. He ate as much as he could without retching. As his eyes got used to the dark, he couldn't believe what he saw. Were these oblong concrete cemetery stalls they had been stuffed into? There were bones all around. My God, the slight pain he felt on his side came from lying on something hard. Had he lain on top of bones all along? The smell that bothered him must have come from the bones he had been sleeping on. He felt like puking.

He saw BB and Marco talking to the leader. Spencer heard him assure BB that Mark's body could temporarily be buried here and would be recovered when circumstances permit. BB was about to say something again, but the leader fell on his knees and pulled him down. He started crawling behind the concrete stalls and motioned for Spencer, Marco and BB to do the same. Spencer took care not to crawl on his wounds. He wondered how they got here in the first place.

Spencer's knees were shaking. He distinctly heard the sound of footsteps coming deliberately toward them.

Now the jig is up, he thought. We're going to be captured after all.

He closed his eyes unable to accept the idea that after all the hiding they would have to surrender anyway. As the steps came closer, the leader got up from behind a stall and whispered softly.

"Everything's okay. These are the rest of my men."

Two guerrilla soldiers came to report that the men on horses raced toward the hills; they had jumped off the horses and somehow eluded the Japanese. They holed out somewhere in the hills.

"But how did we get here?" Spencer was insistent, thoroughly bewildered.

"We made sleds from the fronds and pulled you out of the *nipa* grove. You were in such pain from your wounds and Marco's feet were so badly burned neither of you could have walked far at all. When we got out of the creek into the open, we put you in jute sacks and carried you on our backs."

"How far away from the creek is this place? You couldn't have gone far at all. We're too heavy for anyone to lug around." Marco was dismayed.

"You're right," said the leader. "We had to think of something fast. The Japanese were combing the area we left, so we put you back on *nipa* sleds still in jute sacks. If the Japanese got anywhere near us, we were going to say we had coconuts to sell. Nonoy Ponce, here, knows this area better than anyone. He thought of holing up in this small cemetery."

Nonoy grinned and asked them how they liked sleeping with bones of dead bodies.

"Hey, if that's a joke, I don't like it at all." Spencer spat at the stall; he was deeply offended.

"Like it or not, that was the only way to outwit the Japanese. This is barrio *Calumpang*; some members of my family are buried in this cemetery. I put the dead body we were carrying into my uncle's burial space. That way we'll remember where the body is temporarily buried."

"Thank you for that," BB said, greatly relieved.

"We need to stay here for three more days," the leader said. "It seemed our only chance was to get back to the creek and paddle *bancas* without outriggers to get to the mouth of the river and then walk into the swamps in *Himamaylan*, but we know we can't do that now. The

Japanese most probably anticipate that move; we need to stay put until they decide we've taken another route."

"You can't stay out in the open if you stay here," Nonoy said. The Japanese will still be combing this area. You better get back into your stalls."

Spencer cringed at the thought of sleeping with the bones again, but either that or risk capture. If the guerrillas abandon them, they would starve. At least they could feed on coconut and ripe bananas when they could get out for a spell at midnight. So they holed up in the small cemetery in *barrio Calumpang* for three more days. During the day, they had to lie quietly in the burial stalls stuffed with dead leaves at the opening to hide their presence. Spencer knew BB and Marco were within hearing yet they couldn't talk to each other at all. Three days of this routine and he was ready to scream. He wondered what they were doing here anyway. Maybe they were better off running on their own or surrendering to the Japanese. After all, there are still the rules of the Geneva Convention to guarantee fair treatment of captured officers. Tales about Japanese treatment of prisoners he heard in Australia worried him though. He could hardly stand the stink of the bones and the guerrillas were nowhere to be found or heard from. Were they abandoned? His heart raced and his stomach wounds ached like hell.

After three days of dealing with unsettling silence, he heard the scratching of leaves being removed. Breathing hard, he fought nausea and a splitting headache but he was so gently removed from the stall he held the anger in his chest.

"We're sorry we couldn't feed you for the last two days," the same voice said again.

It sounded so full of genuine contrition that Spencer decided not to say anything. Besides, he saw the ripe bananas. His hand shook as he tried to grab some. Hands that matched the firm voice took his hands, steadied them, put peeled ripe bananas in them, one at a time. He didn't bother to know if Marco and BB ate. He devoured the ripe bananas, and gulped the coconut drink. The scraped coconut meat tasted bland, but it slid fast into his stomach. Topped with juicy, ripe mangoes, sweet, tasty, and very filling, the meal made him completely forget two days of hunger. He belched in satisfaction and asked to be excused.

* * *

Now all three of them were put into a bamboo cart lined with *kogon* grass. Nonoy carefully arranged more grass over them and on top of the grass he put bananas of different sizes and varieties. The thick layer of grass at the bottom of the cart made it look as though it was necessary to cushion the ripe fruit from damage. Before they were smuggled somewhere this way, Spencer wanted to know the danger they faced: "If the Japanese are anywhere near us, isn't this rather an extremely dangerous move? How could we defend ourselves lying down, immobile like this? Besides, the grass tickles my nose. What if I sneeze?"

"Would you rather walk into the Japanese garrison with a gun?" Nonoy asked extremely irritated. "Neither you nor Marco can walk fast enough to hide from the Japanese. Why don't you just shut up and let us do our job?"

The leaves were thick enough to hide their bodies from view. Besides, Nonoy had a hand grenade on top of his head, underneath a tight fitting cap. He was commissioned to drag this cart with the fruit offering into and out of the Japanese garrison at the *Binalbagan* Crossing. In another cart filled with grass arranged exactly the same way lay a choice crop of ripe mangoes. The Americans weren't told where Nonoy was taking the carts. All they knew was, once again, they had to trust the firm voice telling Nonoy to keep them still all the way.

Nonoy (Norberto) Ponce sat on the carabao pulling the lead cart. He was emboldened to attempt this trick because he knew a smattering of Japanese from going in and out of the garrison in *Kabankalan*. He had a friend, a double agent, a loyal *Kempetai* running important errands for the Japanese. This friend, though, knew how to stay out of the way when necessary. He revealed the nature of his errands to Nonoy.

Spencer listened to Nonoy's stories about his run-ins with the *kempetai* but he reserved his judgment about Nonoy's trustworthiness. He didn't like being totally dependent on the guerrilla men, yet they had no choice but to do what they were told. First, they had no idea where they were; secondly, their wounds and the need for food kept them almost helpless. Somehow, he felt that BB was his and Marco's only trustworthy support. He half carried them when they had to run for cover, but even BB didn't know where they were going. They simply had to trust the guerrillas if they were to survive.

Chapter 2—The Route to Nowhere

Spencer counted the days since the emergency landing. They spent the first day hiding in the *nipa* grove on the bank of the creek, and for three days they had holed up in a cemetery. They spent the last two days running, walking, or crawling, resting only when they couldn't go on. They had very little food and hardly anything to drink. The leader kept insisting that coconut milk was better than drinking river water, running the risk of getting diarrhea or dysentery. When it rained, he used the broad banana leaves to catch rainwater and saved it in a bottle he always carried with him to pass out to them every time they sat down to rest. He was right, of course. Somewhere in Australia where the B-29 crew was training, eleven of them were informed that unsafe drinking water carried the possibility of infection from intestinal worms invisible to the naked eye. But they were also told that without healthy drinking water they could get dehydrated and pass out from heat and exhaustion.

By now, Spencer was completely spent; he swore they were back where they started. He noted certain turns he thought they had passed before. Were they going around in circles or had the heat and the humidity affected his brain? He turned to the leader.

"Excuse me, sir," he said feebly, "have we been here before, or am I out of my head?"

"Not really," the leader said. "You're observant, I see. That's good. We're going back to a village where our contacts can keep us safe. The Japanese have been tracking us relentlessly for two days now. We have to get near their garrison instead of going away from it to avoid detection. Here, have a sip of good water. You need it to keep your strength up."

Spencer took the water gratefully.

"But how the devil could getting near their garrison keep us safe? Isn't that foolhardy?" Disbelief lined his face.

"We hope the Japanese will think so too. Simple logic would suggest that we wouldn't make that move, so we're making it."

"I see," Spencer said, though he really didn't see. "But isn't that dangerous?" he persisted.

"Yes, very. But that's our only chance to avoid capture."

"How is that possible?" Spencer insisted.

"The risk is great. But I think if we go on as we planned to do, the Japanese will cut off every route of escape. With their trucks and their motorcycles they can move a lot faster than we can on foot; we have no choice left."

Logic could not offer any assurance that he was right, but Spencer's gut feeling told him this man knew what he was doing. He quit arguing.

"So what are we going to do now?"

"You would have to leave that up to us."

Spencer had gotten used to the sound of this voice, so firm without being overbearing. He was persuaded to trust it implicitly.

"Just tell us what to do," he said finally.

"By the way, I'm Captain Almanzur Villalva. I'm in command of the guerrilla units involved in your rescue and defense. No, that's not quite right. I'm the field command. My cousin, Colonel Alvaro Gomez, older than I and a lot wiser, is my superior officer. He's the chief of intelligence. I consult with him by two-way radio. He gives me orders which I often disobey," he said with nonchalance. "God willing, if my cousin can help it, I hope we can keep you safe from the Japanese."

"May I ask another important question, please," Spencer said. For days now he was desperate to know the answer.

"Could you tell me how many of us are alive and do you know where the rest are?"

"Absolutely," the Captain said with the same self-assurance Spencer had always noted.

"Two of your men died instantly at the crash site. They've been buried in temporary graves. Your aircraft split into three parts; the cockpit was found at the foothills of *Isabela.*"

"That must be where George, Frank, and Robert are, if they're still alive. Are they?" Spencer asked. "Are they anywhere near us?"

"They were found twenty kilometers northwest of where we found you. I'm told by radio communication and by our own crude ways of passing information they're right now in the hills above *Isabela.* They'll circle up the mountains near the Japanese garrison in *Kabankalan.*"

"Maybe I'm stupid, but why are they taken near and not away from the Japanese garrison?" Spencer asked again, really bewildered.

"They're following the same notion I have of confusing the Japanese about our routes of escape. We take you near instead of away from them because that's a move they least expect. That seems to me and my cousin the only move we have left to avoid being captured."

Are we also moving close to another Japanese garrison?" Spencer desperately needed a clarification.

"Yes, we are. And so are Scott, Joe and Valdez. They're running with two of my trusted lieutenants. They're not too far from us. I chose to be responsible for you and Marco because you've suffered the worst injuries. BB insists on helping you and wouldn't be separated from you. Can I answer anything else?" He asked graciously.

"Not at the moment, thank you," Spencer couldn't think of anything else to say.

"We put ourselves completely in your care," he added a few minutes later, thinking desperately, *if I die, I'm certain this man will die with me*.

"Something else I'm sure you want to know," the Captain continued.

"All nine of you are split into three groups of three. I believe that number is lucky. Actually, it's easier to maneuver a few than many in a large group. Besides, three different routes should be more confusion for the Japanese, don't you think," he said with a twinkle in his eye and a very cool smile.

"Much later, we hope to all get together in the swamps in *Ilog*. If we can manage it, we'll all take a nice *batel* (an oversized *banca* with oars, sails, and it's rather unlikely but if we're lucky, perhaps a small engine) ride to *Maricalum* where you can be picked up by one of your submarines. Just think about that ride and believe that anything is possible." The same twinkle escaped his eyes and the smile was effortless and reassuring.

Tired as he was, Spencer began to relax. In his heart he knew he would survive this ordeal. Still, a gnawing fear grabbed at his subconscious; he prayed silently that he'd be able to endure whatever would happen. Thank God for this man. Faith in the rightness of what he was doing and how he was doing it was reassuring. Spencer began to breathe a lot easier.

* * *

BB lay between Marco and Spencer. The Captain thrust a 38caliber revolver in his hands.

"If you hear a grenade burst, that means the Japanese are within shooting distance. You need to get out of the cart and we'll somehow keep you running with us. If you get captured, you need to use the gun. You must decide what to do with it. But I'll tell you the Japanese will never let you live, or us either. They'll keep you for torture; that's a fate worse than immediate death. You have the weapon. You'll know what to do with it if the time comes."

BB didn't know what to say, so Spencer said it for him.

"You mean, we may not kill any Japanese at all, but we can use the gun on ourselves."

"Correct! There are only six bullets in it. Use them well. Whatever you decide to do, do it fast. If you hesitate, you're lost."

BB hugged both Marco and Spencer.

"I didn't know it would come to this, guys, but do we have any choice?"

"Do what you have to do. What's to be done, must be done," Spencer said. Both he and Marco gave him a tight hug.

"What always helps," Captain Villalva said, "is to think of something pleasant and forget about the danger at hand. You have to keep absolutely still, not even a whisper at any time. If you're tempted to say something, swallow the temptation. There's time enough to talk when it's safe to talk. Okay?"

Spencer felt every bump of the cart. They were traveling slowly. Every time the cart went over tall grass Spencer could hear the hiss and he felt the tug as the cart pulled out of the long grass caught underneath. He thought of the ripe bananas and wished they could have more of that soon. He felt so helpless. He wondered what it would be like if they could be in the open with a rifle, or, even better, a .50 caliber machine gun to defend them with. He speculated about what happened to the other guys.

If they are still alive, are they in as grave a danger as we're in right now, or worse?

He shut his eyes tight. Think of something pleasant, Captain Villalva said. He heard his sister recite the Twenty-third Psalm in church in Ohio, so he tried to straighten out the passage in his head:

"The Lord is my shepherd. I shall not want. He leadeth me beside still waters; He restoreth my soul. Yea, though I walk through the valley of the shadow of death, I shall fear no evil for thou art with me. Thy rod and thy staff, they comfort me."

He tried to remember how the whole passage went as he repeated the phrases again and again in his head. Dear God, help us in this hour of need. Desperately, he tried to block out the danger from his mind.

Something pleasant, did the Captain say?

Spencer could hear church music and his sister's voice in the choir. Wow, could she sing! She sang the solo in the Hallelujah chorus. The tears were slowly filling his eyes as he let the sound of Easter Sunday music carry him back to Ohio.

He felt the jolt as the cart came to a halt. He grabbed BB's arm. He could feel a cramp in his leg; he let the pain rise but he didn't dare move a muscle. He heard a gate swing with a creak. The cart moved deliberately, slowly, through the gate. Then he distinctly heard broken English as a Japanese voice broke out angrily.

"No more move. What you got there?"

"This is it," Spencer told himself. "This is the moment." He steeled his faculties, mentally preparing for an assault.

In his most ingratiating Filipino accent, Nonoy answered the guard softly, very subserviently.

"Mangoes ripe now, Sir. Bananas too. Every two weeks I bring. You see ripe fruit, Sir?" He pulled the carabao closer to the guardhouse.

"You give rice, yah? Rice for fruit. Mother very sick. Need rice for soup, please, Your Excellency," came the mock plea.

"Mangoes very good. I put in basket and bring in." Nonoy Ponce said in the best Japanese he memorized with Andres's help.

"Where you learn Japanese," the guard said with a hint of pleasure in his voice and a trace of suspicion on his face.

"Me come two weeks always. Learn little Japanese. *Arrigato,*" Nonoy said rolling his *rrrs*, bowing very low, slowly backing out toward the cart.

"Me no give you no rice, but you bring fruit in guardhouse now," the guard commanded, waving his rifle at Nonoy.

Though he couldn't see, Spencer knew Nonoy was taking the mangoes and the bananas on top of them out of the cart and was putting them in baskets. Someone was helping him. His *kempetai* friend, Andres Kapote, came out and took hold of some of the biggest, most fragrant mangoes and carried these to the Japanese guard. He peeled one and the juice dripped out.

"Hmm, very sweet,"

Andres sank his teeth into one letting the juice run out as he peeled the other and stretched his hand, offering the mango to the guard. When the guard's attention was distracted, Nonoy took out the last of the ripe bananas and put them in baskets too. He ran to take a basket to the guardhouse and kept running back and forth taking basket after basket.

He went to the lead cart standing a ways into the gate closest to the guardhouse. He grabbed an armful of leaves that cushioned the mangoes, ran back, and dumped armful after armful on the other cart, the one the Americans were in.

"You no need grass," Nonoy said almost out of breath. "Leaves make mess. Will take back, Sir? Yes? Grass good for carabao. Will take, sir?" He said standing still, but slowly, he bowed to the waist level, waiting to be dismissed.

"With your permission." Andres said to the guard. He peeled another ripe mango.

The guard took the mango. He shook his head up and down giving his permission without thinking much about it as he helped himself to the fruit.

"Bring more mangoes and bananas in two weeks," Andres yelled at Nonoy. "Bring ripe papayas, and boiling bananas too."

Nonoy shuffled out of the gate, pulling the carabao and the carts when the guard realized what he was doing or, more accurately, what he did not do.

"Hey, you, back here; Come here."

He yelled to Nonoy, pointing down at his feet with the butt of his rifle. But Andres put his arm on his shoulders and pushed another peeled mango into his hand.

"Let him come back next week and bring more fruit. The commandant would like that," he whispered to the guard. "Want to take him some of that juicy fruit now? I'll close the gate for you."

"Colonel hunting guerrilla We no know when he back. You no go *arong* this time?" the guard asked Andres who was playing dumb. The look on his face said he didn't know what was going on.

Andres hurried to close the gate and waved Nonoy away.

"Make sure you come back next week," he yelled. "And make sure you put more grass and leaves so the mangoes don't get squashed in the cart. Hear me?"

He raised a stick and was going to strike Nonoy with it, but he hit the cart instead. Not knowing what was happening, BB heard the stick bang on the side of the cart. He tried to sit up, but Nonoy, aware that the guard was looking, ran backward and pretended to fall on the cart pushing BB down.

"Keep very still down there," he muttered.

"Hey, no mumbling over there," Andres yelled at Nonoy. This time he hit him hard on the shoulder with the stick. The guard beamed his approval.

"That why carts full of leaves!" He finally understood. "I see. Grass good for fruit, good for carabao. Next time he come, we keep carabao, yes?" He roared in laughter, sure that he had put one over Nonoy.

Nonoy was quickly out of the six-feet wire fence. Seeming not to hurry, he skirted the gate, turned left and crossed the railroad tracks, urging the carabao softly to do a steady canter toward the river behind the Japanese garrison. He stayed close to the fence, making sure the carts were in sight so the fruit offering episode wouldn't cause suspicion. He could hear the loud laughter as the guard told his joke to the other soldiers.

"Come back next week with same carabao." He cupped his hands over his mouth and shouted loud so Nonoy could hear.

"Put plenty grass in cart; Grass good for fruit, good for carabao."

He bent over in laughter and could not stop. Andres, laughing hard, joined in the camaraderie. Nonoy saw the glint of the setting sun on the wire fence on the pathway behind the garrison. At the end of the wire fence he turned behind the solid concrete fence. Thick perspiration rolled on the back of his neck. He tried taking off his cap, forgetting the grenade underneath. It rolled to the side and almost fell. Nonoy flipped his hat to catch it and he swung it wide as though he were making a gesture of goodbye.

The guard and his companions still doubled up in laughter yelled in a chorus.

"Grass good for fruit, good for carabao."

"Make sure you bring same carabao next week." Andres yelled as loud as he could.

The guard and the other soldiers didn't stop laughing. They gathered around the guardhouse and helped themselves to the fruit. They never bothered to check the grass underneath the fruit, but as soon as Nonoy was out of sight the guard started to have misgivings about letting him go without further interrogation. He stopped enjoying the fruit; uneasy, he thought about doing something.

Why not keep carabao now? He seemed deep in thought as he quickly walked to the gate and running out called to Andres. "Hey, you, *kempetai,* come with me. We get carabao now."

He ran as fast as he could and didn't stop till he got to the end of the wire fence. Then he unloaded a round from his automatic rifle in the direction Nonoy took. The bullets ricocheted on the trees behind Nonoy. He used a stick on the carabao. The other soldiers in the garrison got nervous. They ran to find out about the gunfire and questioned the guard about his unnecessary misgivings.

"When the Colonel gets back, he'll go out and get the carabao for sure. Hasn't he always done so before?" They reassured the guard. Still the guard unloaded his uneasiness on Andres.

"Hey you, *kempetai,* you no say to Colonel Asaki where fruit come from. Say your wife bring, Oke?"

But the more he thought about the cart, the more disturbed he became. How was he going to keep his comrades from telling the joke about the grass and the carabao?

Nonoy wanted to abandon the carts, but he knew Marco and Spencer couldn't walk faster than the carts so he turned them around to go back in the direction they had come from.

Spencer was speechless with annoyance. "Does this fellow know what he's doing," he began to wonder. But when his eyes got used to the darkness of the empty field ahead, he was aware of objects moving through the grass for sometime. He noticed Nonoy, in the lead, followed the movement. As the grass thinned, the terrain began to change. Now they moved underneath the shadow of trees. It had gotten dark but the moon was rising. They moved in eerie silence through trees with bark glowing white in the moonlight. Then the cicadas began their noise. Full of them, the trees sounded as if their leaves were chanting. The carts slowed down so quietly, it felt as though they were not moving at all, but Spencer saw they were squeezing through tree trunks that lined the edge of a creek. Nonoy motioned for them to get down and follow him as he walked into the darkness ahead. They pushed the carts into the thick *nipa* fronds. Nonoy did not want the carabao to make marks in the mud. He chased them, using his stick. Without the weight of carts behind, the carabao galloped through the grass parallel the *nipa* grove along the creek and waded in the water close to the *nipa* fronds.

Weaving in and out of large cottonwood trees, Marco began to think his feet were burning. BB took his arm and half-lifted him at times. Spencer hung on to BB's belt for fear he would lose both of them. Suddenly, machinegun fire burst behind them in the direction they had left. Spencer calculated the Japanese were about half a kilometer behind.

The sky lit up from the fire spreading through the grass they'd crawled in barely an hour before. Obviously, the Japanese thought they were moving away from the garrison toward the river. The fire scorched the entire field of grass and moved toward the *nipa* grove. Captain Villalva was right again. Colonel Asaki assumed they were escaping toward the river but now they were getting back to the foothills where they came from before they were loaded into the cart.

They could feel a heavy breeze moving through the trees. Now the cicadas were quiet. The chanting ceased; the slender fern leaves growing on the trunks of the host acacias folded together like the fingers of hands in prayer. BB and Marco breathed their relief when Captain Villalva joined them under a huge acacia tree in bloom. Spencer thought the leaves were falling from above. He felt something landing on the back of his neck and his arms. He shook his shirt as something wriggly moved down his neck. He picked it up. A fat caterpillar glowed its greenness in the moonlight.

"Shit, something like pellets are falling on us; it feels so weird," Marco whispered.

"Damn," BB blurted as he slapped something crawling on his arms.

"It's okay," Nonoy laughed softly. Take off your shirts and put them on top of your heads. The acacia trees are blooming and are full of larvae that'll fall off in the dark. They'll be all over the ground in the morning and so would the bloom. The earth will be covered with a pink carpet."

Farther down the creek, Captain Villava's men took off their shirts and tied them together, stretching them on to sticks they carried. They invited the Americans to join them. When they crawled underneath, they could hear the soft thud of the worms falling on the improvised canopy.

BB and Marco breathed in comfort and assurance at seeing the Captain and his men; something else took their breath away. At the edge of the creek lined with the shade of hundred years old acacia trees were Scott, Joe and Valdez lying on their backs and breathing heavily, protected by blankets stretched like flat roofed tents.

"Well, I'll be!" Spencer said in complete amazement. "Where'd you guys come from?"

"About time," Captain Villalva whispered to Nonoy still panting beside Spencer. "We'll rest here. Give them something to eat and drink," he ordered his men.

The three other Americans had a thin rope tied around their torso. They were dead tired from running. Scott, Joe and Valdez (they never called him by his first name) were burning their lungs off from sheer exhaustion.

"We've been everywhere and nowhere, it seems to me." Scott complained. "God, we never stopped running or crawling till now."

"Where are we and where are we headed?" Joe asked. He looked ready to cave in from the steady running.

"If we told you, would you know where that is," Ponsing, Captain Villalva's aide, muttered sarcastically. He was running out of patience with this impossible whining. He threw his *bolo* hard at the trunk of an acacia tree. He swore in the vernacular and asked his *Kapitan* if this lot was worth risking his life for.

Spencer could not follow the verbal exchange, but he thought he knew just how Ponsing felt; after all, he volunteered to throw in his lot with theirs. It must seem like a thankless job if they could not trust them, let alone thank them for what they were doing. He felt like chiding the crew. Though he shared their frustration, he could not understand why they had to question what the Captain and his men were doing. He had done so earlier, but now he was sure of one thing: There are a few things we can't conceive of and we can only look at what they are doing for us from one angle or another. We could never see the entire picture, so what are we bellyaching about?

Yet he understood the feeling of being threatened all the time. For his crew, the uncertainty was overwhelming. He understood their anxiety for they were continually menaced by something they couldn't see except out of the corner of an eye.

Spencer woke up very early the next morning. He sat up and looked around him feeling like a kid treated with some wonderful, magic trick. Nonoy was right; of course, he was always right. So was the Captain or his aide Ponsing (Alfonso) Salcedo, not quite twenty years old, the one with the harelip

Why couldn't we believe in all of them implicitly?

What he saw now overwhelmed him with wonder. In spite of a hell that threatened, a picture of peace and tranquility spread before them. The ground they had crawled on the night before was covered with a pink carpet an inch thick. While they were sleeping, the acacia blossoms had fallen on the ground all night. Their beauty was an incredible sight. Strips of gold peeped through the pink, for at the center of each bloom a cord of gold circled like a crown. Nonoy saw the expression of wonder on Spencer's face.

"Thought you might like it," he said smiling. "First time I saw this annual spectacle, I could hardly believe how beautiful it was. But try walking on this carpet with bare feet. It's gross."

He was right. Spencer saw the limbs arching above, now completely devoid of blossoms. The acacia trees looked like inverted brooms stuck on the ground. Their broad trunks were like thick broom handles left standing on a flat floor. The warmth of the sun slowly transformed some of the worms into emerging butterflies. Spencer began to feel an ache, not from his wounds but from some longing inside.

I wish I were one of these beautiful creatures that could turn around and fly away unharmed. Hell, this world's in trouble; does it take a little madness to make some sense?"

A little madness? He had to straighten out his thoughts. The gigantic piece of metal he'd just abandoned, though it had lost its intended direction, was the largest weapon ever yet designed to fly the skies and wreck destruction on the enemy. When was the madness going to end? How was it going to end for them?

He saw Nonoy, Ponsing, and Pedring, huddled together sharing a joke and laughing softly. When they volunteered to rescue them, they must have known the extreme danger they would face; yet they braved the peril as though for them life had no limit. Where did their inner strength come from? The warmth they shared with one another impressed him. Trust in each other and a complete reliance on their *Kapitan* hung in the air they breathed. He wanted to let his crew see that their offensive lack of faith in this incredible bunch was beginning to annoy even him. He wanted to thank them for what they were doing for him and his crew, but he couldn't find the words. Not yet anyway.

Chapter 3—Moving On

"Time to move on; the sun is rising. It's going to be a scorching day." Captain Villalva removed his shirt.

"I suggest you remove your shirts, too, and tie them over the rope on your waist. You'd be less visible without the shirts; the sun will burn your sensitive skins. That can't be helped; but the darker you get, the less different you'd look from us."

"Cover your blond hair with the straw hats we gave you. There'll be less chance to be recognized with hats on." Pedring looked straight at Scott and BB when he spoke.

"Yep, and I have to scrape off your growing beards too," Ponsing raised his sharp *bolo* almost menacingly. "Filipinos hardly ever grow beards."

Now they think of everything, Spencer thought with a bit of annoyance. Can't blame their caution, though; especially when they've done so much already.

"Well, I'm ready to move on."

He stretched his limbs. Something bristling and dark was beginning to spread on his face. He felt it with his fingers. The stubble was sharp.

"Hey Ponsing, you can start with me."

He made a step toward Ponsing and felt a tight pull on his belly. A quick grimace clouded his face.

"The wound hurts a lot more today, huh," the Captain asked him.

Gosh, nothing escapes this guy, Spencer noted. Somehow, he always felt safer and more assured with him around.

"We need to walk or run a few kilometers today, and we're backtracking again. It must seem frustrating logic to go over what we had covered two days ago, but, as I told you before, it's the only way to outwit the Japanese. We don't intend to get caught so we deliberately think about where we're going,"

"Oh, yeah, it's easy for you to say. You don't seem to care how tired we get, or how hungry. We haven't had much to eat these last two days." Valdez barked his frustration.

"Neither have we, the *Kapitan* least of all. Have you noticed?" Nonoy blazed back but he checked his anger. "We put all the fruit we could find on the cart over these three guys here." Nonoy gestured towards BB, Marco and Spencer. "We didn't want the Japanese to grab them. Is that a good enough trade you think? BB, Marco and Spencer for a cart full of bananas and mangoes we could've fed you?"

The *Kapitan* raised his hand to silence his men and was promptly obeyed.

"Before the day is over, I promise we'll all dine with my friends; that's if we do what we have to do no matter how tired we get or how hungry or frustrated over things we've no control over."

Immediately, Nonoy moved beside Valdez. Spencer saw Pedring moving toward Scott; BB, concerned about Marco's aching feet, moved toward him. Joe nodded to Spencer and walked beside him. The Captain moved toward the first two with Ponsing trailing close by. He was still carrying a black box.

"Ten men should not be seen close together. Keep a distance of ten or fifteen meters between each pair. Run when no one is in sight, especially when you don't hear anything or see any movement around you. Nonoy and Pedring know where to go but Joe and BB don't; that's why they have the rope tied on their waist. If you get too close, the rope will be slack. If you keep your distance, it'll be taut and you'll feel a pull. Move toward that area. Ponsing and I will scout around and decide on the direction we take."

"Don't forget, you must walk quietly if you think someone or something is close, or you have to crawl when you hear something," Ponsing reminded them.

Nonoy and Pedring nodded and started to move. Spencer again observed something about this bunch. Between themselves, they seem to be able to communicate with a few words. They had not gone far when the Captain stopped. Nonoy motioned for Valdez to squat low in the thick *kogon* grass. The Captain passed through toward Pedring and Scott. They felt a slack in the rope. Pedring felt a tug and the rope tightened so he sat down in the grass and motioned for Scott to do likewise. The Captain crawled between Pedring and Joe and moved closer to Ponsing. Spencer saw Ponsing open the black box to listen to the radio.

For God's sake! So this is how they knew what was happening ahead or behind. All the time they moved, they weren't as clueless as we thought they were. Puts us to shame for being so mistrustful," Spencer thought with some misgiving.

They lay under the cover of the grass for so long he was getting edgy. He smelled smoke, but the wind was blowing the smoke away from them toward the Japanese garrison.

Ponsing whispered to his *Kapitan*. "Last night someone had moved the carabao to the path behind the garrison and carried it to the *nipa* grove at the edge of the river. The carabao made visible marks on the mud so the Japanese followed the tracks."

"Well, the Japs got the carabao they wanted after all." Nonoy smirked.

Hundreds of soldiers from the *Binalbagan* garrison and reinforcements rushed from *Kabankalan* waded waist deep into the *nipa* grove, their bayonets drawn. Colonel Asaki had lit the grass. His troops fanned the fire with their shirts and the flames led toward the *nipa* grove. Soldiers trampled behind the flames and cut the *nipa* fronds to ground level. Nothing much was discovered, except the carabao and the carts and small *bancas* without outriggers. The Japanese riddled these with machine gun bullets till they sunk. Evidently, they were empty.

Furious and frustrated, Colonel Asaki marched back to the garrison. When he discovered what had taken place the day before, he had the guard on duty and the half dozen privates who laughed raucously over the joke about the grass and the carabao tied to a stake in the middle of the compound. Andres Kapote had disappeared without a trace but the rest of the *kempetai* in the garrison were herded together, stripped of their shirts and tied close to the Japanese guards. Colonel Asaki's anger knew no bounds. The soldiers and the *kempetai* received two hundred lashes each. The merciless flogging took hours. Japanese soldiers and the *kempetai* were near death when the flogging ended.

Chapter 4—Unleashed Fury

Farther north, another Japanese contingent searched the area. In an hour, sixteen trucks, eight jeeps, and twenty-four motorcycles tramped over the towns of *La Carlota* and *La Castellana* tracing every clue and rumor about the whereabouts of the guerrilla unit that had rescued the Americans. Colonel Nikamura, dispatched from *Bacolod*, led the hunt; he swore no stone would be left unturned till the Americans were captured. His assurance turned to impatience when he found that right from the start he had been misinformed. The blast from the cockpit was so tremendous that calculations from the *Binalbagan* garrison pinpointed the crash at either the town of *La-Carlota* or *La-Castellana* instead of *Isabela*, southeast toward the mountains. The Japanese didn't expect the aircraft to split into three parts. Only one tremendous blast was heard to indicate the dissolution of the entire aircraft so all available vehicles from the nearby garrison sped to the calculated spot: the town of *La-Carlota*. Within that hour, Japanese trucks loaded with soldiers, guns and ammunition covered every major road.

"Each unit must take two trucks, six motorcycles, and a lead jeep. I want every road covered. Arrest every Filipino you find in every area you cover. Take them to the town plaza for questioning. Meet me there in twenty minutes." Colonel Nikamura yelled to six of his lieutenants.

Each lieutenant covered every surrounding barrio. They dragged men, women, and children out of hiding. The soldiers struck them with rifle butts or flogged them with a long, braided rope before they loaded them into their trucks. Most of them bled from wounds inflicted before they were unloaded in the town plaza. Kicked with heavy boots, men sagged with broken knees, and ribs. Rifle butts hit skulls again and again. Women's breasts bled from bayonet slashes. Children suffered the same way without exception. Some tried to run and were instantly mowed down by machine guns. Dead bodies littered the town plaza.

Colonel Nikamura blazed with rage when the B-29 was nowhere to be found in the area. Rushing to move on, he ordered his officers to put the rest of the captured victims in a line; they gunned down more than a hundred men, women and children with machine guns before they could be questioned. His orders were carried out without hesitation. The hunt moved on.

The contingent traveled south to *La Castellana*. Once more, trucks and motorcycles covered every road and lane in the surrounding barrios. Soldiers carried out the same orders. They caught fewer prisoners since the gunfire at *La Carlota* warned people they were coming. They captured less than two dozens, most of them men farming in the area. Tight lipped, they were mangled before they were killed.

Where the hell was the explosion? Colonel Nikamura couldn't contain his anger.

It couldn't be much farther. It could be either north toward *Pontevedra*, or it could be southeast toward *Magallon*, later called Moises Padilla. Maybe the guerrillas were taking the Americans to the nearby mountains at the foot of the *Kanlaon* volcano, closer to Negros Oriental. He had to get there fast or it would be impossible to capture them. He took a seat in one of the jeeps ready to race to Magallon when a motorcycle sped in front of his jeep to stop him. Word from *kempetai* said the aircraft had blown up in barrio *Caridad*, east of the town of *Isabela*. Earlier, one of the captains under his command told him that Colonel Asaki had raced from the garrison in *Kabankalan* to the garrison in *Binalbagan*.

Colonel Asaki had also been misled. He was told that a guerrilla contingent had been at the garrison in *Binalbagan* and some stupid guard had let them go. Without doubt they must have gone to the mouth of the river to the sea and would use *batels* to escape to unoccupied territory in the south. He decided to order gunboats from *Bacolod* to *Binalbagan*, ready to chase the guerrillas in open sea. When Colonel Nikamura heard by radio message what Colonel Asaki was going to do, his anger mounted.

"The stupid fool," he grunted; "he hasn't even located the aircraft but he's ready to go on a chase.

"Stupid bastard," he said aloud. "Send him a message to take the railroad tracks and meet me in *Isabela*. Ask him to cover the entire area in that vicinity, even as far as *Hinigaran*. This time I'm not going to waste a minute. Every road, every lane, must be covered. Track down every possible avenue of escape."

Colonel Nikamura sped south from *La Castellana* to *Isabela*, but his instinct still told him he had to send a contingent southeast toward *Magallon*; the logical route of escape had to be toward the foothills of Mt. *Kanlaon*.

Chapter 5—The Crimson Trail

Manang Simang took the clay pot to boil the last handfuls from the *ganta* (a small unit of measure) of rice she'd been saving for a while. She could make *lugao* (gruel), and maybe flavor it with the last piece of salted fish she'd been keeping too. While the rice was boiling, she dug into her betel nut and *buyo* hoard; she chewed the betel nut and rolled the *buyo* (a green leaf) sprinkling it with *apog* (lime), a favorite concoction she loved to chew when she was nervous. This time she was not just chewing for pleasure; she had to do something to stop the bleeding. The white men were still unconscious, but the one covered with minor scratches stirred.

"Consing," she called her sister tending the kitchen fire, "get water from the well and let them drink; maybe it would give them some energy before I feed them with the *lugao.*"

Consuelo took the bucket behind the *malungay* tree by the well, tied the rope on the metal ring ready to lower the bucket down when Cario stepped beside her and grabbed her arm.

"Sus, *Manong* Cario," (Jesus, *Manong* Cario), she said, and made the sign of the cross. "You really scared me. What's in that heavy sack you're lugging? ."

Breathing heavily, Cario put his load down. "Where's *Manang* Simang?" He asked. "You need to help us hide the American."

"Us? Who's with you?"

"Polding is up the fire trees. He's making sure we haven't been followed,"

"And how did you know about the Americans?" Consing asked, wondering how Cario could've known about the two Americans they were hiding.

"What are you saying, girl? There's only one American Polding and I found in the church. Father Miguel hid him in the belfry." Cario was confused.

"So where's Father Miguel?" Consing lowered the bucket into the well.

"We left him at the church where we found him already dead. The Japanese cut his tongue before he died. I bet he wouldn't tell them anything."

"How horrible!" Consing set the bucket down beside the sack.

"The Japanese left Father Miguel for dead; they had broken his skull with the butt of their guns and the mark it etched meant they tried to strangle him with the rosary hanging on his neck. He must've dragged himself under the belfry with the rope in his hand before he died. When all the trucks left, Polding and I went into the church and found him dead. The rope in his hand led us to the body in the belfry. We figure this American has been half conscious for a while. Help us to revive him."

Polding walked in noiselessly. "*Nong* Cario, ask *Manang* Simang and Consing to feed the American. I think he's too weak from hunger."

"Help me carry him to the hut." Cario loosened the jute sack; together, they carried the load to the little hut. Consuelo still had not told them about the other Americans. She picked up the bucket of water and hurried in with the boys.

"*Agoy, Dios ko (Oh, my God)," she mumbled. "Ano ang himo-on naton sini?"* ("What are we going to do about this?")

Manang Simang boiled water, took a small towel from the *banguera* (kitchen porch) and sponge bathed the unconscious Americans. She scrubbed blood that caked over the wounds of George Miller; moaning, he rubbed his eyes. When he opened them, he stared at *Manang* Simang. Automatically, he felt himself all over.

Thank God he was still in one piece. When his eyes slowly got adjusted to the dark he saw Frank still bleeding from the gash below the shoulder.

"He needs a tourniquet," he told *Manang* Simang who shook her head, unable to understand a word he said.

"*Pasiensia lang kamo, toto, kay wala guid kami mahimo. Ka diotay guid sining amon balay,"* ("Young men, I hope you will forgive us. We can't do much for you. We only have a very small hut here,"). She talked apologetically to George who couldn't understand a word she said either.

Polding and Cario were already on the stairs; the weight made the stairs squeak. They put Robert gently on the mat on the bamboo floor in the corner of the hut. Consing wasn't far behind.

"*Isa pa!"* (Another one!). *Manang* Simang exclaimed. "*Grabi man ina?"* ("Is he badly hurt too?").

"How many do you have here?" Cario asked.

"We rescued these two. The sky was on fire when they fell almost at our feet while we were transplanting seedlings at the rice field behind the old rice mill. You know where that is? We wrapped them in our *patadiongs* and Consing and I carried them here; that was really early this morning."

"Did anyone see you do that?" Polding asked.

"No, we carried them in quickly. I think the Japanese will be looking for them soon."

"They already are. Polding said. The heathens were at the church. They killed Father Miguel I think because he didn't want to tell them what he knew. But they were in a hurry so they killed him quickly, thank God! They cut his tongue, you know. Bastards. God surely will punish them for killing His priest."

"They're not done with killing yet." *Manang* Simang frowned. "We should think about hiding them, but first things first."

She spat out the concoction she was chewing, gathered it carefully in the towel and plugged the hole on Frank's left arm with it. She took the *patadiong* hanging across the window and tore strips from it. Then she wrapped his arm tightly and tied it to his body. When George saw what she was doing, he asked for a stick, gesturing wildly to communicate what he was asking for. Consing ran down the stairs and got a bamboo stick. She handed it to George, not knowing why he was asking for it.

"Thank you; I'm glad someone understands English."

"The three of us understand a little. You have to speak slowly and gesture with your hands so we can understand you. I only finished fourth grade in school," Consing told him.

"We have to cut this stick in two, each a foot long. George measured a foot with both hands. Then we have to put the sticks on each side of Frank's arm and tie it tightly to stop the bleeding." George explained still gesturing.

Cario took his *bolo* and did what George told them to do. When George was ready to put the tourniquet on, he was amazed that the bleeding had slowed down considerably.

"What did the old lady put on the wound? It's unbelievable. The bleeding has almost stopped. It's amazing!"

"What did you put on it, *Manang* Simang, " Polding asked.

"Oh, I chewed some *buyo* and *apog*; an old cure I learned from my mother. I plugged the hole on his arm with it; he's not a bleeder, thank God. It has almost stopped the bleeding."

"Boys, I'm sorry there isn't enough *lugao* for all of us to eat; there's only enough for the three Americans. I hope you don't mind. There's

Saba (cooking banana) I can boil for you, Consing and me," she offered. "Consing, you can start feeding them now."

Consing took the ladle and filled the coconut bowls with the thin *lugao.* She was careful to split the dried fish into three equal parts. Then she handed one coconut bowl to George.

"Eat. This is all we have. It's rice, dried fish and *alogbate* (a variety of spinach) boiled into a tasty soup we call *lugao.* Please feed yourself."

She stuck a coconut spoon into the bowl and made the gesture of feeding herself. George took the bowl from her. It smelled good and made him hungry. *Manang* Simang and Consing each took a bowl and spoon-fed Frank and Robert. The hot soup filled Robert's stomach and he immediately revived. He sat up and, with shaking hands, took the spoon from *Manang* Simang to feed himself.

"Be careful with the fish bone."

Consing tried to warn him, but he had already crunched the fish bone, put the bowl to his mouth and slurped the rest of the *lugao.* He was famished; they had not eaten in more than forty-eight hours. Frank was a different matter altogether. He took in the *lugao* very, very slowly, almost throwing up at times. Consing painstakingly fed him every spoonful of the soup. He, too, revived, but loss of blood from his wound had weakened him considerably. George was tired and sleepy yet he had to stay awake. He didn't remember anything. Where were the others? Had they all died with the blast? Relieved, he had seen two men climb the steps, bring Robert in, and lay him down on the mat at the corner. But how did he and Frank get here? Did they carry them in before they brought Robert? He was going to ask the question but Polding beat him to it. He asked *Manang* Simang how the Americans came.

"I told Cario we wrapped them in our *patadiongs* and carried them here quickly," *Manang* Simang told Polding who translated for George.

"We made sure the other one bled into the *patadiong* and we washed the blood off them right away. His shirt was bloody too, so we washed it; it is drying by the window."

She pointed to it with her hands so George would understand.

"I don't know what to do, Cario," she said. "Where can we hide them? If you listen well, you can hear their vehicles. They're getting nearer."

She had hardly finished what she was saying, when they heard gunfire clearly.

"My God, *Nong* Cario, what are we going to do," Consing pleaded.

"*Manang* Simang, there's no time to cook the *saba*. We need to get out of here."

"I don't think you can outrun their trucks Cario, and there's really no place to hide. Maybe you and Polding can get to the fire trees. They're thick with leaves this year and if you climb the trees, you can hide behind the large trunks. These Americans will never make it; they don't have the strength to climb the trees."

She scrambled down the stairs as she talked. Crouching under the small hut, she took out three of the six large bamboo baskets filled with rice straw she was meaning to tie into bundles to reinforce her thatched roof.

"Quick, Consing, in your best English, tell these young men to go with us down the hillside to the well. Polding take the baskets with you. You, too, Cario, bring the coils of rope hanging on the post."

Consing and *Manang* Simang led the Americans by the hand. Understanding the women's urgency, they ran with them down the hill to the well.

"Tell them to get inside the baskets. Put two baskets together so it would be strong enough to hold them. Cushion the bottoms with rice straw so they can be as comfortable as possible. We have to tie the baskets firmly with ropes and lower them into the well. They have to cover their heads with the rice straw and they may have to stay under water if the Japanese look in there before they decide to leave."

George only half understood what the old woman was saying but he recognized her fear and urgency when the gunfire got louder and motorcycles sounded unmistakably within short distance. He knew they desperately meant to help them so he let them do what they had to do without questioning their judgment. Polding and Cario lowered the baskets into the dark well. George was first, then Robert, and Frank last. Consing had put Frank's shirt over his wound and wrapped him in the *patadiong* drying in the window. The boys tied the ropes on the foot of the *malungay* tree by the well and the women put weeds on top to hide them from view. To say his respectful goodbye, Cario took the old woman's hand and put it on his forehead.

"We have to go now, *Manang* Simang. What are you going to do? Aren't you and Consing going to hide too? We can push you up the fire trees with us."

"*Indi, anak,*" ("No, son,") she said determinedly. If the Japanese catch us, they'll force us to tell what we know. If they find us at home, they'll think we're too stupid to do anything, even to hide. Let's hope they'll not harm two helpless women."

"Go, go now," Consing said in fear. "God be with you. If the Japanese don't find the Americans, and if they give up looking for them here, make sure you come back and get them out of the well and look for someone to take them to some guerrilla hideout somewhere. Hide, please. Please hide well. *"Ang Dios lang mahibalo.."* ("Only God knows what to do.").

Cario and Polding barely got to the fire trees and hid in one where the trunk was large and the leaves were thickest when the first of the motorcycles roared into the vegetable patch by the hut.

Manang Simang was cooking *saba* when Colonel Nikamura ran up the stairs swearing and yelling in anger. Consing cowered on the mat at the corner, her hands folded in the gesture of prayer. In her hand was a rosary Father Miguel had given her.

"Where are the Americans? What have you done with them?"

Manang Simang stared at Colonel Nikamura with a blank face. The face clearly meant to say, "What are you talking about?"

The colonel slapped her face with a savage force. The blank stare infuriated him.

"Answer me. Did you hear what I said?" He yelled at the old woman.

Blood was trickling down the side of her mouth. The colonel was doubly infuriated at the sight of blood. He smacked the other side of her face just as hard. More blood flowed down her face; she held her breath from the pain. She bowed her head. The colonel lifted her face and yelled at the blankness once more.

"Look at me when I'm talking to you."

All the time he was yelling at her in Japanese without any translation. She did not mean to be belligerent. She simply did not understand anything he said. He poked the staring eye with his finger. She screamed in pain, but after that involuntary sound, she cried soundlessly. The colonel was amazed at her fortitude, but he could not accept her rebellion. She needed to be humbled. The eye began to swell and then it started to close. The comb that held her hair in place fell to the floor and her gray hair fell on her shoulders. The colonel took the long hair, wound it around his wrists and yanked it hard.

Consing could not stand it any more. *"Dios ko, tabangi abi kami,"* ("My God, please help us), she prayed. She stood up from where she was cowering at the corner and lunged at the colonel. She scratched his face with her nails, grabbed the hand that held the sword he was about to strike *Manang* Simang with, bit it and would not let go.

"Bitch." He screamed in pain.

He shook his hand loose; then he hit her head with the handle of the sword. Consing fell on the floor and fainted. He dragged her by the hair and dumped her on the mat at the corner where she had cowered before.

"So you have quite a bit of spirit, huh? Let's see what you can do." He grabbed her cotton blouse and tore it, exposing everything to her waist. "Ah, what have we here? Such pretty breasts! A virgin, no less. Today is a lucky day, I guess," he said wetting his lips.

"Get down, all of you." He shouted at his soldiers who were beginning to stare at what was going on. "Get busy with something down there." He roared with coarse laughter. "I'm going to have a bit of fun. Who said I couldn't have fun while working?"

He unbuttoned his shirt very deliberately and began to pull his pants down.

With one eye still open, *Manang* Simang saw what he was about to do. She crawled to where the colonel was quickly removing his boots.

"Please, Your Excellency. Please spare my sister from shame."

She knelt on the floor, tried to take the colonel's hands in hers tearfully pleading.

The colonel kicked her with such force she bent double in pain. "Ah, this your daughter?" He asked in the tone of a statement. "Well, you'll see how she'd enjoy my favor."

He lifted the spiritless Consing from the floor, cupped her breasts with his hands and sank his teeth into them till they bled.

Consing screamed from the pain.

"A bite for a bite, you bitch." Panting hard, he stripped her naked. He stared hard at the almost immobile form, thoroughly enjoying what he saw.

Frightened by the lust she saw on the Colonel's face, *Manang* Simang pulled herself together, ran to the kitchen, took the pot boiling with the *saba* and tried to rush the colonel with it. He turned around quickly, met her directly and run his sword through her heart.

"Hey, you down there," he issued an order, "someone, come up here and take this body away." He pulled his sword out without the slightest tinge of compassion. The blood emptied from *Manang* Simang's body fast. One eye was still wide open, still staring at the colonel.

"Wipe my sword clean. One can hardly have fun at the sight of so much blood."

She had fallen on her face. Colonel Nikamura turned her face up.

"Maybe you still want to see how I enjoy your daughter?"

Consing was slowly recovering from fainting; she screamed when she saw the lifeless body of her sister. *"Ay, Dios Ko,* ("Oh, my God,") where are you when we need you?" She cried in anguish. She was going to rush at the colonel again, but she was no match for him. He was thoroughly aroused.

"Come here, you with the pretty breasts."

He grabbed her hair, threw her on the floor and pinned her down with one bare foot. He rubbed her breasts with the other foot. Drooling, he dropped on her so hard, she screamed in agony.

"That's right, baby; scream for it." He put his tongue out and slobbered over her breasts once more. He propped himself on his hands on both sides of her body, pulled up to her face, forced her mouth open and pushed his penis deep into her throat. Only half conscious by now, Consing gagged in pain. The lead burned in her throat. He was on fire. The soft flesh in her warm throat felt like melting cream on the hot lead; he couldn't withdraw it from the overwhelmingly pleasurable sensation. When he was able to, he very slowly pulled the lead out, dripping semen all over her face. This sight excited him more. Instead of dying out, he burst into redoubled hardness. He trailed this organ over the creamy face down to her neck, and felt her breasts with it. The breasts were hard and hot, but wet with perspiration. In uncontrolled pleasure, he traced a fast line to her navel, pushed the heavy, long pipe on the dark black mound, found her opening and forced it in. She screamed in excruciating pain. The pipe tore the vaginal lining and warm blood soaked the lead to the hilt. She couldn't bear the pain. She tried desperately to sit up but had no strength left to brave the agony. She sagged like a discarded rag doll. The look of helpless surrender and at the same time an expression of utter contempt on her face put out the fire in his groin. He was done and was somewhat exhausted. Consing lay unconscious on the mat. Colonel Nikamura wiped the blood off with Consing's *patadiong* he had ripped off. He had no more use for her. He kicked the almost lifeless body with his bare feet; he felt half way disgusted with what he had done. He put his clothes on carelessly, left his uniform unbuttoned and his fly open, rushed down the stairs, and called for his jeep.

"Let's get out of here; there's work to do." He got into his jeep, intending to speed toward the town of *Magallon.*

"Burn the hut;" he tried to sound savage, but his men heard a slight quaver in his voice.

Colonel Nikamura saw Consing had crawled as far as the steps of the hut. Her fingers clasped the bamboo steps. She was still vomiting blood. He pulled a .38 caliber pistol from his hip holster and shot her in the head. Her body fell on the ground in a pool of blood.

The trail leading to the well sloped down the hillside partly covered by lush ferns. On the upside sweep a clump of trees enjoyed a luxury of greenness. The monsoon season had just started and the soft daily drizzle encouraged a new thickness. Small birds called *mayas* flew in and out of the trees. The hillside looked harmless enough. If Colonel Nikamura hadn't been a bit rattled by his lustful release, he would certainly have ordered his men down the gap by the hill and found the trail to the well, but he was in no mood to waste time. He had spent no more than forty minutes in the hut, but those were a good forty minutes wasted. He told himself he had to torture these people into volunteering pertinent information, yet how could he have side-stepped his investigation on helpless women instead of moving on to confront rebels helping the Americans escape? He needed to get back to the serious task of tracking down the fleeing Americans. He would chase them relentlessly.

He stopped to regroup, ordered his unit to remain in *Isabela* and examine the debris around the explosion. Something was very wrong here. How could the explosion of a large aircraft have left so little to show for it? Assuredly, the answer would come with the capture of the crew who had survived. He figured two important issues must be resolved. Number one: The area around *Isabela* and northeast to *Pontevedra* needed to be monitored. The *Binalbagan* garrison should secure the area then move south toward *Himamaylan, Kabankalan,* and *Ilog,* to prevent guerrilla rescue forces from escaping to the unoccupied southern towns. Number two: If the Americans were taken northeast to *Magallon*, that move was his responsibility. He should take care of the more difficult but most likely route of escape: northwest to *Magallon.* This, he must do immediately. He can't be cheated of his quarry. The capture of the Americans can earn him the rank of General.

An eerie quiet settled in the surrounding hills.

"Spray everything with machine gun bullets." The Colonel ordered. "Uncover all from their place of hiding. I will teach these people to cooperate. They need to know that their lives mean little, if at all."

Machine gun fire blasted the large fire trees. After thirty minutes of continuous spraying, the gunfire ceased. The Japanese did not see blood running down one of the firetrees. Polding held on to Cario as long as he could; when his strength gave out, he could no longer keep his hold. He let go and fell to the ground spilling blood at the base of the firetree.

All the way to *Magallon*, Colonel Nikamura dragged people out of hiding and tortured them beyond endurance. He spilled blood readily, carelessly, with little compunction. The less he discovered, the more he killed. The vicious colonel Nikamura created an infamous "Crimson Trail."

Chapter 6—Nothing Can Get Worse

Cario slid down the tree trunk and jumped beside Polding. He cradled the lifeless body in his arms, and pressed the blood-soaked shirt to his breast. He cried quietly as he held his brother close. His face still dripping with tears, he took Polding's body back to *Manang* Simang's hut. He found only the charred remains of the women's bodies. He cried in despair, took what was left of them and Polding to the well on the hillside and buried their remains. He swore the Japanese would never get their hands on the three Americans for as long as he lived.

He knew he had to do something. Groping for the ropes on the ground, he shook off the weeds that hid them. He hauled up one basket after another. It was getting dark. He could hardly see what he was doing. Afraid the Japanese might still be in the area, he couldn't light a fire. He took the Americans out of the baskets. Their clothes were soaked and their legs were stiff from being underwater for a long time. He had lowered them into the well at nine in the morning. Now it was almost six in the evening. Nine hours in cold water had taken its toll. Not sure if they were alive, he put his ears on their breasts to hear any heartbeat. He heard a faint ticking.

"Thank God they're still alive!" Utterly relieved, he sobbed in guarded joy.

"Don't you die on me now, or *Manang* Simang, Consing and Polding all died for nothing."

He did not have a rag, let alone a towel to wipe them with. He took off his shirt and wrung out the blood from it, but it was too sticky to use. He took off the *patadiong* that Consing wrapped Frank in, took the bucket, dropped it in the well for some water and dipped the *patadiong* in it. He wrung the water out and started to wipe their faces. He began to massage their stiff legs and started in earnest to bring life back.

I wish I had your help, Consing, he sighed. He had loved her for so long and was waiting for the right time to tell her. Acutely aware of his loss, he began to sob softly. Why did you all have to die? He lamented. Thankfully, he didn't know that Consing had been raped before she died. He really didn't know how to start his task of reviving the Americans, for if he attended to one, it meant he was neglecting the others. The wind started to blow. How could he shield them from the cold when he did not even have anything dry to wipe them with? He sat for a minute desperately trying to decide what to do.

I need to take their wet clothes off, but they'll catch a cold if I do that. His nerves were shut. Automatically, his hands twisted the *bolo* he always carried. "I know. I can cut the broadest banana leaves I can find and wrap them in those while I hang their clothes to dry."

He ran back to the banana grove, cut as much leaves as he could carry and hurried back to the well. He laid the leaves on the ground, took the shirts and pants off the Americans, wrung the water from their underpants and put them back on them again. He pulled their boots off and shook the water out. He stuck these on the trunks of the *malungay* tree. He had difficulty removing their socks. His hands were always busy; for an entire five minutes, he would rub George's legs, hands, and face. Then he would switch to Frank, and then to Robert. While he was working on one, he wrapped the other two in banana leaves. He cut soft ferns on the side of the trail up the hillside and cushioned the banana leaves with them. He began to realize how much warmer it got inside the banana leaves when he lined them with the ferns.

What he would give for a blanket! He did whatever his hands could find to do, but there wasn't much he could do for them. Anything he did was hardly any help at all. He sat down utterly disheartened.

Why was he spared to face such a hopeless task? Better to have died with those he loved and his kin. Well, he can only do the best he can. Maybe he just has to leave the rest to God?

Frantic, he scurried from one task to another; the responsibility he faced and the thought of the incoming danger the following day took the wind out of him.

Oh, God, I need some help. I need to sit down and think this through. What must I do before I face the coming day? He was reeling from the weight of his task. He began to pace briskly, feeling guilty that he could not think of anything to solve his problem. Unable to think straight, he put his hands up in desperation. The load he carried the past day and half the night fell on him like a heavy, soggy blanket hung out to dry on a line too thin to hold it. He gave himself up to the night and he lay down on his back letting the weight of his despair hang all over him. As his emotional strength flowed out, he considered with foreboding that perhaps thoughts can get oblivious in the dark. Maybe by morning things would clear up in the light of day? Quickly, he had to find resolve again. He resumed massaging all three with renewed energy. He unwillingly conceded that when things go wrong, they do go wrong indefinitely. In utter frustration, his energy running out, he decided there was nothing more he could do, but he thought there's a certain kind of freedom in being completely screwed up. Nothing can get worse.

Chapter 7—Rescue and Flight

I wish there were someone I could turn to for help. Come daylight, I could be in deep trouble. What am I going to do?

While his hands worked, his thoughts wandered in all directions. He remembered *Manang* Simang offered *saba* to boil. There's got to be a tree with fruit in the banana grove. She also mentioned green coconuts. There were some young coconut trees on the other side of the hill beyond the well.

"If I find something to eat and feed them, maybe they'll regain consciousness. Let me do just that. "

He decided he would scrounge for food; he was getting hungry himself. Not having eaten left him weak and light-headed. Yes, he must find something to eat. The Americans hadn't eaten since *Manang* Simang and Consing rescued them. They only had thin *lugao* hours ago. He decided to look for *saba*, but if he left them here, what if someone should want well water and find them? What if the Japanese decide to get back, or if *kempetai* should look for more victims to turn over to the Japanese? One by one, he carefully moved the bodies underneath some fern cover. In his haste, he forgot the wet clothes and left them hanging everywhere.

He returned to the banana grove to look for *saba,* but he went around in circles in the dark. He lost his footing and slid downhill a couple of meters. He squatted to regain his balance. Something swooshed above his head. What was that? Before he could stand, he heard it again.

A bat? A bat! Sure, bats could smell ripe bananas. What luck! In the dim light of the quarter moon, he tracked their flight to a few meters to his left. He stood to get to the fruit-bearing tree when he heard an unmistakable rustling to his right. He froze in his tracks. A few minutes later, a light flashed near him. The light turned on and off, but moved steadily toward him. Now it was aimed directly at his face. He was blinded. He moved swiftly to his left to dodge the light, but it landed on his face again.

Good God! The Japanese are back again!

Cario cringed in fear. He made an attempt to sprint, but a voice spoke in *Ilongo,* his own language.

"I wouldn't do that. We have you covered. There are four of us to only you. You might as well give up."

Cario turned to his left, ready to move toward the darkness of more banana trunks, but there was someone there to block his move. He turned swiftly to move behind; someone was there too.

"I'm just a few paces to your right," the voice said as it advanced toward him. "Who are you and what are you up to? Why are you traipsing alone in the dark?"

Cario held his tongue. He must be careful not to give information. He hesitated.

"Are you *kempetai?* He asked.

"Are you?" the voice flashed right back.

"Hell, no!" He made no attempt to hide the contempt in his voice.

"Then we're on the same side. Come out of hiding and tell us what you're up to." The voice courteously invited.

"I was just looking for something to eat; I'm hungry, and . . ." Cario hesitated. His voice trailed off.

"And wanted to feed those you left behind?" The voice completed his statement.

"How did you know?" Cario let the tears fall. "I can no longer do it alone. I want desperately to hide them from the Japanese," he said in despair.

"So do we, son. I'm Sergeant Raymundo Valderama. My squad and I have been tracking you for a while now. Was it your idea to hide them in the well? That was smart; it may have been the only way to hide them from those savages."

"No, Sir. It wasn't my idea. *Manang* Simang told us to do that. It was she who saved them, but she's dead now and so are her sister, Consing, and my brother, Polding. They all died for them.." He began to sob. "You have to help me hide them," he pleaded when he got his voice back. "I swear I'd rather die, too, than let the Japanese find them."

"Take it easy, son," the Sergeant said. "My men are doing all they can to revive them but they probably won't be able to walk for a couple of days. After we feed them, we'll put them in jute sacks and carry them on our backs." He continued quietly as if the matter had been decided a while back.

"You may come along too." Someone extended the offer. "You could carry their wet clothes and some food. We found the *saba* you were looking for.

"You have to keep up with us, though. We'll travel fast at night and stop to hide them in daytime. The Japanese can track us down on their motorcycles if we walk in daylight." Sergeant Valderama cautioned.

"We're ready to go now, Sir," another one of the Sergeant's men reported.

"This is Ramon. What's your name?"

"My name is Macario Flores. Cario for short."

"All right, Cario, stay behind Ramon always. When he runs, you run too. If he stops, you stop and do what he tells you to do, okay?"

Overwhelmed with relief, Cario promised obedience.

They walked so fast he had to half run to keep up with them. Moving in complete silence, they skirted empty fields, kept under cover of trees, waded in streams and crossed creeks. He noticed that when they stopped, the Sergeant opened the black box he carried and whispered into it. His men followed him quietly but they all seemed to know where they were going. When streaks of dawn broke through the trees, they were sliding downhill, almost like the one near *Manang* Simang's place. Cario spied a small hut as well. Two men came out of it and met them downhill. The Sergeant's men carried the Americans inside the hut. Men who met the Sergeant's group took them behind the hut and showed them a pile of dead leaves on top of firewood covering a big hole underneath. There were three covered holes spaced fifteen meters apart.

"That'll do very well." The Sergeant told Cario to go to the hut and take care of the Americans. "They know you and have seen you before. If they're awake feed them some of the *saba* you brought in the sack. Open small holes on top of the green coconuts and let them drink the milk. When they finish drinking it, split the coconuts in half, scrape the meat, and feed them that too."

"Don't you ever let them drink water from the stream. I brought a plastic bottle filled with rainwater; give them a drink from that if they are thirsty," the man who met with the Sergeant ordered.

"Cario, the only food we have is in that sack you carried. We have to scrounge for food as we go. We can go a lot farther without eating, but you must feed them enough to let them get their strength back. In a day or two, they may be strong enough to walk on their own. Understand?"

The Sergeant was very firm.

Cario nodded his understanding. It dawned on him that these men communicated much without using words. The Sergeant gave him a pat on the back to show his approval.

Maybe I'm doing something important, perhaps crucial to their escape? He walked into the hut and found George and Robert awake and whispering to each other. He looked them straight in the eye, put his finger on his mouth and shook his head. George tried speaking to him, but Cario cut him off; he covered his mouth with his hand and shook his head.

George pointed to Frank, put a hand on his forehead and on his wrist. He folded both hands together pleading.

Cario understood that George worried about Frank's temperature. He nodded, went down the steps, and came back with a wooden bucket filled with cool water. He took what was left of *Manang* Simang's *patadiong,* dipped it in, wrung the water out of it, and put it on Frank's burning forehead. He did this several times on Frank's neck and upper torso also. He took off the shirt the men had put on Frank and exchanged it with Frank's own shirt that he had stashed away in a sack. Frank seemed more comfortable. George opened his mouth to thank him, but Cario put his hand to his mouth and shook his head. Again, he put his hand on Frank's forehead to check his temperature. Frank's wound had festered from all the moisture in the well and the perspiration on the march. He was burning up.

Cario disappeared for some time. When he returned, Frank's head was on Robert's lap and George was dipping the *patadiong* into the bucket, desperately trying to cool Frank's temperature down.

Cario returned with *Manang* Pasing, a woman slightly older than *Manang* Simang. Her long gray hair was knotted at the base of her head. She wore a faded *kimoma* (a loose blouse) over a plaid *patadiong.* She walked over to Frank's side, carefully took off Frank's shirt, and examined the wound. She went to the kitchen, got a worn-out towel, came back and began to clean the wound. She had a pouch tied to her waist. She untied it and took out what she needed. She prepared a poultice of crushed green leaves, *buyo*, betel nut, and some *apog* (lime). She chewed the nut, put all the items together, pounded and crushed it to a pulp, and applied the poultice on the wound she cleaned. She took out some bed clothes rolled inside a mat, ripped it apart, and bound the poultice on Frank's arms and shoulders with the ripped cloth.

When she finished, she laid Frank's head on Robert's lap where she found it before. When she put the poultice away, she took Cario aside, told him to take care of it and put more everyday till the wound healed. After fifteen minutes, Robert, stroking Frank's forehead, noticed with amazement that Frank's temperature had gone down fast. He was about to thank the woman, but she had disappeared silently.

Remembering the Sergeant's instructions, Cario fed them with the ripest of the *saba*, made them drink from the coconut, broke it in half with his *bolo* after they'd drank the milk, scraped the soft meat and fed it to them. There was nothing else to eat, so they finished what he gave them, for they were famished. Even Frank, sick as he was, ate his fill. Cario took part of the ripped sheet, dipped it once more in cool water, put it on Frank's forehead and wrapped it with the rest of the cloth around his head. Frank dropped off to sleep. Two men took George and Robert away. Cario took Frank gently in his arms and put him in a hole and covered the hole with sacks of dried coconut husks.

"Sleep as long as you can," he whispered. "Keep very quiet. Try not to disturb what I put on top of you to hide you. Good luck, my friend."

He was not so sure Frank heard him when he walked away. Did he understand him even if he heard?

He hid not too far away. He slept uneasily, off and on. The Sergeant and his men had disappeared. He began to fear they had left him with the Americans for good. His stomach ached; he remembered he only had half a saba when he fed the Americans. He was tempted to eat one more, but he heard the Sergeant's voice.

"Cario, that's the only food we have. "

It was about 2:00 o'clock in the afternoon. He was perspiring, was very thirsty and he did what was probably foolish. He crept out of hiding and went to the hut looking for water. Suddenly, he heard gunfire in the distance. Running back to where he hid before he got up, he lay quietly, wetting his lips with his tongue every few minutes. He heard more sporadic gunfire, but very faintly, much farther away. About four o'clock, he could not stand his thirst any longer. He ran up the hill to the stream on the other side.

About two hundred meters from the stream, he heard footsteps. He dropped to the ground and rolled to the cover of some fern. The footsteps grew louder. Six men were running fast; now they were splashing on the stream below him. He looked more intently and could make out the Sergeant and Ramon crawling to the edge of the stream. They dunked their heads into the water, took off their shirts, threw them on the slope and splashed water over themselves. They were breathing heavily, probably from the running they did. He stood to go downhill and join them when he heard a gun crack.

"Freeze," a voice said.

He could not believe how fast they surrounded him with drawn guns and *bolos*.

"It's just me, Cario," he blurted in fear.

"Cario? Why are you here? You're supposed to keep a good eye on the Americans. What happened?" Ramon looked alarmed.

"Nothing. I just came to drink at the stream. I got very thirsty and I haven't had anything to eat since last night."

"Shish, kid. You're getting to be a real nuisance. You had some food in the sack. Why didn't you eat a *saba* or something?" Ramon spoke with annoyance.

"The Sergeant said the food is for the Americans. I dared not eat lest they'd have nothing left to eat." Cario was defensive.

"He's a good kid, Ramon. Let him drink and give him something to eat," the Sergeant ordered.

"Inyong, (Eugenio)," Ramon called, "come and give Cario a couple of those *bodbod* (rice cakes rolled in banana leaves) your cousin gave us."

"A handful of rice and a piece of salted fish would taste really good, huh Cario," the Sergeant kidded.

Cario was on the verge of tears. He was very grateful for the offer of food. Inyong Salazar rummaged into the sack he carried and reported.

"We have quite a bit of food, Sir. We have two large papayas not quite ripe yet, three pineapples, one big *langka* (jackfruit), a couple dozen *bodbod,* and half a dozen dried fish. Wow! That's enough food for a week, if we stretch it."

They always ate sparingly with Cario. They entrusted him with all the food.

Ramon took Minyong (Hermogenio Morfe) and Berting (Roberto Atienza), looked for green coconuts, husked them so they would not be heavy, and put them in the sacks they carried the Americans in a few days ago. Robert and George could walk now; only Frank was put back in the jute sack. They cut holes on each side of the sack and put Frank in with his feet dangling. They took turns carrying him on their backs. The Sergeant did not carry a load. He carried only a black box.

The next day, Cario crept within a meter of the Sergeant to hear him talk when he opened the box.

"Sir, we are now high above *Isabela*. This is the fifth day we've had them. They can all walk now; we're making good progress. Our problem is food. The closer we get to the mountains of *Kabankalan*, the less food we can find. We can scrounge for food less effectively since we'll have difficulty knowing who are *kempetai* (Filipino collaborators) and who aren't. Whom do we trust to give us food?"

Why the hell are we going close to *Kabankalan*? There's a Japanese garrison there. Shouldn't we be as far away as possible? Cario wondered.

More than a week later, there was hardly any food left. Cario knew the Americans were weak and hungry, tired and bedraggled. Their hair got long and matted. He took care of that. He sharpened his *bolo* till it shined, then cut their hair short, uneven, but short. All had not shaved for weeks; dark stubble grew on their faces. They all looked shabby, but there was nothing he could do about that.

Occasionally, they walked into a creek with a natural spring and would all happily clean up. They still had to bathe in a hurry and keep good distance from each other. Talk was forbidden. The Americans learned to communicate without words. If one wanted to give something to another, he would simply leave it where the other could get to it. They maintained a routine governed by silence and almost seemed mute. Obediently, they followed quietly where they were led, ate what they were fed, and did as they were told. They looked to Cario for help.

He served them diligently, happily, and became attached to all three of them. The guerrilla men would come and go. At night, they set their route rigidly and had to walk many kilometers without rest. Cario made the Americans keep their pace. When they stopped to rest, he attended to their bathroom needs. He maintained their strength, feeding them all he could get. But he never really talked with them at all.

By daylight, he led each to their hiding places and tucked them in to sleep. When they had to run out in an unanticipated move, he, pulled them out, prodded, pushed, and eventually hid them elsewhere. The guerrilla unit would mysteriously, quietly, arrive at dusk. Cario pulled the Americans out of hiding one after the other and prodded and pushed them as they run, trotted, or walked with little rest until the coming dawn.

Cario saw the Sergeant keep talking to the black box. After the first week, he discovered they had hooked up with a larger guerrilla unit commanded by Lieutenant Amador Garcia. Twice, the guerrilla men didn't show up for the night trek. When this happened, Cario heard gunfire at close range. Instructed not to take the Americans out of hiding unless someone, usually the Sergeant, told him to move on, he stayed in hiding. Twice, he couldn't even get near them to give them food to eat, but even they were instinctively aware of some great danger and endured their hunger and their confinement willingly.

Cario got used to the regimen of solitude and silence and so did the Americans. They lost consciousness of the days. Time just stretched indefinitely. Automatically, they observed the routine of exhausting walk or run in the dark and hide, sleep and eat in strict silence in daylight. Fear and danger ruled the days, but, somehow, they managed to outdistance and elude the Japanese. How? Many times he thought the Sergeant was out of his mind and was obviously wrong. But after narrowly avoiding capture, he knew it was always a question of following, without questioning, the orders from the black box. So he followed the orders of Sergeant Raymundo Valderama without flinching, as the Sergeant followed orders from central intelligence. The black box etched their route of escape.

Chapter 8—Covenant with a Mountain

Captain Paterno and his unit were deployed beyond *Isabela* on the second day after the crash landing of the B-29. He knew there was another black box somewhere in the vicinity of *La Carlota* or *La Castellana* because the day before, a black box communication told him a guerrilla unit had trailed the Japanese contingent speeding toward these towns.

Today, Captain Paterno's black box throbbed.

"Identify yourself and clarify your mission," Nanding requested.

"Lieutenant Renato Tabligan here; I'm commanding a unit of sixteen men. We just intercepted a *Kempetai* column scouting ahead of Japanese troops and captured the leader. He says the column is led by Colonel Nikamura, a fiendish torturer."

Nanding could hear unintelligible grunts in the background.

"What the hell is that sound?

"It's my *Kempetai* informer." Lt. Tabligan apologized. "He's gagged but is ready to volunteer more information. He says the Japanese haven't found the site of the American aircraft explosion yet. His guess is it may be northeast toward *Pontevedra* or southwest toward *La Castellana.* Evidently, if Colonel Nikamura does not find the wreck there, he'll proceed to *Magallon."*

"Why would he do that?" Nanding asked.

"This Japanese commander thinks our forces are taking the Americans there and then to *Kanlaon.* We're a small group on foot. Where are you and how many of you are there?"

"I have a unit of twenty men; twenty-two including myself and my aide, Lieutenant Honorio San Jose. This is Captain Fernando Paterno. Do me a favor and pinpoint the Japanese troops. We hear them occasionally spraying with machine gun fire."

"I'll use a bamboo catapult to throw a hand grenade. I'll cut some trees, set a small fire somewhere and zigzag close to you. Where are we headed and how long do we do this cat and mouse trick?" Lt. Tabligan answered.

"We can't carry it on indefinitely. They're heavily motorized and would soon catch up with us," Nanding warned. "On flat ground, we're no match for them, but if we get to the hills and reach the caves near *Kanlaon* without a major engagement, we may have a chance. You and I know the terrain by heart. They don't. We have about a dozen horses; they have dozens of motorcycles and numerous trucks and jeeps. Let them chase you toward very steep hills near the caves. Trails there are hardly visible and are covered with huge stones; they have to abandon their vehicles sooner or later."

"Got you, Sir. We'll set traps for them, move stones at the edge of ravines; this may be fun."

"Horses are waiting outside the caves. A dozen more men are riding them in and out. *Ilang-ilang* branches mark the cave entrances. If you're not familiar with the entrances, you can identify them by the *Ilang-ilang* smell," Lt. San Jose said via the black box. "Exits are marked by lantana smell."

"Very clever," Lt. Tabligan replied promptly.

"I know that *Ilang-ilang* trees were once a lucrative business for *Kanlaon*. I heard the leaves of this tree were harvested by the tons and exported to perfumeries in France before the war. On the other hand, I know the lantana, a flowering brush, grows like weeds and has a distinctly offensive odor when crushed." Whoever is leading this outfit surely knows what he's doing, he thought.

Setting a cat and mouse chase, Lt. Tabligan moved to the right and lighted fires there. Nanding moved his men to the left and lighted fires there too. These fires were abandoned as soon as they were lighted. Black box talk kept the pace and the distance between the two units accurately calculated and set their movement accordingly. They were careful to check with each other in the early morning hours before they moved out again.

Considerably slowed down by hit and run guerrilla harassment, Colonel Nikamura's motorized division arrived at the steep hills at the foot of *Kanlaon* volcano after three days.

"Good morning, Sir," Lt. Tabligan reported. "I'm camped beside the first cave just above the foot of the mountain. My men have spotted activity inside the cave. It seems there's a strange ritual going on in there. Did you say a dozen men are riding horses in and out of the caves? Are these your men?"

"No." Captain Paterno denied. "Those are volunteers from the town of *Isabela*. The leader is a grandson of the legendary '*Papa Isio*.' Are you familiar with the legend about this grandfather?"

"You mean the revolutionary leader, a *Babaylan (*spiritual healer), reputed to have had supernatural powers? He was quite a legend in his time."

"The same one. His grandson still leads a cult. Supposedly, they have *anting-anting (*magic powers) and they recite *oraciones (*prayers*)* to the mountain gods residing in the neighborhood. The local people either have a great deal of respect for them or they fear their powers still. Local belief says they're invincible and they walk invisibly in and out of these mountain caves." Captain Paterno told the Lieutenant.

"True or not, I guess we need them as guides. Going in and out of the caves will be very tricky without guides. I'll speak with this leader, the grandson. I'm supposed to meet him soon."

Lt. Tabligan approached the first cave and he was dumbfounded at the sight he saw. The dozen horses, perhaps albino, were as white as the sheets the men were wearing. The men wore tall pointed cloth headdress like those worn by members of the Ku Klux clan portrayed in the U.S. movies about southern prejudice. The horses had flowing manes as white as the capes the men wore. The ensemble did present a ghostly picture.

Mounted on the kneeling horses, men with their heads bowed, chanted an oracion, a prayer, asking mountain gods to pardon their intent to trespass. The prayer over, the chanting ceased. The leader, called *Toto* Isio, dismounted and handed each one of his men a leafy *ilang-ilang* branch. They brushed the leaves on their capes, removed their hats, crushed the tender *Ilang-Ilang* leaves, dripped the juice on their heads, smoothing it on their faces, carefully tracing it on their foreheads, necks, ears, nose, and around the eyes. This done, they took more leaves from an *ilang-ilang* branch and repeated the same process on the horses.

When the ritual was over, Lt. Tabligan approached *Toto* Isio. He formally saluted and the lieutenant acknowledged the formality with the same gesture. The lieutenant was surprised to see this leader of a band of twelve was only five foot, one inch tall, much smaller than all of his men. He had black hair braided and tied down with a white ribbon at the end. His black beard, streaked with white, reached his chest. He looked like an old man but, getting closer, Lt. Tabligan guessed he couldn't be over thirty. His eyes were deep pools of brilliant light. They sparkled though they grew opaque when he turned and his eyes were not directed at anything in particular. Lt. Tabligan shook his hand after the salute. His grip was so strong the lieutenant felt shaken when he retrieved his hand. *Toto* Isio gave an order and the twelve men reined their horses. The horses stood upright; the men unsheathed long *bolos* looking more like swords. The precision with which they brandished their weapons in the air amazed the guerrillas The glint was blinding. They sheathed the weapons back in their cases as they let out a shout sounding like a cheer. *Toto* Isio dismounted.

"We're privileged to work with you. We're ready to rid the mountain of these disrespectful foreigners."

"That'll not be an easy task," Lt. Tabligan answered. "They're very heavily armed."

"Perhaps so, but the gods promised they'd render their weapons harmless. They'll retreat in a matter of weeks," *Toto* Isio predicted.

"By the way," he cautioned, "you must instruct your men to respect the mountain gods. If they want the same protection my men are granted, they must submit to the same ritual we follow daily."

The lieutenant decided to humor this spiritual leader and acceded to his request. Then *Toto* Isio said something that astounded him.

"You know, of course, that the fruitless assault of the Japanese in the past three days was crucial to sergeant Valderama's progress above the mountains of *Isabela*. It has given him time to connect with a larger guerrilla unit and they'll proceed toward the mountains behind the *Kabankalan* garrison without being captured."

"How did you know that, *Toto* Isio?" Lt. Tabligan asked with alarm and amazement. "Did Captain Paterno tell you about that?"

"Oh no, the mountain gods tell us what we need to know."

After this revelation of prophetic power, the lieutenant's men were more willing to listen to this leader of twelve men on white horses. They were less apt to question the reality of the mountain gods.

* * *

Colonel Nikamura found the terrain rough and rugged. His trucks had difficulty when trails narrowed. They had to stop for long intervals to move the large stones out of the way. After no more than a kilometer of this task, the trucks had to be abandoned. The troops marched on foot. Colonel Nikamura used the motorcycles to lead the way, but one after the other the motorcycles ran into traps after jumping over barricaded obstacles. Frustrated, Colonel Nikamura sprayed the hills with machine gun and automatic rifle fire. Dynamite blasted the stones on the way. Captain Paterno and Lt. Tabligan had no difficulty knowing exactly where the Japanese troops concentrated. The dozen white robed riders on horseback intimately knew the mountain. These run in and out of caves and caverns where Colonel Nikamura's men could not follow.

The nature of the terrain eluded Colonel Nikamura. The extensive caves interconnected and in many places millions of bats littered the ceiling. They hung immobile during the day and came out at dusk feeding on the fruit of the *kamagong*, tall mahogany trees in the *Kanlaon* slopes. These bats were essential to the eco-system of the *Kanlaon* forest. When the roar of the motorcycles disturbed them, they whirled around the caves in waves. The Japanese on motorcycles flew into the caves thinking they could trap the guerrilla men easily, but they ran into stone barricades near entrances and as soon as they went in deep enough thousands of bats descended on them, sucking their blood, blinding them as they settled on their heads in hordes. The Japanese soldiers who made their way in got covered with bats. Screaming and howling as they clawed their way out, they were ready targets for guerrilla snipers.

Not realizing what the problem was, Colonel Nikamura marched toward the caves in blistering wrath. Unable to understand what was keeping the motorcycles so ineffective, he stopped short of marching in a cave himself when he saw one of his lieutenants come out covered with bats and screaming in acute distress.

Guerrilla men came in and out of the caves unharmed. The spectacle stunned the *kempetai* who whispered the story of the guerrillas' covenant with the mountain spirits to the unbelieving Japanese. When motorcycle after another came out of caves with drivers screaming in agony and the sight of bats in overwhelming numbers chasing in dark waves anyone coming in, their wall of disbelief began to crack.

The ghostlike apparitions rode their horses into the caves. Japanese motorcycles would follow only to come out with headless corpses on the driver's seat. The Japanese soldiers who saw this horrendous picture inevitably succumbed to fear. They put their rifles down, lifted their hands up in the air, dropped on their knees and bowed, their heads touching the ground. A loud chanting, like medieval music, came out of the mountainside.

An infuriated Colonel Nikamura slapped the soldiers' bottoms with the flat side of his samurai.

"Get up, you ignorant sons of bitches. Snipers will have you spotted in no time and finish you off. Use your guns. Pull that cannon over here.

I'll send these mountain gods to hell." He strutted, and yelled, brandishing his sword threateningly in the air.

Between fear of the apparitions and consternation over Colonel Nikamura's wrath, the Japanese soldiers dragged the 75mm cannon almost in front of a cave.

"Blast these sons of the devil out of the cave. Don't tell me their gods can protect them from this gun," the colonel screamed.

Without his knowledge, the apparitions followed by guerrilla men exited on the other end of the cave and entered an adjoining one. The walls were solid rock.

"Fire the cannons into the mouth of the cave," Colonel Nikamura screamed.

After three salvos, there was a rumbling but muffled sound as though something inside rolled the cannon balls back to the entrance of the cave. A loud blast shook the whole mountain; rocks began to slide amidst smoky dust. A huge boulder fell on top of the cannon directly in front of Colonel Nikamura. The cannon slid off the side of the mountain and became part of the powdered debris below. Colonel Nikamura found himself precariously tottering in front of a naked precipice. A loud, eerie chanting came up the precipice, slowly enveloping the mountain.

After he gained a more secure footing, Colonel Nikamura nervously surveyed what happened.

"Hah! So where are their gods now?" He strutted, putting his hands on his hips, a gesture of a Japanese boast.

An unexpected response came. The sky slowly darkened; a loud humming sound, like an airplane engine taking off, lifted from the precipice and filled the mountainside. In what seemed like an instant, everything turned dark and with a swooshing sound the bats alighted on everything around.

Lieutenant Enoye Matsuki pulled the Colonel from where he stood. His free hand reached for the tarpaulin inside the jeep he drove. They rolled under his jeep wrapped in the tarpaulin. Then as quickly as the sky darkened, it lighted up again. The dark cloud, like an enormous sheet floating in the air, swooshed back into the mouth of a cave.

Screaming in anguish, the soldiers rolled over and over helplessly scraping the bats still stuck on them. The rest who survived the attack ran for cover into their trucks, refusing to come out again. Lieutenant Matsuki unrolled the tarpaulin, picked up the shaken Colonel Nikamura and laid him on the front seat, on the passenger side of his jeep. When the colonel had regained his composure, lieutenant Matsuki said, "What do we do now, Sir?"

"Drop back to the tents below," the colonel replied. He was still angry, but not quite so sure what to do. "Perhaps we should set fire to the entire mountainside."

"I would not do that if I were you, Sir." Lt. Matsuki's instant answer unnerved Colonel Nikamura.

"And why not?" His sharp retort rang out just as quickly.

"Because, Sir, gods or not, something is protecting the guerrillas from harm. We must not underestimate their common wisdom. We need to study and understand the source of their strength."

"You mean you, too, believe this nonsense about the mountain spirits?"

Colonel Nikamura lifted his eyebrows and a deep crease formed on his forehead. He worried that fear had infiltrated even his officers.

"I don't believe in the superstitious nonsense, Sir," the intelligent Lt. Matsuki corrected. There must be a logical explanation for what has happened, he wondered. This location must be the densest forestation in the whole island of Negros.

He stared at the vegetation in deep thought, convinced that this mountain was the home of a rich bio-diversity. At the Tokyo University before the war, Lt. Matsuki majored in the natural sciences for a degree in B.S.Biology. His professor then underlined a natural wonder. He lectured that because of its preserved dense forests more than 510 species of land mammals, birds, reptiles, and amphibians exist only in the Philippines. The forests contain over 15,000 plant species, 5% of the total number recorded the world over. Without doubt, the forests, his professor stressed, are rich pharmacological mines.

Lt. Matsuki wondered if the guerrillas even realize that the Philippines is one of the most biologically diverse countries in the world. Why, this forest must be the home of the Negros Bleeding Heart, the Blue Napped Parrot, the Philippine Hawk Eagle, and the Serpent Eagle that the natives call "Agila." These are some of the world's rarest species that even before the war were nearly extinct. It would be a shame to torch this forest and lose all that. When he was assigned to serve in the Philippines, Lieutenant Matsuki was overjoyed. He hoped he could see some of these rare creatures in one of the military campaigns into the interior. Lieutenant Matsuki's reply came slowly, deliberately, as though he had given the matter serious thought.

"If you set fire to the mountainside, Sir, it may be difficult to contain. Not only will the guerrillas lose cover, we would too. They'll go deeper into the interior and it would be more difficult for us to follow. They know this mountain well. It is their home."

Colonel Nikamura could not stand to be corrected, but this young upstart had a point. Besides, he did save his life. Did he really? He wondered if he could have survived the bats.

"All right, a fire may be too hard to handle, but we need to blast these ignorant peasants with our guns. We need to haul the rest of the canons up this mountain." Colonel Nikamura's reply was just as deliberate.

"We don't seem to do much damage to the guerrillas with those guns as much as we do to this mountain." Lieutenant Matsuki pointed out again.

"Hmm, the colonel paused.

"So what would you do if you were in command?" He was getting disgruntled.

The colonel's attitude shook the young lieutenant.

"Well, Sir," he said very honestly, "We could carry on this campaign for weeks, but we don't seem to know where our targets are. They're very well entrenched. Besides, I don't think they have the Americans, or else they wouldn't have stayed to engage us. If they have them, don't you think they would be on the run, getting away from us more quickly than they have?"

"That sounds like a reasonable assumption." The Colonel agreed. He scratched his head as if distracted from his intent.

"But I'll not abort this campaign until I'm absolutely sure that's the case. I must go back to the drawing board. Let's have a meeting of the officers as soon as possible. We need to assess our strengths as well."

Colonel Nikamura was determined more than ever to trap a quarry that got more elusive each day.

* * *

Captain Paterno had his own doubts. He stubbornly believed that the covenant with mountain spirits was simply a matter of local wisdom. Guerrilla men who submitted to *Toto* Isio's instruction covered themselves in protective *ilang-ilang* branches, careful to crush the tender leaves on their heads. Pure drops kept the bats intoxicated. They kept away from the smell that rendered them immobile, kept their fury on hold. When they approached the guerrilla men too closely, they fell on the ground unable to fly up. As soon as the bats were kept immobile by the smell, the men on horses, moved through the caves swiftly and quietly. Guerrilla men followed their lead. Moving to the other end they sealed the cave with lantana. Lantana smell revived the bats; they flew up and clung to the ceiling once more, but when disturbed by motorcycle roar, they swirled in blind fury. Bats are blind in the day. They see only in the dark, but though blind, they have radar hearing and they clung to any moving object.

Lieutenant Matsuki pondered the problem of the bats. He puzzled over what kept the guerrillas safe from them. He scoffed at the thought of a supernatural power; more likely there was a natural power at work here. These men understood nature more closely than strangers to their habitat had the ability to discern. If a lab were handy, he may be able to test which of the plants around could afford a scientific explanation. Colonel Nikamura wondered why the lieutenant walked around pulling weeds and mumbling to himself. This is a smart kid, but a rather strange one.

Colonel Nikamura did not anticipate guerrilla mobility with horses. When the motorcycles attempted to carry the chase into unknown territory, they inevitably got lost and were thinned out. The twelve ghostly riders ambushed motorcycles; in the dark, they slashed the heads off of the riders with their long swords. When motorcycles propelled by their own power came out of the caves with bleeding, headless corpses, *kempetai* swore this was the deed of the mountain gods. They succumbed to superstitious fear.

When they continued to get into the caves, soldiers driving motorcycles were ambushed by guerrilla men, killed and stripped clean of weapons, even boots that could be useful in the rough terrain. The motorcycles abandoned by the Japanese were stashed in the caves for future use.

Guerrilla snipers sat on the branches of huge *kamagong* trees sheltering the caves. They felt more certain of their aim and never doubted their safety since the ghostly figures half convinced them they were invisible to the Japanese. Private Rueben Inaro told Lt. Tabligan that he balanced himself carefully on the branch of a *kamagong* tree when he aimed at a soldier running out of a cave.

"I moved on a branch too far out and lost my footing. I swear I slid off the branch I was sitting on, but an invisible hand grabbed me and put me back on another branch below."

Toto Isio overheard this confession. He responded quickly.

"You're right. I saw you fall; I closed my eyes and prayed silently. You might think it took only an instant, but I was asking the spirit of the tree earnestly for a minute to restore your balance and save you from certain death. I'm glad my prayer was answered."

Lt. Tabligan doubted the truth of the story, but he remembered he almost stumbled when he was running away from Japanese gunfire. Something unexpectedly lifted him and maintained his balance. Whatever the explanation was, he and Captain Paterno both acknowledged their debt to the ghostly figures. Certainly, they knew the mountain more than either of them or any of their men did. If it weren't for them and their protective ritual, the Japanese would have thinned out their units mercilessly. Why, they even took care of the wounded.

Toto Isio carried with him a special black root. He boiled it in mountain water and asked Lt. Tabligan's men to drink it when they rested at night. It tasted like good coffee and gave them warmth on a cold night. Incredibly, their energy redoubled; their wounds stopped bleeding and seemed to heal overnight. If the wounds were critical, *Toto* Isio bathed the men in special oils and applied leafy poultices. The rest of his men drew circles on the ground, lighted candles, and chanted their oraciones. They put the wounded on their horses and delivered them to women who took them away.

"In a week's time," *Toto* Isio promised, "they would be able to rejoin the unit again. They would be hale and hearty. The ones who were critically injured would take longer to heal, but they would not die."

The uninjured men serving under the Captain and the Lieutenant felt an unshakable assurance of their safety. They harassed the Japanese with more bravado. They seemed to their officers to tread more lightly and endure more nonchalantly what otherwise would have been a fearsome experience.

* * *

"This is not going right." Colonel Nikamura roared, beginning to see his promotion in rank slip away.

"Clearly you are the superior group, with superior arms and weaponry. Do you have to be outwitted by a handful of men? Where's your pride? In heaven's name, use your guns and your vehicles well. Clear these insignificant pests out of the way." He yelled, looking ready to explode.

"If we don't get rid of these vermin soon, heads will roll; dire repercussions will come when the dust settles." He threatened his officers. Once more, he ordered his officers to regroup. "Keep to the open trails and spray the trees with gunfire. Get rid of the snipers."

Again, the motorcycles led the way and the entire column marched behind the trucks. They had not advanced a full kilometer when the trucks rounded a bend on the trail. Suddenly, a half dozen hand grenades fell on the top of two trucks. Soldiers did not see where the grenades came from. They seemed to have floated down from the sky. The superstitious *kempetai* started another panic and soldiers on foot ran around in every direction. Infuriated with the dwindling discipline, Colonel Nikamura climbed on top of the hood of one of the trucks and fired a submachine gun into the air. He arrested all movement by firing in the direction of the running soldiers. His anger did not blind him and keep him from noting that lining the bend where the trucks had been moving were tall *kamagong* trees with thick, broad trunks and branches spanning no less that ten or twenty meters of ground. But surrounding the trunk were smaller trees sheltered by the branches. The thick foliage made it impossible to distinguish trunk from undergrowth. Swinging his samurai in the air, Colonel Nikamura yelled for his lieutenants to spray trees with machine gun fire, but the trunks and branches and the thick undergrowth surrounding the trunks made it impossible to see where sniper bullets came from. Machine gun bullets ricocheted on tree trunks everywhere.

Lt. Tabligan's snipers were snuggly lodged in protective tree trunks; they knew they were difficult to spot from the ground.

"Make sure you don't move together in large groups," Captain Paterno warned. "Always move singly, or preferably in pairs. No more than two of you should be within the parameter of at least twenty *kamagong* trunks."

"Yes, Sir." Lt. Tabligan agreed. "We know the Japanese will spray the trees with machine gun bullets, so we zig zag behind the biggest trees for protection."

Thus Lt. Tabligan and Captain Paterno's snipers eroded the Japanese column. They assembled in the caves at night and spread out before dawn. Even the *kempetai* had not figured the guerrillas used bamboo catapults to hurl grenades at the trucks.

"No one can throw hand grenades at the height and with the swiftness we see. For sure, this is the power of the mountain gods at work," the *kempetai* kept insisting.

After a week and a half, Colonel Nikamura's campaign troops only ventured out as far as the trucks could go. Each week they went farther after they demolished stones in the trails but it was a slow and tedious job. Colonel Nikamura consistently lost soldiers to guerrilla snipers who continued to elude them. Occasionally, a hand grenade found one of the trucks. The other trucks would fire back and soldiers covered the territory around with gunfire inch by inch, but could never find any trace of where the grenades came from. They never knew anything about the ingenious bamboo catapults. Desperate, Colonel Nikamura asked for air support. Airplanes flew low, strafing suspicious areas.

When Japanese airplanes flew over the area, Nanding's men and Lt. Tabligan's unit sat safely with the ghostly figures inside the caves. They could hear the roar of the motorcycles and the drone of the low flying airplanes. Quietly they moved through one cave entrance to another during the night. They were still able to spot the lights on the trucks and would catapult grenades from their posts near cave entrances and retreated into them quickly. Cave entrances were barricaded with huge stones that hid the caves from view. They rendered them impassable at night

Indeed, it seemed as though the Japanese had angered spirits who refused them further passage through the mountain. When the trail they cleared got them close to a spreading *balete* tree, an explosion out of nowhere halted and invariably killed a few of them. The superstitious *kempetai* the Japanese kept at the frontlines ran off in fear and continued to spread the rumor that Mt. *Kanlaon* was haunted. They had no doubt the mountain spirits were angry at the Japanese assault. Colonel Nikamura, in frustration, fired 75mm guns in every direction. He didn't know his guns sealed some cave entrances and came dangerously close to killing Lt. Honorio San Jose, silencing the black box he dropped.

Neither did the *kempetai* know that the explosions near large *balete* trees came from dynamite guerrilla men planted there overnight. Colonel Nikamura thought he saw Lt. Matsuki close to a huge *balete* tree before an explosion, but there was no sign of him anywhere after. The soldiers who manned the cannon said they aimed at the tree and was sure they hit it but somehow, after the first salvo, their gun either misfired or was inexplicably disabled.

The *kempetai* began to hallucinate. They said the *balete* tree was a huge castle and they saw Lt. Matsuki admitted into it by men in white horses with white flowing manes. Colonel Nikamura got furious. He took a sub machine gun and cocked it. Advancing toward the *baltete* tree, he sprayed it with gunfire. Bullets seemed to bounce back from the tree. He took his samurai and started hacking at the tree trunk. The tree began to bleed but the sword got duller with each stroke and the blade melted to the hilt. The submachine gun jammed and a voice boomed in fluent Japanese.

When are you going to learn that you cannot conquer a forest? You cannot obliterate it, for out of its ashes, new growth will sprout. Nor can you dominate a people with force. Hate consumes and erodes. The only force that can subjugate is love, for people yield to love in willing surrender. Go home. Your hate is not welcome here.

When Colonel Nikamura recovered from an apparent blow on the head, his samurai was still in his hands and the submachine gun functioned right. All around him was a display of nature in full and nonchalant power. The *balete* tree shook its branches filled with leaves in resplendent color. Nothing could be greener, but a sullen gust steamed the forest in a broiling summer heat. With extraordinary power, a sudden, angry thunderstorm darkened the heavens and seemed to short-circuit the earth to put the humans in their place. Though the cannon shots falling everywhere discomfited the forest, it was long suffering and imperturbable. After the storm, it stood in impervious majesty. Colonel Nikamura remembered Lt. Matsuki's warning.

"So where is the young lieutenant? Don't just stand around in fear of invisible ghosts. Find the Lieutenant and bring him to me. He has some explaining to do." Trembling with fear, the *kempetai* tried to explain the lieutenant's disappearance saying the last time they saw him, Lt. Matsuki was really admitted into a huge castle in the midst of the forest.

"Don't you dare confront me with old women's tales about castles and fairies. We have enough trouble with a small bunch of guerrillas Now we have to fight invisible beings too?"

Yet Colonel Nikamura wondered how the lieutenant could vanish into thin air. He ordered a thorough search but the lieutenant's body was never found. He scorned the *kempetai's* tale of the lieutenant being admitted into a castle as completely implausible, without doubt a figment of incalculably rich imaginations animated by fear. Perhaps the cannon shots disintegrated the lieutenant's body in the air. Confusion reined over the events of the past two days but Colonel Nikamura clearly heard the voice from the forest. How could he explain that? Perhaps one of the mountain residents or a guerrilla officer knows how to speak fluent Japanese? Is that possible? He wondered.

"Sir," a young *kempetai* dared to remind him, "You tried to demolish the castle with a cannon, and when you could not do it any harm, you tried to force your way into it by using your samurai to open the door, but you were shut out and a voice from the castle thundered at you. I could not understand what it said, but I know you heard it."

"Fiddlesticks." Colonel Nikamura brushed him off. "Your crazed imagination is working overtime. I heard no such voice. A voice from a tree? How ridiculous! Get out of here before I have you flogged. A voice, indeed!"

A plea for reason and a spurt of self-pride battled inside him. The old demon of self-pride won. He will retreat, but not without cost to his adversaries. He would still teach this people how to respect a conqueror. He retreated, but everywhere he stopped he rounded up civilians by the hundreds and exercised his power to kill beyond any reasonable limit. No mountain god can dull his blunted ambition.

Chapter 9—Dream or Reality

Lt. Matsuki looked for a particular plant that rendered the guerrillas harmless against the bats. The sound of soft music coming from a large *balete* (also known in Negros as *dalakit)* tree a few feet from where he stood distracted him. This tree towered over all the other trees. The Lt. thought he was hallucinating. Huge, spreading branches arched down to the ground and large white stones surrounded the base. He turned around to see that the stones around the base were really circular stairs that lead to several floors of a towering castle. Dazed, Lt. Matsuki came closer to the tree at the instant that Colonel Nikamura's 75mm canon released a shot to demolish it.

The *balete* tree had been standing in this forest for hundreds of years, shading approximately three hundred meters of ground. The trunk had grown enormous; numerous aerial roots hung from it. This is the oldest tree in the forest. Before the war, science departments of both Silliman University and the University of the Philippines estimated it to be over a thousand years old. People in *Kanlaon* feared or revered the spirits in this *balete* tree. They believe this tree is a magnificent palace of the fairies and *encantados (*magical beings*)* who are invisible to human eyes. Selectively, they choose whomever they reveal themselves to. At night, this tree is believed to be the gathering spot for fairies. Allegedly, music is always heard from it. At the base of the *balete* tree is a big oblong gap, the door to the home of the fairies.

Colonel Nikamura's cannons could not hurt the *balete* tree. Every time it was fired upon, a door opened, admitting the cannon balls and letting it out through the back door. The chief of the *encantados* opened the door for Lt. Matsuki. Several maidens escorted him inside. A marble stairway led to a hall adjoining a courtroom. Inside, sat twenty judges in flowing crimson robes. Though they were full-grown, mature men, they were only three feet tall or less. Opposite them, a jury of twelve wearing white pointed hats and white robes told the lieutenant why he was brought into their presence. They towered over the judges. Though the leader was only an inch over five feet tall, the rest were at least six feet tall or taller. Led to the center of the courtroom, the Lieutenant saw through walls of clear, transparent glass the view of the forest outside. The judges asked him to sit. Feeling uncomfortable, he sat amazed at the size of his captors. He was accused of attempting to burn the castle and bringing harm to the environs by killing people taking care of the birds and animals in the spacious gardens within its walls. He vehemently denied the charges.

"I have nothing to do with attempting to burn the castle or harming the birds and animals in this forest that is their home. In fact, I urged my superior officer not to set fire to the forest."

The jury of twelve men in white robes talked among themselves for a while. They told him he would be detained for two days to wait for further developments in the case. His work meanwhile was to feed the animals, especially the rare Philippine spotted deer called the *Usa* (cervius Alfredi) and the pigs of the enchanted people, the Visayan Warty Pig that the lieutenant knew was the most endangered of all the South East Asian wild pigs. He had to feed them with corn provided him.

Lt. Matsuki enjoyed the view outside the glass walls of his cell. Noticing his great interest, his jailer, a short fellow with long black hair braided and tied with a white ribbon at the end and a beard flowing down to his chest, pointed with great care the presence of the *Ibid*, the Philippine Sailfin Lizard (hydrosaurus postulates). He really got excited when his jailer pointed out the Philippine Hawk Eagle perched on the branches outside his cell and he almost cried at seeing the Negros Bleeding Heart. He recognized it by the red spot on its breast. He also saw the Blue Napped Parrot and the Negros Fruit Dove. To the right of his cell, he saw the Philippine Eagle Owl, the Serpent Eagle called *Agila,* the *Tularik* (the Visayan Tarictic Hornbill). His jailer called it *gahod,* or noisemaker, because it made such a raucous sound when it flew from branch to branch asking for food regularly at the noon hour, its accustomed feeding time. Perched on a branch to the left of his cell, was a pink-bellied Imperial Pigeon his jailer called the *hagumhom,* for the grunting sound it made, as if it cleared its throat.

These birds had spectacular plumage ranging from dark orange, black, dark brown, beige, gray, pale and bright yellow, pink, and blazing red. Lt. Matsuki asked if he could be permitted to linger by the walls to enjoy the sight of the birds. His jailer, impressed by his great interest, brought a visitor to his cell, a princess of great beauty. Less than three feet tall, she looked like a doll. She brought with her a musical instrument to entertain him. She talked to him in a voice full of sadness.

"I know why you came to Mt. Kanlaon. Why is it that you wish to destroy this land?"

Again, Lt. Matsuki denied the accusation. Noting his earnestness, the princess asked if he knew the legend of Mt. *Kanlaon*. When he shook his head, she decided to tell him about it, but the music she played, put him to sleep as she strummed on till she finished her story. When he awoke, the princess offered him food but he refused the food saying he was not hungry. His white robed jailer, took him aside earlier and warned him if he ate the food he was offered, very likely he'll never be permitted to leave the castle so he just drank plenty of water to fill his stomach. Lt. Matsuki was aware of the magical quality of this castle. He was suspicious that a trick was played on him. Sometimes he thought he just dreamed everything happening to him.

After two days, his court trial resumed. Again, he gave the same reason why he could not be held responsible for the crime he was accused of. Chief of the jurors, *Toto* Isio, confirmed he heard Lt. Matsuki ask his superior officer, Colonel Nikamura, not to set fire to the *Kanlaon* forest, that he should, in fact, respect the wisdom of its inhabitants.

"Yes, I did just that," Lt Matsuki swore. "I have a great admiration for the very rare inhabitants of this forest. I would never seek to harm them or rid them of their home."

The jury deliberated in earnest. Convinced of his sincerity, they found him guiltless. The next morning, the princess came and told him he was free to go, but he must urge his superior officer not to press on with his trespass against the mountain or they would both lose their lives and the lives of those they commanded. He was happy at heart but he dared not show pleasure on his face for fear he might be held longer. For the inconvenience of being detained, the princess gave him a black root a foot long and taught him how to use it for medicinal purposes. She assured him it could heal any kind of sickness providing it was used for people who did no harm to others.

Lt. Matsuki thanked the princess as she led him to the way out. When he was out of the palace, he found to his dismay that he was on top of the *balete* tree that Colonel Nikamura tried to destroy with the 75 mm cannon. He spent the whole day trying to get down. When he touched ground, his breast and his arms were bruised and he lost all his strength. It was beginning to get dark. After resting for a long time he crept towards the trail to the Japanese tents below the foot of the mountain.

Exhausted from being relentlessly harassed by the guerrillas, Colonel Nikamura's troops slowed down the campaign almost to a halt. The Colonel decided he was not getting anywhere. What he thought would be a quick capture of the fleeing Americans turned out to be guerrilla warfare he underestimated. In utter disarray, his men hurried back into the trucks. Their heavy gunfire could not identify its target. On the day he decided to withdraw from Mt. *Kanlaon,* Colonel Nikamura was petrified at the sight of Lt. Matsuki crawling toward his tent.

Half conscious from hunger and dehydration, the lieutenant raved about a castle and a jury that tried him of a crime he had not committed. Everyone who heard him repeat his story over and over thought Lt. Matsuki crazed. Weeks later when Lt. Ishida was dying from wounds suffered during a guerrilla ambush, the Japanese surgeon at the garrison in *Binalbagan* had given up, ready to pronounce him dead. Lt. Matsuki cut off part of the black root the princess gave him, boiled it in spring water, offered it to Lt. Ishida and saved his life, proving, if only to himself, that his stay in the castle was not just a dream. If he had just dreamt the whole story, why was he on top of the *balete* tree? How did he get there? He could not have climbed to that height. Perhaps the force of Colonel Nikamura's cannon lifted him and deposited him up there? But how could his dream be so detailed? Did the cannon jar his brain and was his dream part of an extended delirium? Maybe he had listened to the *kempetai's* superstitious tales so much they became the base of his own imagination? Perhaps he had collected the root himself when he was out searching for an explanation of the guerrillas' immunity to the bats? Had the entire experience in this campaign rendered him psychologically unstable? He could swear he had seen those endangered species. He fed them with his own hands, and yet again he had wanted to see them long before. His college professor had taught him a good deal about them and he wanted so much to see them that perhaps his injured brain convinced him he had seen them? Long before this campaign, he had known of their existence. Shaken by this experience, he could not tell dream from reality. Whatever the answer was, he would never feel whole again.

* * *

More than three weeks of fruitless search for the Americans sent Colonel Nikamura back to *La Castellana* and *La Carlota* empty handed. Frustrated, he carried on a vicious bloodbath. He turned his anger on non-combatant Filipinos. For two weeks more he trapped and captured all he could find in hiding, inhumanely tortured, and eventually executed them.

Filipinos in the area scurried close to Mt. *Kanlaon* for protection.

By the end of the fifth week, Colonel Nikamura returned to *Bacolod* in disgrace. In his defense, he maintained the Americans escaped to Mt. *Kanlaon* and were still in hiding there. He asked that the area be heavily bombed. Fairies in castles or simply trees in a dense forest, Lieutenant Matsuki despaired for the possible extinction of the rare species of animals and birds in the world.

The apparitions continued to roam the mountainside. Their covenant with the mountain saved the guerrillas from certain annihilation and the rare species that inhabited the forests from extinction.

Chapter 10—A Slight Miscalculation

Despite a fierce but silent objection, Colonel Asaki did as Colonel Nikamura commanded by radio and marched his troops on the railroad tracks toward *Isabela*. On the chance the guerrillas took the Americans farther up the shore toward *Hinigaran*, Colonel Asaki split his troops into three. Marching north toward *Hinigaran*, Major Onoki hacked the *nipa* groves and burned the *kogon* grass on the fields adjacent the beaches. Leading several trucks headed by motorcycles, Colonel Asaki himself took the railroad tracks past *Binalbagan* Crossing and raced toward the town plaza in *Isabela*. One truckload and two jeeps commanded by Lt. Ishida eased southwest toward the swampy shores in *Himamaylan*. Colonel Asaki's instincts told him to go southwest toward the swampland in *Himamaylan* and farther south toward barrio *Aguisan* and barrio *Binicuil*.

If we leave these areas unattended the guerrillas may take the Americans there and then race to barrio *Talubangui*, then to *Enclaro* in *Ilog,* he speculated. But Colonel Nikamura pinpointed the aircraft crash northeast of *Isabela* and he wanted the area around secured, so he ordered Colonel Asaki to meet him there. Colonel Asaki arrived at the town plaza in *Isabela* promptly, but though he heard machine gun fire, Colonel Nikamura was nowhere around.

"Where is the doodling fool?" Colonel Asaki complained to his lieutenants.

In the distance, he could see the blaze lighted by Major Onoki moving toward *Hinigaran.*

"No guerrilla activity here," Major Onoki reported. "Should I proceed toward *Pontevedra?"*

"No. Go southwest to *Isabela*. The explosion was in that area. They could still be hiding around there," Colonel Asaki said. "However, if the guerrilla forces swung south, they could be heading toward *Ilog* and then to the unoccupied territory around *Sipalay*."

"That's very probable," Major Onoki concurred, "but if they swing toward the mountains, they could go past *Mabinay* toward the shores of *Bais*, in Negros Oriental."

"There are caves around *Mabinay*. They could decide to hole up there too," Colonel Asaki agreed.

"On the other hand, Sir, what if Colonel Nikamura is right? You know *Magallon* is just a stone's throw from *Isabela,* and then they could be in Mt. *Kanlaon* in no time at all," Major Onoki suggested.

He should not have the entire credit of capturing them, Colonel Asaki thought. What's taking the fool too long? Had he already discovered a significant clue and withheld it from me?

Colonel Asaki decided to circle around the barrios of *Isabela* himself, though intuitively he wanted to speed back to *Kabankalan.* He knew he wasted time here, but he couldn't leave. He felt a spastic burning in his gut. He struggled against the need to unleash this fury inside. He felt an urge to go beyond the limits of power, to go beyond what others did not have the capacity to do: power to kill with impunity. If Colonel Nikamura could burn and pillage, he could do as much, and more. He could device ways of torture beyond the power to endure. Exercising this power to inflict pain was for him a compulsive need that never stopped, not even for a quiet moment of satisfaction as he used up a frenzied energy to reach an extended dimension. So he moved around *Isabela,* rounding up and killing in the most horrendous fashion as many Filipinos as his troops could find.

When Colonel Nikamura met with Colonel Asaki in the plaza at *Isabela,* he decided that, not counting Colonel Asaki's troops, there were already far too many trucks in his command. With his superior troops and adequate motorcade, he could handle guerrilla opposition without any problem. Besides, why should he share the glory of the capture with this blundering idiot, Asaki? Briefly, he conferred with the other colonel and then decided to send him back to his own garrison in *Kabankalan.* He strode to his junior officer with a great deal of pomposity though when he spoke his voice had a false, conciliatory ring.

"You're probably right, after all. There's a possibility the Americans were taken to *Himamaylan,* and then to the sea and south to unoccupied territory. That possibility cannot be dismissed; you need to go back and monitor the area."

Why the hell did I have to come to *Isabela* when I could have gone back promptly toward *Kabankalan?* Was I recalled here simply to confirm that this bastard is my superior officer? Damn him, I have lost good time already. Colonel Asaki fumed, but he hid his annoyance and restrained his urge to lash his outrage.

If I am proved right and am promoted, watch out, you arrogant fool, he thought.

He kept his composure and tucked in his contempt, but he swore silently.

I shall get back to you.

Having exercised his demons to the limit, he could not wait to move on and follow his instincts.

"I need to get back to *Binalbagan,*" he roared in anger. "Radio Major Onoki to come back immediately," he ordered his aide. "I'll wait for him before I move on."

He waited for half an hour, assuring himself that Major Onoki was indispensable for there's always safety in numbers. Inwardly, he mistrusted the soundness of this decision.

"If he does not get here in another five minutes, I'll simply order him to follow."

He chafed at his own dalliance, but he swore he was going to get to the bottom of the unexplained disappearance of the Americans. More and more he felt certain he would capture and crush the guerrillas before they escape to the unoccupied territory. Let the bastardly Nikamura go all the way to *Kanlaon*. He'll not find anything there.

Colonel Asaki tingled with anticipation. He couldn't wait to be on the right trail; he could taste the certainty.

Damn it, the Americans and their guerrilla rescuers are moving south. But they have no transportation so I'll catch up with them in no time at all. I shall wipe out all those in my way of capturing these Americans and when I catch them all, watch out Nikamura. I will become a general and be your superior officer.

Chapter 11—A Shift in Direction

Captain Villalva calculated the Japanese had by now caught on to their plans. Last night he was so sure the Japanese would move to *Himamylan* but for reasons unknown to him colonel Asaki had gone to *Isabela* instead, so he moved his men and the Americans parallel to the railroad. They backtracked all right, but they were moving to the far left instead of straight to the creek and absolutely not to the mouth of the river toward the sea. His runners confirmed the Japanese had cut off escape through the river and the fire behind the Japanese garrison was moving northwest. He was sure the Japanese command would soon enough discover that's not their route of escape.

Captain Villalva knew he didn't have time to lose. He had deceived the Japanese for another day, but they would soon figure out where he was headed and would race toward *Himamaylan* in their vehicles in far less time than he could on foot, dragging along the already exhausted Americans. He didn't know that Colonel Nikamura had ordered Colonel Asaki to meet him in *Isabela* and they had spent time capturing Filipinos in hiding, torturing and killing them when they could have spent the time tracking him and the Americans. Now the black box was humming; he received orders to take advantage of the Japanese miscalculation and move before they had time to set new roadblocks. He had to disappoint the Americans again.

"I know I promised you would dine with my friends tonight. Unfortunately, there's no time for that now. Those who can run must race toward the swamps in *Himamaylan*. No more backtracking. Run in a straight course and meet with Lt. Verzosa. You'll move with him to *Binicuil* and finally to *Andulawan*. Let's hope Lt. Verzosa gets to you before the Japanese do."

Nonoy and Pedring made ready to take Scott, Joe, Valdez and BB with them, but BB stubbornly refused to abandon Marco and Spencer so Captain Villalva split the Americans into two groups of three once more.

"All eighteen of my men are scattered around the *Binalbagan* Crossing between *Binalbagan* and *Himamaylan*. I have to tell them by radio to be ready to join in a large group. If the Japanese catch up with us, we need every man to defend you."

A faint hum of Japanese trucks and jeeps bothered him. Ponsing saw concern on the *Kapitan*'s face.

"Should I get in touch with Colonel Gomez, Sir?"

Before the *Kapitan* could answer, Ponsing felt the throb of the black box as he opened it to listen.

"There's a truckload of Japanese soldiers coming this way, but this seems to be in no particular hurry. What do you want us to do?" Lt. Verzosa was anxious to know what to do.

"Find out how many are in the truck. I'm sure there's a jeep escort. How many Jeeps are there, and is the unit heavily armed? How many machine guns? Tell Lt. Verzosa to set some traps, but ask him to get all the men together. Maybe we can join the Gatuslao household after all. The men can catch up with us there.

A network of fieldworkers protected the Gatuslao hideout. They had supported the hacienda for years; they still looked to Don Domingo Gatuslao for guidance. This haciendero (extensive landholder) had four sons. Two were married and had young children. These maintained the hideout and lived with their parents. The two younger ones were eighteen and twenty. They went in and out of the hideout, but most of the time they lived with fieldhands and their families. They taught these men to tend whatever crops could be raised in the shortest time possible while they were in hiding. They cut bamboos at night and hauled them to the swamps where they were made into fish traps managed by the married brothers. These were also used to build huts for the fieldworkers' wives who made salt beds. They salted and dried fish on the beaches. The younger brothers managed men who took dried fish, shrimp paste and salted seashells their wives prepared, and walked the hills and surrounding countryside to trade these for rattan, rice, vegetables, fruit, and poultry. They smuggled grain and everything else they traded for to the hideout in the swamps. The Gatuslaos had a steady supply of food generously shared to feed fieldhands and their families and guerrilla troops as well.

The guerrillas kept the Gatuslao hideout well informed of Japanese activity. They ambushed Japanese patrols attempting to locate the hideout. One thing more insured the safety of the Gatuslaos; they lived way inside the swamps. Unfamiliar with swamp topography, the Japanese didn't try to penetrate into the Gatuslao hideout. They knew they would be at a distinct disadvantage there. Colonel Alvaro Gomez and *Kapitan* Almanzur Villalva were good friends of the Gatuslao family. They often visited their swamp hideout where they were treated with seafood delicacies. *Kapitan* Villalva sent Nonoy to run ahead and tell Don Domingo Gatuslao he had some special guests coming for dinner that night.

Chapter 12—Disturbing Orders

Lt. Ishida was happy to be sent back to the garrison in *Kabankalan*. Nothing had been more important to the Japanese command than the capture of the Americans the guerrillas had rescued, hidden, and defended. So far, the quarry escaped capture, but the Japanese knew it was only a matter of time before their superior forces would corner the fleeing Americans.

After he crossed the *Binalbagan* Crossing, Lt. Ishida received very disturbing orders

"*Kempetai* spies inform me a guerrilla unit is taking the Americans toward the swamps in *Himamaylan*. Take your truck and jeeps to barricade their progress. If they are taking the river toward the sea, you must pursue. Expect reinforcement soon because I'm going to join you and take over," Colonel Asaki boomed on the radio.

Lt. Ishida was prepared to encounter guerrilla resistance. He knew he had far better arms and ammunition than guerrilla forces had, but why go into the swamps to the mouth of the river? Colonel Asaki knows the disadvantage of going into dangerous terrain. In fact, no one in his command had ever gone into swamp area before. Why now? Why with such a small force as he had? He had better increase his speed and engage the guerrillas before they get to the swamps. His drivers revved their engines to full speed toward *Himamaylan*, but he didn't like the idea of pursuing them into the swamps.

Chapter 13—Out of Flat Land and into the Swamps

The situation was desperate. Captain Villalva had been in contact with Colonel Gomez everyday; in fact, several times a day to confirm every move they had taken. The Colonel knew every little progress in the grass or under trees, every retreat, every zigzag movement necessary to elude capture by the Japanese constantly at their heels. Now, not only were the Japanese close, typhoon weather was moving in. Winds were shifting; visibility was almost zero. A storm was brewing, raising the waters in the creeks and blowing the *kogon* grass flat, taking away cover and concealment.

As they sat waiting for the *Kapitan's* orders, more guerrilla men, as if coming from nowhere, joined the Americans. Three more men detailed to run with Pedring, Scott, Joe West and Valdez replaced Nonoy, assigned to run ahead. These men, alert, wary and incredibly fast on their feet, knew where they were going. They spotted and recognized objects as if they had eyes at the back of their heads. They rushed the Americans with gentle care but with a firmness that surprised and impressed them. When they stopped to allow the Americans to catch their breath, Valdez asked one of them a question that weighed on his mind for a while.

"Who are you? Where did you come from? Who trained you and who do you answer to?"

"Sir, my name is Salvador Larena. You can call me by my nickname, Badong."

Pointing to the guy sitting close to him, he began to introduce the rest.

"This is Sauro. His full name is Rosauro Villegas, and that one over there (the one over there nodded as Badong pointed to him), is Rudi, Rodolfo Munoz.

Valdez introduced Scott, Joe, and himself.

"We're all serving under *Kapitan* Villalva. He trained us. We've been under his command for over a year now," Badong said.

"It's a great honor to be part of his command," Rudi added.

"Is there something special about that?" Scott asked with subdued sarcasm in his voice.

"Yes, Sir. You better believe it. I almost quit when I first joined. Training was so difficult. I went through the most rigid, relentless and consuming discipline I've ever encountered in my life. If you didn't pass the *Kapitan*'s approval, you were weeded out and sent off to some other less demanding assignment," Sauro answered quickly.

"If you had any pride at all, you didn't want that to happen." Rudi said.

"Why was training so hard?" Joe West wanted to know.

"When we were new recruits, the *Kapitan* had little tolerance for our stupidity and indolence. In training, he assigned us to run and pass messages already done by men carrying black boxes. We ran as fast as we could, but when we gave the message, it had already been delivered. The *Kapitan* just wanted to know how fast we could get where the message was intended. The first time we slacked off, we were reprimanded. When we slacked off a second time, we had to run another message. This seemed to us such an extremely useless exercise causing great pain and energy. When some failed to get the *Kapitan*'s approval a third time, they were dismissed from his unit."

"You ask Badong here." Sauro turned to Badong. "He's our squad leader; he answers to the *Kapitan* directly."

Clearly, Sauro was re-living his distress over the matter. "Don't you think that is too much to ask of us?" He stared at Joe intently, but before he got an answer he continued. "We didn't understand how important it was then, but by gosh, we found out it was life saving when we were in combat situations with the Japanese, just as we're in right now."

"Don't you have a junior officer to answer to before you get to the Captain?" Scott asked rather doubtfully again.

"Yes, We do." Badong put in defensively. "Of course there's Lt. Palacios and Sergeant Padriga, though our unit often splits as the circumstances dictate. But the *Kapitan,* he's everywhere. He personally supervises exercises and expects the best from everyone."

"The *Kapitan* is a superb marksman, whether he uses a *bolo*, bow and arrow, a rifle, or a submachine gun. He can throw a grenade farther than anyone and with great accuracy. He even fires a bazooka. He thinks very clearly. He's beyond compare and quite a legend in the guerrilla forces around here," Rudi continued with passion. "You ought to try competing with him one day."

"Don't forget," Sauro interrupted, "he has ambushed Japanese forces so many times successfully. Colonel Asaki at the garrison in

Kabankalan has put a special price on his head. He's the most wanted guerrilla officer in this region."

"The ambushes he organized required surprise, stealth, daring, and speed and has earned him the nickname of Quick Silver, after a long, silver fish found in *Tanon* strait, (pronounced *Tanyon*) the body of water between this island and Cebu. The Quick Silver is a fish that strikes its prey and disappears with lightning speed," Badong declared proudly.

"The *Kapitan* is probably over thirty years old; he is much older than most of us in his command. I'm only twenty-two, but I can never catch up with him. He can run faster and farther than any one in any guerrilla unit. To save our own lives in any encounter, he expects us to have the same resource in energy he has. He says we need an energy reserve greater than is expected in any situation of danger." Sauro was very proud to add this bit of information.

"Not only that," Badong insisted, "He has trained us to be very observant, to think clearly, independently, and quickly, to respond to changes in expectations, and to react with level-headed common sense all the time."

"Forget being too proud because you can be humbled in an instant by changing circumstances beyond your control, the *Kapitan* always tells us." Rudi put this in quickly while he had the chance to say something. He continued somewhat tearfully.

"We do the best we can every time we do anything for him. He's like a father to us. We'll do anything for him because we know he'll give his life for any of us, if necessary."

Pedring came from nowhere. He came in very quietly and wanted to know what the talk was about.

"We were just talking about the *Kapitan*," Rudi said.

Suddenly, they were tight lipped again.

Scott, Joe, and Valdez were also quiet after this, but there was a new spring on their feet and a new quickness to act in response to command from the squad.

Pedring thought, perhaps talk about the *Kapitan* had something to do with it? It always does to all of us.

After they had a chance to catch their breath, Pedring led them unerringly through ditches and dikes in rice paddies where there was still some cover. He knew how much time it would take to clear spots without cover, and, running fast, they made it to the line of coconut trees in the distance. The coconut grove stretched into lanes hidden by clumps of bamboo. Quickly they made it to the end of the coconut grove and as they lost the cover of the trees, they began to crawl through grass blown almost flat by wind and rain.

"Couldn't we rest under the trees for a while? Valdez asked.

Pedring apologized quickly, but he explained why it wasn't wise to do so. "Stopping every now and then would take away five minutes of valuable time. We need to clear the flat land and get into *nipa* groves by the creek that leads to the river and into the swamps."

Pedring seemed to know exactly when to switch from grass to ditches to dikes and then run once more for cover of still another coconut grove till they got to the edge of the river at the outskirts of *Himamaylan*. There, they hugged the riverbank where they waded through *nipa* groves and were met by men in *bancas* without outriggers. As suddenly as the heavens darkened, a light broke through. Through a heavy drizzle, the sun shone. They were all drenched; their straw hats soggy with water.

"Take your hats off quickly and squeeze the water out of them before you put them on again. It's no good to catch a cold from the rain," Pedring warned.

Their boots were heavy with water but it was no use to take them off for they walked almost knee deep in water at times. Their shirts clung to their bodies; the humidity was high. They were wet but not cold. The wind slowed down to a pleasant breeze. Tired and hungry, but knowing they made good progress to where they were supposed to dine, they felt relief and anticipation.

Scott and Joe both heard the sound of running vehicles a while back. They asked Pedring if he heard it too.

"That must be the truck led by a couple of jeeps. Earlier, our men reported seeing those and were preparing to engage them if they stopped and went on foot in our direction. These men with the *bancas* are tenants of the Gatuslaos. They'll paddle us to the narrow waterway leading to the Gatuslao hideout. Thank God we've made good time and we're getting into swampland where the Japanese never venture," Pedring explained.

"Besides, " Badong remarked, "this wind and rain may be a sufficient difficulty. They better know where they're going or they'll be in deep trouble."

Chapter 14—Back in *Binalbagan*

The stormy weather presented a disadvantage to the Japanese as well. Their heavy trucks slowed down on muddy roads unimproved since the Japanese occupation. Bridges became unstable and hindered trucks crossing with heavy equipment. Rain blew into trucks drenching the soldiers. When it poured, visibility decreased to almost zero.

"Damn this rainy season," Colonel Asaki grunted under his breath. "Well, at least this delay will give Major Onoki the chance to catch up with us."

The trucks pulled in the garrison and piled into the yard at the back of the barracks. Before the war, the barracks were houses of chief executives of a sugar milling company. One after another trucks parked close to the concrete fence surrounding the compound. Water in the yard was at least six inches deep, in some places even deeper. The men got soaked when they ran out of the trucks into the buildings for shelter. Wind and rain lashed on their faces fiercely.

Filipino workers in the garrison served in four-hour shifts. Some wielded dry mops on wood floor. They made sure the floor was dry and clean despite mud tracked in by wet, dirty boots coming in from the pouring rain. Cooks worked in the kitchen, making sure hot coffee, tea, or *conji* (hot rice gruel), and the condiments needed to mix in it (sautéed garlic, finely chopped green scallions, minced onions, chopped green and red peppers) were in good supply.

The officers jammed the lounge, a tiny room in the far corner next to the stairs leading out of the officers' quarters. The lounge, open and airy, let the smoke clear quickly. Tonight, though, the wind blew in in unwelcome gusts. Colonel Asaki hated cigarette smoke, cigar smoke, any kind of smoke, so officers huddled in the lounge, away from the sala (receiving room) close to his quarters. He occupied three of the most spacious rooms to the west. A narrow veranda ran alongside the rooms and he often came out and walked the entire length when he couldn't sleep, or when he was in deep thought. His officers watched out for his mood swings. When he was jovial, drink, loose talk about women, and reminiscences of Japan flowed freely. When he was dour, they learned to keep out of his way or risk being a scapegoat for whatever bothered him. Tonight, his ire blazed in uneven spurts. Clearly, he was mauling about a problem he wrestled with since he left Colonel Nikamura's company. He was wading through a private hell and he needed his space.

His aide ordered the Filipino women he toyed with when he was tired and restless to bring in plenty of drinks. Colonel Asaki drank heavily in the privacy of his quarters. He had a penchant for women, slim, firm breasted brown virgins, or plump, running-to-fat, middle-aged prostitutes he needed to cool off his lust. Alternately, he fondled them or battered them with his fists. Tonight, he was exceptionally vicious. The women softly moaned in pain. They didn't dare exhibit their fear or disgust, for then he would use a whip instead of his fists. The more he drank, the more abusive he got. His officers could hear the thud of bodies falling on the floor or thumping against the walls after Colonel Asaki got going. Major Onoki arrived when Colonel Asaki had spent his energy and he sat limp in a chair on his veranda. He got up when he heard trucks and jeeps come in. He walked out of his rooms in full uniform into the sala yelling for service.

"Where the hell are the men with mops? Why can't they keep this floor clean?"

When the Filipinos rushed in to clean the mud Major Onoki and his men tracked in, Colonel Asaki grabbed a mop from a cleaning hand and poked the handle into his stomach so hard he staggered and fell on the floor. Roaring in anger, the Colonel kicked his ribs with his heavy boots.

"Take this inefficient beast out of my sight; bring me men who know how to clean."

Other men with mops scurried in and soldiers dragged half-conscious workers out of the room and threw them out into the rainstorm. Colonel Asaki asked Major Onoki if he and his men had eaten. He yelled in the direction of the kitchen.

"Bring food into the dining room and be quick about it. Don't you people do anything all day except bite your nails? Bring some *conji* this instant . It better be steaming hot, or I'll pour it on you if I have to teach you how to keep it hot."

When the food was brought in, he took a bowl and tasted the *conji*. He spat the first spoonful out in distaste. Trembling with fear, the cook was brought in. Colonel Asaki took his bowl of steaming *conji* and poured it on top of the cook's head.

"You call yourself a cook? Get someone to teach you how to prepare edible *conji* before you cook for me again."

The hot gruel burned into the cook's flesh. He endured the pain and dashed out of Colonel Asaki's reach. When the cook was out of the room, Colonel Asaki took another bowl and helped himself to the *conji* again.

"Actually," he asked Major Onoki to agree with him, "this isn't bad at all; am I right?"

Major Onoki was embarrassed. He didn't risk a reply, but he wished Japanese high ranking officers, would behave like decent human beings.

"As soon as you're done eating, I'll call a conference of all officers to assess the emergency situation we're facing. We need to outline a plan of action and decide how to proceed," he said coherently despite the smell of alcohol on his breath.

Major Onoki couldn't agree more strongly. With *conji* in his mouth, he was unable to say anything, but he nodded his head in agreement.

"Let's see." Colonel Asaki stroked his chin as he spoke. "Let the Filipinos clean the trucks and wipe them dry," he demanded.

"At this hour, Sir, and in this weather?" Major Onoki asked in amazement.

"And why not? If you put fear in them, they'll find a way to do it," Colonel Asaki snickered. He ordered his officers promptly into his study. On the wall behind his writing desk hang a large map of the island of Negros. With a red marker he encircled seven different towns and barrios, then drew a line with a black marker and connected the red circles: *Himamaylan, Aguisan, Binicuil, Kabankalan Crossing, Talubangui Bridge, Vista Allegre, Enclaro.*

"I see what you're trying to point out, Sir," Major Onoki said with enthusiasm. "We must get to these points soon if we hope to capture the Americans, right?"

"Absolutely! Officers assigned to cover these locations must secure the area and establish roadblocks to make sure the guerrilla bands do not pass through. In a day or two, I expect to see the Americans in my garrison at *Kabankalan.* Am I understood?"

"Even if they get to the *Talubangui* Bridge, they can't get to *Enclaro* if we catch them thereabouts," Major Onoki, remarked. "I'll guard the *Talubangui* Bridge," he volunteered.

"That's crucial to their last recourse: to get to *Enclaro* where they can paddle to the sea and escape by sailboat to the southern unoccupied territory." Colonel Asaki clarified. "The rest of you take turns to pick your assignment at random. Draw a paper from my hat over there." He pointed to his officer's cap on the coffee table by his easy chair.

"Your duties are specified on paper. Anything you don't understand or anything you need to carry out your assignment, you can communicate to me by radio. It's getting late. I want each of you to leave in the order of your assignment from the *Talubangui* Bridge to Himamaylan by six o'clock in the morning. I expect immediate success. Don't disappoint me."

When he was about to dismiss them, they heard a noise, a loud thud, as though someone had jumped on the balcony outside the study.

Major Onoki was prompt. Out of the room in an instant, he came back in with a grin on his face and Colonel Asaki's pet cat on his arm. The checkered Angora jumped from his arm to the floor with the same thud they had heard. It ran between Colonel Asaki's legs as it purred its affection.

"See you tomorrow morning, at six. Hopefully, the weather will clear by then. You are dismissed." Colonel Asaki gestured his dismissal; he closed the door to his study fondling the cat in his arms.

Someone dressed in rags commonly worn by the Filipinos serving at the *Binalbagan* garrison sneaked out of the officer's lounge into the pouring rain. Walking toward the trucks parked in the back of the barracks, he joined four men and a mechanic who hotwired one of the trucks. The cook and half a dozen men wielding mops earlier had come out of nowhere to see what they can do to help. They picked the truck nearest the back gate and pushed it, inching slowly and soundlessly out the gate. Someone slit the sentry's throat and dumped him behind the wall. Twenty meters out of the gate, the driver turned the engine on. In low gear the truck made its way to the main road toward *Himamaylan.*

For the past three days, the sky had been overcast. The wind howled in the trees as though a chorus of mourners wailed its grief in a wake before a burial ceremony. It was only forty-five minutes after eight o'clock, but wind and rain kept everything dark. Thankfully, the howling wind muffled the sound of the truck's engine.

Weary but comfortable in his bed, Colonel Asaki thought he heard the sound of a truck minutes after he retired, but he was too sleepy to get up. Probably Lt. Ishida came back from *Himamaylan,* he thought. Damn it, he forgot to issue a recall for Lt. Ishida to come back from *Himamaylan* yesterday. Surely, he didn't proceed to the swamps as he was impulsively ordered. So why was he so late in getting back and where did he park his truck? He hadn't heard anything since he turned on his side a few minutes ago. He looked at a wristwatch he seldom removed, not even when he slept. It read fifteen minutes after ten p.m.

Did Ishida come in? Why was everything so quiet then? He tried hard to wake up when, still in a daze, he began to realize something. He bolted in alarm.

"What the hell's going on?" He yelled. Did Lt. Ishida come in with his truck or not?"

Chapter 15—Trouble Following an Order

Lt. Ishida was in deep trouble all right. Thirty minutes after his truck left the *Binalbagan* railroad crossing, the jeeps ahead careened and were out of control. The road was gutted with deep holes covered by dead leaves and the lead jeep fell into a depression half a meter deep on the right side of the road but not far from the center. Water splashed from the hole, making the road behind sleek. Following, the second jeep slid on the water-splashed, slick road and careened into a shallow ditch. The driver, trying to get control, managed to swing the jeep back onto the road, but it slid sidewise and stopped short of running into the other jeep. It blocked the truck behind. The front end of the lead jeep was so severely damaged; it would take at least a half hour to get it out of the hole.

"God knows how long it would take to repair the front bumper and the engine," the sergeant grumbled in disgust.

Lt. Ishida wondered if he should abandon the lead jeep. Sitting in the second jeep, he hit his knee on the dashboard and it got badly bruised. Thank goodness there wasn't much damage to the jeep. Only a flat tire! That could be fixed in minutes. The lieutenant wasn't sure if the road shoulder was firm enough to let the truck pass on that side. He didn't dare order the driver to try that maneuver for fear the truck would get stuck as well.

The wind rose and the rain poured relentlessly. In the Philippines, he was informed earlier, things begin to slow down when the rainy season starts. He ordered the men out of the truck. He heard the men grumbling but he issued a command.

"Take the chain from the back of the truck and wrap it around the front wheels of the jeep." He ordered four men to do it.

"The rest of you go up ahead and look for trees with big enough trunks to use as a lever and raise the front end of this jeep out of the hole," When he heard more grumbling he spoke with authority.

"Either do that or stay here in the truck all day."

The men got out and took their sharp bayonets and swords and started hacking at the trees lining the road ahead. In three quarters of an hour they got the jeep out of the hole and dragged it to the side of the road where the others could work on the engine.

Two hours passed, but the rain never let up. The wind banged on the truck top. The men huddled close to each other, smoking to keep warm. Lt. Ishida paced back and forth, from the jeep to the truck. He was thinking in distress.

Just my luck to be out when the rest of the men are lounging at the barracks, enjoying hot tea, coffee, and *conji*.

Then a disturbing thought hit hard.

The hole didn't just happen to be there. It must have been dug to slow us down. Perhaps there were guerrilla men in the area or have they sped out of the area taking the Americans with them? He had to get out of this predicament fast. Certainly that was why he was ordered to pursue them into the swamps. He didn't dare inform Colonel Asaki of his delay. There was no help for that. He needed at least a half hour more before he could move. The holes had to be covered, of course. Colonel Asaki must not encounter the same trouble.

Shit, that would take at least another hour.

When the unit was ready to move, the rain had not abated. Stronger winds and pouring rain in the past three hours rendered visibility minimal. From *Binalbagan* Railroad Crossing avoiding mud pits and clearing debris from trees blown on the road by strong wind, Lt. Ishida had not made good time at all. Finally arriving at Crossing *Aguisan,* he had to make an educated guess. Should he continue on the highway to *Himamaylan* or veer to the right to get to the river and the swamps?

Either way, he could encounter guerrilla ambush.

Chapter 16—Toward the *Gatuslao* Hideout

The river runs slightly north toward the sea, but bends back south around thick *nipa* groves that hide its direction. It flows south for a kilometer, and turns straight to the sea. Halfway toward the sea, dozens of narrow waterways extend from the river into the heart of the swamps. One of these leads to the Gatuslao hideout. Lush growth clinging to the base of mangrove giants overshadow interconnected deltas that can only be accessed by *bancas* without outriggers.

Made from a huge tree trunk with the heart carved out, the *banca* doesn't have a flat bottom like the native Indian canoe in North America. The sides of those canoes are made of bark. The *banca*, on the other hand, is carved from the natural thickness of the tree trunk. The heavier sides make it difficult to handle. It could easily roll and capsize unless balanced by an expert paddler or supported with outriggers.

Badong, Sauro and Rudi made the Americans lie comfortably in the bottom of a *banca* paddled by Gatuslao fieldhands. Freshly cut *nipa* fronds concealed and protected them from rain. Pedring paddled another *banca* some distance behind, making sure they weren't followed.

The Gatuslao household hummed with expectation. Don Domingo Gatuslao welcomed Nonoy at noon. He was disappointed at the short notice, but knowing it couldn't be helped he went in and out of the kitchen urging his wife and her helpers to prepare a feast for *Kapitan* Almanzur and his guests. Nonoy told him there were eight privates, a lieutenant, the *Kapitan*, and six very special guests. He wondered who they were, but knowing Almanzur, he looked forward to meeting them.

The weather worried Nonoy. He paced underneath the house where firewood for the kitchen was stacked. Would the *Kapitan* be able to make it at all?

The three Americans with Pedring made good time, but the two injured ones inevitably delayed the *Kapitan*. Nonoy asked if he could take two rowers and go downriver to meet him. He took Don Domingo aside and explained why the *Kapitan* might be late.

"You can tell your wife," he cautioned, "but other than those you trust implicitly, you must keep the fact about your guests a secret."

Of course he must guard the secret. His own household could be in danger if he didn't. Don Domingo could not believe his ears.

"Julita," he whispered to his wife, "make an excuse to give the servants time off. You and the girls will have to do all the work."

When she found out why, she let all the servants go on the excuse that the wounded *Kapitan* needed privacy.

"But, Senora," *Manang* Rosing objected, "I have helped him before; perhaps I can again."

Dona Julita thought the matter over carefully. Indeed, it would be suspicious if even this most trusted servant couldn't stay to help.

"Okay, *'Nang* Rosing, prepare a healing poultice for deep burns."

Her daughters-in-law and Dona Julita cooked the food and set the table. Excited to meet the guests, everyone felt on edge. On the likelihood that Almanzur was chased (it wouldn't be the first time), Don Domingo ordered sentries posted at the river bend, a kilometer from the hideout. His fieldhands were armed with sawed-off shotguns crafted in their native smithy. They had bows and arrows, *bolos* of various lengths and weights. Conrado, the eldest son, had a hand grenade, a gift from *Kapitan* Villalva. He zealously guarded this to use only in the most extreme circumstances.

Nonoy was relieved to meet his guerrilla comrades in the waterway. He hacked the undergrowth and urged the rowers to make better time as he prepared to go farther to meet Pedring. The sun was setting; Pedring anticipated in two more hours the river would be in complete darkness.

When the two met at the river bend, Nonoy couldn't conceal his anxiety.

"Where do you think the *Kapitan* is now?" He asked Pedring.

"Your guess is as good as mine." Pedring replied. "I'm more worried about the truck we heard early this afternoon," he said. "Why hasn't it been seen in *Binicuil*? It should have been there hours ago. Even the Americans heard it after we crossed the highway and were halfway to barrio *To-oy*."

"I heard Lt. Verzosa say it was in no particular hurry," Nonoy said. "But where was it headed?"

Chapter 17—Unearned Compassion

Lt. Ishida veered to the right and took the road to barrio *Aguisan*. The wind and the rain muffled his approach so people usually fleeing at the sound of Japanese trucks were still around preparing to fish in the sea. Using lighted lanterns fueled by coconut oil, the fishermen used *bancas* with outriggers to fish in groups of three or four. The lieutenant lost no time rounding all the people they could get their hands on. It was now fifteen minutes past four o'clock in the afternoon. The Gatuslao fieldhands had just swung into the narrow waterway en route to the Gatuslao hideout. It was turning dark.

Wind and rain showed no signs of abating. The Japanese took people they'd rounded to a large bamboo building used as a public market before the war. The building had roof but had no walls. Falling apart from disuse, bamboo ledges once used as stalls to show people's wares: vegetable, fish, meat, fruit, etc. were piled high on one corner, looking as though someone had stacked them preparatory to taking them away. The roof was leaking badly. In some sections, the rain poured in buckets and water muddied the ground floor. At one corner, the floor was concrete. This was once the meat and fish section of the market. The Japanese brought the people, mostly men ranging from late thirties to early sixties, to this area. Two young boys, ten and twelve years old, huddled close to this group of poorly clad fishermen. An old man was carrying an armful of ratty fishing nets so old it was filled with holes he was attempting to sew together with *kogon* grass soaked in salty water.

The group sat on the concrete floor, but a Japanese private swung his gun, demanding they stand. The men spread their arms and joined hands, pushing the boys toward the center to protect them from the butt of the guns. Seeing what they were trying to do, the sergeant rushed quickly to the group, broke it up, and pulled the boys out of the protecting circle. With hands on his hips, the sergeant bent low to intimidate the ten year old.

"All right," he said, thinking that young ones are better at telling the truth, "let's begin with you. You better tell the truth. Do you know what will happen to you if you don't tell the truth?"

The boy began to whimper. The sergeant slapped him hard on the face and kicked him viciously. The boy lost his balance and staggered backward. The men caught him and stood him up straight. His mouth started to bleed. Glaring at the sergeant, he stood straight.

"That's better; now you tell me where the Americans are. Where did the men take them?"

The boy did not understand the question asked in Japanese. Someone from the group tried to coach an answer. The sergeant wheeled around and grabbed the man he thought tried to answer for the boy. He yanked him hard and dragged him to the corner where the rain poured heavily.

"You stay here and keep your mouth shut. Your turn for questions will come soon."

The man tried to wipe the water from his face.

"Stand still," the sergeant yelled. "Don't move a finger or I'll use this."

He waved a .38 caliber pistol at the man's face. The man tilted his head a little to let the water pouring on his face drop to the side. He could hardly breathe through the downpour. The sergeant inched backward toward the man and, with a wide swing, hit him on the side of his face with the pistol. The man fell down on the concrete floor. The sergeant was swinging his leg to kick him as Lt. Ishida limped fast toward the scene.

"That's enough of that, Sergeant." Though he was in pain because of the bruise on his leg, he stepped forward quickly to stop the kick.

"I'll do the questioning now. How did you expect to be answered when these people don't understand Japanese?"

"That's not my concern," the sergeant grumbled. "You're just a softie; that's your problem. If you let me handle these people my way, we may get some answers fast," he registered his objection with some contempt.

"What are you saying? Say it to my face clearly, you coward. You seem to be effective with defenseless people. Let me see you face the guerrillas one-on-one and prove to me that you're right. I have had enough of your attitude. Send me a *kempetai* interpreter. At once!" the lieutenant ordered.

The *kempetai* interrogator, no better than the sergeant, unleashed his anger at the lack of cooperation from the group. He pushed his face as close as possible to the men's faces as he yelled his questions in *Ilongo*. He pushed and shoved and used his fists when the lieutenant was not looking.

Lt. Ishida knew they were not getting anywhere. These men were local fishermen tying to eke an existence from the sea. It's possible they had not seen anything at all. He stopped the questioning, ordered a supply of fish, and asked for supper to be made ready for all his men. He made the rounds in the barrio and took the best huts, ones that leaked the least, and ordered his men to take possession. He still didn't know what to do with the prisoners so he left them on the concrete pad they sat on.

They can sleep there till morning. Then I can decide what to do with them, he thought.

It was too dark to proceed to the swamps. He asked the *kempetai* men to confiscate as many outrigger *bancas* they could round up. He instructed his non-commissioned officers to take all the ammunition necessary to protect themselves in the swamps; but if the guerrillas had taken the Americans into the swamps, they certainly knew where they were going and where they could exit. The best he could do was to track them down in blind pursuit. How could Colonel Asaki issue such an unreasonable order?

But an order was an order. He wondered what Colonel Asaki would think if he deliberately disobeyed. He was uneasy with his own answer. The arrogant bastard would get into one of his uncontrollable fits of frenzy. All hell would break loose; he would kick, scream, and carry on, and lash his anger on whoever was closest. He would be the first of those, of course. The Colonel would then drink heavily in his own quarters, but he would most certainly abuse all the Filipinos in the garrison, not exempting the hapless privates in his command and even some of his own officers.

Hell, something is wrong with the Japanese chain of command, Lt. Ishida thought. Colonel Asaki was a classic example of the behavior of high-ranking officers he had served under, with the exception of Major Onoki. But he was only a Major and often his hands were tied. Both of them could only offer a simmered objection to the senseless abuse that was often going on. But what was there to do?

Before they retired at night, Lt. Ishida clearly delineated to his men the danger of unfamiliar territory and difficult swampland topography. They were assigned to pursue the guerrillas into the swamps and they better prepare for the worst. He thought long and hard about the impending danger of penetrating the swamps, but he was tired and miserable, and his knee began to throb.

The rain pelted and shook the flimsy rafters of the bamboo hut he picked to stay in. The *nipa* roof leaked in so many places and the wind blew through the holes on the walls. Feeling cold and wet, he drew his soggy raincoat over his leather jacket. This rainy season would be a constant irritation, he knew. Perhaps, though, it would induce a necessary slowing down of the punishing, rapacious harassment, the inhumane and unprovoked torment of the poor, starving natives. Thinking of their need for food made him hungry. He had not eaten much of the boiled fish they served him and his men for dinner. Colonel Asaki would have asked for the impossible, and would have used their inability to supply the food he wanted as justification for inhumane torture.

Suddenly, something reasonable suggested itself. He would use those fishermen to paddle the *bancas* to the swamps come daytime. He was glad he did not release them. Gosh, it must be miserable to try to sleep on that concrete pad with the wind gushing in on them underneath that leaky roof. The building was without walls! The poor wretches! But they could be of good use. They could paddle *bancas* and serve as good guides.

Human compassion has its limits, especially in a war, he conceded.

Chapter 18—A New Insight

Exhausted beyond endurance, Scott, Joe, and Valdez welcomed the boat ride from the *nipa* grove to the Gatuslao hideout. Scott stretched in the bottom of the *banca*, grateful he didn't need to run, crawl, or squeeze through grass and mud. The *nipa* fronds they piled on top of him were small protection from the wind and rain pouring all day long, but though he got wet, he was not cold. The air grew thick and humid. He perspired though he was wet.

So this is the swamp in the tropics, he thought.

He heard their host extending his welcome before Badong removed the fronds that covered him. Badong extended a hand and pulled him quickly underneath the house into an enclosure with bamboo slats for flooring. An earthen jar filled with rainwater sat on one corner; beside it was a coconut dipper Badong said he could use to bathe with. Cleaning up was such a luxury impossible to describe. This felt as exhilarating as the thought of an expected dinner. Boy, the dinner had better be good!

He was shocked to discover a thin, faded towel, a shirt, an underwear, loose, but dry and some pants that came to six inches up his shins. He put these on in a hurry because Badong said he had only fifteen minutes to get ready. He rubbed his hair dry with the thin towel and since he couldn't find a comb, he smoothed his hair over to the side of his head with his fingers. My! His hair had grown long. He had not shaved in weeks, but he felt so good from the bath and the clean, dry clothes he couldn't care much how he looked. Such a simple thing as a bath took away most, if not all, of the feeling of exhaustion. Man, he was getting hungry.

Before they were ushered into the dining area, he saw Joe and Valdez had had a bath and a change into dry, warm clothes as well. Joe's shirt hardly came down to his waist and his pants looked more like long shorts. Only Valdez looked good in clothes that seemed to fit well.

Badong, Sauro, and Rudi were still in their own clothes but they must have washed them and wrung them as dry as they could. They didn't seem to mind at all.

A Petromax lantern hung at the center of the dining area and small coconut oil lamps brightened the room more. Scott figured it was close to five o'clock in the afternoon, but it was already dark outside. He noticed the elaborate spread on bamboo tables.

Green coconuts were opened at the tops for drinking. A jar of rainwater sat on a table at the corner. Bottles filled with rainwater were made ready for them to take when they leave. According to their host, Nonoy conveyed this request from the *Kapitan*: "Feed them well, but be very careful about what they drink. They must not drink well water. Better for them to be thirsty than to drink impure water."

Scott hovered around the table curiously. Don Domingo's daughter-in-law explained the dishes:

"This is Red Snapper and Blue Marlin fried in garlic and coconut oil. This is *Sinigang*, a dish of boiled fish heads cooked with sour Iba, a green sour fruit used for flavoring. It's a favorite dish among the guerrilla men; it goes well with plain, steamed rice. We have a single chicken broiled in coconut charcoal and a sharp knife beside it, ready to cut it into preferred pieces: the wings, the thighs, the breasts, the neck, the backbone, even the innards (heart, liver, and gizzard)."

She pointed to another dish. "Here is another tasty fish dish we call *Pinaksiw*. It's fish boiled in vinegar, garlic, ginger root and coconut oil thickened into delicious sauce as the dish is simmered."

She was about to turn to the other side of the table but her mother-in-law gestured to her.

"I'll take over from here." She lifted a round, shallow, woven bamboo food container.

"Here's a platter of large salted shrimps fried in coconut oil with sliced green mango strips, cucumbers, and tomatoes at the center."

She took another food container just like it. "Here's sweet potato sliced thin and fried crisply."

Scott couldn't resist nibbling on it. It reminded him of potato chips.

"Tastes good, doesn't it? I fried it myself." She threw another one of those ready smiles. Here's more sweet potato of another variety; they're boiled and so are the cooking bananas. Of course, a table is not complete without rice, both steamed or fried with small shrimps, onions and garlic. For dessert, we have fresh fruit: mangoes, ripe papayas, bananas (the small finger variety), guyabana, *caimito* (star apple), and even sour *santol*. You are lucky the mangoes are in season. We can only get this fruit this time of the year."

Nonoy stood aghast for some time. Even when *Kapitan* Villalva and Colonel Gomez visited here, Nonoy had not seen such a spread. He was awestruck, amazed beyond belief.

Scott's eyes took in everything. He didn't know what to say. In more than three weeks that they had been running here and there, they hadn't seen a fraction of the food on this table. Scott noticed that Dona Julita and her daughters-in-law were filled with pleasure as they saw the delight on the faces of their guests.

"If you are ready to eat, we'll pass the bamboo plates around after my husband says grace," Dona Julita said with a gracious smile.

Her husband said grace and ended with the sign of the cross. Immediately after, the women went around the table passing bamboo plates covered in green banana leaves to the host, Don Domingo, first, then to Scott, Joe, and Valdez, and to Nonoy, Badong, Sauro, and Rudi, and then to the rest of the Gatuslao family.

Scott was famished but didn't know where to start. He hesitated.

"Oh, please help yourselves. Filipinos always start with the rice, but you can start anywhere. There's plenty of seafood, vegetables, and fruit, but hardly any meat. If we had more notice, our younger sons could have bartered for pork and more chicken, but the single chicken is all we have today," Dona Julita apologized.

"This is very gracious of you; you need not apologize at all," Scott spoke very warmly. "We don't have the words to thank you for the kindness you're extending us. These clothes are warm and comfortable. I know this is hardly the time to introduce us. We should've done that before, but our Filipino friends gave us little time for that. I'm afraid we just barged in on you with little notice."

"You have no need to apologize for that either," Don Domingo responded just as warmly. "In a war, there's seldom time to pay attention to formalities. But let me introduce us to you. I'm Domingo Gatuslao. This is my wife, Julita. This here is our eldest son, Conrado, and his wife, Nenita. This is my second oldest son, Francisco, and his wife, Conchita. Our two other sons are somewhere busy trying to supply us with what we need. We wouldn't have what's here tonight if it weren't for them."

As he spoke, he walked around touching each one he introduced. They all flashed warm, wide smiles and nodded their heads in acknowledgement.

Scott Rankin returned the courtesy by introducing himself first, then Joe West, and Romero Valdez.

"I assume you know Nonoy, Badong, Sauro, and Rudi," he said.

"Ah, yes, Nonoy has been here many times before, but we're glad to meet the other three. *Kapitan* Villalva rarely has the same men with him. Too bad he's not here to join us at the moment," the elder Gatuslao replied.

Nonoy quickly added that Pedring went to the main river to wait for the *Kapitan* and three other Americans. He could be here any moment, he said. Don Domingo took Nonoy aside so they could go on with the meal.

"We can start without them, but we are prepared to feed the others later."

Scott felt a great deal more at ease after the introductions.

"Please don't wait on us. We can serve ourselves. We would feel more comfortable if you enjoyed with us what evidently took you much time to prepare," he said easily.

"We don't mind preparing the food for you or waiting on you either. No, we don't mind at all. This is the most pleasurable company we've had in a long time. It's not everyday we entertain guests like you."

The entire Gatuslao family, and the guerrilla men too, had a hearty laugh at this, so Scott, Joe, and Valdez joined in the fun. The laughter that flowed freely felt so comforting. It cancelled the anxiety they had felt for weeks.

"Besides," Dona Julita added, "we want to make up for your sacrifice and the risk to your lives. I'm sure it must feel so unfair to risk your lives for people you don't even know."

Amen to that, Scott thought. The Captain and his men must surely feel it unfair to risk their lives for us. What a bunch of ingrates we must seem to them!

In an instant, the enormity of his arrogance and lack of graciousness came home to haunt him.

"Please forgive us if you're not used to the dishes you're served tonight," one of the daughters-in-law shyly said.

"It's our pleasure, most certainly," Scott assured her. "In fact, you have to excuse our appetite, for this is, indeed, an unexpected feast. The Captain was not exaggerating when he told us we would dine with the best tonight."

"Thank you so much for your hospitality," was all Joe and Valdez could say.

They ate slowly and leisurely, enjoying the food and the developing friendship. They talked as they ate and exchanged pleasantries as though there wasn't a war outside the swamps, as if there was no need to escape the pursuing Japanese, and as though hate and suffering were exempt from life in hiding.

Finally, close to seven o'clock, the darkness moved in. The oil lamps began to flicker, and wind and rain seemed to take on increasing fury. Nonoy brought the company back to reality.

"Please try to understand, Sir," he addressed his host. "I hate to put an end to so much enjoyment, but I'm afraid the *Kapitan* and the others have been inevitably detained. I have no idea how soon and where we must proceed. These men should rest, for we don't know what the next few hours would require. I must contact the *Kapitan* for orders."

"You're quite right, Nonoy. I'm sure Almanzur would expect you to do so. We don't have as much comfort for rest to offer them as we have good food, but we have native mats for them to lie on, a few cotton sheets, and k*apok* pillows to share," Don Domingo regretfully said.

"We have slept on the ground under the trees for so long we don't know how a mat would feel," Scott said. "Thank you very much for your generosity."

"Good night to you all."

Enjoying the company very much, Don Domingo seemed unwilling for this happy day to end.

Soon after the hearty dinner, exhaustion overtook them. Scott, Joe, and Valdez slept like babies. The rain pelted the *nipa* roof and the wind shook it as if it would fly off the rafters. Wind and rain regardless, the comfort of warm sheets and soft pillows put them into sound sleep.

Nonoy didn't sleep at all. He spent the next few hours under the house, on top of stacked firewood, his rifle lying on his arm. He was still worried about the *Kapitan,* Pedring, and the rest. At twelve thirty in the morning, a message from Ponsing relieved him. The *Kapitan* ordered him to take the Americans quickly to the highway past Crossing *Aguisan* to the river before the town of *Himamaylan*. Nonoy took as much provision as they were offered.

"For the *Kapitan* and the rest who missed out on this feast!" He expressed his gratitude.

There was time only for hot ginger tea passed out in bamboo cups. They were offered to keep the dry clothes they put on the night before. Their own clothes were washed, wrung dry, folded, and pushed into a cloth knapsack they each could alternately carry on their backs.

Nonoy rushed them out of the hut before they could say goodbye to the women. Don Domingo agreed there was no time for heartfelt goodbyes, but the family would keep them all in their prayers. At one o'clock in the morning, all were ready to run again. Carefully hidden in the *bancas* once more, all three were quiet but watchful. Scott looked back at the bamboo house with much emotion.

The moments shared here were intense realities that spoke volumes.

He mentally said his goodbye with so much longing for peace in his heart. For him, the world suddenly assumed a clearer contour. Such heartfelt welcome these people extended supplied a special clarity of meaning. The eye of memory averted itself from the violence of war to gaze at this unlimited hospitality of spirit. Here was unreserved help and genuine friendship for total strangers. Scott's mind rambled into his past. He recalled a stanza of a poem by Edwin Markham, a thought that painted itself into his awareness right then:

"There is a destiny that makes us brothers

None goes his way alone:

All that we send into the lives of others

Come back into our own."

He also remembered an eastern thought from a reading of Khalil Gibran:

"I discovered the secret of the sea

In meditation upon a dewdrop."

As Nonoy rushed them out of this hideout, Scott saw clearly that these people reflected Captain Villalva's attitude. He had the same generosity of spirit that all three of them—Joe, Valdez and, especially, him—selfishly doubted at every turn. Scott saw that the Captain and the men who loyally served him were making every attempt to help them despite their unmasked distrust. He felt a pain in his chest as he dwelt on their ingratitude. He was suddenly aware that the Captain moved them about, on the hem of life, as it were, for they seemed always within the grasp of death. Slowly, Scott began to realize that the Captain always displayed the conviction that pain, any pain, was endurable. Obviously that included even the pain of being undeservedly mistrusted? As he moved them through persistent, impending danger the Captain's reassuring presence lent unbelievable courage to his men; he gave their lives immeasurable substance. He tried to extend it to those he rescued as well, for they hung like fragile items on the quality of his decisions.

His men were right. The Captain didn't hesitate to give his life to save theirs. Scott remembered the conversation the men had the day before. How much devotion these men had for the Captain amazed him. They worshipped the ground he walked on. They were willing to risk their lives for him, and what he was willing to risk his life for. Now Scott was certain he was ready to surrender his will to the wisdom of this manager of his survival. From now on, he unequivocally promised a complete turn around.

No more questions or complaints, just a grateful acquiescence! God, what miserable ingrates we must seem to them.

No wonder they were often tight lipped when we wanted their opinion. With some misgiving, Scott asked himself why he had not seen this dimension before. Suddenly, he felt an acute need for the Captain's presence. Without the slightest regard for his own safety, the Captain worried about Marco, Spencer, and BB. He wondered if he would ever see them again. Yet if they were with him, they were probably much safer.

The Captain had taken special care of those two who were wounded. And BB was remarkably, unselfishly, loyal to them. He could have been here too, tonight, if he weren't so concerned that neither Marco nor Spencer would be able to make it without his help. Such unselfishness was a rebuke to Scott's soul. He felt diminished in stature. Recent circumstances had weighed him and he found himself wanting.

Why was the Captain unable to join them when he said he would? When and where would they meet him again? Wherever, Scott knew the Captain would be with them soon, for in the midst of so much uncertainty, his men looked to him as the most constant fraction in an unstable equation. This unselfish human being accorded them one most certain consolation. He did keep his promise to the three of them. They had been starving for the longest time, but last night he made sure they dined in the heartiest of circumstances with his friends. Scott began to wonder if the Captain kept his promise though he could ill afford time they took to detour from the straight route the others took. He began to feel really apprehensive. What price had they made him pay for that extravagant dinner? He felt like a spoiled brat needing to be catered to because he would have sulked otherwise. Now, he was feeling really small. The ultimate truth of the matter shook him to the core: *The Captain, Nonoy, Pedring, and the three with them now are sacrificing their lives to keep them safe!*

Chapter 19—Keeping a Tight Rope Balance

As soon as Scott, Joe, and Valdez sped with Pedring toward the swamps in *Himamaylan,* the Captain knew it would be impossible for the three others with him to catch up with them. Marco's blistered feet kept him in agony. BB carried him on his back but after a few hundred meters his strength gave out. Crawling on their bellies would relieve Marco's feet of pressure, but it was murder for Spencer's wounds on the belly. Either hindrance slowed them down considerably.

Something had to be done to alter the circumstances. As the day progressed quickly, BB realized they were in greater danger than they'd been for days. They were putting the guerrillas at risk because of their incapacity to travel fast. BB began to despair. He heard a Japanese truck and two jeeps at a distance and he realized how crucial it was to get to the river and to the swamps before more trucks and more troops would arrive to block their route of escape.

"This is a hopeless situation, isn't it Sir," he asked the Captain. "You have outwitted the Japanese for nearly two weeks now, but they've caught on to your scheme, haven't they? George, Frank, and Robert are completely cut off from us, aren't they?"

Are they in less danger than we are? He wondered; he wasn't sure of anything anymore. At least Scott, Joe, and Valdez will most certainly make it to the swamps by nightfall. I'm certain, we wouldn't, not at the rate we progress.

"We're putting you guys at risk. Of this, I know for sure," he said ruefully.

"Why don't you just take BB and join the other three and make better time," Spencer put in. "Marco and I will hide as long as we can. Just give us something to defend ourselves. A sub machine gun will be fine. I can still use one."

"If you save seven out of nine of us, that would still be a record," Marco quipped almost cheerfully.

BB listened to this nonsense long enough. "If you think I will abandon you after all *we* have been through together, you really don't know me yet, he thought.

"I hope you both know I will never leave you," he said feeling the tears well in his eyes.

"Don't you all give up so quickly," the Captain said still with so much assurance in his tone. "This is all a tight rope scheme," he said confidently. "If you put too much weight on your right, you might lose your balance, so you need to shift your weight, ever so slightly, to the left. You have to learn to keep your balance."

"And do you still have enough rope to hang on to?" BB caught on to his good humor. "You don't give up easily, do you?"

"If you have room to skip in, you can keep the game going," the Captain answered BB with a trace of a smile on his face.

At that moment, it seemed to BB as though the Captain caught the thread of an idea. A thought crept on his face and brightened it like a dark room admitting light from a curtain drawn on the side.

"This wind and rain can still work to our advantage," he said, still thinking. "Just give Ponsing time to connect with Lt. Palacios and some of our men around this area. The lieutenant can take care of you while I'm gone. With some luck, I'll be back with something."

He was gone for the rest of the day, but Ponsing, connected with Lt. Palacios who brought Sergeant Roming (Romeo) Peralta, and privates Tonio (Antonio) Rodriquez, Pedoy (Alfredo) Concepcion, Petong (Ruperto) Atienza, and the brothers, Sisong (Narciso) and Mario Salazar.

Lt. Palacios took over the tight rope situation. He took charge of the men carrying the two wounded Americans over flooded rice dikes, crawling through *kogon* fields, and seeking cover under coconut and bamboo groves. It looked to BB as though there were never more than three men running with them, yet when the group sat down to rest, the men seemed to have alternated.

BB lifted Marco some of the way, and Spencer sometimes leaned on him when he ached and felt his energy ebb. The lieutenant tried to make as much progress as possible, but towards late afternoon, BB's strength waned. He could hardly manage to move on. They had covered no more than a third of the way to *Himamaylan*. Nevertheless, BB insisted on inching their way on.

Half an hour before midnight, BB begged Lt. Palacios to call it a day. He sat with Marco to eat a few bananas and drink from the last green coconut Sisong carried. He shared the grated meat of the coconut with Marco and Spencer but though it gave him some energy, he felt as though he never had enough to stop his stomach from growling. He wondered if Scott, Joe, and Valdez had by now dined with the Captain's friends. What did they have to eat? Perhaps they had some meat, chicken or pork fried to perfection? Of course, they must have eaten rice, for that seems to be standard fare here. Well, boys, eat hearty and eat for the three of us, too.

Thinking about the food, he recovered some of his strength. Though Marco and Spencer looked like they had reached the end of the line, BB knew Lt. Palacios was uneasy about stopping before they had crossed the highway.

The wind had picked up again and blew right through BB's jacket. He knew Spencer had just about all he could take. The pouring rain raked his wounds mercilessly. BB stood up calculating he had enough energy left to lift Marco across the highway. He had rested sufficiently and he was determined to use his last ounce of strength to cross the highway so they could get to the swamps the next day. They couldn't stay where they stopped. The location wasn't safe. His eyes penetrated the darkness. He realized why Lt. Palacios didn't want to stop here. It was still the edge of an open field; they were too exposed. He looked up once more to estimate the distance from here to the cover of the trees across the highway. In an instant, he thought the worst possible event was about to take place. A Japanese truck was speeding towards them. He saw the headlight through fierce wind and blinding rain.

BB's legs lost all their power instantly. There was no way to outrun the vehicle. Lt. Palacios ordered everyone to seek cover. They anxiously waited for the headlight to get closer.

"It is a lone vehicle," Ponsing observed. Why is it traveling alone? Japanese trucks never travel without escorts.

A garbled message gurgled from the truck. Despite tremendous static, Posing thought he heard this message:

Captain Villalva. Tight rope walking cancelled. Get to the highway fast and hop in. Ponsing doubted what he heard, but though fading, the message repeated.

Captain Villalva . . . . Captain Villalva

Get to the highway . . . . to the highway

Lt. Palacios listened with Ponsing intently. He heard the message twice before he galvanized the group into action. He wiped water trailing across Marco's face, dripping from his nose. He took off his jacket and slung it across Spencer's shoulders. He pulled his long, sleek hair to the back of his head and embraced BB with a joy that lighted the darkness.

"Today is your lucky day," he said to BB with a sob caught in his throat.

Then BB thought he heard a dog bark persistently. He turned his head in time to see the Lieutenant stop barking.

All at once, seven men took turns lifting Marco and Spencer and guided BB unerringly as they raced toward the highway. They could see the headlights of the truck blinking off and on in the distance as it prepared to slow down for them to hop in.

The *Kapitan* was still dressed in rags; a *buri* (woven palm) hat covered his hair and he had a wet mop with a long handle beside him. Sergeant Roming Padriga was in the front seat with him, grinning from ear to ear. The hunt was still on, but the *Kapitan* more than evened the score. His men didn't ask how he managed this trick up his sleeve, but as they pushed the Americans into the back of the truck, despair shifted into pure joy.

BB had difficulty comprehending what was happening. Think about a last minute incredible rescue that's supposed to happen only in the movies. Even that couldn't top this one.

"Your prayers must have worked," sergeant Peralta said, pumping BB on the back. "Were you praying for a miracle? You couldn't have carried Marco for another hundred yards," he teased. When he saw the look of utter exhaustion on BB's face, he apologized instantly.

"I was only kidding, Sir," he said, regretting his insensitivity. BB and Lt. Palacios turned to the *Kapitan* and to sergeant Padriga with a look that asked for an explanation.

"Never mind how. We just stole it from the garrison while Colonel Asaki was busy torturing the help." The *Kapitan* let out a sigh of relief he was unable to stifle.

"Right under his very nose too!" Sergeant Padriga hit the dashboard with his fist. Now that they had done it, he had a hard time believing they did what they had done.

"How did you know where to pick us up, Sir?" BB asked, still unable to comprehend the miracle.

"Simple calculation," the Captain answered, not offering further explanation.

"The *Kapitan* times all our moves He figured how much time it would take you guys, to reach the vicinity of barrio *To-oy*. As usual he's accurate, give or take a few minutes," Sergeant Padriga explained. Marco and Spencer were asleep in the back of the truck, oblivious to the jovial exchange among comrades and the excitement of the rescue.

"They're too exhausted to stay awake, Sir," BB apologized.

"No problem. Let them rest while they can. We still have a long way to go.

"One crisis at a time, I see." BB breathed a sigh of relief. He marveled at the faith and assurance of this man who kept the Japanese at bay and their lives out of their reach for as long as he was able.

How long can he keep going like this? God help him and us to endure, BB prayed earnestly.

Chapter 20—Trouble on Four Fronts

The *Kapitan* had planned for everyone to get together at the Gatuslao hideout, but the three with him were too slow to make the rendezvous. The stolen Japanese truck altered his plans. The truck could transport the three slow ones to barrio *Binicuil* faster than a *banca* could so he sent a message to Nonoy to leave at once and meet him at the riverbank in *Himamaylan*. For sure *Himamaylan* was one of the red encircled spots on Colonel Asaki's map, but the delay at the *Binalbagan* Crossing and at several other points would make up for the delay of waiting for the three from the Gatuslao hideout.

The next stop for the stolen truck would be Crossing *Aguisan* where Lt. Ishida had turned right toward barrio *Aguisan*. It puzzled him that the vehicles had not been seen passing through to barrio *Binicuil*. Where were these now? His most accurate guess was that these were presently holed up in barrio *Aguisan*. Careful that the truck they drove wouldn't be heard, he told Tonio to put it in very low gear and drive slowly as they approached Crossing *Agusian*. The Crossing was about eight kilometers from barrio *Aguisan*. After the change of plans, Ponsing sent message after message to Lt. Verzosa.

"Don't set your traps before we go through. We're speeding to *Binicuil* in a Japanese truck the *Kapitan* stole from the garrison in *Binalbagan*."

The *Kapitan* wanted to leave Lt. Palacios, Sergeant Padriga and all the privates at this point.

"Tell Lt. Verzosa we will rendezvous at the bend west of Crossing *Aguisan*. He'll hear the sound of barking dogs," Lt. Palacios told Ponsing.

"Be careful. That truck you heard yesterday may be in barrio *Aguisan*," the *Kapitan* warned. "Don't get too close before you are certain of Lt. Verzosa's back up."

"Sir, the holes on the road south of *Binalbagan* Crossing were dug again. Our men worked on the road after you passed through in this truck." Ponsing was excited.

"Just about five hours from now, Major Onoki (I heard Colonel Asaki address him with that name) would be having trouble there," the *Kapitan* said. He was looking at his wristband.

"I hope the men dug deeper holes all over. The other officers must be slowed down too."

In his mind's eye, he saw all the red circles marked on the wall of Colonel Asaki's study: *Aguisan, Himamaylan. Binicuil, Kabankalan Crossing, Talubangui* Bridge, *Vista Allegre, Enclaro*.

"If all the lead vehicles will have trouble, they could block the way of the others. The delay would make Colonel Asaki so furious he wouldn't be able to think straight. Anger clogs his brains worse than alcohol can. When he is drunk, he can still keep his thoughts sharp," the *Kapitan* smirked. "When he is angry, watch out! He loses his balance. I like to keep him furious. Then he issues orders unmindful of the consequences." The *Kapitan*'s eyes were sparkling pools of mirth.

"Speaking of orders, Sir," Ponsing interrupted, "I have a message from Lt. Verzosa. He says he came from barrio *Binicuil* and is close to Crossing *Aguisan* now. Colonel Gomez sent a fully armed unit to *Binicuil*. They are waiting for you to tell them what to do. Lt. Verzosa left *Binicuil* without touching the road. He said the unit that replaced him must be told what to do. They're waiting for your orders."

"Tell them to dig holes from *Binicuil* and get as close as possible to *Kabankalan* Crossing without alerting the garrison. We need to pass through to *Binicuil* before they can do anything to the road from there to here," the *Kapitan* said. "Gosh, I just thought of something. I hope it isn't Major Onoki driving the lead vehicle, but Colonel Asaki himself. If he falls into the first hole, the bastard may get injured or he may, somehow, escape injury. Either way, he'll be madder than a hornet. It'll be fun anticipating what he's going to do. I bet he's already fuming at the loss of this truck." The *Kapitan* enjoyed this thought thoroughly but, in another minute, concern creased his forehead.

Think, Almanzur; what is the bastard going to do then? He talked to himself.

"He'll not have the patience to wait for the road to be repaired. He'll order the garrison in *Kabankalan* to drive up to *Binicuil* and secure the area," he said aloud. "Quick, Ponsing, tell the unit in *Binicuil* on second thought we need to leave the road from *Kabankalan* to *Binicuil* alone."

He got out on the road and paced back and forth.

"We either have to drive now and leave the others or can we afford to wait another two hours? What do you think we should do, boys?"

"I see what you are thinking, Sir, Sergeant Padriga said with a frown on his face."

"Do you, really?" The *Kapitan* seemed deep in thought now.

"Yes, Sir. You are thinking that if Colonel Asaki orders his troops out of the garrison in *Kabankalan* to secure *Binicuil* and post a road block there, **the garrison in *Kabankalan* would be thinned out.**" Sergeant Padriga and Lt. Palacios blurted aloud together. Lt. Palacios had caught on too.

"Now you are thinking smartly," the *Kapitan* nodded in agreement.

"Time for a concerted all out assault? Too bad we're here now," Lt. Palacios said.

"Don't forget, you have a truck load and two jeeps to take care of right here," the *Kapitan* warned him again.

"Sir, Colonel Gomez is on the line. He wants to talk to you at once," Ponsing handed *Kapitan* Villalva the black box.

"Yes, Sir, Cousin," he teased. "I know you're thinking the same thing I'm thinking, or you wouldn't talk to me directly. Gosh, I can hardly think a step ahead of you."

"Almanzur," his *Manong* Alvaro boomed, "Our hands are full. Everything is happening at once. Without doubt, Colonel Asaki will order his troops to move out and get to barrio *Binicuil* to secure the area. I sent one of your younger cousins, Lt. Poping (Procopio) Balinas, to *Binicuil* already. Although Poping is from *Andulawan*, he knows *Binicuil* just as well. Lt. Verzosa is preparing to engage the truckload and two jeeps in Barrio *Aguisan*. Are Lt. Palacios and Sergeant Padriga already there to help?"

"At the moment, they're still with me. We're at Crossing *Aguisan*."

"I know Nonoy and Pedring and three others are taking the three who dined with Doming to join you. When are they going to get there?" his *Manong* Alvaro asked.

"It'll be a while before they get to where I want to meet them in *Himamaylan*. I wish they were here with us now so I could send Lt. Palacios, Sergeant Padriga and six others to *Kabankalan*. But I'm short handed without those five and I can't wait another two hours. They'll have to follow on foot and try to catch up with us as fast as they can. My, but a hearty dinner does exact a great price," the *Kapitan* remarked somewhat perturbed.

"We can wage an assault in *Kabankalan*. We know it'll be thinned out. The problem is there's no way to know how far reduced it'll be in numbers. However, if we attack there, too, we could complicate Colonel

Asaki's problems. We can keep him busy defending himself on all three fronts," Colonel Gomez said.

"Correction," The *Kapitan* retorted. Don't forget Nick De Guzman and about nine others are near Crossing *Binalbagan* and will be taking pot shots at the vehicles stuck there. Colonel Asaki will be beleaguered on all four fronts."

"I hope De Guzman still knows how to use the bamboo catapults to throw hand grenades from a distance. Colonel Asaki is strongest at that point. De Guzman can't afford to get too close," Colonel Gomez warned.

"Why the heck did I send those three to Compadre Doming's hideout? If they left there at one o'clock this morning, they should be in *Himamaylan* at about half past two. Hmmm, that isn't bad. How about it, guys, do you think I should wait?" he asked.

"It's not those guys fault that you sent them to dinner at your friend's place, Sir," Lt. Palacios volunteered. Pedring didn't know you could steal a truck or he would never have taken them."

"Right now, though, we're all in need of three of the most important requirements in a war," the *Kapitan* voiced a reminder.

"And what are those?" Lt. Palacios asked.

In a chorus, from the back of the truck the privates and Sergeant Peralta intoned: *SPEED, FLEXIBILITY*, and *TIMING*.

Chapter 21—Speed

After the *bancas* got to the bend in the river about a kilometer from the hideout, Pedring realized they would save time if he put all three Americans in one *banca* and Nonoy and he and Badong, Sauro and Rudi paddled together.

"Young man, my son and I would not mind helping you paddle all the way," Don Domingo's fieldhand said. "Besides, my son knows a short cut. If you're in a big hurry, he can take you to a trail and you can run the rest of the way. You can probably get where you want to be in half an hour less time."

"Thank you so much, Tio Boni; my *Kapitan* will thank you for the help."

Pedring sent the two other *bancas* back and all seven men paddled in earnest. Getting to the short cut and running the rest of the way took forty-five minutes less. They arrived at the rendezvous point forty-five minutes less than the *Kapitan* calculated. Hurray for speed! The *Kapitan* was getting restless and would have left in another fifteen minutes. When Pedring and the other three Americans arrived, he was elated.

"So far so good. Things are working out better than I expected. We'll go full speed ahead to *Binicuil*. Sorry Nonoy. You have to backtrack to join Lt. Verzosa and Lt. Palacious. You need to take a black box to them so we can talk to them and they can report back to us."

The truck left for barrio *Binicuil* without Nonoy.

The *Kapitan*, Ponsing, Sergeant Peralta, Pedring, Badong, Sauro, and Rudi and the six Americans were finally on their way to *Ilog*. At quarter to three a.m., another thirty-five minutes more, they arrived in *Binicuil* where they had to turn over the truck to Lt. Procopio Balinas.

Once more, Scott, Joe, and Valdez led the way on foot with Pedring, Badong, Sauro and Rudi while the *Kapitan*, Sergeant Peralta and Ponsing followed with Marco, Spencer and BB. Marco and Spencer were on a bamboo cart pulled by a carabao.

"If we can make good time, we can make it all the way to *Enclaro* as planned," Sergeant Peralta whispered to Ponsing.

"I hope so too," Ponsing answered. "If we make it to *Andulawan* by noon, we can get to *Ilog* and take the river to *Enclaro*. We have to do it or we'll be in trouble again. So far the *Kapitan* has managed one more crisis well, but I'm afraid the hunt is by no means over."

Chapter 22—Flexibility

Lt. Ishida woke up from uneasy sleep. The rain was still pouring hard. Although it was five o'clock in the morning, the sun still hid behind dark clouds. He put his jacket on to look for the sergeant. The sound of barking dogs disturbed him. Perhaps the thunder and lightning frightened them? Going over to the concrete pad where the fishermen were huddled, he assumed they were awake for he heard them coughing. Poor wretches! They surely must have spent a cold night for they clung to each other. He looked for the *kempetai* interpreter to give the order to get the *bancas* ready. Looking for any excuse to delay action, he was glad the interpreter was nowhere around.

Did he really have to get into the swamps? What was he looking for anyway? Ah, yes, the Americans were supposed to have escaped in this direction. He had no stomach for torturing these innocent fishermen into telling him what he wanted to hear though there was no truth to it, so he asked the sergeant to give the orders. He would go downriver as far as he can and then get back to report he had not found what he was ordered to locate. Then he could get back to *Kabankalan* sooner. Let the Colonel make as much of that as he can. He walked toward the truck and the jeeps. His men were up, awaiting his orders.

The dogs barked louder.

"Get ready to move toward the river," he yelled at the sergeant.

The driver revved the engine of the truck. With clothes dripping from the rain, his men huddled close to each other, smoking to keep warm. As he climbed into his jeep, the dogs yelped even louder. Then a hand grenade exploded close to his jeep.

"Where the devil did that come from," he asked.

"Everyone, take cover," the sergeant yelled.

It was too dark to see anything clearly. Automatically, he grabbed a can of gasoline and torched the hut closest the vehicles. The fire spread to the other huts and lighted the area around. His men were deployed in the ditches and under the truck and behind the jeeps. The fishermen were screaming in fright. The sergeant took a sub machine gun and fired in their direction. Lt. Ishida didn't want them killed.

"Those are nothing but helpless men," the Lt. yelled. "Quit firing at them. Fire in the direction of the yelping dogs instead."

The sergeant fired in the direction of the dogs. There was absolute quiet after that.

This is senseless, Lt. Ishida thought. Torching the huts did give them light, but it also got rid of some cover. To hell with Colonel Asaki's orders, he thought. Until this rain and wind stops, we won't see anything. We better get into the vehicles and get as fast as possible back to the garrison in *Kabankalan*. We're sitting ducks in this weather.

The dogs started barking again. Machine gun bullets hit the side of the truck. His men fired back in the direction of the dogs. The truck followed his lead. He sped out of barrio *Aguisan* toward the crossing on the highway. His option was to go back to *Binalbagan* or speed towards *Kabankalan*. He was in no mood to face Colonel Asaki's wrath, so he sped towards *Kabankalan.*

Between the yelping dogs and the new guerrilla unit that arrived in Crossing *Aguisan,* Lt. Ishida was trapped in a tight ambush. The bend that curved toward the highway was littered with fresh leaves and broken branches. When the driver swerved to the side of the road to avoid what he thought was the scattered debris from the wind, he ran right into a deep hole. The lieutenant bounced several feet up before he was thrown in the hole with the jeep. Several hand grenades exploded behind and on the side of the speeding truck.

"Damn it. Why doesn't he ever learn?" The sergeant was angry with the driver. "We're in the same spot we were earlier yesterday. These holes were dug to delay us."

The sergeant pulled the unconscious Lt. Ishida out of the hole. He had a bump on his head and his left arm was crushed. The yelping dogs were closing in but the sergeant mounted a machine gun at the back of the truck and started spraying. The dogs were quiet for a while, but machine gun bullets hit the front of the truck. The soldiers scrambled out and mounted three other machine guns surrounding the truck in all directions. They fired wherever the dogs barked and kept them quiet, not knowing they kept the guerrillas at bay. The sergeant wanted to send the other jeep back to *Kabankalan* but he knew there would be more guerrillas to ambush it. He had no other choice but to keep the seriously wounded Lieutenant Ishida with them until reinforcement would arrive. He radioed the *Binalbagan* garrison for help. Major Onoki answered the call.

"Colonel Asaki has the same problem with holes on the road; it would take at least a couple of hours before we can move but we'll be there soon. Three truckloads from the garrison in *Kabankalan* are coming to reinforce you. Meantime, hold on and make sure you keep the guerrillas from advancing south to *Ilog,* " the Major said.

Lt. Verzosa and Lt. Palacios pinned down Lt. Ishida's men just south of the bend beyond Crossing *Aguisan.*

"Hold fast Roming. We have to keep harassing this unit to keep it from moving toward *Kabankalan*. I'll throw the grenades at the truck and keep it busy while you get close and use the machine guns. Get closer and surround the truck. Keep the dogs barking from different directions so they'd think a large contingent has pinned them down." Lt. Verzosa sent this message through the black box.

"Damn it," the Japanese sergeant swore, "if help does not come soon, the lieutenant could die."

But every time the truck tried to inch out, a grenade fell a few feet from it.

Commotion reigned in the garrison in *Kabankalan* as well. Because Colonel Asaki took two columns to *Binalbagan* a week earlier, only five trucks were left in the garrison. They could not possibly send all five trucks out and leave the garrison lightly attended. Desperate, they radioed Colonel Asaki for orders. Pinned down just beyond Crossing *Binalbagan,* Colonel Asaki was impatient to chase the escaping Americans. He hadn't recovered from his anger at the missing truck. He suspected it was speeding towards Ilog, even towards *Enclaro.*

"These guerrillas have to be blocked at barrio *Binicuil* or at the latest at Crossing *Kabankalan*," he yelled. "Radio the garrison to send three trucks to barrio *Binicuil.* Tell them we have to hold the guerrillas there at all cost."

Chapter 23—Timing

Colonel Alvaro Gomez and Kapitan Almanzur Villalva put their heads together.

"We're not making much progress with the second group; they're too exhausted to catch up with the first group. If we don't get to *Ilog* today, Colonel Asaki's forces will be too difficult to avoid," the *Kapitan* complained to his cousin.

"At least the three traveling with Lt. Garcia and Sergeant Valderama are now behind the garrison in *Kabankalan*. We need to make an assault at the garrison so they can avoid detection. They'll be paddled to the *Hacienda Luzuriaga*. The tricky move is to get them to join you." Colonel Gomez answered.

"Half of the unit in *Kabankalan* had been ordered to set a road block in barrio *Binicuil*. They've not been told about the missing truck so they don't know we're getting ready to run out of Binicuil. What are the plans for ambush there? Is Poping prepared to engage the troops speeding there?" *Kapitan* Villalva asked his cousin.

"Yes, Lt. Silverio Singson wanted to join Procopio but now he has to lead the assault on the garrison in *Kabankalan*. Procopio will have his hands full in *Binicuil*. He needs to keep the trucks busy there and make sure they don't proceed to barrio *Aguisan*. If they join the Japanese troops in *Aguisan*, the boys there would have trouble. There are only a few of them and they're not too well equipped." Colonel Gomez explained. The cousins exchanged information, intending to keep the Japanese busy on all four fronts.

"We have to delay Colonel Asaki's progress toward *Enclaro* and get the nine airmen together. Our biggest problem is keeping all units with enough ammunition to accomplish their missions. I have to turn over this stolen truck to Procopio, take to the woods and run toward barrio *Andulawan*. From there, we'll proceed to *Ilog* and to *Enclaro* as fast as we can," Almanzur told his cousin.

"You could travel faster if you use the truck, but that would be a clear give away of the presence of the Americans. By now Colonel Asaki must surely be aware of the missing truck. The garrison in *Kabankalan* would do anything to prevent the truck from passing through Crossing *Kabankalan*. It would be too dangerous to use it," his cousin answered.

Pedring herded his three charges, Scott, Joe, and Valdez, together for a last minute talk.

"From here on we'll run for dear life as long as our energy would last, swiftly, quietly, without verbal communication. From barrio *Binicuil* to barrio *Andulawan,* we'll run under good cover. Wind and rain could slow us down, but we have to get to *Andulawan* then to *Ilog* proper before the Japanese trucks could block our route to *Enclaro.* We need speed, and timing, and nothing short of a miracle to arrive where we're expected before the Japanese get there."

The second group of three did not move as fast. Sauro and Rudi often relieved BB of carrying Marco on his back. Sometimes Sauro got hold of Marco on the shoulders and Rudi got hold of his legs; together, they would run with this burden till their energy gave out. They had to spot the best cover before they could sit and rest for a spell. Badong stuck to Spencer like a leech. When Spencer flagged, Badong tugged, pulled and half lifted him till he got his energy back. Marco felt he was getting to be too much of a burden.

"Why couldn't you just leave me here," he pleaded. Slowing down the progress of the group was too much for his pride to bear,

"Next time I hear this nonsense from you, I'll slug you to keep your mouth shut," BB hissed at Marco. "Now you have made me break the code of silence so shut up before the boys get too disgusted with our impertinence." He had to say something to keep Marco from being depressed. Spencer, too, had the same problem, but either Badong or Sauro insisted on silence; often, they simply lifted him on their shoulders. When Sauro and Rudi carried Marco, BB followed close.

Towards noon of the day after they left barrio *Binicuil,* the second group caught up with the first group in a hut in barrio *Andulawan.* Here they rested for a full thirty minutes and were served a brew of hot ginger root and honey. Wind and rain never abated; in fact, it escalated almost beyond endurance for both Marco and Spencer. The *Kapitan,* always aware of every detail on this march, ordered additional time of rest for this group. Miraculously, while both groups rested, bowls of rice soup, flavored with sautéed garlic, onions, and ginger root, laced with chunks of chicken meat, came from somewhere. A change into warm, dry clothes given to Spencer and Marco lifted their spirits beyond belief.

When the first group escorted by Pedring and a few guerrilla men with sub machine guns and automatic rifles left, the mood changed from desperation to stirring hope. Marco and Spencer had half an hour more to sleep for they were at the point of utter exhaustion. BB continued to hover over the two, but he, too, finally slept a troubled sleep. He kept twisting and turning. Before the thirty minutes were up, he heard the distinct sound of motor vehicles in the distance. He sat up when he heard gunfire.

Chapter 24—All Barrels Bared

A road from the highway in barrio *Binicuil* veers inland towards barrio *Andulawan* for about a kilometer and ends in a creek. The rain filled the creek to the brim and the water overflowed about a meter above the banks. Below the banks, the water was muddy. Tall heavy-bodied reeds residents cut, dry, and weave into mats and baskets line the banks.

Kapitan Villalva ordered his men to use the reeds for cover. They followed the creek winding through tall cottonwood and coconut trees stretching along the borders of the swamps. The swamps blanket the shoreline behind barrio *Andulawan* for more than five kilometers thick. In some parts, narrow waterways reach into the heart of the mangrove fastness. The shoreline from *Himamaylan* drops sharply toward *Ilog*. There, the swamps broaden in depth to over five times the width of the swampland on the shoreline of *Himamaylan*. *Ilog* marks the beginning of the curve of the heel of the island of Negros that is shaped like a sock. Swamp cover the shoreline thickly behind the town then thins down as it borders the highway going in a straight line to *Cawayan*, the next town south of it. The highway extends all the way to the back of the heel, then drops off as it curves toward the towns of *Sipalay*, *Hinoba-an* and *Maricalum*, just a few kilometers to *Basay*, the town nearest the border of Negros Occidental and Negros Oriental.

Halfway between *Ilog* and *Cawayan*, a secondary road runs through barrio *Dancalan* in *Ilog*; it climbs up the mountains to *Candoni* and bends back toward the shoreline at *Sipalay*. Just behind *Kabankalan* below the caves and natural springs of *Mabinay*, less than a hundred kilometers below the mountain range that divides the two provinces, lies the source of the *Ilog* River. The caves of *Mabinay* extend toward the source of the river and feed it with hundreds of natural springs. Unknown to the Japanese, this cave system is the second longest cave system in the entire Philippines. The river flows downward to the foothills above *Kabankalan* down to *Ilog* where it branches into two directions forming a huge Y that encircles the town. The river has two mouths (the tops of the Y) that lead directly into the sea. Dense mangrove forests extend from the banks of the river beyond the town toward the shoreline where, before the war, enterprising business families bought the land rights from the government to construct extensive fishponds. These supply the commercial fish markets in Manila.

The smallest section of these fishponds range from a hectare (2.48 acres) to a fourth of a hectare, depending on what it cultures: bangus (milk fish), prawns, or crabs. The biggest fishpond belonging to a single owner covers about one hundred and twenty hectares of swampland. The dikes that frame the ponds rise to two meters high and are two meters wide, again, depending on what they enclose. At high tide, the frames admit a brackish combination of salt water from the sea and fresh water from the river and fill up the enclosures to raise fish, prawns or crabs. The smaller and shallower enclosures raise oysters and varieties of seashells. Kapitan Villalva and Colonel Gomez's aunt, *Nanay* Luciana, owns ninety hectares (approximately 200 acres) of fishponds in the swamp area across *Enclaro*. Nanay Lucing's tenants still operate some of the ponds on the sly to feed the guerrilla forces who come down from *Cawayan* to take seafood to guerrilla headquarters once or twice a month.

Japanese troops once attempted to cross from *Enclaro* to the fishponds, but the elevation of the riverbank and the dikes provide protection for guerrilla forces to ambush the invaders and the proximity of the swamp cover furnish the guerrillas a formidable defense and retreat shelter. Thereafter, the Japanese learned to avoid this area and rely strictly on the towns north of *Binalbagan,* by the sea, for their source of seafood supply. There they terrorize fishermen and take away their catch by force. Anywhere from *Binalbagan* going north are coastlines that have far less swamp cover than *Himamaylan* in the south. Often, Japanese gunboats use captive Filipinos as subservient fishing crew to obtain sufficient sea catch to feed them. They have it made in the north so they avoid the risk of going to the fishponds in *Ilog*.

At this particular time, however, the fishponds became a strategic defense spot for the guerrillas Kapitan Villalva asked Colonel Gomez to send three men with binoculars, a black box, and a .30 caliber machine gun they mounted behind a hut on top of the fishpond dikes opposite *Enclaro* to anticipate their arrival there. The Colonel also hid small outrigger *bancas* in the *nipa* groves ready to transport them to the *batel* at the mouth of the river beyond *Enclaro*.

To minimize his anxieties, Colonel Gomez summarized the situation facing *Kapitan* Villalva. ALmanzur was getting edgy when he heard gunfire as they left barrio *Andulawan* to run toward *Ilog* and catch up with the first group that had left a half hour earlier. He had all the speed he needed, because now there were about eighteen men who took turns to give the wounded Americans a hand. Still a gnawing unease took the *Kapitan* by surprise. He didn't like the sound of the vehicles nor the gunfire he heard.

Kapitan Villalva was distraught. Torn between wanting to go back to help Lt. Balinas, or proceed to *Ilog* as quickly as he could, he vacillated. The Lieutenant would have a better chance with his help. But he needed to get out of *Andulawan* to join the first group that had already left. If he went back to barrio Binicuil to help his young cousin, Lt. Procopio Balinas, he would risk the capture of the American airmen, but in the back of his head, he could hear the pleading voice of his elderly aunt, *Nanay* Julit Balinas.

"Please, Almanzur," he heard her say over and over, "Procopio is the youngest of my boys and the most attentive to me. I can't afford to be without him in my advancing years. Please take care of him and make sure the Japanese don't kill him before this war is over. Promise me you'll not send him on an assignment without you supervising his men with him."

Why of all the officers at his command did his *Manong* Alvaro send Procopio to barrio *Binicuil?* He assessed the danger for Procopio. He knew the Japanese at the garrison in *Kabankalan* were determined to hold on in barrio Binicuil. Colonel Asaki probably ordered them to secure the area at all cost since they believed the guerrillas hiding the Americans were still in the area. Procopio needed his help. He decided that Pedring and sergeant Peralta would take care of the Americans while he determined how much trouble Procopio was in.

He gave orders on how to proceed to *Ilog*. Meantime, he decided to go back to barrio *Binicuil*. Badong, Sauro and Rudi got hold of a submachine gun and automatic rifles and went running back with him. *Kapitan* Villalva's pants pockets were bulging with hand grenades. When they arrived at the road that extended to *Andulawan* they saw heads bobbing in the reeds.

"Where is Lt. Balinas," the *Kapitan* asked one of the bobbing heads.

"Sir, we got separated. The last thing we know is that the lieutenant drove the Japanese truck you stole toward the direction of the *Kabankalan* garrison. Two Japanese trucks that came from the garrison in *Kabankalan* raced to overtake him. Sergeant Bobbie Lucerna threw a hand grenade at the truck left behind near the highway, but he missed."

"Yes, but he blew a hole right in front of the truck, so it has not moved. They pinned the sergeant down with a machine gun and are still doing it; I mean, spraying with the machine gun," one of the other bobbing heads surfaced and informed the *Kapitan.*

"Four of us ran toward this direction. We were trying to get back to help the sergeant, but his guns have been silent for a while. We don't know what has happened since," another bobbing head added.

"Okay, you boys cover me. I'm going to circle around those tall trees over to the right. Don't waste your ammunition; crawl closer and see if you can fire at the truck," the *Kapitan* ordered.

"Sir, I will crawl with these guys. Maybe Badong can follow close to you and cover you," Sauro answered.

"Good idea." The *Kapitan* started to sprint towards the nearest tree cover. "Badong, get ready to cover me. I'll throw a hand grenade at the machine gun. You can see where it is from here, right?"

"Right, Sir. Be careful, please." Badong ran shoulder to shoulder with the *Kapitan,* but pretty soon, the *Kapitan* out-distanced him. Badong ran toward the nearest tree cover and started shooting to distract the machine gun. In the corner of his eye, he saw the *Kapitan* run toward the tree behind the truck. As the *Kapitan* pitched the hand grenade, the machine gun started spraying at Badong's direction. Badong managed a few rounds on his automatic rifle before he heard the explosion. The grenade blew the machine gun in the air but shortly after, Badong's gun was silent.

Sauro, Rudi, and the four bobbing heads had crawled towards the rice dikes to the left of the truck and were shooting sporadically. Still, there was no sound from Badong's gun. The *Kapitan* got furious. Not knowing how many Japanese guns were left, he ran with his submachine gun cocked.

You bastards, he thought. First Procopio and now Badong. I'm going to get you all if it costs my life. These kids don't deserve to lose theirs.

He ran on a zigzag towards the truck, blasting with the submachine gun. Sauro knew why the *Kapitan* ran though there was hardly any cover. He knew that Badong's gun had been silenced. Sauro stood up from his crawling position. Rudi and the four others followed him, firing their weapons at the truck. Getting near the truck, they saw the *Kapitan* climb up the hood still blasting with his sub machine gun. They saw several Japanese soldiers pasted on the truck walls. Sauro did not even know he was bleeding till he fell down from sheer exhaustion and loss of blood. He had been hit on the right shoulder. Rudi lifted him and ran for cover.

"Boys, see if you can help Sauro," the *Kapitan* yelled at the three others still running. He raced toward the direction where he left Badong. When he got there, he picked up the near lifeless body. Badong got hit on the abdomen just below the heart. His eyes were closed but he was still able to whisper.

"We got them all Sir, didn't we?"

"Yes we did, Son. Yes, we surely did," the *Kapitan* answered through his tears. With Badong's lifeless body in his arms, he went back toward the truck again. He lost one, but he wasn't going to lose Sauro too. He rummaged in the Japanese truck looking for first aid material and sure enough he found several kits. With Rudi's help, he set Sauro's shoulder in a tourniquet as quickly as he could, then he talked to all three that followed Sauro to cover him.

"Rudi, I want you to promise me that you'll take Sauro to my Tia Julit's house in *Andulawan*. Tell her for me to do the best she can to keep him alive, for I'm going to see what happened to her son, Lt. Balinas."

They took all the medicine kits with them and left as fast as they could, knowing the Japanese trucks could be back in the area anytime at all.

Meantime, eight of Lt. Balinas's men behind a rice dike near the highway joined the *Kapitan*. Two of them were hit, one on the leg and another on the elbow. The man hit on the elbow had to be sent back with Sauro, but the man hit on the leg asked for a tourniquet and insisted on coming along with the *Kapitan*.

"Sir, I want to know what happened to Lt. Balinas. I have to come along," he said.

"If we have to walk, you can't come along, for you will slow us down," the *Kapitan* answered him. "But we will see what we can do about this truck here."

The Japanese truck was battered but still operable. The windshield had shattered from the *Kapitan's* submachine gun. Bullet holes lined the truck in many places. It was leaning on its side. The men straightened it, took all the guns they could salvage, threw the bleeding but dead bodies of the Japanese out, made sure the tires were okay, and the engine still functioned. They pushed it behind the hole on the road and climbed into the truck.

"We're ready now, Sir," Sergeant Lucerna shouted. He and another private had fiddled with the engine. "

"She's in good enough condition. Don't know how fast she can run, but she'll run all right," the sergeant assured the *Kapitan.*

Nine of them climbed in. The *Kapitan* would not leave Badong's body behind. He would take him wherever he ended up. He grieved for this faithful comrade silently, but he was still worried about his cousin Procopio. He really had no time to think what to do. All he knew was that the quickest way to locate him was to follow his route with this almost broken down truck.

"Boys, from here on, I have no idea what to expect. All I know is that I have to see where Lt. Balinas went and what happened to him. The odds are against us. Some of us may die like Badong here. I would have given my life to save his. I only know I did what I could, but that wasn't good enough. You have to weigh the odds. If you think you've had enough, now is the time to say so. Anyone who wants out, just say so and I'll stop the truck to let you off."

No one said anything.

"Are you saying something with your silence? Does it mean you want to be with me, come what may?"

"Yes. Sir," came the spontaneous chorus.

"Okay, then. Let's all seriously think about what to do before the circumstances stop us," the *Kapitan* said, trying to stifle the quaver in his voice. He was obviously much moved by this show of loyalty. He couldn't discount their willingness to sacrifice everything to help him. For the first time, he noticed that Ponsing wasn't with him. He remembered Ponsing was way ahead with the wounded Americans when he turned to go back to *Binicuil.* Without Ponsing's black box, there was no way to get in touch with Procopio. He didn't even know if Procopio's unit carried a black box. The truck swung right at the *Kabankalan* Crossing. They were now just three kilometers north of the *Talubangui* Bridge. The truck radio sputtered static. Sergeant Lucerna fiddled with the knobs. In a few seconds everyone heard a message in Japanese.

"Sir, the message is ordering this truck to hold fast and is asking if everything's okay," Mauro, who lived in *Kabankalan* and had studied Japanese, translated.

"Answer. Say *Arigato*. Repeat three times, and use the static to cover your voice.

Evidently the message was received for after a few minutes Colonel Asaki's voice came through the static.

"This is Colonel Asaki. I'm stopping for a few minutes by Lt. Ishida's unit. I'll join you in *Binicuil* as soon as possible then proceed to *Talubangui* Bridge and on to *Enclaro*. Over and out."

Once more, through the static, Colonel Asaki's angry voice demanded a report of the situation.

"Turn off the blasted radio. Put in all the speed this truck's good for," the *Kapitan* yelled over the static.

After that, the *Kapitan* was quiet, too quiet in his seat. He keenly felt the danger they were in. Every step he took demanded serious consequences. An instant of focused self-awareness threw him into a corner where he was all by himself. In that moment, a decision began to flash clear in his mind. It came as a wave of instinctive recognition as he looked intently at the landscape through the shattered truck window.

I cannot let these young men die out of sheer bravado. I can't throw caution out this window.

"Wait a minute," he said aloud. The shaking of the truck seemed to jolt his memory. "Isn't there a short cut between the *Malabong* Bridge and barrio *Talubangui* that goes to barrio *Andulawan?* Slow down, we have to find it. Let's not push our luck. We're no match for the heavily armed Japanese detachment in two fully loaded trucks."

The *Kapitan* spoke very slowly as though he were talking to himself.

Retracing recent events in his thoughts he started with the basic statement of fact. Procopio knows Adulawan by heart. He lived here all his life. Then his mind lit up with a subsequent thought. I bet a million that's why Procopio raced in this direction. He must have veered back to *Andulawan* through the short cut. He knew the same thing I know now. He had to retreat when he needed to. What he did was the best way out of a predicament. Bravo for Procopio. He's too smart to throw his life away.

"I know exactly where he is now." The *Kapitan* let every one hear.

The truck slowed down carefully. They found the short cut to *Andulawan* and sure enough the tire marks in the mud clearly indicated Procopio's truck passed this way. The truck inched its way over Procopio's tire marks. The group cheered.

The *Kapitan* asked for silence. He didn't want the two Japanese trucks to hear them. He ordered the driver to cut the engine and let the men out to push the truck from the highway all the way to *Andulawan*. The *kogon* grass provided some cover. The wind slowed down and the rain receded to a drizzle. The sun was slowly peeping through the clouds.

As they approached Andulawan, several of Lt. Balinas' men came to meet them and helped push the truck beside abandoned fishpond dikes to a depression underneath tall cottonwood trees. Procopio, himself, came waving his automatic rifle in the air.

"*Hoy*, (Hey) *Nong* Almanzur, how did you know where to find me?" he said with a wide grin on his face.

"I didn't Not until the very last minute. I remembered you took us on this road from *Talubangui* when your *Manong* Alvaro was looking for a farm tenant shortly before the war. The road was better kept then. We had trouble spotting it now. The Japanese must've overshot you. Did you cut off your motor when you turned into this road?" He asked Procopio.

"Oh, yes, I had to; we also pushed the truck all the way in. What a memory you have. I never expected you would find us."

In half an hour, they could hear the Japanese trucks zooming back on the road from the *Malabong* Bridge and racing toward the *Talubangui* Crossing. They didn't find the truck in barrio *Malabong* so they assumed Procopio's truck had somehow crossed the *Talubangui* Bridge. The *Kapitan* found out later that the Japanese truck didn't want to cross the unstable *Malabong* Bridge. They didn't trust its condition to bear their weight.

Ponsing came ambling toward the *Kapitan* like a pet dog with its tail between its legs. "Sorry I lost you, Sir. It will not happen again."

"All is well that ends well is what they say, Ponsing. Next time, you stick to me like glue, okay? We missed your black box. Have you been reporting to my cousin?"

"Yes. Sir. He says you must hurry to get to *Enclaro* because Colonel Asaki's trucks are now racing to get there before you do."

"Tell him Pedring and sergeant Peralta and four of the eighteen men now with them went ahead on foot. They probably have already crossed the river in barrio *Malabong* and are closer to barrio *Diot* in *Ilog*. Tell him also that the Japanese trucks that chased us have raced to the *Talubangui* Bridge. I assume one of those proceeded to *Vista Allegre* to see if we have gone there. If they don't find Poping's truck there, my guess is one will go back to *Malabong* and see how they could have missed it."

"Yes, *Kapitan,* right away, Sir," Ponsing answered. "Sergeant Lucerna has camouflaged the short cut you took with more *kogon* grass. He has six men to guard it and make sure those bastards don't find it,"

"Okay. Just make sure Crispin and Benito stay behind at *Nanay* Julit's. We have to catch up with Pedring as fast as we can. We'll make better time since there are enough of us to carry the wounded Americans. We have to run with them. No time for them to limp and slow us down."

"Sir, Colonel Gomez says you have to send Lt. Balinas' unit to the *Hacienda Luzuriaga* to wait there for the arrival of the three other Americans. I'll radio Lt. Balinas right away," Ponsing relayed another message.

The *Kapitan* and his men tried hard to get to *Enclaro* in *Ilog*. Before they got to the town proper in *Ilog*, another message from Colonel Gomez stopped them. Colonel Asaki's trucks had passed *Kabankalan* Crossing and were running full speed to the *Talubangui* Bridge. It wouldn't take him long to get to *Vista Allegre* and join the first truck that now arrived at *Enclaro*.

"Looks like the end of the line for us, Almanzur. What in God's name are we going to do?" Colonel Gomez's voice sounded desperate.

Kapitan Vilalva's unit was very proud to have been selected for this most exciting and dangerous mission of hiding and protecting the Americans. Now, they had mixed emotions about it. The prevailing feeling was that this was what they had been training so hard for. This was the ultimate test to their courage, the highlight of their combat encounters but they began to realize that from here on, the mission had taken a suicidal turn.

The mood was somber. Badong, much regarded by the *Kapitan,* had died. Sauro and Crispin were seriously wounded. There was no guarantee anyone of them would live. Benito was barely able to limp to safety in *Andulawan*. Lt. Balinas' unit almost got annihilated, except for his fast thinking and daring. The *Kapitan,* too, almost died as he risked his life for Badong and Sergeant Lucerna and his men.

They were very quiet now, for they realized they would not make it to *Enclaro* at all. The next encounter could be nothing short of suicide. Still, no amount of persuasion could dissuade them to quit being part of it.

Chapter 25—A Desperate Decision

Colonel Gomez laid the cards on the table: "All routes to *Enclaro* are now blocked. Colonel Asaki is determined to stop us. What do we do? Where are you now? Which way is left for you, short of running into overwhelming odds? From now on, keeping the Americans would require your lives. You can shoot it out and get to your *Nanay* Sid's hideout, but think of the consequences. It would probably mean they would be wiped out too. Your *Manang* Aning and my kids are there. Almanzur think hard before you do anything. Whatever you do, let me know. Please."

Kapitan Almanzur Villalva heard despair in his *Manong* Alvaro's voice. His entire cousin's family: father, mother, three siblings, and his wife and two sons, lived in the hideout. So did two of the *Kapitan*'s younger sisters. How can he expose them to a possible massacre? Colonel Asaki commanded heavily armed combat troops from two of the biggest Japanese garrisons in southern Negros Occidental. He was determined to capture the Americans and the guerrillas who rescued them. They had eluded capture thus far, but despite the recent guns, two-way radios and ammunition they had received from the last surfacing of the submarine from Australia, they were still no match for the heavily armed Japanese.

"We almost made it. Darn it, we can't just march into *Enclaro* now. That bastard Colonel Asaki would be waiting there. He couldn't ask for anything better." *Kapitan* Villalva gritted his teeth in frustration.

They were inching along the pathway north of the *Ilog* town proper that had remained abandoned for more than two years. *Kapitan* Villalva sat down to rest and think. He was biting his lips in anguish. Every move he made this last week had been blocked with a counter move from the Japanese. The typhoon winds and heavy rains three days ago had slowed down their progress. Colonel Asaki, now wise to their plans, has arrived at *Enclaro*. Exit from there to the sea was now impossible.

His cousin Alvaro's plan was simple and would have worked. But they didn't have time to execute it. If only they had reached *Enclaro* before Colonel Asaki got wise to the move. At *Enclalro,* Alvaro was waiting in the largest *batel* (an oversized outrigger *banca* with oars, sails, a small engine and a small cabin) he could find. If the Japanese didn't catch on to the plan, this *batel,* loaded with the Americans, would have left for *Maricalum*, for the rendezvous with the American submarine. Now this plan had to be scrapped.

What was he to do? In desperation, *Kapitan* Villalva was always alone and quiet. Time had run out. He knew the men with him were battlewise, but he could not lead them to certain death. He needed their input. He called a halt at barrio *Diot*, outside the *Ilog* town proper a few hundred meters north of the point where the other branch of the river extended in another mouth to the sea. He asked for immediate confirmation of a report that a radio technician and two of the best shots in his reconnaissance unit from *Cawayan* were holed out in a small *nipa* hut on the opposite bank of the river at *Enclaro*. They trekked there from the *batel* the day before. They were anticipating the arrival of the Americans; instead, they almost run into the Japanese contingent that arrived in force. The *Kapitan* received another message.

The two trucks had to return to the garrison in *Kabankala*n to reinforce the remaining troops there, but a large unit of Japanese soldiers, approximately fifty men, six machine guns, two 75mm guns, and a few motorcycles were now deployed on the riverbank at *Enclaro*. In fact, all small river craft have been intercepted and dragged to the commandant's presence for questioning and inevitable torture. Radio messages also said *kempetai* were seen proceeding to the other branch of the river to determine what's happening there. They most certainly report to *Enclaro* and could ask for reinforcement to block that other exit to the sea.

The Japanese at *Enclaro* were certain *Kapitan* Villava's men were moving in their direction. They set a trap for them. This time, Colonel Asaki swore the Americans the elusive *Kapitan* was hiding would finally be bagged. Already, the first platoon were spread out northeast of *Enclaro* to block exit in that direction. Colonel Asaki would no longer be cheated of his quarry.

Kapitan Villava decided it was time for a clinical discussion because no heroics could answer to the situation.

"I can no longer make decisions alone. I want you to assess our chances. Given the circumstances, what are our options? We could paddle to *Enclaro* where we would be expected by several Japanese platoons armed to the teeth. What would our chances be? Nil. That's unthinkable! Besides, it's not just our lives we're risking. We have the Americans to consider."

"Going on the other branch of the *Ilog* River won't solve our problem either," Pedring interrupted. Once the *kempetai* find out we're headed there, they won't lose any time telling the Japanese to follow us there. Your *Nanay* Sid's hideout will be wiped out in no time."

"The danger is double-edged, really," Sergeant Peralta clarified. "If we're not seen proceeding to *Enclaro,* the Japanese will think we have shifted direction. They'll speed with their vehicles following our new route and cut off escape."

"Both branches are being watched by the Japanese and the *kempetai.* We're outnumbered, outgunned, and, right now, outmaneuvered," Rudi said desolately.

"Gosh, I'm surprised at you all," Ponsing remarked. "You talk as if we have no other option but to surrender."

"Surrender? Surrender is not an option, had never been an option no matter how desperate we were. So far, we've not risked our lives for nothing. Are you ready for Colonel Asaki's maniacal torture machinery before death? Not me. I'll never submit to that sadistic bastard."

Pedring brandished his sub machine gun in the air and was out of breath after he said all that.

"Heck," Sergeant Peralta objected. "The Japanese are at *Enclaro*; they're not yet here. Isn't this the more logical option? We can hide here somewhere."

"For how long?" Ponsing asked?

As was his custom, *Kapitan* Villava seemed alone and too quiet. Responding intuitively to the gravity of the situation and calculating all the detailed data concerning their position, his mind rapidly brought several unnoticed details into a brilliant clarity. He was operating on a kind of mental geometry, a special awareness, thought that was extra rational.

"What can we do, Sir? You always think of something. You're so quiet; are you thinking of something we don't know about," Rudi asked anxiously.

The *Kapitan* felt the veins bulging on his forehead. They were now very close to the possibility of capture or certain death.

"Of course I am." *Kapitan* Villalva promptly realized that perhaps the solution to this final crisis is no longer just a matter of combat readiness but a masterpiece of trickery on top of that? With a twinkle in his eyes, he asked his men to call the Americans into the circle of discussion.

"I don't know if you've watched the movie cartoon 'Tom and Jerry?'"

"My nephews loved to watch that incredibly funny match of wits. What about it?" BB asked. He remembered the episodes but was unable to connect his recognition with the Captain's trend of thought.

"I loved to watch that cartoon with my kids. I enjoyed it with relish," the *Kapitan* said. He started to explain to his men who could not follow his thinking either.

"In a series of episodes, Tom, the cat, chases Jerry, the mouse, and corners him. He's ready to pounce. Gerry stares at him and, somehow, he always has a trick up his sleeve to avoid being devoured. I just thought about it now; funny, we're exactly in the same situation. Some plan of diversion is imperative."

He walked around in circles, his men still waiting for him to say something incredibly out of the way. Finally, the *Kapitan* stopped pacing and dropped down on his knees.

"What we need now is a neat trick, and I can only think of the most outlandish one. If this does not work, it'll be my last one too."

He stood, closed his eyes, and leaned on a coconut trunk. He spoke to his men in *Ilongo* so that the Americans would not understand what they were talking about.

"Remember those oversized jars we made to transport guns from one camp to another without being detected? You know, the ones with the false bottoms and a top that would hold grains for cover? We pretended we were trading grains for salt, right?"

"I know, Sir. They're still in the *batel* with Colonel Gomez," Ponsing remembered.

"Yes, and we're not too far from *Mang* Kari's well either. What if the tops of those jars were sealed and we filled them with water from *Mang* Kari's well? We could have *Manong* Alvaro drill fine breathing holes on the false bottoms and we could fit our human cargo in so they could breathe. It wouldn't be easy. Gosh, it would be excruciating to lie inside for hours before they can be delivered to *Nanay* Sid's hideout."

"Would it be possible for the Americanos to survive that ordeal?" the men murmured.

"What other choice do we have, much less them?" *Kapitan* Villalva asked. "It's their only chance. The only other problem is a very crucial one. Who can paddle the jars to *Nanay* Sid's hideout without being stopped by the *kempetai?* They're now posted on this branch of the river. They'll most certainly stop any male paddler."

As if this were another Tom and Jerry situation, the *Kapitan* came up with an incredible answer.

"My small cousin, Delia, is the only answer. She's an expert paddler; she had paddled "The Undefeated Seven," a group I had trained, for all their races. She also has nerves of steel. She has survived Japanese torture. I rescued her under the most adverse of circumstances. Boy, did she ever lie her way out of that situation!"

"But can she paddle alone with all the weight?" Pedring asked the *Kapitan*.

"That I don't know," the *Kapitan* thought hard. "Everybody in the swamps knows her oldest sister, *Inday* Choling (Soledad), is going to have a baby."

"Isn't your *Inday* Choling, now almost forty? My cousin's wife died unable to give birth to her last child because she was almost forty," Ponsing said. "They cut up her belly to save the child."

"That's why *Inday* Choling must have safe well water for the childbirth. The other women in her household are staying home and tending her. Delia's Papa is sick and *Inday* Choling's husband and her son are scouring the swamps in search of a midwife because *Inday* Choling has already started labor. I'm not inventing this. I heard the women talking about her, even in *Andulawan*. I know Delia. She can embellish reasons that would lend credence to her desperate errand. But I don't know if she has the strength to paddle alone."

The *Kapitan* walked toward the riverbank. He came back with a frown on his face.

"I'm really am not too sure that what I'm thinking of is feasible, but I noticed that the river is swollen. It has rained hard here too. The current is in her favor. She might be able to make it," he hesitated.

Kapitan Villava's men trusted his judgment. In their past maneuvers they had implicit faith in his last ditch plans to avoid capture, but leave the fate of the Americans in the hands of a ten year old? That's going a bit too far! It would almost be certain suicide on the part of the girl.

The *Kapitan* saw the thought on their faces, but he persuaded them to consider that he was suggesting a desperate gamble, and they had no other option. Besides, six of them will still have to risk their lives, for they have the most difficult job of following her on the opposite bank of the river. If the *kempetai* stop her and hold her longer than three quarters of an hour, the six will have to engage them in combat and rescue her and the jars she's risking her life for.

"I'm fully aware of the danger she faces, but I know this girl's mettle. I would trust her with my own life, if it depended on her. What no one realizes is that she's far too intelligent for her age, and is very wily and strong-willed. If any one has a chance to outwit the *kempetai*, it would be her." He mumbled as if talking to himself. He paced in circles again as his men waited for his final word.

"This sounds too bizarre I know, but there's no other way. Is there?" He quit pacing and looked at everyone intently. Shaking his head, he spoke rather sadly.

"I wouldn't risk my cousin's life if I were certain she doesn't stand a chance, but as improvable as it seems, I have this gut feeling that she alone will make the trick work."

He walked a hundred meters to the riverbank and came back and spoke again.

"The wind is blowing toward the sea; both wind and current are in her favor. It's flooding. The water's muddy and the current moves swiftly toward the sea. There's good reason why she needs to fetch this water; it's an imperative errand, one she couldn't do alone if the current and the wind were working against her. Desperate problems need desperate measures. Delia will manage the rest. I'm positive."

His men couldn't think of any other way out of the desperate situation, so they looked to the *Kapitan* in blind faith, trusting his judgment despite their nagging doubts.

This wasn't the first time *Kapitan* Villalva faced a crisis and a near capture. Every one of his men knew they were grossly outnumbered and much less equipped than the Japanese who were now almost at their heels, but, like the *Kapitan*, they weren't prepared to lose. They all looked to him to decide what to do. He was desperate for he was keenly aware that the lives of these men hang on the quality of his decision.

He commanded this special reconnaissance platoon organized in 1942 during the mid months of the second year of the Japanese occupation of Negros Occidental. This unit had now expanded to one more platoon and had ambushed several of Colonel Asaki's patrols in more than one encounter almost simultaneous with the one he led himself. This duplication made it seem as though he were in two places at once. News of his feats had spread fear among the *kempetai* who regarded him almost as a legend but Colonel Asaki considered him an upstart. He swore he could easily push him out of the way. Nevertheless, the *Kapitan's* continued success in eluding capture was a constant assault to the Japanese colonel's pride, a threat to his reputation and a challenge to his command.

Colonel Asaki vowed to hunt him down and eliminate him, for despite the fact that he thought Captain Villalva's notoriety was most certainly exaggerated, he was a known conduit of unequaled courage and had provided in-depth loyalty and unity among the guerrilla bands hitherto scattered, unorganized and, therefore, ineffective. *Kapitan* Villalva was a thorn on the Japanese command's side. His successes depended on men fully devoted to him. They worshipped the ground he walked on despite the fact that many of them paid their lives against the Japanese effort to track him down. His men knew he didn't hesitate to risk his life for them. At no other moment was his decision more crucial than the one he was about to make. He had no time for continued persuasion and argumentation. The *Kapitan* outlined the details of the plan he had in mind.

"I wish there were more of us to carry out this plan. Six must follow Delia. That leaves only twelve of us. Oh, yes, there are the three others already at *Enclaro*, behind the hut on top of the fishpond dikes."

"You mean that crazy American with all that technical equipment? Is he American or just a Filipino born in America?" Sergeant Peralta almost spat his sarcasm.

"Knock it off; he's very dependable. He's a sharpshooter. He can challenge anyone here anytime of the day. Not even the Japanese would be a match for him, given equal circumstances." Ponsing got irritated at their attitude for it seemed to him they were bragging about themselves.

"You think he's a better shot than Caesar or Rafael? Rudi challenged. Rudi referred to the two men who had joined the unit in Andulawan.

"You should just be glad he's on our side," Pedring closed the argument.

"Anyway," the *Kapitan* continued, "We would take two *bancas,* paddled by two men on each end. We would pile thick *nipa* fronds in the middle and paddle deliberately as though we're unaware of the Japanese presence there. We have to let them believe we think we're not expected."

"But wouldn't they be suspicious if there are only two men paddling?" Ponsing was not at all convinced with this plan.

"I know what you're thinking, Sir. We'll put up sticks shaded with *nipa* fronds and put hats on top of the sticks and make them look like camouflaged paddlers. Perhaps a half a dozen in each *banca?*" Sergeant Peralta got excited.

"That's the general idea. I'll paddle the first *banca.* Who'll ride with me? I prefer to take only the best swimmer, for we have to jump off at the right spot and swim fast to the other side of the river. Any takers?"

So it was determined Caesar will paddle the other *banca* with Sergeant Peralta at the other end. Rafael will ride with the *Kapitan* who'll sit on the front end.

Eight men must move stealthily on the opposite bank carrying the submachine guns, half of the grenades available, and Ponsing with the black box. Before they move, they have to send a message to the three men already hold up on the fishpond dikes at *Enclaro.*

"Those on the riverbank must stop about three hundred meters from the men behind the hut. About five hundred meters before we get within range of the machine guns of the Japanese, Rafael and I and Caesar and Sergeant Peralta will quickly dive below the *bancas*, give them a good push, swim underwater, and get to the opposite bank at the spot where you leave guns and grenades wrapped in banana leaves. Make sure you hide them with red markers in the thick grass on the riverbank. Then let hell break loose," the *Kapitan* said.

"We'll open fire only when we know you've reached the riverbank, " Rudi assured the *Kapitan.*

"After you let them have it, you don't stand a chance if you stay put, so run the hell out of there and circle back to *Mang* Kari's well. Whoever gets there must wait for all the rest before we head to *Nanay* Sid's hideout."

Assigned to lead six who'll track Delia's progress at the opposite bank of the river, Pedring wanted to know how long before they open fire at the *kempetai* if they stop Delia's *banca.*

"I wouldn't know about that for sure, but you have to rescue her and the jars at all cost only if she gets in trouble," the *Kapitan* told Pedring. "Watch her very closely but give her time to negotiate her way out."

Ponsing had to send a message to Colonel Alvaro Gomez, to deliver the jars to the hideout before, on, or shortly after midnight, depending on how fast the *batel* can manage the trip to the other mouth of the river.

"I'll tell him to drill holes on the bottom; but to save time, he'll have to do it on his way to the hideout," Ponsing promised the *Kapitan.* "I'll warn him that sealing the tops is his most important concern for if the tops leak, the Americans may not survive the ordeal."

"Tell him timing is essential. The six men at the hideout must paddle to *Mang* Kari's well right after midnight. The *kempetai* won't be too concerned about *bancas* leaving the swamps as they would about those going into the swamps. The jars and Delia must be *at Mang* Kari's well hours before dawn. They have to put the Americans in the jars, and let Delia paddle back before noon. Tell the colonel to return the *batel* to where it was anchored before and convince *kempetai* spies that he had been anchored there all along. Got it?" The *Kapitan* wanted to make sure Ponsing sent his devious message accurately.

When they were told about the plan in some detail, the Americans were too exhausted to object. Before this crisis, they had been guided and led through enough obstacles. Too grateful for what these men had done and are still doing to save their lives, they've learned never to ask any more questions. This time, though, they felt much like lambs led to slaughter. Yet left on their own, they would be dead or, most likely be captured by the Japanese anyway. They meekly surrendered to do the impossible. The chess game of move and counter move was near its end. The next move to checkmate was in Japanese hands. The *Kapitan* began his one last hope to prevent a checkmate. Using this crucial trick up his sleeve, Jerry was about to avoid being devoured by Tom. A message was sent to *Manong* Alvaro. The message read:

Use the other spoon; sit on the other side of the table and ask the kitchen for another dish. Get back on your side to eat it. Enjoy it while it's hot. Ask your youngest sister to get water for you and the boys.

It was easy enough for *Manong* Alvaro to understand that Almanzur wanted him to move the *batel* to the other mouth of the river and obviously ask someone in the hideout what to do before he got back to where he was waiting originally. But he couldn't understand what his young sister, Delia, had to do with the plan. If he knew Almanzur, the other spoon meant a change in plans was inevitable. He wouldn't know what it involved without going to the hideout right away. He sailed to the other mouth of the *Ilog* River into the main trunk, and in a small *banca* paddled into the waterway that coiled into the hideout in the swamps.

What was presented to him was a desperate plan. Who else but Almanzur could dream of it? Past events had taught him to regard Almanzur somewhat off beat. Often, he had to temper his younger cousin's bravado but Almanzur was a master planner of impromptu and unusual solutions. Alvaro had difficulty anticipating the direction his mind took, much less understanding it, but when situations were desperate, he watched Almanzur follow his intuitive solutions as decisively as a gambler who asks for a hand and nonchalantly hides behind an impassive face to win his bet.

Chapter 26—The Big Earthen Jars

Colonel Alvaro Gomez didn't like the risk. He hated putting his sister's life on the line, but Almanzur convinced him that he would never suggest that Delia alone could do the job if he felt she were not equal to it. Almanzur loves this girl dearly, so *Manong* Alvaro explained the plan detailedly to her.

"Delia, your *Manong* Almanzur said you've paddled your team, "The Undefeated Seven," in all the races. He convinced me only you are familiar with this river route. You're the only hope remaining of paddling the jars from *Mang* Kari's well back here. Are you up to it?" He went over, and put her gently on his lap.

"I know it's too risky and too scary for anyone, let alone a little girl all on her own, to do this job. Your *Manong* Almanzur says there's nothing more important than this deception. We have considered everything; this is our last hope. One more day in the open and the Americans will surely get caught. Your Manong Almanzur has risked his life for these men. We've been hiding them for over a month now. It's too painful to give them up to the Japanese without trying one last thing."

He gave his sister a tight squeeze in his arms and reluctantly pleaded. "I don't want to put you in danger, Delia, but I don't want these young men to die either. Even death is not so bad, if that's God's will, but we know what Japanese torture is like. You of all people know they can devise the worst means to inflict pain on the defenseless."

Manong Alvaro turned his head so Delia wouldn't see the tears that threatened to fall. He didn't want to lose this girl. He loved her energy for life and her keen mind.

"I know the *kempetai* will stop me. What do I tell them, *Nong* Varo?"

"Tell them your *Inday* Choling is going to have a baby and you're the only one available to fetch the water she needs. You have to be convincing. They'll stop you but you mustn't let them keep you long. Your *Manong* Almanzur's men will watch you from the right bank and will open fire if they hold you until dark."

Delia gave in to this final appeal. If it hadn't been for *Manong* Almanzur who risked his life to rescue her, she would be dead by now anyhow. But how could she outwit full-grown men? She swallowed hard. Yes, she could. Men are such idiots sometimes. They assume women can't think, let alone young girls. She worked the problem over and over in her head in the past hour as she paddled hard.

If they stop me, when they stop me, I must pretend utter helplessness and let them think I need their advice. I must complain hard of the futility of having been sent to do this task alone. If I succeed in letting them think they're in full control, they may let me pass.

During the races, Victor, had carefully coached her to pay attention to the rhythm of the river.

"You should never miss a beat or the water will work against the hull of the *banca* and keep it straight on the long end like a log floating on its own, bogged down by its weight, unable to move forward. One curve of the paddle at the precise rhythm will move the bow and keep it on a slant and the current underneath will heave and let the *banca* glide in its direction."

She let the paddle lie against the wood frame and straightened the *banca* in time for the continuing beat to allow it to move once more on a slant. Over and over, she repeated the process in consistent timing, without pause, so the current could do the rest of the job. She concentrated.

The *banca* drifted downriver for a good two hours without any incident. Another hour later, Delia passed a coconut grove and turned around the banks densely covered with *nipa* palms. She paddled briskly knowing someone was watching her. She saw the branches on the bank move slightly. She steered towards the middle, making sure the outriggers were as far away from the brush that covered the muddy banks. The river was considerably narrower at this point. If the *banca* snagged any of the branches, keeping a straight course would be difficult. She could capsize, or be stopped easily. Her human cargo was lodged in the large, wide, earthen jars with stoppers sealed tightly at mid point and filled with water to the top. Occasionally, she pretended to accidentally tap the jar nearest her reach twice or she tapped the side of the *banca* with her paddle twice and hope it would be heard from jar to jar. That was her signal to tell them everything was okay, that they could sneeze, cough or make any noise they needed.

The current was strong and in her favor and the *banca* moved almost effortlessly. As she steered it around the river bends, she heard the rustle of the brush behind her, warning that whoever was watching was moving to catch her as she sped around the bend. When she increased her speed enough to lose the eyes on the bank, she would hear a birdcall and then an answer a little farther down river. Then she knew there wasn't only one but a few eyes on her. Anxiously, she waited for them to come out of hiding to stop her.

Her arms were heavy with the ache of paddling. With heart racing and pumping, she pushed farther from the bank then slowed down to let those watching her know she was very tired. She stopped paddling, stood up, and walked a few feet to the nearest jar. Because she was no longer using her paddle for movement, she was simply drifting with the current. She knew the change of pace would allow those on shore to watch her more closely. Deliberately, she lifted the cover from the first jar and picked a coconut cup hanging on the seat beside, dipped it in and took a long drink all the while kicking it three times, her way of saying there was trouble ahead. She drifted this way for a good ten minutes before she decided to use the paddle again, but she tapped another jar three times with the paddle before she moved on.

Would they stop her at the next bend? She wondered. They waited till she turned past a shallow, sandy bend where she would be within easy reach. Someone came out of the brush and waded toward her.

"Hay Inday," "hey honey," *"Nga-a ikaw lang mag isa?"* "Why are you alone?" *"Ano na ang carga mo?"* "What's your load?"

"Oh, my father isn't well and my mother and my sister, you know they can't swim so they're afraid of being in this outrigger monstrosity. Besides, they have to be handy because my oldest sister's going to have a baby. Her husband had to stay home because she has started labor. My sister's son went to look for the midwife to make sure she'd be there to help my sister-in-law when it's time for the baby to come out. Because we ran out of drinking water, I had to go up river clear to *Mang* Kari's well and had to fill these jars. Do you know how far away that is? I'm so tired and so hungry, but I've finished the rice and salted fish I carried for lunch. Salted fish makes one thirsty. Do you know that? I take a drink every now and then. I know my mother would be so angry if one of these jars gets partially empty so I drink from all of them.

Two men held the outriggers firmly at both ends. The *banca* came to a dead stop. Delia moved from jar to jar, tapping them with her palms three times.

"Gosh, I hope we wouldn't drink this water too fast. I hate to have to go back soon to fill these dumb things again." She kicked a jar here and there three times when she could. Message: keep very still in there.

She just kept rattling on to calm her fears.

"The trouble is my sister-in-law says we have to boil clean water for the coming of the baby. We can't just boil muddy water from the river. That's too risky because there's no disinfectant available. Anyway, I'm no good in the kitchen. My other sister stayed home to make sure a fire is going on all day. Besides, she knows next to nothing about paddling a *banca*. They're waiting for this water to boil for the coming of the baby.

She spat to register her disgust.

"Why do they have to have a baby, huh? Isn't there enough trouble just to hide in these blasted swamps? Thank God, I'm good with paddling a *banca*. As for filling these jars, I had plenty of help. *Mang Kari* and his neighbors pitched in when they heard my sister's having a baby."

She addressed the man at the far end, trying her best to make him trust her:

"Would you like to take a drink, Sir? Here——"

She offered the coconut cup to the man. She lifted the cover of the second jar.

"I've already drank enough from the other jar; if I let you drink from this one, my mother wouldn't know the difference."

She gestured to the other man, and extended him the cup.

"Let's drink a little from each jar, then she wouldn't see that I wasted anything from being thirsty."

She forced a laugh and with a tomboyish grimace, she lifted the covers from each jar and tried to dip the coconut cup into each one.

"If I put any germs into this water, I'm sure boiling will kill them anyhow, don't you think?"

Running out of things to say, she thought of shifting the conversation to the men. Hesitantly, she asked them questions.

"Have either of you guys ever had a baby? Have you seen your wife give birth to a baby? That must be scary. Everyone at home thinks my sister will have so much difficulty this time because she's past thirty-five, past the age when babies come easy. Is this true? Heck, I'm so scared so I was glad to get away and do the only thing I do best, paddle these monstrous jars home by myself."

Getting no immediate answer, she tried to pry them more.

"Do you live anywhere around here? I'm not too familiar with this location. I think I'm still a few hours away from home so if you don't mind I have to go soon, okay?"

The man nearest Delia let go of the outrigger he was holding. He had moved to the side of the *banca* getting as close as possible to the jars, noting, as Delia slowly lifted the covers of each, that, indeed, they were filled with water to the top. When Delia got to the last jar, he shook his head saying he had enough to drink.

"It seems such a shame to send a slip of a girl to do a man's job," he said.

"Oh, you better believe it," Delia answered quickly. "But I didn't do any of the heavy job. The jars were fitted into the *banca* by my brother-in-law and *Mang* Kari and his neighbors did the heavy job of filling them. All I had to do is to paddle and I'm used to it. We do it for fun all the time. We have *banca* races when the moon is bright."

She raised her paddle and offered it to him for inspection.

"See, this is as sturdy as they come, right? Test it." She looked him straight in the eye without blinking, but she had to move her legs apart; they were starting to shake. He handed her the paddle back.

"Yes, this is good; very light, and wide at the tip."

Delia retrieved the paddle and inched toward another jar, patting it lightly three times. "Thank God we have enough jars here not to go back for water too often; but for the strong current today, the strongest it has ever been I think, I wouldn't be able to make it home by myself." She bent low to put her hand on the river current.

"Two of our neighbors helped me paddle up river; they had heard someone wanted to trade bamboo for shrimp paste. They need bamboo to make a fish trap. They told me that they couldn't come back with me, but they assured me with this strong current, I wouldn't have too much trouble paddling home alone. I have learned how to let the current do the job and I'm very good at steering. I do the steering at the races. Do you two ever race?"

They ignored her question.

"I agree; you surely do a good job at a man's job," the other man said. Tied on his head to keep his long hair in place was a blue bandana with white flowers.

"I'd hate to race against you and lose."

Both men laughed.

"Are you sure you don't want some more to drink?" Delia asked to steer away from the drift of the talk. She was ready to lift the cover of the middle jar again, but the men turned her down.

"I'm sure we had enough." The older man replied.

"I'm sorry but I have to go now," she said. "Would you please give me a push?"

"What's your hurry, little one?" The man with the bandana said. He was no longer disposed to kid with her. He nursed a nagging suspicion that there was more to this young girl's trip than a need for water. He was torn between giving the *banca* a push and detaining her for further questions. What would happen if they returned to the Japanese garrison with nothing to report about the whereabouts of guerrilla men who were supposed to take the Americans to the swamps? Is there a reason for a lack of activity here with the exception of a small girl's errand to fetch water to make birthing safe? But to turn in a little girl on his suspicion was ridiculous.

"I don't trust it that your father would let you to do this errand all by yourself." He turned around to look at the sun now sinking below the trees.

"Are you sure you're not carrying anything else?" He spoke looking at her sternly to try and frighten her.

"Why don't you get in here and check for yourself?" She hurled the challenge though she could bite her tongue for saying it. If he climbed in and checked as she suggested he could perhaps see the holes at the bottom of the jars?

"This *banca* is only big enough to hold these jars. What else could I be carrying?"

The girl is too naïve to lie; nothing else has happened here all day. The sun is setting down fast and we're wasting our time." The older man was irritated.

Think fast, do something; make another objection before he really gets in, Delia told herself. She tried a little sarcasm: "I can't believe you would come up here from where you are. You can easily tip my jars. Why don't you pull the *banca* on that sandy bottom there to steady it before you climb in?"

She hoped he would ignore this rather dangerous challenge. Perhaps she had gone too far? Not only was the sun sinking fast, the wind was picking up. Feeling a bit cold, he finally relented,

"What the hell, let's give her a push." A nagging doubt still persisted but he let go his impulse to check the *banca*.

"Next time have a man with you to do a man's job. You never know what can happen if some people decide to help themselves not to your water but to one of these jars. They look unusually big. Where did your father get them?"

"My mother traded two *cavans* of rice and three *gantas* of *guinamos* (shrimp paste) for them; we paid dearly for these jars." She blurted this with a careless haughtiness.

"I bet you did. Yep, I bet you did. They look very expensive. Honestly, I have never seen jars as big as these. I think if your sister's not going to have a baby, we would be tempted to keep one of those."

Though she had drifted far enough for him to do anything now, she answered him with genuine alarm.

"Oh, please, you can't do that. My mother would be very angry with me. I wouldn't be surprised if she'd beat me or let me go without supper. Could I go now, please?" she pleaded with real concern. "It's going to be really dark before I get home."

Disgusted at the waste of time and the useless banter, the older man gave the outriggers a very hard push and waded toward the bank. The younger man ducked under an outrigger; he got into deeper water and slipped. The blue bandana fell and was drifting out of reach. Delia extended the paddle to catch it as it floated by, deftly turned the handle, and flipped the bandana. It landed on his chest.

"Thanks, You certainly would have lost one jar in payment if I lost this." He wrung the water dripping from it, and shouted. "Hope you paddle hard to get home before dark. Tell your sister to hurry up with the baby. It's getting more dangerous these days, even in the swamps."

Without another word, Delia paddled as hard as she could. With shaking hands she tapped the nearest jar rather loudly twice, signaling that the danger was over. She hoped it was really over and that her cargo heard her message. Several minutes later, she heard the same bird's cry and then the answer farther down. She could hardly keep a lid on her fear and she couldn't control her shaking as she paddled hard, once again keeping the *banca* out of reach in the middle of the river. She was in a desperate hurry to get her human cargo to where they could be relieved of the pain of being cramped in the jars beyond belief. She must hurry. She felt their pain in her own body.

Delia looked at this freak who would trade a life for a raggedy blue bandana and a fierce anger stirred inside her. Again, a vision flashed in her mind's eye. She saw the heads drop into holes and heard *Tia* Caring's desperate wail. She was looking at her empty eyes and her bleeding wrists as she broke free of the rope that tied her to the fence and dropped down to hug a wriggling, headless torso. Delia turned her head and closed her eyelids tightly for a minute to shake away the vision. How could she ever understand how human beings could do what they did? The anger inside blazed at this bastard now helping the Japanese catch these nameless Americans and kill them in the same horrible way perhaps. Not if she can help it! Over and over she heard the voices of those who could no longer articulate their pain. She talked to herself.

If *Tia* Caring knows what I'm carrying now, she would paddle with me. And if she saw this idiot, this ignorant Japanese collaborator, she would use the paddle and break his head with it.

The anger gave her the strength to paddle with more energy.

In another half hour, everything got very quiet. The sun sank fast and all around quickly turned dark. Where are *Manong* Almanzur's men, those who were supposed to track her progress? Where are they? She wished they could come out of the darkness to help her get home. Delia had not heard a sound from the jars for a long while. Are the breathing holes big enough? She was not too sure the Americans were still alive. She had been delayed long enough.

She only half realized that her *banca* ride was almost the last leg of the planned escape for her human cargo. The Japanese had been very busy. They scoured the countryside. In the week they kept going this way and that after a false tip from those they caught and tortured, the Japanese were more furious than ever. They killed hundreds from pure frustration. They knew why the Americans could not be found. Among these people, they should be conspicuous enough. People are, of course, helping to hide them. So each time they searched fruitlessly, they killed a dozen or tortured to force them into confession. Some confessed to something they knew nothing about, just to avert the senseless, unbearable torture. But the more the Japanese killed and tortured, the more tight-lipped the people became.

The Japanese had never gone far into the swampy areas where access was difficult and fraught with the danger of inability to get out of the dark, unfamiliar terrain. But they were closing in because the *kempetai*, were desperate to find the Americans or risk their families' lives and their own as well. In the mood they were in, the Japanese had no scruples and *kempetai* who were sent out to track the quarry were often handy scapegoats when they returned without results. In a mean mood, the Japanese didn't care who they inflicted pain on.

Delia couldn't believe the *kempetai* let her go as easily as they did. Her sixth sense told her these men were up to no good, but, unwilling to be stopped again, she paddled with redoubled energy. Now paddling was not for fun anymore but for dear life.

"Dear God, please let me have the strength to get home," she prayed.

She never understood why she was allowed to get home, but she didn't know that guerrilla men had circulated a rumor that the next day, *Kapitan* Almanzur was going to transport the Americans to a coconut grove at the opposite branch of the *Ilog* River by outrigger *bancas*. In fact, two outrigger outfits were seen being filled with *nipa* and coconut leaves for camouflage and were proceeding in that direction.

As for Delia, two taps at the jars and her human cargo could sneeze or clear their throats or make the necessary breathing noises, but three taps anywhere meant trouble. Delia and her cargo had to be instructed into understanding and following the code. As she turned into the narrow opening going into the hidden passageway, it was getting pitch dark. Exhausted, she felt rather than saw the hands that pulled the outrigger as *Manong* Almanzur's men took them off the *banca* and steered it through the narrow waterway. She knew she was now out of real danger herself, but what about her cargo? How have they endured the agony of hours in the jars?

It was difficult for her to realize that *Manong* Almanzur's men were watching her progress, but what would they have done if her real task were discovered. Was she really the only hope they had of transporting the Americans to her home in the swamps? She was totally shaken. Too weak from physical and emotional stress, she allowed herself to be lifted from the *banca* into her mother's arms.

Mama Sid cried from pure relief because Delia was finally home safe and her father gathered all the family for a prayer of thanksgiving. Delia stayed awake long enough to see the Americans removed from the jars.

They were wet and cold from water slowly dripping on them from the top of the jars. Too weak to speak and hurting beyond words, they tried to stretch their cramped legs in the huts prepared for them. Only half conscious from the pain and agony of lying in the same position for hours, their legs had gone numb and were as stiff as wooden boards.

"Quick, Esperanza, you and your cousins take out the cotton blankets dipped in hot water and wring them dry. Wrap their legs with them, but make sure they're not too hot. Take off the blankets every fifteen minutes and massage their legs to restore the normal blood circulation." Mama Sid gave efficient instruction.

Delia's sister and cousins followed this process for hours till they themselves were too exhausted to do anymore. Two of the Americans had high fever and were given medication. The one with deep burns was shaking like someone with malaria seizure. His temperature was very low. Mama Sid asked Delia's cousin, Milka, to lie down beside him and wrap her arms around him to extend sufficient body heat and stop the shaking.

Mama Sid prepared a fragrant mixture of Eucalyptus and *Ilang Ilang* tips and imposed a breathing exercise for all of them. Despite their fatigue, she forced every single one to stay half awake and breathe hard to get the lungs back into normal function. This home remedy was very effective and after long hours of breathing in the cooling mist from the mixture, much like breathing in Vicks vapor rub ointment melted in hot water (a remedy Mama Sid gave her kids for the cough when they were growing up), the Americans finally succumbed to deep, restorative sleep. Somehow, breathing in this mixture alleviated the lung congestion they suffered. The food prepared for them lay untouched. Though starving, they couldn't eat, not even the soft gruel cooked with ginger root and very soothing to the stomach. They wouldn't be able to stand let alone be able to walk till perhaps the next day.

Manong Alvaro had taken the *batel* back to the other branch of the river. He had to convince the *kempetai* watching it that he was waiting for the Americans at that end. Fortunately, the weather had started to change again. Rain was pouring hard and the sea was getting rough. It was difficult to notice that the *batel* had just sailed back to where it was anchored the night before.

Chapter 27—A Day in the Hideout: A Respite from Danger

The six Americans were still exhausted. They didn't know where they were because they were virtually carried in by *Manong* Almanzur's men and deposited in the small hut where Mama Sid ministered to their condition before they collapsed into deep sleep. They weren't aware of the services that restored their capacity to function normally. They didn't know that the women had worked on them for hours and had just recovered from exhaustion, too.

Finally awake, they staggered and looked around. Though dead tired, they focused on the almost storybook look of the compound. The tall mangrove trunks supported vines that laced the branches extending and overlapping, forming a natural roof over the three small huts huddled together at the far end. The trees shadowed the huts so completely for the overhead vines were thickest at that end. So thick was the foliage that smoke from the makeshift stoves clung to the leaves and couldn't give away activity underneath. The narrow waterway flowing from the big river swirled around like a coiled hoop of rope. Eyes unused to the contours defining the spot would fail to distinguish exit from entrance and would exit almost immediately after entering. But those who lived here glided unerringly into a fairyland nook. The landing curved around the mangrove trees in three separate turns, each hiding the cove from view. The small clearing sat on top of mangrove roots filled in with sand tightly packed to keep the surface dry.

One by one the Americans filed outside the hut they slept in and saw a clearing formed like a perfect oval, looking like a natural landscape. Only a much closer observation would reveal a meticulous design. At the edges of the clearing, large vines trailed from tree to tree in a tight braid, but smaller vines had been trained on the larger ones, giving the effect of natural growth. The leafy roof was the handiwork of Victor and Delia. At first, the vines resisted the daily twirling and broke here and there in the heavy monsoon rainfall. But slim and strong *barasbaras* trunks were strung across branches and the vines trained on these grew lush in time and completely hid the trunks from view. Another layer of vines hung studded with small, marble-sized berries swamp birds loved. Delia had to chase these out of the clearing continually.

Initially green, the berries turned yellow and then grew bright red as they ripened. Now the mangrove roof hung studded with green, yellow and red marble sized berries looking like jewels on display, but the smell of swamp mud when the tide was high betrayed the fairy tale paradise. The tide washed the sand into the sides and bottoms of the waterways. *Banca* after *banca* load of sand had to be tediously carted from the beach at low tide and brought into the hidden cove and packed into the crevices for the sun to bake before it once again caved into the waterway with the tide.

Silence stretched like a blanket over the place, beautiful but rather eerie. When some of them ventured farther, they saw what looked like a kitchen busy with food preparation. Then the sharp pangs of hunger hit full force, too difficult to contain.

There wasn't much to offer because no one really knew what the Americans preferred to eat. Everyone agreed surely fried chicken is enjoyed everywhere. Fortunately, Mama Sid had bartered precious rice for chicken weeks before. Fattened and killed only his morning, these were fried in coconut oil. Sweet potatoes were boiled till they were soft. Bananas of different varieties, yellow with ripening, hang at the rafters of the mess hall. Mama Sid with the help of *Kapitan* Almanzur's men fed the Americans. They ate ravenously. The three that had not dined at the Gatuslaos were fed hot food for the first time in about two months. They had eaten canned food, dehydrated eggs and potatoes and other items the quarter master corps tried to pass off as food before they took off on this mission.

After their incredible rescue, they ate on the run. Sometimes, all they had was a handful of peanuts, ripe bananas, mangoes, and coconuts. Once in a while they ate cold rice, and part of a bony fish. They ate the feast they were served here as if they had not eaten a full meal for weeks, which, of course, was the sad fact. The meat of the fried chicken clung to the bones, but even the bones were crisp and the meat was marinated in a delicious sauce. They crunched meat and bones with relish and devoured steamed rice served on woven bamboo plates covered with banana leaves. They noted how tasty bananas were when boiled, and marveled at the variety in size and color of fresh bananas. There were green, yellow, orange and purple bananas, some as small as delicate fingers. The ones that had to be cooked were as big as Delia's arms; these were quartered in sections before being boiled for eating.

Mama Sid shouldn't have worried about what to feed them. They would have eaten dog meat if cooked hot and if they weren't told it was dog meat. *Manong* Alvaro's sons had gathered, washed, and drained the sand out of clams, stuck them on coconut leaf midriff and roasted them on coconut charcoal. Curious as children are, they peeped through windows but weren't allowed underfoot. Their clam kabobs were eaten fast and thoroughly enjoyed.

"This would have gone very well with cold beer," Scott Rankin smacked his lips and belched with relish.

The boys were happy they did something the big Americans enjoyed. Smoke from the kitchen fire gave a feeling of warmth. It broke the fairy tale spell and lent the place the air of home.

By mid afternoon, the Americans were restive. The food had restored their strength but they were unaware of the restorative measures, like the breathing exercises and the massaging administered when all of them were only half-conscious from being crammed in the jars. Now breathing normally, they noticed how badly they all smelled. Their hair had gotten matted and unkempt and a dark growth covered their chins. When they saw women around, they felt embarrassed and scurried back to the hut.

Mama Sid realized their predicament. She produced T-shirts of different sizes and colors as well as pants and underpants. She put them on a pile by the door of the hut.

"These are the biggest of my son's and my nephew's clothes; some belong to my husband. They've been washed and ironed. They're clean. You have to get in these somehow. Perhaps they're too short for your size, but all of you have to undress and put your clothes in a tin can by the waterway used for bathing. We'll wash and iron them quickly. We need to get you ready for traveling as soon as we get word from my son, Alvaro."

She walked over and gave each of them pat on the back.

"There's no need to be embarrassed; we know what you've been through. Our place here is like a guerrilla camp; no one unrelated to guerrilla men can come near here. The sentry at the waterway entrance sees to that. When your legs are steady enough, you can go directly to the bathing fixture a few yards away and take a bath."

She pointed to the facility and urged them to go there. She didn't have to do much urging.

"There's a single bar of soap you have to share because that's all we have. These past three years we've had to go to the seashore, bring enough coconut trunks there to burn into lye to make soap. We simply bleach our clothes by spreading them on bushes and let the sun do the trick. Soap's a rare commodity here. But there's enough river water to wash with; no one stays dirty and the children swim like fish all day long. By the way, we also have makeshift toothbrushes. You can take this to the bathing quarters with you and see how it works. Let me show you how."

She took the green husk of a beetle nut in her hands. The nut was cut in half, quartered, the end beaten to a pulp and cleaned so the rough edges served like a toothbrush. She proceeded to clean her teeth with it.

"This is a war-time alternative. There's nothing like using our native wit to serve our purpose. Another thing, after you've used the soap to wash your hair, my daughter, nieces, my son, and I will give you each a haircut. I think you'll be more comfortable with short hair. You can shave yourself with the sharp knives we have, or if you don't trust yourself with the task, my daughter and her cousins will help you with it."

"Thank you ma'am," BB spoke for the group. "I beg your pardon, but, please, who am I speaking with?"

"People around here call me *Tia Sidra,* short for my name, Isidra. My kin call me Mama Sid. I'm the mother of the guerrilla Colonel and the aunt of the *Kapitan* who managed to have you brought here."

Again, the slender American who obviously outranked everyone spoke.

"Mama Sid, we're very grateful for what you, your son, and nephew have done for us. We know we wouldn't be alive if not for them. Please accept our gratitude. We'll do as you say and get ourselves clean. After, when we smell better, we'll come back here and introduce ourselves formally, if that's okay with you?"

"No. Not here. Go to the mess hall when you're ready." She smacked their bottoms with her hands, as she playfully does with her son, nephew and grandchildren. Then she put her hands on her nose and pretended to be offended by the smell.

"Okay, get going. We'll wash and mend your clothes as fast as we can." She turned and closed the door to the hut before they could say anything more.

The waterway she spoke of was like a giant bathtub. The water ran so clear they could see the bottom inlaid with trunks of slender trees put side by side and tied together like a raft. At one end, water flowed into this tub-like fissure from a large bamboo pipe designed to make washing the hair easy.

"Hey, you all," Scott used his southern drawl, "what a marvel of native ingenuity this is. The water's warm too; it's fabulous."

One by one they used this improvised gadget to get clean. They saw wide strips of cotton cloth to dry with before getting into what Mama Sid gave them. They were embarrassed to have the women wash their clothes now ragged and filthy from having been in it for weeks without being cleaned. What they were given to wear didn't really fit but they did as they were told.

Vines trained on bamboo stakes screened this bathing feature from the rest of the compound and provided a natural privacy. What they saw here astounded them beyond belief. The entire hideout didn't look like part of the swamps. Truly, this seemed like a fairy-tale scene.

"This reminds me of the illustrated *Hansel and Gretel* story book I enjoyed in Kindergarten," BB said.

"No, it's more like a Caribbean resort in the middle of a dark forest," Joe West remarked.

"This is too difficult to believe," Marco quipped. "Besides, everyone in this compound speaks English. Well, perhaps a tad slow and with an accent, but easy to understand. Even that kid, Delia, who paddled us in is easy to talk to. She can't be much more than ten years old."

Where is she now? Marco decided she would be the best to interview.

The tin can with their clothes quickly disappeared. Even their boots were gone and in their place were slipper-like clogs made of wood with strips of thin leather.

"What the heck are these?" Scott Rankin asked. The clogs were varied in size but mostly rather small.

"Those are for us to wear while our boots are cleaned, *stupido*." Romero Valdez teased. They have these also in El-Paso, near the Mexican border."

"They're not big enough for my big toe," Spencer Ridley kidded. "I see the girls have them on, but the men are barefoot. I think I'd rather go barefoot myself."

The leather straps were elastic. The others, not used to being barefoot, stretched more than fit into these. As soon as they were in dry clothes, they gawked at the wonders of the hideout. When Delia came to tell them to go to the mess hall, she couldn't help laughing at the sight. The pants were too short and came just below the knee, exposing hairy shins. The shirts were way above the waistline. She stared at a huge belly button. Joe West, a six foot-four hunk, grabbed her and tossed her eighty-two pound frame in the air as if she were a bag of peanuts. He was laughing with her and as she landed on solid ground, a little embarrassed; she asked if they were comfortable and to please excuse the hurry but they need to get ready.

"To the mess hall for group hair cut," she said laughing.

They all trooped toward the mess hall, a rectangular building with *nipa* roof, triple thatched to keep the rain out, but not the sun. The sides were open. Flaps of *nipa* thatched into bamboo-bordered sections to cover the openings when it rained were raised to open the sides for air. Here it was again, the slender tree trunks, round and about two inches in diameter, stacked tightly on top of each other like cabin logs, rising two feet from the ground. They were doubled up a foot apart and filled with garden dirt, holding the most beautiful, variegated green and white leaves with a shade of gold along the edges. The moisture in the swamps must be good for these because the leaves were long and thick. The longer leaves flowed gracefully over the sides of the supporting wood and the young, yellow tendrils stayed on top like flowers. The color brightened the bare rectangle with sand floors. Bamboo strips held together and tied with rattan vines served as tables. Polished tree stumps, six on each side of two bamboo tables were used as chairs, making a mess hall for twenty-four.

Six tree stumps were moved outside of the building, put on top of bamboo matting and on top of each was a strip of cotton cloth, woven with big, brightly colored stripes, like those they used to dry with.

"These are *patadiongs,*" Delia said. "They are locally woven. My mother sold these before the war. Women use these as wrap around skirts. We saved them and use them for every purpose. Please wrap them around your shoulders to keep your hair from falling on your clothes, making you itchy. Sorry, we don't have towels here; we use *patadiongs.*

From the kitchen adjoining the mess hall, four young girls ages fourteen to twenty-four, wearing the *patadiongs* as wrap-around skirts came out presently. Over the skirts, they had short-sleeved loose blouses, called *kimonas*. Delia introduced them.

"The tallest and oldest is my sister Panching, short for Esperanza, Spanish for *Hope*. She's hoping her betrothed who served in Bata-an would come home after the war. Next, is my cousin, Melcha. It's a Biblical name, but we call her Milka because she has a milky complexion. She's the fastest swimmer for miles around here. She even swims faster than my brother, Victor."

Delia walked over to another girl as fair as Milka.

"This is Socorro, a second cousin; *Socorro* is Spanish for *help*. Don't count on that, though," she teased. "Coring is very standoffish and is very conscious of her good looks." Coring playfully stuck her tongue out at Delia.

Delia moved to a taller teen-ager.

"This is Sondra, Milka's younger sister. She's only fourteen, two and a half years older than I, but she's almost as tall as my *Manang* Panching. Sondring enjoys good humor. She tells good jokes in Filipino, especially to *Manong* Almanzur's men who eat here often."

"My brother, Victor, is over by the table." Delia pointed to him and he waived his hand in greeting. "Mama Sid will be here to cut hair too. I'm clumsy at these things so I'm exempt. Sit down, all of you; they will start as soon as you are ready."

The girls were standing back and giggling at the awkwardly dressed Americans. When Mama Sid and Victor came to join the girls, the Americans stood up to greet them. Once more, the slender, six feet-four Air Force Captain, about twenty-six years old, took command. His blond hair was very fine and badly matted, needing either a comb or a cut. He had blue eyes; he looked rather funny in loose khaki pants that came down inches below the knee. He wore the borrowed red T-shirt much too short for his lanky figure.

"Good afternoon Mama Sid. My name is Bradley Baker. I'm the co-pilot of the plane that crashed. My buddies call me BB for short. I'm from Livonia, Michigan. I went to school at the University of Michigan in Ann Arbor. I played basketball there. I don't know if you've heard of Ann Arbor. It's a pretty little town."

BB was at a loss. What was one supposed to say to these folks? It was very clear to him this was a well-educated lot. Mama Sid who can't be more than sixty and the young girl, Delia, both spoke fluent English.

The girls weren't talking but all eyes were on him, waiting for his introduction.

What am I saying this for, he thought. What do they care where I come from?"

He wanted instead to compliment them for the accommodations and the very considerate efforts they did to take care of them. His eyes moved over the buildings in the compound. How could they be busy making this place look the way it does when there's a war just beyond the waterway to the river bend? He couldn't think of anything else to say so he extended a handshake to Victor and felt how rough his hands were. He towered over the sixteen years old, only five feet, six inches tall.

"Hello there son, I hear you're giving me a hair cut."

"Yes, Sir, I will." Victor managed a shy smile.

"Do you suppose you can cut my hair as short as yours? It would take some time for it to grow out before we get back to duty again, if we ever do. Well, let me introduce the rest of us before we start."

He was glad to shift the attention to his other companions. He went over to Marco, the gunner.

"This is Marco Yablowski, our tail gunner from Chicago. Marco's feet are badly burned. He could hardly fit in that jar, even though I think he was in the biggest one. He might need a cane for walking. His feet have been bleeding from all the walking and running we did. He never complains, but his stomach's grumbling all the time. He dreams of Chicago style pizza and I swear that's all that keeps him going."

All six of them laughed at this, but they could see the joke went overboard; no one laughed with them. Panching looked at Marco's blistered feet. She quickly noted he needed help.

"My sister-in-law is a nurse. She'll know what to do with those blisters on your feet as soon as she's done tending to my older sister who's going to have a baby any time now. But come suppertime, my sister-in-law will join us here. My sister's house is just around the bend behind the thick mangrove brush, and my sister-in law's hut is the one near the kitchen. Smoke is still rising from the fire I'm tending to boil water just to make sure it's purified and safe for the baby."

She moved tentatively toward Marco.

"My sister's not supposed to have this baby, but to lose it will break her heart. It comes thirteen years after her last one, a daughter who died of cerebral malaria fever at the start of this war. They lived on Papa's farm in the foothills of Galicia, some fifty kilometers from here." As

Panching explained, all the while she thought. *Is food all they can think of?*

"We're sorry to hear that," Marco replied. He almost fell from the tree stump he was sitting on as he attempted to stand on his blistered feet.

"I'm glad you all can still laugh after your ordeal." Mama Sid joined in. "I can tell you had a very rough time, even before being confined in the jars."

"Yes, but I think the jars take the cake," said the young stocky gunner, about five feet ten inches tall, the shortest in the bunch. He was darker than the rest and could almost pass for a Filipino.

"I'm sorry if you don't understand the expression," he added quickly. "It means, being in that jar was the worst I have experienced. It wasn't only the pain and discomfort that I didn't like. Fear of the unknown gets me all the time. Mama Sid, my name is Romero Valdez; I'm the front gunner and I come from El Paso, Texas. My parents are Mexican Americans. I went to school at the University of Arizona, in Tucson, Arizona, with our pilot who's still out there, somewhere." He simply followed BB's lead; he didn't know what to say either.

"I know exactly what you mean," Delia interrupted. "I was hoping all the while you could hear the taps I made on the jars, though you couldn't have known what the danger was. I still don't understand why those *kempetai,* let me leave without more investigation. You have no idea how frightened I was and what a relief I felt when they gave the *banca* a push and said I could go."

Marco looked admiringly at this girl, thinking, how self-possessed she was. Back home kids this age don't have half her sense, without doubt because they're spoiled, and over protected and when they're young we treat them as though they have no brains to think with.

"You're very brave and sharp witted," he told her. "I was in the first jar and I knew opening every jar and drinking water from each one convinced those men water was all you carried. I held my breath; inside, I could hardly stay put when you tapped my jar three times, but I knew there was nothing I could do."

Waiting for his turn to be introduced but impatient because of the pain he was suffering, Spencer Ridley spoke. "Mama Sid, I'm still in a daze; I don't think I'm fully recovered from all we went through, but the beauty and calm in this place settles my nerves. I'm truly grateful. I'm a gunner too. I man the gun above the belly of the B-29. When our pilot force landed, my friends, these brave young men, pulled me off the burning plane. I suffered severe burns on my stomach. I couldn't keep up with them when we had to run and go hide and seek from the Japanese patrols."

"Spencer certainly had a rougher time than any of us had," BB said.

Spencer took a deep breath before he continued. "These kind friends had to carry me on their backs many times when I didn't have the energy to run on my own. The skin has all but dried up but the wound is still infected. Maybe your daughter-in-law can look into it tonight? We stopped somewhere where very kind women smeared some herb juice on my burns and helped ease the pain. My name is Spencer Ridley. I'm from Columbus, Ohio." Once more, he tried to follow the trend of the introductions. "I went to Ohio State University and played football there. I was a receiver. I guess the running I did then prepared me for this run-for-your-life experience. If it isn't for the fact that I look forward to being hospitalized so my wound would heal right, I'd like to stay right here and wait for the war to end. If you'll excuse me, I would please like to have the hair cut right now so I can go back to the hut and lie down. I think I don't mind skipping supper if you would send your daughter-in-law to the hut to help me."

Spencer was four inches taller than Valdez, but he was big boned, not lanky looking. He was more muscular but the girls saw he was losing weight from the pain he suffered.

Milka offered to cut his hair immediately. "I'll take you to the hut after the hair cut and make sure to bring you some supper. If you would let me, I'll feed you some hot soup with rice in it; we call this soup, *arroz con caldo.* After, I'll ask *Manang* Aning to come and take care of your wound."

"Excuse me for asking, but what does *Manang* or *Manong* mean? I hear Delia say "*Manong* Almanzur*"* and just now you said "*Manang* Aning.*"* Spencer waited for an answer.

"The literal translation is older sister, for the feminine, and, older brother for the masculine. However, when there's no sibling relationship it's used only as a term of respect. So you could address my cousin as *Manang* Aning. You can call her husband *Manong* Alvaro or my brother *Manong* Almanzur. Respect for our elders is taught and expected in our culture. It's naturally woven into our language," Milka explained.

"Thank you, that's good to know; thanks for offering to bring me supper, but that's really not necessary. Thank you anyway."

"Oh, but I insist. I'll not take no for an answer. Come sit down for a haircut, right now."

This was an urgent command, but there was no sharpness in it; somehow, it felt comforting. Spencer did as she asked. He sat on one of the tree stumps immediately.

I don't have the energy to argue, and, gosh, how very pretty she is.

The sincerity of her offer to take care of him sat on her face visibly. He was fiercely touched. Her fingers rumpled his hair gently. Somehow, he felt he knew her touch. He didn't know that she had lain with her arms around him for hours to give him warmth when his temperature was too low and she had to keep him from shaking. In no time at all most of his hair lay on the bamboo matting. He felt for the mess on the top of his head, but his head was lighter, his hair just an inch long on the side and at the top of his head. Without hesitation and with a smile, she handed him a broken glass for a mirror.

"Be careful with the glass; it could cut you. That's all we've got. You can see how the loss of that matted mess suits you. Already, you look younger and stronger. I wish you well. God be with you for the rest of this war."

Spencer turned his head as he handed her back the glass. He didn't want her to see the emotion on his face. Something about this young girl's genuine compassion burned in his heart. God, he wished he could stay to get to know her better. For sure, they were going again somewhere the next morning. Thank God, they were to be taken by boat again. He would be spared the agony of running. They were assured they'd not be put in jars again either. Before training for the Air Force, he was a student in the art school at the University of Ohio. He noted the high cheekbones and the creamy complexion on her. There must be some kind of mixture here, he speculated. If I had some charcoal and paper, I could sketch her face.

He walked slowly up to the hut while she went to the kitchen to get his supper. Dusk was settling on the trees and the approaching shadows made him lonely. He was glad the girl was coming to keep him company. As he walked, he was taking in the huge mangrove trees and their greenness gave him hope. Trees are always looking up, reaching for the sun, never giving up hope, always reaching out where light is and, where it is blocked, branching in new direction. Some change the color of their leaves as if the last surge of splendor would make it easier to endure losing all a little later.

He was thinking about autumn in Ohio. There the trees are beautiful in autumn They also shed seeds that split in the ground under the warmth of the fallen leaves blanketing the earth. The seeds sleep through rain and sunshine of Indian summers, through cold of dreary winters, till little limbs sprout to reach out again to the eternal sun that tickles the buds to open in glorious blossom, wrapping the earth in beauty in the springtime. It must be spring here, for he noticed at the outskirts of the compound, just beyond the huts, red and yellow berries dotted the vines hanging on the shorter trees bordering the waterways.

I must sketch this place, he mused. I need charcoal and paper; maybe a pencil will do. I wonder if they have crayons?

Later, Spencer learned there are only two seasons here, wet and dry: six months with extreme humidity and heat, and six months with heavy rainfall. This is almost the end of the dry season. The westerly winds already brought heavy rains that drenched them and slowed them down several days ago. With faltering energy, he walked to the hut. Later, quiet as a whisper, she came in with a wooden tray on which sat two wooden bowls and a coconut spoon. She found him sitting up on a reed mat with a blanket and a pillow.

"Shouldn't you be lying down and resting?" she asked solicitously.

"I'm fine, really," he protested.

"Okay, but I'll feed you myself. Tell me if the soup is still too hot and we'll let it cool down."

She stirred the soup and put more rice in. Then she slowly lifted the spoon to feed him.

"Be sure to take the soup in slowly and chew the rice. Don't just swallow it; savor it. The hotter the soup is, the better for you. It'll nourish more. Mama Sid got the rice from the mountains. Especially soft and fragrant, this variety makes a meal by itself."

He was slow to respond to her spoonfeeding.

"Open up. You can do better than that. Wider."

He felt like laughing. Why does she have to baby me?

Aware of his embarrassment and hesitation, she urged him to comply. "It'll do you no good to resist. Settle down like a good patient. You're getting good hospital care here in the swamps. Pretty soon *Manang* Aning will be here and she'll not be as gentle. So enjoy the pampering while you can."

She laughed, a bit too loud he thought, but there was no derision in it, just plain, heartfelt enjoyment. He started to laugh with her. He let her feed him and the warmth of her kindness was a balm on his wound and a fire in his heart. "Oh, Milka, with the milky complexion," his heart sang. "Your beauty is not skin deep. It's soul reaching."

Hastily, before he lost his courage, he spoke. "Can you please do me one more favor?"

"What is it?" She replied with some concern.

"I know you've lost a good deal in this war, but surely you have kept some pictures of yourself. I'll remember your kindness always and your image will be in my mind always. But I would like to have a picture of you to treasure always."

He repeated himself to assure her he was serious. "I feel as though I've known you before, but I'd like to know you better. Would you let me write to you wherever I'm sent after we leave here tomorrow?"

"Mr. Ridley, you are being facetious," she said. Now it was her turn to be deeply embarrassed.

"No, I'm not. I'm deadly serious. You know as well as I do this war makes things happen without rhyme or reason. Yesterday, I felt only pain; now just joy and elation and some sadness that I must leave here before I can do anything about my feelings for you. When we were running without really knowing where we were, I almost lost interest in life. Now, I'm very much alive again. There's a war going on, Milka, but I'm not going to lose the gift of knowing you because of it. Can you, please, do me the favor I ask?"

Softly, the tears came. She put the bowl down by him and left as quietly as she came in, but not without feeling his fervor.

Now I have lost her, he thought. But he did not regret what he said. Though she had gone, he still felt her presence. Her tenderness lingered in the room she left. Much like a spray of perfume, the scent pervaded though the spray had dried.

When she got back to the mess hall, everyone had had his haircut and a shave. The other Americans were introduced to her. Joe West said he was part Swede, part Norwegian. His grandmother was Swedish; she came to America in 1923. He, too, was tall, not gangly, but well stocked. Light red hair also cut to a mere inch, hugged his head. Joe was a top gunner. He handled the machine gun at the turret. Deep scratches criss-crossed on his arms and around his neck, marks left by barbed wire fences and the sharp *kogon* grass they crept through in the dark as they run from Japanese soldiers only several hundred meters behind them. He, like Marco, displayed a lot of humor and congeniality, a guy not too hard to know still rather private. His voice was strong and hearty. As his friends say, he's a typical Swede from Wisconsin, a straight shooter, very positive. Sure of himself but not self-conscious, he grinned when he introduced himself.

"With this name, how American could I be? How is Spence getting along," he asked Milka lightly. He meant this only as banter, but she took it hard. She flushed with embarrassment, feeling once more the weight of Spencer's passionate outburst. She turned and didn't answer, but when *Manang* Aning asked her to come and see how Spencer was, she was ready to go.

"Excuse me, this is Scott Rankin," Joe said. Scott rose to shake hands with her

"Somehow, when it's a good thing, I always seem to come in last, but not the least, I hope. I'm from Raleigh, North Carolina. I wish I were back there right now. My sister's about to be married, and in North Carolina weddings are very special, very lavish affairs. I could use some of that champagne to forget whatever it was we ate just before we got here; something boiled with bamboo shoots and covered with green slimy stuff. Only the smell of coconut milk on it made it easier to swallow."

Manang Aning snickered. "I guess they fed them with some *bagongon* shells with *saloyot* which is a lot like okra. Okra is slimy if it's boiled and not fried.

"Maybe that was all they had to eat," Milka said, slightly annoyed.

"Oh, I'm not complaining," Scott said quickly. "Gosh, we're lucky to be fed so generously. I know we had a lot to eat today and I smell fried chicken again. This is wonderful, but wine and champagne would be heavenly. Maybe we could have more of the clam kabob?"

"Oh, sure," *Manang* Aning said. "We have more clams in our hut. The boys would love to roast them for you."

"And why is it that we have not met your boys?" Scott asked.

"We don't want them to bother you. They're very curious and have incredible energy. They can be more of a nuisance than help. But you can meet them tomorrow," she promised.

"Scott, we have wine from *bugnay* trees, or, even stronger, some *tuba*," Victor offered.

"Well, let's get to it," Scott exclaimed jovially. "That would top this off. By the way, what's tuba?"

"Would you like to try some before supper?"

"Don't get them tipsy before supper. Maybe some sweet *tuba,* but it's too late in the day for that. *Tuba* is a fermented drink from the coconut tree. It seems harmless, but it has a strong kick." Mama Sid warned. "The more it has fermented, the stronger the kick."

Manong Almanzur's men bustled about at the mention of *tuba.* One of them brought in from the kitchen a long bamboo tube containing the coconut drink. He hummed as he passed bamboo glasses around and a very festive air fell on the place. Someone brought out a guitar and softly strummed a *kundiman,* a lovesong. The girls started humming and urged Coring to sing. Her lovely voice floated at dusk and Delia, joined in with a soft second voice.

Scott was overwhelmed with emotion. He turned to his friends. "If someone were to tell me this would happen after all we have gone through, I would call him a liar. I swear, after the war, if I survive that long, I'll come back to hunt for this place."

"Amen," said Joe West. Despite of, or because of the *tuba,* he, too, was hoarse with emotion.

"May I please borrow the guitar?" Valdez asked. "I can sing an equally plaintive song from Texas."

Someone passed the guitar to him and he started a Mexican melody obviously sang with nostalgia. It was beginning to get dark. The oil lamps were lit and hung at the rafters of the mess hall. The seats were put back and the bamboo matting with all the hair was disposed of, for in the improbable event of a raid, these would be tell tale evidence that the Americans were hosted here.

Manang Aning and Milka returned from dressing Spencer's wounds. She washed it thoroughly with hot, boiled water turned lukewarm. Using cotton-like material from *kapok* seeds, she rubbed coconut oil mixed with healing herbs gently on the wound. After placing cool, young fronds, the heart of the banana trunk, on top of the healing mixture, *Manang* Aning cut strips from a bed sheet to wrap around his body.

"Now you'll be ready to travel with less pain," she told him.

Again, Spencer was overwhelmed with gratitude. He couldn't thank them enough. He closed his eyes and relief rolled in. "God bless you both," he managed to say before the weight of sleep overcame him. He was dead tired.

Milka was silent but very much moved by the inert figure lying helplessly on the floor. When she was finally alone that night she wept that he should care how she fared. "God bless you," he said, but she heard not just the words. In a blinding moment of understanding, she felt the warmth of his passion, and she found herself suddenly more alive than she had ever been, breathing slowly and heavily as if she was swept like a swimmer by the undertow of the tide of her dreams.

She walked into the mess hall misty eyed. She didn't know that everyone there felt the pressure of the unknown though they tried to comfort each other with surface assurances of their safety.

Mama Sid put a stop to the drinking and singing. Not wanting to spoil fun, she nevertheless knew they had to be overly careful. The Americans must be alert the next day, maybe their last day here. She had to discipline Almanzur's men. When allowed, these men were marathon drinkers. They had to keep watch this night as they waited for three other Americans, the pilot, the navigator and another gunner expected to join the resting crew. All would be taken to a guerrilla camp at the southern tip of Negros.

When the dishes were taken away and the tables were cleaned, the girls bid the men goodnight. Mama Sid stayed to make sure the men would go to their hut and rest, but BB and Marco wanted to know how long the hideout had been in operation and who engineered and landscaped the place. Mama Sid called Delia and Victor back to the table and asked them to tell their story.

Victor started with this explanation: "Before we moved here, we lived close to *Mang* Kari's well, but the Japanese, and the *kempetai,* always managed to get close. We moved farther to get away. I figure on an average, we moved every three weeks. They were always at our heels."

"Sometimes," Delia interrupted, "we got away by sheer luck. Once, the Japanese went on a rampage, furious because *Manong* Almanzor ambushed a patrol and killed a few soldiers. That time, we almost got trapped."

"You can't imagine how tiring it is to move so often," Victor said with a sigh. "When we moved farther into the swamps life became difficult. Water and food were hard to get. If we stayed close to the well, the Japanese tried to get us. That was our problem for almost a year."

"What made you decide to move this far then?" Marco was all sympathy.

"*Manong* Alvaro finally told us to get as far away as we could and cut the constant moving."

"So how did you find this place?" Marco asked again.

"It wasn't easy. Months ago, Delia and I decided to follow this twisting, narrow waterway. It stretched and coiled into a swampy darkness. Most of the other waterways, like this one, dead-ended into thick, impassable, mangrove brush. We decided to cut the brush on this one. We needed firewood anyway. As we cut through, we passed into what seemed like a corridor connecting with another wider passage into yet another coil of waterway. We moved on and then we paddled around and around as if in a maze. We had to cut bark to mark our trail. We were getting confused and somewhat lost."

"I got out of the *banca* and waded across the next waterway," Delia interrupted again. "I fought my way through the brush with a *bolo* and came to the bend of the coiling corridor of the same passageway. I moved farther on. The same corridor coiled one more time. I thought I had gone much farther from the spot where I left *Nong* Victor, but I could still hear him paddling. Then I realized I had been running into the same waterway; it just coiled four times around the same spot."

"Delia has a keen instinct for hiding places, I think because she often plays hide-and-seek with our small nephews and some neighbors. She convinced me that if we widen the waterway by clearing the brush from the banks, it would be passable," Victor continued.

"That must have taken hours and hours of clearing," Marco exclaimed. "When one sees this place now, it's hard to imagine what you must have done."

"*Manong* Almanzur's men helped us. All we had to do was bribe them with fried chicken, clam kabobs, and *tuba*. Look at them now. They'll get stone drunk if Mama Sid doesn't take away the bamboo flask of *tuba* right now." Delia grumbled.

"We had one major problem. The rise and fall of the tide coated the ground with muck; it smelled so bad, it drove Delia crazy. We either had to move again or do something about the mud." Victor revisited the problem.

"You notice the tree trunks we've piled around the edge of the compound?" Delia went over to the nearest edge and pointed them out to Marco.

"It keeps the white sand we've piled and pounded inside it to raise the ground level. Over some time, a considerably long time the sun baked the combination of mud and sand dry. We've put more sand on top of that since." Delia, too, was remembering the hard, hard work.

"All because Delia is tireless and very restless," Victor ribbed his sister.

"Yes, but very intelligent and resourceful, right?" Marco chipped in.

"Stubborn and pig headed, is more like it," Delia joined in self-deprecation.

"Delia took all the small boys, nephews and cousins to the seashore to help her cart the sand. Somehow, she tricked them into doing much of the work."

"I didn't stop with the sand either." Delia was proud of what she had done. "Do you see the work we've done with the vines and the leaves? Look well, Marco. I trained the vines to wind around the *barasbaras* saplings and bamboo lattices. When Mama Sid went to the foothills to trade shrimp for rice, I tagged along and traded my portion of shrimp paste for young bamboo and rattan vines."

She pulled Marco aside and prodded him to look at the vines she trained on both bamboo and *barasbaras* stakes looking as if it were a wall of thick brush, as though the waterway ended there.

"Look," she pushed the wall of vines and brush. "We can push the *bancas* without outriggers through. If you don't know this magic getaway, you can go round and round, till you seem to get lost. That's just an illusion. This waterway simply skirts the place. It's like a narrow corridor leading from room to room, but circles back to the living room of the house. This hideout is like the ancestral home my grandfather built in town before the Japanese burned it. It had a network of decks that encircled the structure, but led into separate rooms with private entrances. This is our permanent home now. We hope the Japanese will never find it." Delia released Marco's hand and tried to walk away.

"Hey, wait a minute," Marco called her back. "Show me. What's this *barasbaras* you are talking about?"

Victor pulled a slender sapling more than three meters long, lying on a pile by the kitchen wall.

"This," he said, "grows straight and tall and has no branches. When full grown, some are three meters long. You can't find them anywhere except in the heart of the swamps. There, they grow under the shelter of huge mangrove giants so old their trunks are hollow. See how long and slender they are. No more than two inches in diameter, they're good for building walls and floors of these huts, including the one you slept in."

"But, if I'm not mistaken, we slept on wooden floors?" Marco raised a question that was more a statement.

"Oh, no; those are wooden doors we took out of our house and the Baptist Church in town before the Japanese burned the buildings. We always carry those with us when we move from one hiding place to another. *Barasbaras* floors are good floors but are impossible to sleep on. We put the doors over them to use as beds. Every hut has at least one. We put four in yours to make you comfortable."

"You don't know how lucky you are. We've slept on the ground, on cement stalls, on *kogo*n grass, on coconut husks and *nipa* trunks; everything but wooden doors." Marco laughed at the irony.

"We've been lucky so far. The Japanese have not ventured anywhere near. Delia says she'd rather die than leave this place, but I know better. When it's time to go, she'll help me find another place again."

"Knock on wood, Victor. That's what we say when we wish to hold on to good luck." Marco said with a broad smile.

"In these three years that we had to make the swamps our home, I can see character shape in my sister. She little knows the depth of her own vitality. She's driven by a fierce hunger to see, to know in her heart the entire sweep of the swampland from river to seashore. She has lived with the smell and texture of mud, the sting of mangrove roots on bare feet, the lash of twigs in narrow inlets, the protection of giant mangrove during a senseless air raid, the sound of the wind in the tall, thin, straight *barasbaras* saplings, and the slap of water on the paddles as an outrigger *banca* moves quietly out on the river to its mouth in the sea. Without her, this dream place wouldn't be as you see it now. It's her way of surviving the war. Though she often thinks like an adult, she's still a child at heart. I think making this place as beautiful as she could was like playing doll's house for her. I know even when the war ends this place will ring a vibrant tone in her consciousness.

Aware that talk about her was going on, Delia moved close.

"Why do you talk about me as though I were not here," she said, very much annoyed. "All I did was to follow you around." She addressed her brother. "I got bored when you went off somewhere without me so I paddled everywhere, careful not to wander too far away. I made sure I wasn't followed and I kept close to the banks, ready to hide the *banca* and scramble up to get inside a mangrove tree trunk when I heard the sound of an airplane."

Delia started to leave, but Marco stopped her once more.

"Don't go yet. I want to tell you about where I come from." He was so homesick for Chicago that he wanted to talk about it.

"I was born in Chicago but my grandparents immigrated from Poland. Chicago has a lot of immigrant Polish residents. I worked as a security guard for one of the banks downtown. On weekends, I took my younger brothers and sister to the museums in downtown Chicago and when I got paid, I took my older sister to the opera. I wish I could take you to see Chicago, Delia. It's funny how this war we all hate for the violence and the havoc it has done to our lives, has brought us together like this."

As he spoke he looked up at the sky and noticed the moon that threw a deep color on the trees and lighted the entire compound. "This same moon that shines on us here, Delia, shines on Chicago too. I know my family is looking at the same moon right now wondering where I am and wishing I would still be alive. One day, after the war, I wish you could come to Chicago. I'd love to take you around to see the parks, visit the museums, or listen to an opera."

Delia brightened when she heard this; she could not wait to interrupt Marco.

"I know all about the museums and the Lake Shore Drive. I saw pictures of those museums and the lake in a book Victor took from the high school library before the Japanese burned the school. Mama Sid gets angry when we use the oil lamps late in the night to read those books. She says we waste too much coconut oil and the flickering light is bad for our eyes. But even Mama Sid enjoys looking at the pictures of the museums and what's in them."

Marco brimmed with excitement and asked her to show him the book that has the pictures. Delia promised to show it to him in the morning. "I know a little about your government and your justice system, "she said tentatively

"Our what?" Marco exclaimed. "Did I hear you right?"

"You heard me. I said your justice system. She got out of breath with their connection and talked with renewed vigor.

"There's a book that contains the court decisions of a Justice Brandeis. I don't know anything about him except what I read in this book. He must be very important because he writes about constitutional rights and civil liberties. Papa had to fully explain what these meant. We've decided that since you have judges like Justice Brandeis who passionately serves to protect the peoples' rights, your country must be a most ideal place to live in. Here, no one really cares about people's rights. Judges are bribed all the time and the poor go to prison not because they're criminals. They're punished because they're poor. The rich take advantage of them and rob them of their rights."

Marco could hardly believe his ears. How could someone as young as this little girl be aware of things way beyond kids her age in the U.S.?

Delia continued the discussion with great enthusiasm and energy. "You know what makes Papa so sad is that in our country all the politicians care about is taking advantage of the poor. The rich get richer because they steal land from the poor people, and steal money from the government."

She tried to shift the talk afraid Marco would get bored. "It gets dark very early here in the swamps. Have you noticed? When it gets dark and we're not sleepy and have nothing better to do, we talk about everything, especially about what we read. It's the only way to pass the time.

"Do you understand everything you read?" Marco was incredulous.

"No. But Papa very patiently explains things we don't understand. He's delighted we happened to save Justice Brandeis's book. He says we need to study the ideas of intelligent writers so that even though our schooling had been interrupted by the war, we would still keep our minds sharp enough to be well informed and to distinguish fact from superstition and falsehood from truth."

"So what does your Papa think about the East Asia Co-prosperity Sphere the Japanese say this war is about?" Marco asked.

"Oh, yes, we've heard about that so we asked Papa to explain what it means. He says it's Japan's excuse for conquering other countries in East Asia so they can take away their natural resources by force. For instance, the Japanese are excellent farmers, but they don't have enough land to raise rice. In Asia, Papa says, rice is not just a crop; it's an industry. Rice is staple food for millions of Asians and is the base of the economy of Asian countries. All Asia could learn about farming from the Japanese but the equality that Japan promises is nothing but hot air."

"Yes, just look at what they have done to us." Victor could not help interrupting. "They don't even permit us to till the land. That's why we have no food to eat. People all over the Philippines are starving. Is that what they mean by equality? They don't treat us as equals. They torture and kill all over the place. They treat us like dirt. That's why Papa won't let us come out of hiding."

"I heard Captain Villava say the Japanese are after your Papa. They want him to come out of hiding and be Mayor of *Ilog.*" Marco repeated what he had heard from guerrilla soldiers.

"Papa will never do that. If he does accept that position, people will go back to town and *Ilog* will be occupied territory, just like *Kabankalan* is. But Papa says there's no dignity in that position. He believes people in occupied territory have surrendered their God-given right to be themselves and are nothing more than slaves. We feel very strongly about that so we live in the swamps rather than suffer Japanese torture and indignity. Don't you think Papa is right?"

Marco agreed and marveled at the intelligence of this young girl. He felt keenly the pain she held inside.

"I think a great deal about studying law. I could be a lawyer for the poor. Maybe after the war——." Her voice trailed off

Silent for a while, she slowly turned around and sadly heaved a sigh.

"I'm just what *Manong* Alvaro calls *wishful thinking*. I want to be as smart as Papa, you know. No one I know is as smart as he is; perhaps the former Justice of the Peace, the honorable Vicente Riego. Before the war, he would come and visit us every night almost, just so he could talk to Papa and exchange ideas with him. I loved to listen to them but the Judge was not as fluent in English as Papa, so they spoke in Spanish. I know a little Spanish, conversational Spanish, that is, but the Spanish those two spoke was too deep for me to follow."

"Where's the judge now?" Marco asked.

"The Japanese caught the Judge's family and forced them to live in town, but the Judge refused to act as mayor so they tortured and killed him. *Manong* Almanzur and his guerrilla band helped the rest of the Judge's family escape. People refused to come out of the swamps and live in town. The Japanese abandoned it, but they burned down the entire town to punish the people for staying away."

"They're after Papa too, I know. Victor intruded again. *Manong* Almanzur and *Manong,* Alvaro, watch over us attentively. If the Japanese catch us, I'm sure they'll kill our Papa too, and all of us, no doubt."

There was a moment of silence again, and Delia added with great emotion welling in her voice. "That would be a shame because people like Judge Riego and my Papa are like Justice Brandeis. They serve the people, both rich and poor alike."

Filled with filial pride, she continued. "Before the war, my Papa was superintendent of public schools in Negros Occidental. He served in that capacity for thirty years before he retired. He has trained hundreds of teachers and the United States government pensioned him for life-long service and my mother will receive his pension when he dies. That's a great honor, yet if we speak with pride of him to others, Papa gets angry with us. He says people shouldn't be proud of what they have accomplished. They haven't accomplished it by themselves alone. It is a gift from God, so there's nothing to be personally proud of, grateful, yes, but not proud. I don't entirely agree with this. Do you?"

"I think he's just very humble, Delia. I had no idea how great a reader you are. Why did you choose to read the books you read," Marko asked, very much impressed with her intelligence and her sensitivity.

"I didn't choose them. They just happened to be the ones Victor salvaged. I read simply for entertainment, to pass the time away, you know. I've already told you that oftentimes we have too much time on our hands with nothing to do, especially in the evening. The sun goes down early in the swamps. Darkness, when it does not threaten is like a blanket that comforts. With little light, we lie in the dark and begin our discussions about this and that. In daylight, I wonder around in a *banca*, but at dusk, when it turns dark rather quickly, we light the lamps and read to pass the time," she repeated herself. "When I don't understand the words I read, I look them up in a small dictionary Victor also happened to save. Or, I ask my Papa who can explain quicker than a dictionary. Papa is not only smart, he's a very deep thinker and he's very well read."

"He must have had a good education," Marco interjected.

"In Spanish, yes, but in English he's self-taught. I think his wisdom comes mostly from reading. Papa's curiosity is inexhaustible. Before the war, books lined the walls of one room in our big house. The books were arranged under categories so it would be easy for Papa and his guests to find the books they needed. There were books on religion, theology, history, geography and philosophy, though almost nothing on literature. Papa says he doesn't find value in make believe," Victor once more tried to help Delia explain.

"But *Manong* Alvaro, disagrees with Papa about that," Delia corrected. "He says stories and novels are not merely make believe. If they are well-conceived, they're based on the author's understanding of life, though the language is often lyrical and poetic and the characters are *larger than life*. I didn't understand how that could be, so I asked *Manong* Alvaro what that meant. He said sometimes writers exaggerate the qualities of the characters they imagine. They often glorify them."

"Does your *Manong* Alvaro come home very often?" Marco wanted to know.

"Not too often because he spends his time with the army. When he's home he spends the day with his sons and his wife, but we have the same discussions with him as we do with Papa from dusk to almost early morning. I enjoy these sessions the most. It takes me away from my anxieties and from boredom."

"Boredom? Aren't you always up and about, enjoying paddling around?"

"That only goes so far. It's awfully boring here. Without the books we read and the discussions we have from time to time, it's hard to endure the war. I wish you could speak with Papa or *Manong* Alvaro. He's fascinating. He can quote lines of poetry from the best English and American poets. Whatever he quotes to us, I try to put to memory, too. Oh, but I'm boring you with this endless prattle."

Marco was overwhelmed. He couldn't believe what his ears heard. Who can expect such a depth of maturity in one so young? Evidently, this family pampers this youngest child, but the way they do it is by pumping her with adult ideas. What a rare experience it is to hear about these discussions in the swamp! That they've read the writings of Justice Brandeis he wasn't even aware of was very humbling. The subjects they mentioned weren't usual topics for discussion among the middle class, and, clearly, not for the poor. Yet this family endures more poverty in this war than the poorest of the poor at home. Half the time, they must be starving. No, not really. There's always fish, seashells and all sorts of seafood. Hardly any meat or starches, he noticed. No fat in their bodies at all. Above all, they carry themselves with an air of grace and dignity, and even with compassion that's very uncommon. Whew! What a humbling discovery; learn something everyday!

Already, he was ready to forget the very harrowing experience of being chased by a ruthless enemy. He had been fed generously, not just physically, but much, much more. He had just shared their innermost intimacies. What a family! Yes, after the war, they must find this place again.

"I'm not wasting your time, I hope. I apologize for talking too much, but I have never had as good a listener as you," Delia said with mischief in her eyes. "Mama Sid says you have to rest now," she reminded him. They had been talking for a while before they noticed that BB, Valdez,

Joe and Scott were also attentively listening to Victor who was still talking about the compound and explaining how it operated.

"There's a place even Delia does not know about" Victor was telling them. "We store our supply of food there."

"Don't you keep everything here?" Joe was surprised.

"No, we keep the rice elsewhere. Food is difficult to get here and in every place that the Japanese control. At least here one can fish, or dig for shells at the riverbanks and make kabobs and never be hungry; but rice, which is our staple food, is at a premium here. Other people in the swamps eat the starch from a root they dig, dry in the sun, and pound into flour. Some of the roots are poisonous. Sadly, it is difficult to tell roots apart. Some die from eating root flour.

"So where do you get the rice you eat and feed us with?" Scott got concerned.

"We don't get any rice unless we walk to the farmlands at the foothills beyond the Japanese occupied places."

"How do you get there?" Joe asked.

"We walk for almost a day and a half. My mother has the same vitality Delia has. At her age, she can walk as far as any person my age can."

"That's incredible. Do you do this often?" Joe asked again.

"As often as we can make shrimp paste and salt. My mother is a good trader. Before the war, she had a flourishing business that sent us all to school. When war broke out, two of my older brothers were in Manila studying at the University of the Philippines. One was in Law School; the other was an intern at the U.P. College of Medicine. We have no idea where they are now; we pray they are still alive somewhere."

"What was Mama Sid's business? Was it a family business? I mean, wasn't your Dad involved in it too?

"Papa was too busy with the farm to help, except he kept Mama Sid's accounting books. She hired about thirty *bordaderas*, women who embroidered *kimonas* for her. They matched the designs on the skirts on the *kimonas*. Her products were often exported overseas, to Japan mostly. Ironic, isn't it? The embroidery in the Philippines is among the finest in the world, comparable to fine lace made in Belgium. Later, she made ready-to-wear clothes for men, women, and children. She made money so my brothers went to the best school in the country, the University of the Philippines."

"Interesting, but we're getting side-tracked here. What I want to know is how do you transport the rice from the foothills to the swamps," Scott asked.

"Simple," Victor answered. Mama Sid exchanges a portion of the rice she gets from trading for a carabao ride to the mouth of the river. We meet her there with a *banca* and bring the rice here."

"So do you have enough rice to last for a while?" Scott persisted in asking.

"Papa says it's impossible not to share food with hungry neighbors, but we manage to hide some of it somewhere in the heart of the swamps. Only my cousin Rodney and I know where. Not even Delia has been there. When I'm home Rodney is over there to guard the rice and I go there when Rodney comes home. I built a small hut there, big enough to store the rice and for one person to sleep in. I did what Delia has done here. I trained the vines on *barasbaras* to hide the hut and make it look like there's nothing there but a clump of trees. Around it, I built dikes that look like natural canal walls. In case someone learns about the place and tries to steal the rice, I have a sawed-off shotgun and I store long, sturdy *barasbaras* saplings sharpened at one end to use like a lance, particularly on wild hogs that are drawn to the hut by the smell of the rice. Would anyone like to take a look before *Manong* Alvaro takes you somewhere else?"

All four accepted Victor's invitation eagerly. BB, Joe, Valdez, and Scott were raring to go, but Marco and Spencer had to stay. Mama Sid was angry and forbade them to go in the dark so Victor agreed to take them before the sun rose the next day.

This was a hot summer day, the last hours of one. The day was beautiful but it was humid and damp. Mama Sid was in no particular hurry to let the day go. The sight of the American boys reminded her that her son was coming to pick them up. He had entrusted them to her care, making sure they were well fed. She was counting the days he had been absent. He was away so much; he was home very briefly the night before, but had to leave immediately. They didn't have much time to visit or talk about his plans. Suddenly, she was anxious for him to come back again and in the pit of her stomach crept a queasy feeling for his safety. With the absent-minded look of someone not quite sure of what he was saying, he promised to be back.

"If Delia delivers her load, I'd be here as soon as I can." There was no mistaking the anxiety on his face when he said that. Mama Sid was certain he would come the same day, or the next, if he could. She was sure he was on his way.

This was the next day, what could be keeping him? Some impossible obstacle perhaps? Maybe the weather, for she had heard some rumbling and the clouds darkened fast, but please not another encounter with a Japanese patrol. She hurried to the kitchen to make sure the girls were making breakfast for the boys. These are very likable boys, respectful, polite, attentive, but weary and always watchful, especially Marco.

At the mess hall last night, Marco saw the girls feed them the best food, always passing them chicken, roasted shells they liked, choice parts of the fish, fresh and ripe fruits. But he noted the girls, the small boys, and men who hovered around with their firearms slung on their shoulders had only rice and fish. Marco would pass back the dish of meat.

"How about some of this delicious chicken? What do you call this dish?"

"*Chicken adobo*. It's chicken marinated in vinegar and boiled in garlic till the marinade simmers into a thick, savory sauce." One of the men volunteered the information.

Marco noted the girls would smile back at him, take the dish from his hands without taking anything from it, and manage to pass it to Scott, BB, Valdez, or Joe. Not to make anything look obvious, Mama Sid would take a small piece, but she would reach out to place what she had taken on Victor's or her husband's plate. Marco stepped out of the girls' way politely, sat down on the tree stump, and finished what he had on his plate. He must tell the others about his observations. They have to learn how to be as inconspicuously considerate, as these people. Somehow, the girls always put his comfort or the rest of the crew's over theirs. Though their stay is most assuredly an invasion of these people's privacy, they're treated as though they're a very privileged group. What gives them the right to be an imposition? They were always served with uncommon generosity, though they have been nothing more than a threat to these peoples' safety. He felt the need to discuss his observations with the rest of his crew.

He saw Mama Sid hovering about in the kitchen this morning. He was about to let the boys hear what he had to say, but Spencer met him and said the boys had left with Victor who wanted to show them a special place.

Mama Sid was worried about the breakfast. "It's not real coffee," she apologized. "It's a drink made from corn kernels shelled out of the cob and stirred in a clay pot till it's roasted black. Then it's pounded into fine powder and boiled in well water. Doesn't smell like coffee but has its own aroma, and with a bit of sugar saved from Delia's unfortunate trip to Central Palma, it's not a bad breakfast drink at all."

She moved some dishes closer to Marco. "This is *suman* (rice cakes wrapped in banana leaf and served hot), fried *camote* (sweet yam), fried chicken, boiled eggs and rice."

She was worried this was not exactly the kind of menu these boys were used to, but that was all they had. Delia was already in the kitchen feeding *Manang* Aning's boys. The men with the firearms were fed separately in the kitchen. The girls excused themselves; they said they would join him and Spencer with a drink and some rice cakes, but they had already finished part of their meal. Mama Sid was perturbed. She apologized for serving practically the same menu they had the day before, except for the eggs and rice cakes. If they were tired of the same menu, at least they must have some eggs and rice cakes, and, of course, the native corn drink, a substitute for coffee. Marco was protesting and apologizing strongly as Spencer sauntered in. He declared he had a good night's sleep and now he was hungry enough to eat a horse. Once more, they were served what Marco was certain the rest of them didn't have for breakfast. He would be glad to get out of here and move on to that guerrilla camp they said they would be taken to. He evidently enjoyed their company, but he was getting guilty and embarrassed over the preferential treatment.

The girls started to clear the dishes. Delia brought out the book that had pictures of the museums and the lake Shore Drive in Chicago and was going to show Marco the extent of her reading. One of the men with the firearms offered Spencer a cigarette rolled in paper, but Spencer declined. Instead, he asked the man to show him his firearm.

All at once, hell broke loose.

Chapter 28—The Hut in the Heart of the Swamps

At the first cockcrow, Victor got the gang ready to go. He fixed breakfast early and fed them in a hurry. Mama Sid had their uniforms cleaned, mended and ironed and their boots were brushed and dried. Victor said they had to wear these just in case the *Batel* arrived to pick them up. He had a small *banca* without outriggers on hand to take them in the narrow waterway. Quietly, they pushed it out of the compound before Mama Sid and the rest knew they had gone.

Joe West helped with the paddling. This is like paddling a canoe in the lakes in Wisconsin, he thought. They had to duck the twigs when the waterway got too narrow. The sun was already out. They smelled sea air but didn't see any water except that in the very shallow waterway soon covered with mangrove brush making it impossible to go any farther. They got out of the *banca* and left it wedged between two large mangrove trees. Their boots sank in mud that smelled probably the same smell that drove Delia crazy. They must have walked an hour before they saw the vines that trailed on the *barasbaras* wall hiding the small hut. Rodney jumped out and was crouching below the dikes Victor built behind the hut.

"Get out of there," Victor called "I just brought you some company."

Fear visible on his face, Rodney came out of hiding.

"Come, meet the guys."

Victor introduced him to the Americans. Younger than Victor, Rodney was six feet tall, unusual for a Filipino.

They sat for a while looking at the sacks of rice Victor had stashed away and they examined the *barasbaras* saplings neatly piled behind the hut.

"Want to try one of these? I hope a wild pig comes along so you can target practice and we can make *lechon* out of it." Rodney said.

"What is l*echon?*" Joe asked.

"Pig roasted on a spit," Rodney answered.

"Hey that would be a feast!" Scott pumped him on the shoulders.

Rodney cautioned them to keep quiet and wait in the hut because he did hear a noise the pigs made last night. He figured they would still be around. Several minutes later, they saw a small one rubbing its behind on a small tree about twelve feet away. Joe and BB sneaked out, grabbed *barasbaras* lances, and got ready to hit the target when it moved closer to the hut. Simultaneously, they threw *barasbaras* lances and hit the target. It snorted its last breath. The pig squealed and rolled eight feet from the hut its mouth wide open exposing sharp tusks. The eyes were bulging out in a dying rage. One lance hit the stomach and another pierced the neck. Blood oozed on the mud.

"What a hit!" Rodney shouted. "You guys are good shots. We'll take a quarter sack of rice and I'll put the pig in a jute sack and carry it to the compound."

"You must hurry or Mama Sid will be furious. We left the compound without her permission," Victor said.

"Man, this is some fun," Joe rasped. He was still breathing heavy from his feat. "Wish we could stay for another hit."

"Can't do that," Victor told him. "The others must have heard this one cry. Already, they're probably out of range and wouldn't come back. Besides, you do have to get back."

Victor was reluctant about staying behind, but Rodney didn't want to miss the *lechon.* All four walked back to the *banca* with Rodney.

They were about to push the *banca* into the waterway when they heard the explosion. A shell from a 75mm gun landed about twenty meters away. Where it sank, mud splattered the trees around. Rodney dropped the jute sack and the rice in the *banca* and pulled it behind thick brush. He heard Victor sprinting from the hut with his sawed-off shotgun. All four Americans were behind big mangrove trunks ready to run for life again.

Chapter 29—The Improvable Event

Colonel Inuro Asaki was furious. He raised his samurai and brought it down hard on the table full of food brought in for him by women he captured. Cups flew; wine, soup, steamed rice and cooked meat spilled on the floor as the table split in two.

"Bring in the *kempetai* spies and the Filipinos from this area," he bellowed. "I have a lot of questioning to do."

His face turned red and his breathing hard. His eyes were bulging with suppressed rage. Like a piece of machinery that had been given one ounce of pressure too much, he looked ready to explode.

"Don't just stand there like an immobile gecko. Get women to clear up this mess and bring the men in here quickly. Have the column ready to move; find out which fork of the river the guerrillas have taken the Americans and make sure everything's ready for a chase. The bastards think they've outwitted me but it's not over yet."

He brandished his sword carelessly; even his men got out of his way. Livid with anger, he ordered his lieutenants to pull out of position, load all the machine guns and ammunition and hook the 75 mm guns on trucks ready to roll out of *Enclaro*. He tortured the Filipinos that were brought in for questioning but no one volunteered any information about the whereabouts of *Kapitan* Almanzur and his men. After he was done with the men brought in for questioning, they were hardly alive. Colonel Asaki hit a skull, broke a nose, cut an ear, a hand or put out an eye. All he could find out was there's another branch of the *Ilog* River that also empties to the sea, leading to denser swampland than the one they were in presently. To get there, they have to get out of *Enclaro*, go toward the town proper in *Ilog,* circle it and follow the bank of the river as far as their trucks could go without getting mired in swamp mud.

This information was nothing the *kempetai* didn't know before. The torture was senseless, done simply to spread fear and let Colonel Asaki unload his frustration. The *kempetai* were ready to guide the column to their objective. After calculating distance and range, Colonel Asaki ordered his men to use the 75 mm guns to indiscriminately shell in that direction prior to his arrival there.

"I'll teach these bastards there's nowhere they can hide from my guns even if I have to mow down every tree in the swamps."

The first volley of 75mm shells were undirected and only served to warn people in the swamps to hide.

The Japanese vehicles roared through *Ilog* proper, barrio *Diot* and eventually to *Mang* Kari's well at the outskirts of the swamps, a distance of approximately twenty-five kilometers. *Mang* Kari's place was the last clearing bordering the swamps. A grove of coconut trees shaded the riverbank. The well in the middle of the coconut grove gushed water from deep fresh water springs. From *Mang* Kari's place Mama Sid's hideout was in easy range of the 75 mm guns. Since neither Colonel Asaki nor the *kempetai* knew its exact location, guesswork sent the shells farther into the swamps clear to the hut where the rice was stored.

A shell landed twenty meters away from Victor's hut; the explosion was deafening. A few more indiscriminate volleys of shells landed here and there. Then the shells fell much farther down. In a few minutes, they smelled smoke and fire. Victor knew one of the huts in the compound must have been hit and was on fire, but which one?

Was it a direct hit? Please, not where my *Inday* Choling is lying helpless or where Marco and Spencer are resting, Victor silently prayed.

"Take the Americans to the hut and let them sit behind the canal dikes," he shouted to Rodney. "Keep them very quiet. Intruders may be deceived to think there's nothing here but swamp brush. If the hut is discovered, wait till whoever are coming are almost on the dikes, then use the *barasbaras* lances as bayonets for self-defense. I have to go back to the compound to see what has happened."

Victor was overcome with guilt.

Why did he leave his mother and father, his sisters and cousins at a time when he was needed most? And what about Marco and Spencer? How could he leave two of his American charges unattended? They need to get away and join the other four.

It was too late for outrigger *banca* rides now; too late to get to the main river. The Japanese must already be all over the riverbanks. The only route of escape was the heart of the swamps. The Japanese can never find their way in this mangrove forest but *Manong* Alvaro would never forgive me if they get hold of these Americans. And what about Delia? Her brave gesture of exposing herself to the danger of being caught is now perhaps in vain!

He didn't bother to take the *banca*. He ran as fast as his legs could go over the thick mangrove roots not paying heed to the pain as the roots pierced his feet. The closer he got to the edge of the compound, the more he realized that the shells fell more often, that a roaring fire was blazing somewhere. A menacing fear crossed his mind. Something was beginning to get clear to him. It was at first too subtle to grasp. It began merely as a disquieting thought, but now he knew that the shells were no longer falling at random.

The Japanese could pinpoint the compound!

The shells hit the giant mangrove trees hanging over the huts. Dry as kindling, they caught on fire; the burning branches dropped on the thatched roof and fueled a blaze. Where the shells hit the ground, gaping holes as large as a *banca* dotted the once flat space. Mud splattered all over. A shell fell on the bathing area, and demolished the vine covered bamboo wall that screened it. The hut close to it, where the Americans slept the night before, caught fire. The fire devoured the thatched *nipa* roof and the structure collapsed and filled the bathtub-like fissure with debris that burned and steamed the water to boiling temperature.

Delia couldn't comprehend the destruction. She sat on the bamboo steps of the last standing hut; it didn't burn because there was no large tree over it. Papa tried to console her. Shaking with anger and despair, she couldn't stop sobbing. A calamity she had no power to stem raised its ugly head and swept over this ingeniously created paradise like an avalanche, consuming everything on its path like a forest fire driving headlong over all obstacles.

Marco organized a brigade. He put everyone on line: Mama Sid, Papa, Spencer and the girls were passing old rusty tin buckets from hand to hand and at the end of this line, Marco dumped water onto the hissing blaze.

"More, more; faster, faster," Marco cried desperately.

Victor could hardly hear the sound of his voice over the roaring fire.

"Stop it Marco," he shouted. "It's a hopeless task. Girls, get everything you have saved and throw them in the *banca*. We have to get out of here, *NOW*!

The urgency in his voice spurred everyone. With little thought, he detached the outriggers and threw them into the flames. The action threw Delia into motion. Just as instinctively, she gathered what they couldn't take in the two *bancas* and threw them into the flames as well. They couldn't save even the wooden doors they always carried when they moved from one place to another. They were too wide and too clumsy on the *bancas* without outriggers. They could only take them when they used the main river route to move on. It was much too late for that. As she threw them into the flames, she had a feeling she couldn't shake, a finality, as though this was the end of a fast vanishing dream. In half an hour, a wave of destruction demolished everything they had worked hard for, and at its wake, blotches of mud and ashes from the burning huts covered the ground.

The blazing trees became a compass leading the Japanese unerringly to the narrow waterway, the entrance to the compound. The sputter of machine gun fire was unmistakable. Victor was in the lead *banca*; Delia followed close behind. They had just gone around the first bend when the automatic rifles of *Manong* Almanzur's men answered the machine gun fire of the Japanese. The first *banca* loaded with Japanese soldiers came close to the entrance. A shout rang clear as one of *Manong* Almanzur's men was spotted sitting on a branch of the huge mangrove tree that hid the entrance waterway. Before he fell, he let go of a hand grenade and hit the *banca* below. Bodies of Japanese soldiers flew all over. Boots still on severed legs drifted past Colonel Asaki's *banca*. Enraged beyond his power to control, he ordered several rounds of machine gun fire and sprayed every inch of the trees on the riverbank. Two more of *Manong* Almanzur's men fell into the water. As the *bancas* filled with Japanese soldiers entered the narrow waterway, machine gun fire ceased for sometime before it was heard again.

It was imperative to get to the end of the waterway that narrowed to a bare ribbon and disappeared into the lush bushes. They were barely half way out when he heard more grenades explode. He knew the Japanese were now at the compound. It would not be too long before they too have to get out of the *banca* and walk, no, run toward the *barasbaras* trail. He noticed that Spencer lay on the floor of the *banca*, concerned that it might tip over. Milka and Panching were using *barasbaras* poles instead of paddles to push the *banca* in the shallow water.

"Where is Coring?" Victor asked, trying to account for everyone.

"She went home down river very early in the morning," Panching answered.

Turning around to see who was with Delia, he missed his Papa. In the rush to flee, he had taken for granted that his Papa was with Delia, but he wasn't with her. Could he have gone to see about *Inday* Choling? They were fleeing without any thought of them. There hadn't been time to check what happened to them.

"Why the hell didn't you check where Papa was?" His voice cracked, heavy with accusation.

"You could have done the same thing," came Delia's angry retort.

"My God, I have to go back and find Papa. This won't do at all. We're making very slow progress as it is. Sondra, jump out of there; come here and take my job."

Then he realized that both *bancas* were overloaded. They weren't fast enough to outdistance the Japanese and they may be caught before they get to the point where the water was barely a foot high and the brush completely covered the waterway. There, they would push the *bancas* through, hide them, and everyone could follow him on foot to the *barasbaras* trail. If he turned back, who would lead them? Delia saw the silent question and the shadow of desperation on his face.

"Don't worry, I have followed you many times almost clear to the hut when you weren't looking. We can get there by ourselves. Just, please, find Papa and don't you get caught. Go. Cross the bend that goes in circles. You will make better time then."

Panching realized that they were making little progress, if at all. Sondra was not capable of moving the *banca* quickly over shallow water. Soon after Victor jumped out to go back, Panching and Milka got out too. Without hesitation, they ran where the trees were thickest. They had to get out so Sondra could move the *banca* faster. They had to run into the swamps and hide from the fast approaching Japanese. They expected Spencer to stay with Sondra, but when he saw the girls jump out, he followed them. He didn't know what else to do. He trailed the girls. Sinking into the mud, he scrambled helplessly. Marco looked behind and saw what the girls were trying to do. He sat up when he saw Spencer follow.

"Don't you dare go too," Delia snapped at him.

She was beginning to wonder if it was worth bringing them to the swamps. Their coming certainly brought an end to the comfort of the compound, an end to the sanity and quietude that could have lasted till the end of the war?

Marco read her thoughts and agreed in silence.

To begin with, why were they brought here? Better that they continued running and risked danger only to their own lives and not jeopardize the lives of these people. Perhaps they should stop escaping and surrender to the Japanese. They are the quarry, not these unfortunate civilians.

Delia read his thoughts too. Her answer came in the way she harnessed her energy to her purpose. She used the paddle like a pole to push the *banca* through the waterway that had now narrowed to a ribbon of clear, shallow water.

"Look out for the underbrush," she warned Marco and Mama Sid. They had to duck low, almost lying down at the bottom of the *banca* to escape being snagged by the swamp brush that became almost impassable. Delia began to feel a loss. No one followed behind them. It hit her instantly. She knew she had lost Sondra. Unfamiliar with the terrain, Sondra simply followed the waterway and instead of turning right on the fourth bend she turned left because it was the wider branch. She must have gone around and around almost half way back from where they started. She didn't know that the smaller, narrower waterway was the path leading out of the circle. Delia had gone several hundred meters after the last bend. If she were to go straight across the circling waterway, she would not be more than five hundred meters ahead of Sondra, but she checked the impulse to cry out to her, for if she did, the sound would carry and would betray where they were and reveal how they got there.

God, these circular waterways seemed like endless corridors that lead away from pain only to connect with other corridors that ushered in more pain. When will this endless trail of escape ever end? They have lived in the swamps for over three years now, but, by far, the events of the last three days were the most intensely dangerous attempts the Japanese have ever made to try and root them out of the swamps. Dimly, Delia understood that this savage attack was made not only to cut down *Manong* Almanzur's and *Manong* Alvaro's families but primarily to capture the Americans. Using *kempetai* guides, it wouldn't be too long before they'd find Sondra's *banca*. They once caught Delia, though they didn't know who she was. At the thought of being caught again, she redoubled her speed. She was getting close to the end of the waterway where they have to push the *banca* through, hide it, and continue on foot to the *Barasbaras* trail.

Why did *Manang* Panching and *Manang* Milka get out of the *banca*? Perhaps if they follow their instincts, they would go as deep into the swamps as they could. They might even eventually get to the *Barasbaras* trail.

"Please, Lord, lead them to the trail."

She prayed in silence. But she had little faith in her prayer for it was clear to her that trudging on the mud was not easy and the pain from the roots that pierced through the skin of the feet was difficult to endure. If the girls got tired, they would be tempted to sit down and rest and lose the energy to go on. Why did she not anticipate this danger and look behind her and urge them to stay in the *banca* and follow her? Why was she too intent on her own danger to act with more concern for the rest of them? And what about Victor and Papa? What about *Inday* Choling and her family? If *Manong* Almanzur's men responsible for *Manang* Aning and her sons had taken them somewhere for safety would they have taken Inday Choling and her family, too? *Manang* Aning was taking care of *Inday* Choling before the shelling of the compound began. Perhaps Papa had gone back there to see how they were. Maybe Papa was safe with them. Maybe Victor went back on a needless search?

She answered her own questions with a series of self-accusations.

Victor was not thinking only of himself. Despite the danger, he went back for Papa. That's what I should have done too. I should have waited for Sondring and made her take the girls and Spencer with her. Is this what I am reduced to, to think only of myself when I face danger? So much for this war and the shaping of character. Oh God, why is all this happening? What happened to the guerrilla plan of escape, and where is *Manong* Alvaro?

Chapter 30—Escape, Rescue, and Complete Rout

Manong Alvaro arrived at the mouth of the *Ilog* River in a *batel* full of guerrilla soldiers armed with rifles, submachine guns they call Garands, Tommy guns, and hand grenades. On the way to his parents' hideout, they heard the first round of shells from the Japanese patrol at *Mang* Kari's place. Immediately, they anchored in a small tributary and left the *batel* hidden there with only a crew of three. The group split and used two outrigger *bancas* they had pulled behind the *batel* in case they had to get into narrow waterways. The men paddled hard to get to the entrance to the compound before the Japanese could get there.

Manong Alvaro hoped Almanzur and his men had arrived from *Enclaro* and were now in the hideout to protect the Americans. Obviously, Colonel Asaki was really furious. By now he must have discovered he had been tricked again.

Earlier, *Kapitan* Villalva had split his men in two groups too. The smaller group of six trailed Delia and her load of Americans. Delia had arrived safely and the six men ordered to follow her to the compound escorted her in. They ate and drank *tuba* with the Americans and waited for the rest of *Kapitan* Villalva's unit. When the first shell hit the compound, the six men who only had one Tommy gun, five automatic rifles, half-dozen grenades and bows and arrows, positioned themselves as they were instructed. Two men were on trees at the entrance waterway; two more were at the point where the waterway forked into the compound. Pedring and Martin went to find *Manong* Alvaro's wife and children. *Inday* Choling's family were with them and so was her Papa so they took them too and proceeded by outrigger *banca* toward the mouth of the river where they eventually found the *batel.*

"What happened to the other six who had too much *tuba* to drink last night? Pedring asked.

"I think they're up in trees guarding the compound," Martin answered. So are the four who came with us.

Meanwhile, the *Kapitan* and his band of twelve barely reached *Mang* Kari's place. Exhausted from running fast, they were drinking at the well when the sound of trucks warned them the Japanese found out that *Enclaro* was not the path of escape. The three men who holed up at *Enclaro* before the *Kapitan* and his men got there also ran to *Mang*

Kari's to join them. On foot and running fast, it had taken them all about an hour and a half to get to the well.

Colonel Asaki raced to *Mang* Kari's well also. On a straight line, it would have taken him no longer than thirty minutes to get there. Unfortunately, his trucks had to use the road that circled back from *Enclaro* to *Vista Allegre* back to barrio *Talubangui* and to the narrow bridge at *Malabong*. The bridge wasn't only narrow; it wasn't sturdy enough to support the heavy 75 mm guns. Soldiers had to cut trees beyond the riverbank, haul them with their trucks to the bridge and fortify it so the guns could cross. Colonel Asaki got more furious by the minute. It had taken him almost two hours to travel the twenty-five kilometers from *Enclaro* to *Mang* Kari's clearing.

He had ordered Major Onoki with his truckload of men to stay put at *Enclaro* in case the guerrilla band was proceeding there. He left in full force because *kempetai* spies informed him the guerrillas were taking the Americans to a hideout on the other branch of the river.

"If they don't turn up here, and you hear my cannons blasting away, go by foot and join me at the other branch of the river. If they do turn up here, I want that guerrilla band annihilated and the Americans captured dead or alive."

* * *

Major Onoki had no doubt he would quickly eliminate the small band approaching in two outrigger *bancas*. Through his binoculars he observed the *bancas* were swiftly paddling close to the other bank of the river. He ordered his men to cross the river and intercept the guerrillas there. He wasn't aware of the topography across the river. Nor was he aware that three men had already mounted a machine gun behind the broad mud dikes of the fishpond at the top of the riverbank. On the lead, the Major picked his way up the steep incline. He didn't expect any opposition from this side of the river.

Paul Lindsey, the American *mestizo* (half American, half Filipino), saw the Major clearly through his binoculars, but he held his fire. He waited till he was sure Captain Villava and three men who paddled the camouflaged decoy *bancas* had jumped out and were swimming underwater. Getting anxious, his fingers itched to open fire. The Japanese lieutenant mounted a machine gun halfway on the riverbank intending to open fire on the *bancas* that now swerved towards the bank they'd left.

Major Onoki was more than halfway to the top of the riverbank. Paul's radio equipment blared the signal. The Major was in easy range; Paul opened fire, spraying wildly. The elevation of the machine gun on the dikes on top of the riverbank was a perfect advantage. The Japanese were easy targets. Within minutes, the Major and half of his men fell. The rest rushed back below scrambling for cover.

The lieutenant swung his machine gun to fire at Paul Lindsey's position but two of the eight guerrilla reinforcement running five hundred meters below Paul Lindsey were now only a few hundred meters from the Japanese lieutenant. They threw hand grenades and hit his gun while it was swinging to start firing at Paul. The impact sent the lieutenant roiling down the riverbank but the men handling the gun lay dead or dying on the spot.

When the *Kapitan*, Caesar, Rafael and Sergeant Peralta reached the riverbank. They quickly recovered the rifles and grenades left by eight men now running to join the three at the fishpond dikes. The *Kapitan* was three hundred meters below Japanese soldiers firing at the eight men running toward Paul's direction. He started pitching hand grenades to divert attention from the mounted machine gun. The explosions from the grenades threw a smoky racket and slowed down the Japanese climbing to get to the top of the riverbank. Four of the half dozen grenades thrown hit the target. Then the eight men reinforcement used their submachine guns to fire at the Japanese getting out of cover, desperately trying to reach the top of the riverbank. They ran to the machine gun behind the hut, dismantled it and helped the three carry their equipment. They slid down the dikes, running full speed toward the other branch of the river to rendezvous with *Kapitan* Almanzur at *Mang* Kari's clearing. With telescopic rifles recently supplied by an American submarine, Caesar, Rafael and Sergeant Peralta picked off some of the Japanese attempting to get back to the other side of the river in outrigger *bancas*. Totally stumped and utterly surprised, most of the soldiers scrambling for the *bancas* got blown to bits by hand grenades the *Kapitan* accurately threw.

An hour and a half later, all of the twelve men singly or two and three together staggered at *Mang* Kari's well. *Kapitan* Villalva was the last to get in, making sure all have come in safely. Thank God, Colonel Asaki's trucks pulling heavy 75 mm guns couldn't go over the bridge at *Malabong* fast enough. The delay at *Malabong* gave the *Kapitan* and his men time to get to *Mang* Kari's well before Colonel Asaki's troops roared in.

Colonel Asaki hadn't expected the delay. Besides, he was counting on Major Onoki to arrive promptly from the opposite branch of the river. He never found out what happened at *Enclaro*. He didn't know till much later that Major Onoki died and his unit, much reduced in number, took time to gather the dead and wounded, crossed back to the other bank of the river at *Enclaro* and vacillated. The lieutenant couldn't decide whether to go back to the garrison in *Kabankalan* or radio Colonel Asaki for further orders.

* * *

When the compound was pinpointed and shells were directed there, *Kapitan* Almanzur knew the Americans were in grave danger. The same *kempetai* men who stopped Delia finally did an curate calculation of the distance from *Mang* Kari's well to the hideout. Earlier, they had also argued about what to tell Colonel Asaki on the location of the hideout.

"There must be an entrance waterway to that hideout. We have to find it before Colonel Asaki gets here or we'll be in deep shit. If the guns hit the buildings in the hideout, the fire will lead us to it," one man said.

"I know. We should've looked for it yesterday, but we didn't dare get too close. I bet you a million pesos the girl we stopped had something to do with the hideout. What was she carrying in those huge jars?"

"You know damn well she was only carrying water. She opened all the jars and you saw there was nothing but water in it," the older man argued.

"Yes, but I should have gotten into the *banca* to see what else she carried. She was the only one who passed here that night. Somehow, something still tells me she has something to do with guerrillas," the man wearing the blue bandana with flowers on it insisted.

"Bullshit. Just keep telling the soldiers on the guns to hit the same spot. When a blaze burns, we'll know we've found it," the older man retorted.

* * *

Before the Japanese arrived at *Mang* Kari's well, *Kapitan* Villalva was prepared to take a short cut in the swamps to join the rest of his unit at his *Nanay* Sid's compound. But *Mang* Kari had an imperative message.

"Almanzur," *Mang* Kari anxiously pulled the *Kapitan* aside, "a boy, from *Andulawan* told me to tell the guerrillas three Americans have arrived at the *Hacienda Luzuriaga.*"

"When? Almanzur asked. "How does he know?"

"He said to look for *Kapitan* Almanzur and tell him his cousin, Lt. Balinas from *Andulawan*, had gone as fast as he could to the *Hacienda Luzuriaga* to protect the three Americans taken there by *banca*." *Mang* Kari delivered the message breathlessly.

"Thank you, *Mang* Kari. Is the boy still around? Can I talk to him?" *Kapitan* Almanzur asked, anxious to find out.

"No son," the old said. "He went back immediately. He said if Americans were around, it wasn't safe for him to be on the road."

The *Kapitan* had strict instructions to get to his *Nanay* Sid's hideout at once but he knew Lt. Balinas needed him at the *Hacienda Luzuriaga*. The pilot, navigator and tail gunner were stranded there. Knowing Procopio had enough men to defend the *hacienda*, the *Kapitan* took only two men and sent the rest with Paul Lindsey and the two others with him to his *Nanay* Sid's hideout. They and his trusted men in the swamps could protect the Americans. Besides, his cousin Alvaro was expected to arrive there shortly. The Americans at the *hacienda* were in greater danger than the ones in the swamps. They had to be taken out of there before the Japanese discover they were within easy reach. Without hesitation, the *Kapitan* disobeyed orders again.

* * *

Two of *Mang* Kari's neighbors who helped fill Delia's jars were at the well when the Japanese trucks arrived. At the sound of the trucks, they tried to hide, but the already half-crazed Colonel Asaki was prepared for such an event. Disregarding any risk, he pulled a motorcycle and was in hot pursuit. Pidong was not as fast as Ensiong. The commandant swiped him, tied him up, and dragged him like a dog on a short leash.

Ensiong ran to hide in the *nipa*-covered border, crawled under the brush and crossed a small creek where one of *Kapitan* Almanzur's men fished him out. Furious that he couldn't spot Ensiong, the commandant drove the motorcycle out of the open clearing to the edge of the *nipa* grove. Ponsing, up in a tree, couldn't resist his luck. He pulled out his bow instead of using his rifle. He didn't want to give his position away. Carefully taking aim, he released an arrow. It got caught in the shaft of the wheel, turned the motor cycle a hundred and sixty degrees around and sent Colonel Asaki flying. He landed about thirty feet from Ponsing's tree. Ponsing shot a second arrow and pinned Colonel Asaki's leg on the ground. The roar of pain was instant. The truck edged close to the helpless commandant, now grossly humiliated. In the commotion that followed, Ponsing slid down the tree, inched into the dense *nipa* grove, and crawled into the swamp.

Now they were in for it. The arrow missed the bone. Actually, Ponsing was aiming for the heart. After the flesh wound was cleaned and bandaged, Colonel Asaki decided merely frightening the people in the swamps with shelling wasn't good enough. He must root them out of hiding. This charade had gone far enough. He issued an order to Major Onoki at *Enclaro* to get to *Mang* Kari's well at once.

The lieutenant answered to report that Major Onoki had died.

"I took time to gather all the dead and the wounded and I'm driving back to *Kabankalan*."

"You fool. I'd have you flogged for desertion if you do that. Ask for direction and drive your truck to join the men at the guns. I expect a full report later."

Colonel Askai's anger mounted beyond his control. If a truckful of dead and wounded arrived in *Kabankalan*, he would be discredited.

"How could a handful of guerrilla men overwhelm a fully armed unit?" He roared at the lieutenant on the radio. "I want no excuses. Give me a full and detailed account. How could Major Onoki let this happen? I expected only the best of him. What an absolute disappointment!"

Colonel Asaki was extremely irate. Though he couldn't think straight, he determined not to lose face. Rounding up the *Kempetai* informants, he struck his boots with the flat side of his samurai and demanded they locate the exact waterway entrance to a hideout they were talking about or else they would pay for his humiliation and his injury. It was now almost three o'clock in the afternoon.

"Sir, it wouldn't be wise to get into the swamps this late," the *kempetai* with the blue bandana informed him. We don't know how many guerrilla men are in there. They're too familiar with this terrain. Swamp cover would be to their advantage and a threat to our safety. Besides, rumors say they're well armed and in a few hours more darkness will cover the swamps. "

Too incensed to listen to common sense, Colonel Asaki bellowed, "If they're well armed, why didn't they use guns instead of arrows? Take all the *bancas* you can find. All *kempetai* will paddle. I'll teach these resisting bastards a lesson they'll not forget."

* * *

Ordered to protect it, *Kapitan* Almanzur's unit arrived at the hideout, hoping Colonel Gomez would come on time to reinforce them. But there was nothing to protect. The place was an inferno of burning huts, burnt, splintered trees, and large gaping holes.

Before the *Kapitan's* men arrived at the hideout, the burning trees had lighted the Japanese unerringly to the spot.

"Radio the lieutenant at the guns to shell the hideout to kingdom come," Colonel Asaki roared. "Send a volley on the same spot every fifteen minutes."

The shells accurately fell on the hideout. Colonel Asaki simply followed the trail of flames. Every fifteen minutes they, too, had to dodge the shells falling around them. A shell hit a tree where one of *Kapitan* Almanzur's men was poised; the body fell on the ground minus a leg and an arm. Colonel Asaki wanted to finish the job, but when he came out of the brush a volley of machine gun bullets caught him off guard. He crawled back to the safety of the brush. Now every Japanese soldier had to look out for himself!

* * *

Kapitan Villalva knew the shelling had to be stopped. But he had only two men left with him and there were at least sixteen Japanese soldiers guarding the guns. Colonel Gomez, too, decided the 75 mm guns had to be silenced. He sent half of his men to stop the shelling. The group took a short cut in the swamps at the other end of the same trail Ponsing and Ensiong had taken. Both had trouble keeping up with *Kapitan* Almanzur's men. Before they could cross the main river, they met Colonel Alvaro's men looking for the guns. This turned the tide for the guerrillas Ensiong made the sign of the cross at this stroke of good luck. Given an automatic rifle, he led the guerrillas swiftly but stealthily back to *Mang* Kari's well. Now they made good time, for Ensiong and Ponsing knew exactly where they were going.

They circled the trucks covering the guns from view. Ponsing climbed the same tree where he sent an arrow hitting Colonel Asaki on the leg. He threw grenades when Colonel Gomez's men opened fire with the M2 sub-machine guns. Sensing they were outflanked, one of the two trucks roared out of there. The truck full of dead soldiers from *Enclaro* was abandoned. The other truck had no time to escape. As the driver revved up the engine, a bullet from an automatic rifle hit him. The Japanese soldiers manning the 75mm guns had no chance. The fight was over shortly after it started. Ensiong hacked those who hadn't died with his sharp *bolo* as they lay dying. Each time he raised his *bolo*, he cried with a sob.

"This one is for Pidong, savages."

Kapitan Villalva kicked the driver out. Caesar drove in pursuit of the fleeing truck. Half a kilometer down the road, the escaping truck halted to assess its loss. The lieutenant from *Enclaro* needed immediate attention. He was slowly dying. The unscheduled stop gave *Kapitan* Villalva, Caesar, and Rafael time to catch up and execute a hurried plan of attack. The narrow trail, covered with potholes, wove around coconut trees. The *Kapitan* asked Caesar to slow down; he unbuttoned the uniform on a dead Japanese soldier in the back of the truck, put a Japanese shirt and a cap on to hide his shaggy hair, raised his machine gun and in guttural imitation of Japanese talk shouted at the men in the other truck. The men waited for what they thought were their soldiers coming to help them. As they came close, the *Kapitan* opened fire. All six, including the dying lieutenant, fell instantly. The bullets ripped their guts and a trail of blood marked the ground where two tried to run out. *Kapitan* Villalva riddled the gas tank with bullets; quickly, it caught fire and in minutes exploded.

"Damn, what a shame! I wasn't thinking straight. I wish we could've saved this truck, too."

The salvaged machine gun rattled at the back of the truck. Rafael and the *Kapitan* kicked the dead soldiers out. He stripped the shirt off, threw it and the cap in the truck, and Caesar stepped on the gas on the way to the *Hacienda Luzuriaga.*

* * *

In the swamps, the Japanese found the compound completely deserted. All the huts burned down and only one was left partially standing. Delia was long gone; she had made good progress with only two others in her *banca* but Sondra, unable to follow Delia, circled the compound. Knowing the Japanese were gaining on them, the girls jumped out of Sondra's *banca* and ran for the trees. Confused, Spencer followed them. Lost and helpless, Sondra decided to hide in the underbrush in the narrow waterway. There were only ten left of the *Kapitan's* men, but with Paul Lindsey in command, they zig zagged behind mangrove trees at the heels of the Colonel and his men. Beyond the burning flames, the Japanese didn't know where to go. Those who hesitated were picked off one by one. Colonel Asaki stayed close to the brush in the waterway beyond the huts; he saw that it continued into the swamps so he and what was left of his column kept trailing the banks for shelter in the underbrush. They didn't know it, but they repeatedly circled around the edges of the compound, as did Sondra.

They stumbled on her *banca* in the undergrowth. She was crouched inside with her arms thrown over her head waiting in agony for a shell to hit her. Jubilant that he found something to crow about, Colonel Asaki lifted Sondra from her crouching position, stood her five feet four inch frame up, squared her shoulders and pushed her against a tree trunk. Then he saw despite her height she was no more than a gangling teenager. She turned her face away, afraid to look into his eyes. She heard the anger and frustration in his loud, guttural tone as he issued an order to the nearest soldier.

"One more a time." the soldier shouted in broken English, pushing his head very close to her face. "Tell us where are Americans."

She saw the butt of his rifle from the corner of her eye; the blood turned like ice in her veins. The rifle butt landed on her left cheek, crushing that side of her skull. She crumpled like a rag doll. She heard everything they said as if they were very *far, far away*. The soldier lifted the rag doll once more and tried to shake some response from the almost unconscious figure. He stepped aside. The Colonel hit her again and again, breaking her ribs at will. She tried to scream but no sound escaped her swollen lips. Only one eye glared at him; the other was closed from the swelling on her left cheek. The other eye stared straight at the squat and stocky commandant daring him to take her life, all that was left of it.

Every time she didn't answer, Colonel Asaki hit her on the side of her head with his pistol. Blood ran freely down her chest. He hit her on her stomach and smashed her lips with the pistol butt. It swelled so she couldn't spit out the blood in her mouth; she swallowed it. Seeing she was almost gone, he decided she was of no more use, gave her one last kick with a heavy boot and broke her knee.

She was all but dead when Victor, beside himself with grief, found her. Rustling close, the Japanese had no idea they were circling back to the hideout. Victor crouched beside Sondra and opened fire with an automatic rifle he had taken from a dead Japanese soldier. The other Japanese soldiers and the *kempetai* clawed their way out of the brush, trying to get away from this raving maniac. Blocking their retreat, Paul Lindsey used a submachine gun. Also in pursuit, the rest of the guerrilla unit scattered, climbed on mangrove branches and used telescopic rifles to spot Japanese soldiers not knowing where to go. The only way out seemed to be the narrow waterway. They had no way of knowing that it circled three times around the compound. The *kempetai* realized it was certain death to go back to the hideout, so they ran blindly into the swamps. This was the worst mistake they could've made. Incensed with grief, Victor followed in pursuit.

A few hundred yards away, Spencer was unable to keep up with the girls. He tried to overtake them, but when he pulled himself up from the deep mud, he had no strength in his legs, his arms, and shoulders. He staggered to the nearest tree trunk and sat down at its foot. He sat immobile; the strain was too much for his now emaciated frame. His arms were limp, his legs felt rubbery; he ached at every joint. He felt the skin tighten around his wound and when he attempted to get up, every muscle on his stomach tugged and pulled him down. He wondered if the scar would be permanent and the skin would never be smooth again.

Panching and Milka had no idea where they were going but they stopped when they saw Spencer sit down to rest. They sat down not fifteen feet away from him, knowing he was in great pain. Milka spied the *kempetai* through the mangrove trees. Deliberately, she moved away from Spencer. If she hadn't moved, they probably would've been missed, but she didn't like the thought that Spencer might get up any minute to join them and be easily spotted by the *kempetai*. She motioned for her *Manang* Panching to stand and they tried to make a run for it. The mud slowed them down. They were barefoot now; their feet bled from roots that stung beyond endurance.

Stretching to look over his shoulder was pure agony, but Spencer saw Milka get up and run out of a clump of trees. The Japanese gave chase.

Oh, Milka, why do you have to run? They will surely overtake you. Spencer agonized.

In a moment, Milka was out of his sight. Unable to do anything, Spencer began to cry. He felt miserable, tired and bewildered. His body wouldn't do anything but a thought came at once.

I will hate myself all my life if I don't do anything to stop the beasts from harming these helpless girls.

Sheer will power supported his legs as he leaned against the tree trunk and a final surge of adrenalin pulled his body erect. He steadied himself. In another minute, he, too, was chasing Milka behind the Japanese. He must have run about twenty feet when his rubbery legs stumbled over an obstacle. His boot got caught in something like a metal trap. A gun! His brain sent a message to his knees that buckled down to retrieve the incredible find. He managed enough strength to unclasp stiff fingers from the handle of an automatic rifle.

Knowing *Kapitan* Almanzur's men were getting too close, the Japanese made a desperate effort to catch the girls. They caught Panching first; she was breathing hard and with a sob, she gave up running. When Milka saw this, she quit running too.

"Please don't hurt her; she has a heart condition," she begged.

"Come here you guerrilla supporter," said one *kempetai*. "You lead us out of here."

He pulled Milka by the hair, pushed and half-dragged Panching and delivered them to Colonel Asaki. In a desperate attempt to save his own life, he used them as a shield. Spencer came charging, hitting a few soldiers. In the corner of his eye he thought he saw Victor carrying an identical rifle.

"From one of their dead," he shouted and waved the rifle as Victor came running close to him.

"Use it to plague these living monsters," Victor yelled back.

But as they came close to Colonel Asaki, they saw that he squeezed himself between the girls. Victor couldn't open fire. Neither could Spencer. Realizing the girls were a protection, the Colonel pushed and pulled them, careful that he was always behind them as he inched back to Sondra's *banca*. He knew this was his only way out of the swamps. As soon as they got back to the *banca*, he pushed the girls in and again squeezed between them.

Victor couldn't open fire on the commandant and the few Japanese soldiers near him. He was afraid he might hit his *Manang* Panching or Milka. He decided to go back to Sondra. She had fallen on her left side, lying in her blood on the mud where the commandant had dropped her. She was unconscious from too much loss of blood. Victor picked up the almost lifeless body and cradled her in his arms. Sobbing, he closed the glaring eye and asked God to please, please save her life.

Three of *Kapitan* Almanzur's men came running to see if they could help. There was no immediate need to chase after the retreating Japanese. Colonel Alvaro's men had arrived to reinforce them and would take care of the remaining Japanese soldiers. Now their concern was to find what happened to the people in the compound, especially the six Americans. They found Spencer crumpled where Victor had left him, fighting the pain in his groin and dabbing his eyes in frustration that he couldn't save Panching and Milka from obvious harm. He thought the crazed Japanese commandant must have killed them. Nothing could console him.

Hours later, more guerrilla men arrived at the thoroughly devastated compound. Spencer surveyed the damage. Like Victor, he was overcome with grief. Leaning on a tree stump that had escaped the fire, he gave way to the tears he was trying to suppress. In a few minutes, a *banca* arrived at the landing. Through his tears he saw Panching and Milka step out with a guerrilla officer, obviously the much-awaited Colonel Alvaro Gomez. As Milka stepped on solid ground, she spotted Spencer. Without a thought, she rushed to embrace the dazed Spencer who fell into her arms.

* * *

Three guerrilla soldiers helped Victor drag the hollow tree trunk with Sondra on it; they were going to take her back to the compound. Although she looked dead, they could still feel a very slight pressure at her pulse. One man volunteered to guard her until Colonel Gomez and his men would arrive, but Victor picked up the almost lifeless body. He was going to take her to Mama Sid. Surely she would be able to perform some miracle to restore Sondra's life. Mama Sid's prayers could still work, he told himself. She is closer to God than anyone he knew, except his Papa, but he couldn't find him.

"We can carry her for you, son," one of the men offered.

"No, I have to get her to my mother." He put her head on his shoulders and held her as though she were a sack of precious rice. The men followed him closely.

"If you want to help, go look for Spencer, the wounded American. He had picked up a gun from a dead Jap. I have no idea where he went. He either went into the swamps or back to the compound looking for *Manang* Panching and my cousin, Milka."

One of the soldiers tried to reason with Victor. "You have to let us help you, son. Why are you going into the swamps?"

"I must take this unfortunate one to my mother; I have to find out if my sister, Delia, my mother, and Marco managed to get back to Rodney and the other Americans. I know my sister Delia must have gone there. That's where I'm going."

* * *

Later, when Colonel Gomez and his men gathered at the compound, Milka gave an incredulous Spencer an account of what happened to her and her *Manang* Panching.

"There was no room in the *banca* for more than four soldiers, *Manang* Panching and I, and the commandant. He ordered his men to paddle and kicked the *kempetai* out to lead the way. Because it was low tide, the waterway was shallow. The commandant ordered his soldiers who couldn't be accommodated in the *banca* to wade in the water and follow close behind. He was intent on protecting himself. The soldiers raised their rifles above their shoulders and fired into the trees though they couldn't see anything. They were in full view of *Manong* Alvaro's men above. They couldn't see where the bullets were coming from; they couldn't see what hit them."

"You must have been terrified," Spencer interjected. "What did you do to keep from being hit?"

"We were very frightened," Milka cried. We kept very still, afraid we would be hit if we moved, but we were screaming for dear life. The Colonel tried to slap us to keep us quiet, but he was afraid to move, afraid the *banca* would tip over.

"Did you get to the main river?" Spencer asked.

"Not right away. We didn't know that half way out of the waterway to the main river, *Manong* Alvaro's men had created a barricade. Tree trunks littered the waterway, blocking passage. There were snipers in the trees who picked out the soldiers in the *banca* as it slowed down to avoid the barricade. One by one the bodies fell from or dropped inside the *banca*, except for the commandant who put himself between the two of us as if we were posts to shield him. Bodies hit by bullets covered the waterway; blood spouted out and turned the water red. We closed our eyes in horror. The commandant put his rifle on my head and ordered us to pick up the paddles and paddle hard. When the *banca* cleared the narrow passage and we were out in the main river, some of *Manong*

Alvaro's men dove from trees, swam underwater, and capsized the *banca*. The men helped us swim to the bank, but the commandant, wounded on the leg, helplessly thrashed around and was an easy target."

Triumphant guerrilla soldiers riddled his body with machine gun fire and didn't bother to fish him out. Two days later, his body, already rotting, bloated and smelly, drifted down the river.

* * *

The *kempetai*, still in the swamps, ran this way and that, till they wandered upon the *barasbaras* trail. Victor knew they would come out when the swamps turned dark and eerie. They would get hopelessly lost in the dark and sooner or later they would turn back following the same waterway out to the main river.

It was beginning to get dark as the dusk swallowed the sun at the edge of the swamps. The four uninjured Americans were sitting around the hut in utter emotional exhaustion, listening to Marco relate the incredible, complete destruction of the compound. Marco was desolate. Over and over, he sobbed his apology to Mama Sid. She was anxious to go back to search for her husband, her daughter and nieces. Rodney wouldn't let her go so she took a clay pot from the corner of the hut and asked him to get some water. She nursed Marco's blistered feet and dried it gently with her *patadiong*.

"I know my son would be glad to know you are safe for a while. We haven't heard any more shelling or gun sounds. I bet the Japanese have gone back to their garrison. They wouldn't stay longer in the swamps or my son and my nephew would finish them."

"We need to find out what happened to Spencer and the girls and to Victor and the rest of the family at the hideout," Marco said still sobbing.

"We'll find out soon enough. I'm sure Victor will be here before long. He'll be worried about all of you." Rodney answered.

After a while, everything turned completely quiet. Rodney knew the immediate danger was now over. Knowing all were hungry, he took the clay pot from Mama Sid and boiled rice. The pig BB and Joe killed earlier lay by the pile of *barasbaras* trunks where he had thrown it. He took the tin can used for catching rain water to drink and boiled more water in it. When the water was scalding hot, he poured it on the pig a little at a time and scraped the hair from the skin with a sharp *bolo*. The Americans were fascinated by this procedure. When the pig was scraped clean, Rodney slit the stomach and cleaned the insides. He took a large *barasbaras* trunk to use for a spit.

"Help me cut four equal trunk lengths and make two stakes in the shape of an X to support the spit at both ends. Tie a foot long *barasbaras* stick at each end of the spit. Two can sit and turn it at both ends like a rotisserie. Watch the coals don't burn into a fire or the pig will be scorched. If you turn the spit slowly the pig will roast evenly."

Delia sat disinterested on a pile of *barasbaras* trunks. Why had her brother not returned? And what happened to Sondra? Delia couldn't get over the thought that in just a matter of minutes she had lost her. Why was Sondra unable to follow her at all? Where was Papa? Where are *Manang* Aning and her boys, and where were *Inday* choling and her family?

In her mind, Delia sorted out the events of the last two days. Her thoughts flew around like fireflies on a dark night and events flickered in and out bursting in her mind's eye like fireworks that lighted the sky briefly and floated down to nothing.

In a flash, she saw the shiny boots and the geyser of blood from black, to purple, to red. This vision exhausted her, pitting her youthful faith against the weight of the violence that seemed to happen purely for the pleasure of men who play God. The Japanese trampled her world. They exercised absolute power, creating as it were a time and place in which savage murders occur as senseless random acts and those who would deal with it were limited to inconclusive gropings in the dark.

It seemed to Delia that God who ordered events permitted a physical reality without causation. Things went round and round in circles and life was a matter of sharp conflict without resolution. To side step violence, she and Victor created beauty despite the chaos; now it had disappeared in flames, and mud returned to mud. If the order in our lives can be a key to God's purpose, as Justice Brandeis says in his rulings and court opinions, how can this God reverse or cancel that order and allow us to live in a lawless world? Are we merely pawns in a world devoid of meaning?

Struggling with inchoate experience, the pattern of her thought denied the existence of a benevolent God. No matter how hard she worked at tying and retying the significance of events, reason seemed to end in a hopeless tangle. She could not clarify the extent of her involvement with these men for whom her *Manong* Alvaro risked his and his family's lives, even her own, to save. In her mind's eye she saw again how the clear water in the narrow waterway was muddied with blotches of swamp earth. Then she saw how it turned red as the tide raised the water level and pushed the blood from dying bodies to color the water estuaries.

Before the Americans came, before the destruction of the hideout, she and Victor paddled into the heart of the swamps in the narrow waterways, exploring splendor under the dark trees. Mud dikes, *barasbaras* saplings under the sheltering protection of giant mangrove trees with protruding sharp roots were all part of nature. The twisting, coiling waterways trickled or flowed in calm and quietude. They were welcoming entrances into the heart of God's creation. When they followed these to get away from the threat of Japanese capture, the natural passageways coiled around the hideout protectively. Now they were choked with lifeless bodies ripped by hate and violence. No more than mere avenues of escape from death and destruction, they were dark, blood drenched corridors of pain.

Delia was unmindful of the smell of meat permeating the area. Two *kempetai* men, lost, tired, and hungry, followed the smell leading them to the end of the *barasbaras* trail to the sight of Delia sitting apart from the rest as though she were alone. The *kempetai* smelled the aroma of the cooking meat and heard voices coming from somewhere they couldn't see. Thick brush screened the group of Americans, Rodney, and Mama Sid sitting and talking behind the small hut. Caught up in her thoughts, Delia didn't notice the *kempetai* approaching till they were almost upon her. The blue bandana crossed her vision. Instant recognition flashed and then the realization came. These men stopped her *banca*. Obviously, they guided the Japanese into the compound. Consumed with anger, she lashed at them.

"You are men without conscience," she yelled. "You prey on your own countrymen. Do you think you can get away without retribution? God sent you here so you could be punished. An eye for an eye."

She raised a pointed *barasbaras* to use as a lance. A *kempetai* pulled out a 38 revolver, raised his hand and aimed for Delia. At the moment when she released the lance, a shot rang out. Delia's lance struck the man with the blue bandana on his side. The man with the revolver fell at the sound of the shot. One of *Kapitan* Almanzur's men who followed Victor several meters away fired with a telescopic rifle. In minutes, guerrilla men rushed to Delia's side. Blood gushed from the man she tried to kill and splattered over her. She let out the same scream she did in her vision.

She passed out, but guerrilla soldiers caught her before she fell from the pile of *barasbaras* saplings she leaned on. They brought her to Mama Sid immediately.

Victor, cradling Sondra in his arms, heard the shot. Shaking with sobs of helpless grief, he ran and handed her over to Mama Sid. She took the unconscious Sondra, washed more blood away and prayed and cried alternately. Much, much later, in a hut on the main river, Sondra lay like a crumpled, twisted rag doll, all energy and color drained out of it, surrounded by her sister and cousins, and a very furious *Kapitan* Almanzur Villalva who vowed revenge.

The man Delia had struck with a *barasbaras* lance suffered only a flesh wound; later, he hung on a tree in front of the Japanese garrison in *Kabankalan.* It was never certain who killed him. Perhaps *Kapitan* Almanzur's men did. On the other hand, it could have been the senseless act of the completely routed Japanese who tried to save face.

Chapter 31—An Uncanny Silence

Without doubt this swamp encounter, despite the destruction of the hideout, turned in favor of the guerrillas. This was their most successful engagement with the Japanese, ever. For the first time, the Japanese were at a total disadvantage; unaware of the new supply of arms the guerrillas had, and unable to realistically assess the advantage of swamp topography, they suffered the worst loss in numbers. Not one soldier returned to the *Kabankalan* garrison. Four trucks were missing and two 75 mm guns hadn't been pulled in. Late in the evening of the third day, when the column of soldiers hadn't returned, the major in charge of the garrison got worried, but assumed the commandant must've stayed another day at *Enclaro.* The sound of guns had carried back to the garrison two days ago but there was only silence now. Smoke rose at the horizon so the major assumed the commandant was still pursuing his delight to burn and pillage. Still, a nagging worry worked against such logic. Why didn't the commandant send word through his *kempetai* spies? Why such inconsiderate failure to communicate? He always bragged about his exploits and his successful encounters against the guerrillas before. Major Takasaki couldn't understand this silence.

In keeping with the Japanese army's practice of rotating officers from time to time, he had just been transferred to this garrison to assist Colonel Inuro Asaki as second in command. Unfortunately for him, he couldn't hide the sharp contrast he created beside this harsh, mean-looking tyrant. Shuji Takasaki tried to unsuccessfully hide his military record from this senior officer who flaunted rank in his face.

Why is a graduate from college, from Tokyo University no less, assigned as a subordinate, to the son of uneducated farmers? Maybe he can learn a thing or two from this mentor that he hadn't learned in school?

The commandant didn't try to cover his sarcasm yet he couldn't help but like this aide who, despite his youth, was very knowledgeable about matters he had no stomach for. Major Shuji Takasaki was only 29; the colonel was a good fifteen years his senior. Before his transfer to the garrison in *Kabankalan*, Major Takasaki was in charge of maintaining accounts for supplies and money, for securing food for the garrison in Central Murcia, a suburb of *Bacolod*, the capital of Negros Occidental. He was meticulous in other matters of camp administration as well. He had been promoted and transferred as Colonel Asaki's aide because of his efficiency. No matter. Colonel Asaki liked the fact that the lad had polish and personality, and he didn't flaunt his talent. He was most respectful and always bowed or saluted whenever he approached him or when he was in speaking distance. He would recognize his presence with a slight bow and would stay at attention.

"Is there anything I can do for you, sir?" He would ask.

He had an air of gentility, accentuating his politeness that was disturbing to the older officer. Somehow, he took away from the luster of his command, for the major, who stood at six feet, two inches on his stockinged feet, towered over his five feet, six inch frame. He would often order him to sit down when he felt he had a matter to take up with him.

"Sit down," he would say. "Look me in the eye when I talk to you."

On the flip side, Major Takasaki was too soft for his taste, but he was attentive to his needs and often he seemed to anticipate his wishes. Major Takasaki was in many ways a sharp contrast to the commandant. He treated his fellow officers with courtesy and even made allowances for privates when they failed to bow at his approach, a breach of discipline the commandant would never tolerate. Colonel Inuro Asaki demanded full respect. He threw his weight around. He exploded at his fellow officers and kicked the privates when they failed to measure up to his standard of behavior. He despised the Filipinos and hated their regard for the Americans who apparently were *managers* in their country before the Japanese invasion and conquest. His mannerisms were typically Japanese. He spoke no English and could not understand *Hiligaynon,* popularly known as *Ilongo,* the native language of Negros Occidental and the neighboring island of Panay. He always counted on Major Takasaki when he needed a translation in his dealings with the Filipinos who spoke English and used this foreign language well whenever they couldn't be understood otherwise.

The commandant wasn't a well-educated man. In fact his ignorance, brutality and meanness were the badge of his command. In Japan, he went to a trade school before he enlisted in the army and rose through the ranks by patient persistence and abject obeisance and service to his superiors. He had been where Major Takasaki is now. He admired and hated him for this. He was an alcoholic who drank to excess but never passed out except in the privacy of his quarters. The alcoholism exacerbated his penchant for cruelty and sadism. He was old school in military conduct and got promoted to his rank only because of expediency, for the need to subdue the native forces resisting Japan's right to rule despite the fact that it had overrun the country. Now he was out there putting the stamp of conquest on the Philippine countryside though the garrison had yet to hear from him.

Oh, well, the major conceded, give the brass another day or two to enjoy his favorite escapade: harassing the luckless natives. Whenever Colonel Asaki came marching in, weary of a one-sided encounter, he would order all the weapons cleaned and readied for the next chance to butcher more. The poor wretches! Why don't they know how not to suffer senselessly?

When the commandant came back physically weary, one would expect him to crawl into his quarters to recover lost energy. But, no, he would ask for as many as a dozen women, usually young virgins, sometimes prostitutes. He spent the ceiling of his desires deflowering all the virgins first before he would ask for the prostitutes to match his appetite. He can pick the choice beauties and manhandle them till they looked like dolls that had lost their spark. They aged overnight.

What a pity!

Colonel Asaki told his aide he could have the choice of his leftovers, but Major Takasaki declined, saying he is happily married.

"So what about it? What has that got to do with it?" The commandant would growl. "Marriage has nothing to do with gratifying your appetite. That is proof of your manliness. Your wife ought to understand that. Denying your own pleasure for the sake of a woman who is thousands of miles away is foolish. It's a sign of weakness. You better shape up fast, young man."

Major Takasaki only smiled and bowed low to acknowledge the older man's wisdom, but inwardly he cringed at such despicable ethics.

Pity is something one can't expect from such a pig. Ironic, though, that such a pig demanded everything about him be immaculate.

Daily inspection had to yield shine in every inch of the barracks. Like the working staff at a hotel, Filipinos came in at four a.m. to mop floors with coconut husks, clean latrines, fill water tanks and polish all the trucks and motorcycles. The women came in an hour later to dust the furniture, make the beds, tend to the kitchen, make sure coffee or chocolate or *conji* was steaming hot, and fried rice, boiled eggs, and whatever else the commandant required waited on the table when he came in followed by his troops. In most camps the privates did all these. Not here.

"What are we in power for?" the pig would yell. "Conserve your energy. Show you're masters. Make the poor wretches work for their ration of food."

Major Takasaki couldn't understand why Filipinos willing enough to work couldn't raise food in the fields instead of slaving in the barracks. It was brutal and sadistic to restrict food rations to the barest minimum when tons of produce filled the storage sheds and the land around could be highly productive if tilled. Major Takasaki noted the irrigation system apparently working before the war was inoperative now. The pipes were rusty and everything about it was in disrepair.

Why not clean that up and make it work instead of making the barracks spotless and the privates lazy? Is this what we waged this war for? Is this the East Asia Co-Prosperity Sphere Policy in action? Is this learning a thing or two from a high-ranking officer?

Perhaps. But despite the general conception of Japanese penchant for cruelty and sadism, Major Shuji Takasaki wasn't without compassion. He was of the younger generation who opposed the war but got conscripted into service to win it for the military leaders of Japan, and, of course, for the glory of the Emperor.

There were poultry and produce farms in the neighborhood, but meat, grain, and vegetables were strictly for the garrison's tables. Fruit and vegetables Filipino farmers brought in sometimes rotted uneaten or the guards put them in their pockets and traded them for rings, earrings, pins, and practically worthless Japanese paper money. Ironic that the son of farmers could not understand the basic rule of farming: make the land yield what it could. In Japan, farmers made the land yield as much as possible to feed the populace. But there was not enough land to increase the yield and raise enough to feed everyone. Before the war, Japan had to import rice from Thailand to feed its population. That certainly is why they were all over Southeast Asia: to teach Filipinos, Thailanders, Indonesians, and Taiwanese Japan's values and expertise in agriculture. Farming was crucial to Japan's economy.

A greater irony: *kempetai* who worked in the garrison stole all the food they could get and sold it at exorbitant prices to their fellow Filipinos not permitted to till the land. When natives worked on the land, they were not even allowed to keep any share of the produce. They had to buy what they raised from Filipino *kempetai* who exploited their fellowmen. Had the meanness of the commandant rubbed on them too? The commandant used food supply as a means of enforcing discipline. Food supply was rationed but the ration was minimal. More irony: in the midst of what could have been plenty, the people were starving! Surrounding the garrison, the land lay fallow. *Kogon* grass took over the once fertile rice and sugar cane fields.

The greatest irony: everyday the Japanese patrols went out to scour the neighborhood for people who have to be pushed back into occupied territory by force, and were made to stay against their will. Almost daily, people got shot for trying to get away.

The Major felt this senseless disrespect for humanity pushed the privilege even of conquerors. He hated cruelty, sadism, and, the erosion of human quality. But he couldn't do anything about it, not while he was a subordinate to this inhuman monstrosity! He had better be busy scouring the edges of town for women or the commandant would be irate. Preoccupied with the non-military task of providing a brothel for his superior officer, the Major let the military matter slide. Little did he know that at the moment the commandant was floating down the *Ilog* River stripped of his rank, and his authority, smelling like the hog he was. The stench of death surrounded him, alive or dead.

No one returned to the garrison in *Kabankalan* to report what had taken place. *Kempetai* spies shied away. They knew the vengeful soldiers at the garrison, right or wrong, would hold them responsible for this disgrace. They would torture them.

Without the commandant's presence, the garrison got restive. The junior officers pressured Major Takasaki for orders. He was getting really anxious.

What the Devil was keeping the pig away so long?

He, too, was getting restive. He despised the commandant's methods of control, yet, damn it, the commandant kept a tight rein. In the few weeks he served under his command, he saw how he imposed control over the towns and barrios south of *Binalbagan*, with the exception of *Ilog*. He burned it to the ground to punish people for their stubborn resistance.

How much longer should he wait? Should he send troops to trace the ground the commandant covered? Perhaps he should send out *kempetai* spies first to ascertain his whereabouts. As second in command, Major Takasaki knew he had to do something soon.

Chapter 32—The Aftermath of Violence

After the encounter in the swamps, Colonel Alvaro Gomez realized the great danger facing the people. His cousin Almanzur had disregarded his orders again, but he was proud of the rout at *Mang* Kari's well. Almanzur had done his best again. Japanese soldiers lay in their blood all over and the burning trucks and the guns were undeniable evidence of the rout; but if the garrison in *kabankalan* discovered their loss, more soldiers would be back with a vengeance.

Two imperatives were clear to him. "Papa," he said, "the people must be warned of impending massacre and should be asked to hide. I'm sorry to tell them they have to move farther into the swamps. Hopefully, the Japanese would realize they could only go as far as *Mang* Kari's, and no farther."

"True," his father agreed. "But there's no guarantee frustration with their defeat would not make the Japanese go deeper into the swamps to root the people out."

"Oh no," the colonel argued. "I'm sure this is a hard lesson for them. They know better than go into the swamps again. In this terrain, they are not safe from us." He turned to his mother and pleaded.

"Mama Sid, I'm afraid our family has to be moved farther away again; not close to the seashore where the Japanese could land with their gunboats, but farther into the heart of the swamps."

Colonel Gomez wanted to take his endangered family with him to unoccupied territory, but the *batel* had room only for the Americans. To transport them immediately was imperative; anxiously, he waited for three more to arrive.

"Pedring, search the ground around the hideout for dead Japanese soldiers, load them in outrigger *bancas* and deliver them to *Mang* Kari's clearing. We have to dump them in a mass grave with other dead Japanese scattered there," the colonel ordered.

"Yes, sir. We have to do something to this compound too. We need to restore its function as hideout

"About time. Bring the *batel* here so better provision and shelter for your men and the American boys can be devised. I have to ask your men to work to earn their keep. The ground where the huts stood before needs to be leveled and a makeshift kitchen must be set up," Mama Sid told her son

"Ma, there's plenty of *barasbaras* lying around. I'll salvage everything useful and we can set up temporary structures. My men can cut *nipa* fronds from the main river to use for roofing. But you can't demand much. You have to get out of here soon."

The men immediately helped Rodney bring back to the compound some of the sacks of rice Victor hid in the depths of the swamps. They set these on tree trunks they cut in the surrounding area and spread the sails from the *batel* on top, creating a makeshift sleeping facility for the men. At the end of the day, the women went with kind neighbors on the banks of the main river to sleep in their houses overnight.

From the *batel* where she was taken with her boys, *Manang* Aning came back and looked after Sondra. Still shaken with grief and guilt, Victor sat in silence, near at hand, not even minding the Americans. Delia sat listless beside him. Nothing could stir her into action either. She surrendered to a deep depression robbing her of the will to act.

"Victor," his *Manong* Alvaro pleaded, "quit feeling sorry for yourself. You and Delia have to think about moving the family to a safer place. You know you can no longer stay here. We can't be sure what the Japanese would do if they find out what happened here."

Victor sat immobile for a long while. Both Panching and Milka nursed wounds on their feet; they were extremely shaken. All of the family, some more than others, had a near encounter with death. None of them had the will to defy the brutal indifference of the physical universe. What would they do, where would they go, how would they survive? That was the unspoken question in everyone's mind.

"Did you hear what I said, all of you?" *Manong* Alvaro said exasperated. "You have to do something."

"But *Nong* Varo, if we move much farther what are we going to do about water? I'm thinking about moving to the hut in the *barasbaras* trail, but getting enough water to drink over there would be very difficult," Victor answered.

"The rainy season's almost here. You can catch rainwater and store it in the earthen jars we will patch up for you. Or you will have to use the *bancas* to get water up river at night. You must do whatever you need to survive. Perhaps much later, after the danger is over, you can come back here again."

Only Papa had the unbroken faith that God would provide. God would define the nature of the final rescue. Mama Sid was still by Sondra's side. She wept and prayed for Sondra to regain consciousness.

No one seemed to care where the next meal was coming from. Only Rodney had enough energy to do what had to be done. He did the unexpected. He took charge. Rodney's first thought was always of food. No one would survive without sustenance. So he asked *Manong* Alvaro's men to help him guard the precious rice they had brought out of the swamps, to scrounge around for any unbroken container, for anything that could be used in the kitchen, for pieces of clothing left unburned, no matter what the condition. He put anything and everything into a pile to be taken to the place Victor and Delia would choose, and they could all begin to put their lives in some order once more.

Delia was dismayed that she threw what she couldn't take away from the compound into the fire. Thankfully, those were mostly objects that pertained to construction, like the door boards they used for sleeping, and the outriggers. Miraculously three large earthen jars rolled, unbroken, into the shallow waterway. The irony struck her as something funny; laughter involuntarily spilled from her lungs. When Victor realized what she was laughing at, he, too, perked up, though his laughter would come long, long after.

Tired though Mama Sid was, she ordered the girls to clean whatever clothing Rodney had gathered and whatever Papa had saved of his. Again, the girls washed and ironed the uniforms of the Americans. Once more they cleaned and dried their muddy boots. Fire burned in the makeshift kitchen; the steel shafts on which the earthen pots were set for cooking were salvaged and used. The small boys roasted seashells on coconut charcoal; the older girls cooked rice, and kindly neighbors brought in fish. They had no coconut oil for frying, so the girls boiled the fish with salt and vinegar. Nothing but ethnic menu could be served to the Americans who were grateful to share whatever there was. Marco was more comfortable about getting only what Mama Sid's household did have. Little by little, energy for life, for love, yes, even laughter, would come back as the family would bid their guests and charges goodbye and God speed.

Papa did the rest. He called the family for the usual prayer gathering after a calamity that threatened life. He prayed for the preservation of life, especially Sondra's. He asked God to restore her health. He prayed in earnest for the safety of the other three Americans on their way to the swamp. He thanked God for using his son and his nephew to save all nine airmen and take them to the appointed rendezvous that would take them home.

"For all of us who have to remain here, help us to accept Thy will and guide us daily to do what we have to do," he concluded.

Delia listened to her Papa pray but she was no longer certain about God's care. She had outworn the consolation of prayers, yet she could not discount the force of her father's steady and unbroken faith in some power over and above their own strength that could fortify them in their continued struggle to survive. Too, the six young Americans felt the force behind such faith; so far, they had had an extended rendezvous with death, but they were never more certain of life and their appointed destiny. No doubt they would be taken wherever the submarine would pick them up.

Chapter 33—Resistance beyond Mama Sid's Hideout

Long before Colonel Alvaro Gomez arrived at *Mang* Kari's place to set things right, the people living around the area knew they had to clear out, away from the possibility of a Japanese maneuver. If they stayed, they would face a massacre. *Mang* Kari explained their alternative.

"Listen, everyone," he tried to counsel the residents. "The guerrilla units commanded by *Kapitan* Villava and Colonel Gomez routed the Japanese column, but they would be no match for a whole garrison. Every household in this open clearing must take outrigger *bancas*, and be ready to move farther away into the cover of the swamps. But before fleeing, Colonel Gomez says something must be done about the guns the enemy had left behind. If the Japanese discover what happened here, they would leave no stone unturned, would raze the entire place and reduce it to nothing. They would most certainly destroy my well, and cut off your water supply."

Mang Kari did not anticipate the events that took place. He hated to be put in danger, but now that danger was imminent and reprisal was certain, he appealed to all his neighbors to help him do what was needed to save his well.

"Good neighbors," he called everyone, "fresh water from this well serves everyone who cares to ask. This water is a necessity for survival. Sometimes, water is all that's available to keep our strength up. We all have to come together and do what has to be done to save this well. All of us on the riverbanks must help."

Quite a number of men had gathered to listen. *Mang* Kari continued. "*Tia* Sierra's son, Colonel Alvaro, says we have to hide the guns. The Japanese must not know what happened here. Besides, the guns could be kept for possible use of the guerrilla forces in the future. We have to bury the dead and get rid of the smell of death. We need to make sure there's no trace of the conflict that happened here. If the Japanese come here, they must not find any evidence of their defeat."

"*Mang* Kari is right; what needs to be done is too much for a few individuals. It has to be a community project. My men will help. I can provide resources and leadership," Colonel Gomez assured them. "*Mang* Kari will supervise the cutting of coconut trees on his land for us to tie or nail together and use as sleds. We'll mount the heavy guns on these, and use the abandoned truck to push them to the edge of the swamp. The swamp muck would make it easier for us to drag everything in and hide them under dense trees. Lush brush underneath can complete the concealment."

The task was not simple; it required planning, cooperation, and muscle, but filled with the fear of reprisal *Mang* Kari, all the men, *Kapitan* Almanzur and Colonel Gomez's guerrilla units worked with frenzied energy to move the heavy load. The Colonel knew the people had hardly anything to eat, so he asked Mama Sid for two sacks of rice and created a provisional community kitchen. Older women, mothers or wives of the men working, and Mama Sid managed the kitchen. She put her girls into action. They helped women cook rice, boil salted fish with vegetables contributed by those who stored them for their own use. They prepared *mongo* beans with *malungay* leaves flavored with coconut milk, a favorite *Ilongo* dish, and *pinaksiw nga isda*, fish boiled in vinegar and ginger root. They boiled and roasted seashells and made a feast for those who had not eaten this much of a meal in months. Men, women, and children were treated to this feast that gave pleasurable compensation for the work and made the gathering, a unifying community event.

News of the free meal persuaded those who were ready to flee to stay and help with the task of subterfuge and concealment. People were coming out of the woodwork, as the expression goes. They participated with enthusiasm and felt that what they enjoyed was not charity but good will. Despite the urgency of their task and the possibility of a Japanese attack while they were at it, people toiled together as a unit, something that had not happened at all for the past three years.

Two sleds dragged the guns into the swamps. Paul Lindsey, a technical expert, used the abandoned truck to push the sleds to the edge of the swamps. Then it was easier to push the sleds on the mud. *Mang* Kari was meticulous and detailed about his efforts at concealment.

"Pour fuel on these freshly cut coconut stumps," he told the men. "We need to make it look as if the coconuts were cut long before to build something. The Japanese must not discover they have been freshly cut for some other purpose."

"We'll cut some of the mangrove trees edging the swamps and slice the branches into four feet long pieces and arrange those around and on top of the coconut stumps. It would make it look like you've piled firewood," the men told *Mang* Kari.

"Excellent. I'll burn the roof over the well and you can put the same pile of wood around it to conceal it. Then I'll put a sign that says **For Sale or Barter** on top of the pile. Let's hope *kempetai* spies would read the sign and interpret it for the Japanese.

Women and children used tools *Mang* Kari and the guerrillas supplied them to dig and shovel dirt. When there weren't enough tools to go around, other women and children used sticks sharpened or flattened at the ends, scooped the dirt with their bare hands to dig a mass grave.

"Make sure that water would not seep into the large hole in the ground. Use thatched *nipa* we have for roofing to line the walls. We must dig it close to the *nipa* grove bordering the clearing so that the mud smell of the swampy ground could mask the odor of death," *Mang* Kari instructed.

Three *banca* loads of dead bodies from the hideout in the swamps and those floating in the narrow waterway were gathered and dumped into the mass grave. So were bodies scattered on *Mang* Kari's land and the truckful of dead from *Enclaro*. All trace of blood had to be meticulously obliterated. A most unpleasant task, it was done with care and accomplished with both satisfaction and disgust.

Mang Kari's wife, *tia* Josefa, suggested something the women approved of as something really clever.

"We need to take the leafy sections of the coconut and young *nipa* fronds and tie them together. We'll use these like huge brooms to sweep the area to make it natural looking so the Japanese will not suspect that anything had happened here," she said.

Her married daughter, Rosalina, made a suggestion. "We should pick up the coconut leaves and coconut parts, small and large branches of mangrove trees, and broken swamp brush and small twigs and scatter these around to make it look like debris from the monsoon storm the week before."

The women congratulated themselves for being effective with details. After the finest detail was devised and carefully put in place, people scurried to get ready to leave.

"Please help yourselves to the left over rice. It will be equally distributed to all who stayed to help," Colonel Alvaro Gomez announced. He signed I O U receipts stipulating payment for service rendered to the guerrilla forces, payable by the government as soon as the war was over. He asked Mama Sid for two more sacks of rice to be doled out to every helping hand regardless of age, to men, women and children alike. An almost festive air floated over the tragedy of unwanted flight till nightfall came with its deep silence. All sound of receding paddling gave way to a total though unwanted abandonment of the open clearing on the riverbank.

Chapter 34—A Brief Investigation: A Change of Command

The Japanese patrol came five days after the rout. Greeted by a mysterious silence, they never found the guns. No sign of life lingered in the abandoned clearing, but a peculiar smell permeated the area though they could not distinguish it from the smell of mud in the surrounding swampland. No doubt there had been a mass exodus here but it had to be expected on the wake of a massive attempt to uproot people from their hiding place. Japanese soldiers came to confirm the disappearance of their commandant, Colonel Inuro Asaki, and his probable death at the hands of guerrilla forces, but they couldn't ascertain where he had fallen and how. The silence seemed sinister. Though they came to inflict punishment and revenge, they were wary and hesitant to take the fight into the impervious swamps.

"The Colonel must have gone deep into swampland against the warning of the *kempetai* and his subordinate officers," Major Takasaki speculated. "I'm certain he encountered guerrilla forces more familiar with swamp topography. They must have split the column, picked them out from the cover of the trees, and blocked their retreat."

"Why wouldn't he listen to *kempetai* warning at all?" Captain Akagi argued.

"You certainly are not unaware of the Colonel's temper. You heard him say he would teach those who opposed his will to respect his power. He said he would root them out of the swamps 'if it took spraying every single tree with bullets.' Haven't you heard him say that?" Mayor Takasaki reminded the young officer of the commandant's viciousness.

"But where are the guns and the trucks, and the machine guns?" The other lieutenants were unconvinced.

"It could be that while the commandant was engaged in the swamps, another unit of guerrilla men pulled the guns and the trucks from the unstable *Malabong* Bridge where the colonel had left them, drove them across the *Talubangi* bridge and on to unoccupied territory beyond *Vista Allegre* and south to barrio D*ancalan*." Captain Akagi also speculated.

"Yes, but if the colonel left some men to guard the guns, some of them may have died in defense. Where are their bodies? Where are the men? The other lieutenants were still unable to understand the mystery. After lengthy discussion, the officers decided that the guns were taken on the way from *Enclaro* to *Vista Allegre*. Yet if this were so, how could the column be routed in open farmland without the cover of trees? And where are the bodies of those who died in the conflict? Further speculation continued.

"Perhaps the commandant left the guns on the other side of the *Malabong* Bridge when he discovered that the bridge couldn't take their weight and he led the column on to the swamps in motorcycles. But where are the motorcycles now? And why did he take time to fortify the bridge? New lumber on it indicates he did so," another lieutenant said.

Major Takasaki decided this time Colonel Asaki had unwisely sacrificed not only his own life but also those of dozens under his command. Major Takasaki was most certain this was the case. The commandant had gone too far and got what he deserved. The brutal pig lost a whole column! Had he survived he would never have outlived the shame. To save face, he sacrificed so many under his command. What a victory for those whom he despised but underestimated, Major Takasaki silently concluded.

Surely, it was time for a more conservative defense tactic. Major Takasaki decided *Mang* Kari's place was the end of the line for him. He could not order his men into the swamps to meet the same fate. To save his own men from undue danger he could take some humbling.

The three lieutenants under his command anticipated his reluctance to wage as fierce a campaign as the old commandant did. They were ready to disobey his orders. They forged on deeper into the swampy terrain beyond the bend at *Mang* Kari's clearing. They tested the depth of the mud underneath the *nipa* groves. They were blowing up rubber boats to attempt crossing the river to the swamps across. By God, they would avenge the commandant's death!

The current was as strong as the day Delia paddled the Americans in. It would quickly take them to the other side, but not directly across. It would push the light, inflated boats perhaps half a kilometer across to the huge mangrove giants overhanging the river's edge. They were preparing to push the boats off the *nipa* grove; in fact, the current swiftly pushed one boat. Already, it drifted out of reach from the bank into the middle of the river. Machine gun fire from the mangrove shadows ripped the boat and two soldiers bloodied the water. The rest tried to swim back but the current carried them swiftly past the bend into the swampy area beyond the clearing. The Japanese soldiers at *Mang* Kari's clearing answered the machine gun fire, but they were too far away from the mangrove overhang to do any harm. The lieutenant who lost two of his men was furious and was ready to override Major Takasaki. The Major yelled his objection.

"Don't you men realize their extreme advantage? Only fools would want to meet the same fate the commandant's column obviously did. You have already lost two men. You don't know this terrain; guerrilla men do. They may even live here. You have to wait till the odds are in your favor. Here, you don't stand a chance. You would be playing right into their hands."

Though still very angry, the lieutenants heeded Major Takasaki's caution. They reluctantly pulled the boats in, but not before they thoroughly sprayed the other bank with more machine gun fire and sent several rounds from the 75mm guns that almost bogged down in barrio *Andulawan* and were slow to follow after. Once more Major Takasaki asserted his command.

"You are only wasting ammunition; you're not going to kill anyone by shooting in the dark."

"How do you know it will not damage their hiding places," one of the lieutenants contended.

"Is the unmeasurable damage worth the loss of ammunition? We have not received any more additions to our diminishing supply lately. My requests to *Bacolod* have not gotten any reply. Think and think well before your anger gets away with you. The commandant allowed his anger and his cruelty to overcome caution. Look where it got him. Obviously the guerrillas now receive better supply of arms from somewhere. They also successfully get some from our ambushed and abandoned troops. Where could the commandant's guns have gone? Have they simply vanished into thin air or have they been added to guerrilla hoard? We have to conserve our ammunition for the time when we need it to really defend ourselves."

The lieutenants reluctantly faced the truth about Major Takasaki. He's no show off. He doesn't blow his top as Colonel Asaki did. Obviously, he's no coward but a more prudent tactician. He's wise in his decisions and more deliberate about his commands.

In a way, though, the lieutenant was right. One of the two shots from the 75mm gun landed a few hundred meters from the *batel* anchored in the waterway close to the hideout. Major Takasaki's order to desist, though not unwise, came just in time to save the hideout from more destruction, an irony not uncommon in wartime. On the way back to the garrison, Major Takasaki skirted the *Malabong* Bridge, knowing it was still too unstable to sustain the large guns he carried. Again, he took the longer way to barrio *Andulawan.* The troops lingered around the barrio, but everything was quiet and deserted. Though the officers gave in to Major Takasaki's decision to return to *Kabankalan*, they were angry, frustrated and restive. "Someone has to pay for the missing guns and trucks and above all for the disappearance of the commandant. This loss is unacceptable. Something must be done," Captain Akagi insisted.

The feeling among the officers was that the swamps needed a blood bath and if the Major had no stomach for revenge, he must be replaced, the sooner, the better. Captain Masumi Akagi was most irate. He had a change of mind about Major Takasaki. Captain Akagi gathered the junior officers together and unloaded all his frustrations. "What was the trip to the outskirts of the swamps about if we weren't going to hunt and massacre the perpetrators? Why was the search too brief and abandoned so readily? If the old commandant himself had marched to look for the missing troops and the military equipment, he wouldn't have ordered a return without results. Loss of ammunition, indeed! What about loss of face, perhaps loss of purpose? So it's dangerous to go on foot into the swamps. So why doesn't the Major order gunboats and scour the swamp covered areas of the *Ilog* River? We certainly have the manpower and the superior arms to go into every nook and crony. We need to leave no stone unturned until the mysterious disappearance is explained to everyone's satisfaction."

To quell the unrest among his troops, Major Takasaki, against his better judgment, agreed to let Captain Akagi take a patrol to *Enclaro* to look for more answers to the unresolved mystery. After arriving at *Enclaro*, Captain Akagi lost no time to radio headquarters in *Bacolod* and report his misgivings. Though Captain Akagi found no answers either, headquarters in *Bacolod* immediately ordered another investigation and assigned a new commandant to relieve Major Takasaki of his command until the investigation was completed. Once more, Major Takasaki became second in command to another superior officer whose ethics duplicated those of the missing Colonel Inuro Asaki.

Chapter 35—The Pilot, the Navigator, and the Tail Gunner

In the past several days, God, how long had it been, three or four weeks, maybe? George had lost all sense of time; he didn't know what day of the week it was. Trying to count the days, he cut a long blade of *kogon* grass and folded a notch each day, but the blade had grown brown and brittle lately and the notches fell off the end. Maybe it had been a few days over a month now. Time couldn't be accurately accounted for. His wristwatch no longer worked. His legs ached from the brisk walk on pitchblack nights, the pace escalating into a trot or a run on rough trails as his eyes adjusted to the dark. The guide hacked a path through the undergrowth. Twigs lashed his arms, neck, face; the welts itched and burned at the touch. He couldn't stop, except when he or one of the two others fell from loss of balance or sheer exhaustion, or when the dawn caught up with them and etched their shadows on the hillside.

Going uphill sapped his energy and drained whatever was left of the coconut meal or the mong bean soup with green leaves floating on top. It didn't look too inviting, but he was often weak from hunger. Surprisingly, the greens in the soup tasted good, like spinach in a green salad, only wet. He was the only kid on the block who liked spinach. On the farm, his dad grew it for commercial sale and his mom insisted it was a good energy source. A few times, an eternity in between, he was served cold, steamed rice with a slice of salted fish on the side. Once, he even had a hardboiled egg. That didn't stay too long in the stomach, especially in the cold sting of an unforeseen rainfall. The rain blinded him and strong winds came with it. The fury of the wind blocked all other sound, separating him from the others. Blinded by its force, he had little sense of where he was going. Unrelenting, the rain poured for hours till he was drenched and chilled to the bone, but he had to move on or had to be prodded and pulled. As long as the dark held, he moved steadily, quietly, like a blind man on the prowl without a cane. When he was safely hidden during the day, the wind and rain sometimes abated, but the sun rose in blazing fury. Not a breeze stirred. High humidity drenched him with rancid perspiration just as much. His clothes stuck to the skin.

Dawn echoed with extraordinary sounds of wild life. He wished he could hit the birds in the air or lizards crawling by his feet with a stone and start a fire to roast them. The thought only made him famished. When the sun came up, he could hardly move a step farther. He was tucked beneath stacks of *nipa* leaves, hidden underneath mounds of coconut husks, pushed into holes covered with the long leaves of wild grass called *kogon,* or with freshly cut coconut fronds. Only when the guerrillas had cordoned off a place so that no one could approach them within five hundred meters were he and the others allowed out of their hiding places. Then they could stretch their legs, walk around, or lie down inside a hut, on woven mats of reed. Exhausted or hungry, they gave in to fatigue, their legs often too weak for continued use.

When the sun set and dark claimed the hills, they followed the same routine: briskly walking, or running away from motion or sound of any kind. It would have been a two-day walk in the flat plain where people planted rice, corn, or *camote*, (sweet yellow yam), or *cassava*, a root crop eaten with fish or an occasional fowl. That would be nothing short of suicide, knowing the Japanese were on the hunt and natives, interested in trading information for scraps of food, or freedom of a loved one, would perhaps chance upon their path of escape. So they were led on a long, circuitous route on the hills beyond the farms. The objective was to traverse a series of hills that circled the plains and then climb up high to the mountain source of the *Ilog* River. On the riverbed, a *banca* was waiting to be paddled swiftly downriver to the outskirts of the *Hacienda Luzuriaga*, two kilometers away from the abandoned Central Palma.

Days ago, he smelled so bad he embarrassed himself. His hair was matted, unkempt, and small bruises marked his arms, neck and face. When they finally got to the *banca,* he lay quietly beside Frank Defacio and Robert Coleman. With mounds of *nipa* and coconut leaves over them, they hardly knew whether it was day or night. They were distraught, too weak from hunger to speak.

At the time of the crash, people living in the area generously hid them. George had only a vague recollection of two women who rescued him and Frank and took them to their hut on a hillside. Not long after, some men brought Robert to join them. At the time Frank was badly wounded but the women helped to heal the wound with native remedies. George recalled being lowered into a deep, dark well for hours. He remembered how cold he was and how famished. At nightfall, he was brought out of the well. Having passed out, he couldn't figure how. When he regained consciousness, he shook with exhaustion. He was fed with *saba,* banana that was hard and filling, a variety he had never eaten before.

Too exhausted to walk, he was put in a jute sack, slung on the back of a guerrilla soldier and carried away from the site of the crash. Still suffering from his wound, Frank couldn't walk. Guerrillas carried him on their backs a few more days. Sufficiently recovered, Robert and he walked with their rescuers. At daybreak, he was hidden away from the others so any chance of conversation was remote. He rested uneasily, unable to visualize the real danger of capture. Sometimes, he could hear dogs barking and almost immediately hear gunfire. Once, the barking dogs ran too close. Dead silence came after and he lay quietly, speculating that someone close was somehow guarding him. At times he could hear that someone breathe. When dusk rolled in, he would hear motion in the tall grass next to his hiding place. Then a shape outlined in the dusk approached and whispered.

"Get up, please; we're ready to go. Follow me."

When he was unable to move, a hand was extended to lift him up and prod him on. He knew that Frank and Robert were not far from him because when he stopped and was told to sit down for a while, the two caught up with him. They were handed whatever there was to eat: banana, rice or something usually wrapped in banana leaves. They were offered green coconuts with holes cut at the top. They drank the juice and the tender coconut meat, scraped when the coconuts were split, tasted bland. After they got used to it, the taste improved. They could hardly finish drinking when they were asked to move again; then prodding hands separated them once more.

In hiding, the silence was as difficult to bear as the exhaustion from walking or running. At dark, they moved on. When a cock crowed somewhere and the first signs of dawn filtered in the hills, he was pushed into a hole again, hidden in a thicket, or covered with leaves. Sleep was a welcome renewal. He would wake only because of hunger or thirst. As soon as he moved, a hand would thrust something wrapped in banana leaf or a coconut bowl with soup in it. With a hint of danger, he would hear a soft shssssssss. He would lay quiet for hours until he discerned some motion close by. It was a relief to see the dark drift in; then walking, trotting, or running until dawn was another night as punishing as the workouts designed for recruits in an army training camp. Only, there was no yelling sergeant here, just someone's anxious, helping hands that pulled or prodded.

All roads and pathways on the plains were teeming with Japanese soldiers. They had to be taken to the hills beyond the town of *Isabela,* to the mountains above to circle back behind *Kabankalan,* one of the biggest Japanese garrisons in southern Negros. The Japanese didn't anticipate this move. They were chased but never found. Going forward, circling, or retracing routes, they had traveled a distance of one hundred and sixty-eight kilometers from the crash.

The guerrillas were careful to avoid detection, even by friendly eyes. The first two days were the hardest to endure. After the initial ordeal, the routine became commonplace, except once or twice when the dogs came very, very close, a warning that capture was imminent. At some distance, an exchange of gunfire told him there was a fight of some kind. That time, no hand had prodded him to move despite the complete darkness that descended.

He didn't have an inkling of where they were being taken. He only felt a sense of urgency when the guerrillas knew the Japanese were too close on their heels. But this day, after the long *banca* ride, they ran a long distance along the narrow dikes of waterlogged rice fields. They had arrived on the outskirts of the *Hacienda Luzuriaga.* For the first time, they ran in broad daylight; their guides made no effort to hide. As they approached the compound, fieldhands met them. They did not prod but lifted them gently, an arm on each side, carried them into one of the bedrooms in the main house of the *hacienda* and deposited them on reed mats and *kapok*-filled pillows with the softness of cotton. They slept the rest of the day till early evening when they were awakened for a big meal with their host.

Assisted by fieldhands, he was first in line to bathe. He was ushered into a four by four feet enclosure with walls of thatched palm. Water in a large earthen jar sat at one corner and a small tin can lay beside it. Given a strange smelling soap, but soap thank God, he scrubbed himself vigorously to get rid of a baked-in body odor. He felt unbelievably refreshed as he scooped tin can after tin can of lukewarm water and poured it over his head, and on his body. A coconut shell filled with fresh coconut oil was within his reach. He was told to rub coconut oil on his bruises. With oil on the cuts, he could no longer feel their sting, but he traced the welts that stayed on.

He accepted a loose silk shirt that had seen better days. Faded, it was still soft to the touch. The pants were loose. He tied it with a belt of braided cloth lying close. They made the pants stay on. He wished his own ragged clothes could be washed and ironed. When they had all finished bathing, he met his navigator, Frank Defacio, and was amazed to see he had lost several pounds in the last three or four weeks. He wondered if he was just as skinny. His gaze shifted to Robert Coleman, his gunner. Days of wordless suffering lined his face. To Start with, he was heavier than the two of them. Running, trotting, and even walking must have been unbearable because of his weight. Strange, but in the three or four weeks they had walked or ran together, they had hardly spoken a word among themselves. Just now they found their tongue and, unashamed, they hugged each other and cried. For the first time, they realized they had been taken to a place of greater safety, for now they were allowed more freedom to move about and talk freely.

Chapter 36—The *Hacienda* Luzariaga

The *Hacienda Luzuriaga* is one of many land holdings owned by wealthy *mestizos,* half-breed heirs of old guard Spaniards who married Filipinas or kept them as concubines. Some of these families own almost all the land around the *sugar centrals* (sugar mills and refineries). The landowners are usually respected for their wealth but are looked down on as bastards bred by women who yield to the foreigner, not always out of love but for property and prestige. They are cut off from their own people, though if they are generous, they are acknowledged as heaven-sent providers of work and opportunity for the less fortunate to get beyond the drudgery that is the lot of the poor.

Don Mauricio Luzuriaga, *Tio* Mauring to fieldhands, tenants and friends, is landed. He's accepted because he married his chief tenant's daughter, Nora, the prettiest native woman in the area. She bore him three daughters whose beauty is legendary. The Eurasian mixture sharpened the features and mellowed the color line into a stunning tone. Dark hair on creamy skin, a thorough blending of white and brown, is clearly nature's best handiwork. No make up is needed to accent an already perfect hue. Leticia, the oldest daughter, nineteen years old, is tall, slim and shapely. She's a head taller than most Filipinas and is two and five inches taller than her younger sisters, Laura, and Maria Elena,

During the Japanese occupation of Central Palma, the Luzuriagas fled south to *Hinoba-an*, way beyond Japanese occupied territory. Deprived of the comforts they had been accustomed to, the girls learned to wait on their parents as their servants did before the war, but Dona Nora took care of the necessary comforts in the household. A few months before they were asked to host the escaping American airmen, they returned to their *hacienda* considerably humbled. Dona Nora passed away a year before. The youngest child and the only boy, Carlito, died of cerebral malaria fever not long after.

Guerrilla intelligence took the Americans to the *Hacienda Luzuriaga* for several reasons. They could be better fed there. Tio Mauring wasted no time planting rice instead of sugar cane. Also, the family could speak English as well as Spanish or *Ilongo*, the native language in southern Negros. Language exchange made the airmen less frustrated, less nervous. They were expected to join six others at this *hacienda* a week before but the guerrilla unit that rescued the six others had not been very successful at eluding the Japanese who chased them day and night for over four weeks. After a change in plans, Guerrillas fortunately spirited them to the swamps by *banca*. They await their arrival there so they could all be transported by *batel* to *Maricalum*.

When the three airmen had scrubbed themselves clean, they realized that their hair was a matted mess. Robert felt sorry for the younger boys.

"I used to give my kids haircuts. If we can get hold of scissors," he said, "I can do it for you two. Let's go back to the main house and ask for scissors."

They marched to the house and ran into *Kapitan* Almanzur and *Tio* Mauring going up the stairs to the house. They introduced themselves formally as George Miller, the pilot, Frank Defacio, the navigator, and Robert Coleman, the tail gunner. One look at them and *Kapitan* Almanzur knew what they needed before they could get up enough nerve to state their request.

"Yes, there would be time enough for a haircut before supper time; we can wait."

Kapitan Almanzur made them feel welcome. The smell of cooking drifted from the kitchen and he, too, got hungry.

"The meal can wait. You must have a haircut before you get ready for a *banca* ride to the swamps," he said.

Tio Mauring called for a barber among his help. After their haircut, the airmen joined their hosts at the dining area. The *Kapitan* was glad to make their acquaintance. Except with the other Americans he rescued, he had not spoken much with people for whom English was a native language. He couldn't say much while they were on the run. He was proud to use the tongue. Though the flow of words was slow and deliberate, it was not broken.

"Hey, Joe," he addressed George with the name associated with all Americans, though George had introduced himself clearly earlier.

"What would you like to eat? Do you like rice and chicken?"

"How about some fries and hamburger?" Frank answered for George and all three of them laughed.

"What are fries? I don't think we grow them on this island, and as for ham, *Tio* Mauring has plenty of pigs. Maybe the girls can make some pork *adobo* instead.

They were all sorry for the joke at the captain's expense so Robert explained rather lamely that fries are potatoes fried in very high heat.

I haven't seen potatoes since before the war started. We used to import them from Hawaii." The *Kapitan* apologized. "But we have sweet potatoes that can be cut thin and fried in high heat. They'll taste just as good, if not better."

"I'm sure sweet potatoes will be fine," George assured him. "Just about anything will do. Fried chicken's excellent. I'm not so sure about *adobo*. I haven't had that in years."

Again, all three started to laugh at another joke they couldn't resist, but *Kapitan* Almanzur jovially joined in the laughter.

"What a shame," Leticia said with a smile.

She walked in carrying a pitcher of young coconut meat soaked in its own water and sweetened with brown sugar.

"We have pork meat marinated in lemon mixed with garlic and shrimp paste. We had been cooking pork *adobo,* but if you don't care for it, I can serve more fried chicken."

The men offered their excuses all at once. They never expected such graciousness though tinged with sarcasm. It served them right to be cut to size. They were all gawking. She wore her hair flowing to the waistline and her slim figure was draped in a long, plaid, wrap-around skirt. She had a thin blouse on, organza embroidered with bright colored flowers. The sleeves went below the elbows in the traditional *Maria Clara* style. They didn't hear her come in; though she was barefoot, she wasn't self-conscious about it.

"I hope you're thirsty, and if you're hungry and can't wait for the meal, the coconut meat will fill you up before supper." She spoke in slow but perfect English.

"May I help you with the pitcher?" George eagerly offered as he approached close, his eyes glued to her figure with admiration undisguised.

"Oh, no. I can manage. Besides, Papa will be angry if I put you to work."

Embarrassed at their laughter about food, George was all apology. He moved toward her to help her with the pitcher she was extending.

"It's no problem, really," she heard him say.

He moved quickly and as she tried to avoid his outstretched hand, the pitcher fell from hers. She felt clumsy but she could not quiet the hot flash that traveled from her hand to her heart.

Why did he have to move so fast?

She was unable to move her foot from the puddle that was the coconut milk.

Deftly, in the same movement he did to grab the handles in the plane's cockpit, George reached for the ladle sticking out of the pitcher, but, unable to bear the weight, the wooden ladle broke. Aware of a greater danger, he dived to catch the falling object sailing in the air like a football passed to a receiver attempting to catch the ball while desperately trying to maintain balance. He caught it as it fell close to her head. Thank God her foot slid on the now slippery bamboo floor underneath her. The pitcher missed her head by inches, but as he caught it with one hand, he tried to shield her with the other. His weight twisted her completely off balance. Now she couldn't tell if the pain was the same flash as it traveled from her heart instantly to her legs and her foot. He tried to pull her up as gently as he could but he saw the grimace on her face now very close to his.

Did she not flash that indescribably inviting smile an instant ago? How could he have misunderstood it? How could it turn to revulsion in a flash? Overwhelmed by his own emotion, he couldn't see her pain. Unable to stand on her feet, she fell like a limp towel into his arms. He caught her; the contact made him dizzy. He cradled her tenderly when he understood the source of her pain.

"Good God! What have I done? What can I do?

"You can set me down on a chair, please?" she whispered softly. "Something is wrong with my right foot."

He was all attention, but he couldn't manage to pull the apology from his throat. He pulled her skirt as he gently rubbed the ankle with his hand.

The pain was unbearable. She put her hands on his head gently. She did not want him to misunderstand her a second time. "Please don't do that; it hurts to the touch. You can call my sister. She would know what to do."

"Oh, I will. I will. But can I do anything to make it feel better?

"My sister is in the kitchen preparing supper. If you help me up, I can walk with you there."

"Let me take you there this instant."

He could not quell the quaver in his voice. He lifted her up as if she were weightless. She put her arms around his shoulders and laid her head next to his. Her cheeks touched his so softly he would remember the gesture for years. He had not felt so alive in all the time they raced from one hiding place to another in the hills, to the river, and now to this unknown haven. His heart beat in joy and agony at the same time. The anxiety brought by the need to escape did not matter at this moment. He no longer cared what would happen next. Here in his arms was all the reason for life. He saw the edge of a blush on the face next to his. Though they had just met, he was certain the circumstances held little importance for her as well. He knew the moment he held her she felt the whole weight of his feelings and couldn't struggle against it. This magic of instant recognition, an intensely irresistible force, was as compelling as the war he fought in. The war negated all certainty except this one. In a universe of ambiguity, this kind of certainty comes only once, and never again, no matter how many lifetimes they'd live. George's tenderness was a magnet that drew Leticia to a place she'd never been, but a place she knew she dared not miss despite all her resistance.

He took her to the kitchen where she said her sister prepared food. A thought flashed. It brought him back to harsh reality. In the back of his head the thought of how much people had sacrificed to protect them flashed again and again. Those in the hills gave up food so they could be fed. No matter how little they gave, the people who served them did without. Did his own hunger make him callous and indifferent to those people's sacrifice? Those who hid them risked their own lives as they exposed themselves to the danger of discovery. He hadn't even spoken to the young man who had helped them, pulled and prodded them when they had no energy left to move on. Where was he now? The enormity of his own insensitivity struck him just now when they were attended to so graciously and fed so extravagantly.

It embarrassed Leticia to admit him into the kitchen. The chicken *adobo* smelled good, but she couldn't hide the dirt stove, clay pots, and kerosene cans storing water from the river. There was no plumbing here. Eight kerosene cans zealously kept from rust lined the wall nearest the stairs. Water was carried up to the hut in these cans and was stored for the day's use. Polished coconut shells attached to wooden handles were constantly dipped in and out of these cans either for washing or cooking. Drinking water came from large tanks better sealed, placed directly under the eaves to catch clear, rainwater. Even so, Leticia was careful to serve only fresh coconut juice for fear the rainwater wouldn't be clean enough for their guests to drink. Little did she know that for the last four weeks the Americans often had to catch rainfall on broad banana leaves to drink.

Frank, carrying the offending object still half filled with the grated coconut meat, followed the two to the kitchen.

Laura stopped in her tracks when she saw her sister in George's arms.

"Put her down at once," she demanded.

She was afraid her father would see how forward a daughter in his house was to allow such intimate contact, no matter how kind the intent. A servant girl ran to fetch a chair and George reluctantly surrendered the warmth that enclosed his heart. He couldn't understand the impropriety, but he didn't want to offend his host.

Laura soaked a rag with the dipper, squeezed the water out, and tried to wrap the swollen foot around the ankle. Her hands were trembling. Seeing her agitation, Frank held the trembling hand and gently helped her finish wrapping the foot.

"It'll swell a lot."

He found her as stunningly beautiful as her sister though she seemed surrounded by a different aura. Her hair wasn't flowing. It was carefully braided.

"Not if we find something more soothing,"

She took a *bolo* from the kitchen shelf and handed it to the servant girl as she blurted her urgency.

"The old remedy," she said."

The girl seemed to know the rest of the unspoken command. In what seemed to Laura an eternity, Lina, rushed back with the heart of a banana trunk, smooth and cool to the touch. Again, Frank held Laura's' hands as she took the rag off, encased the foot in the cool banana trunk and wrapped the rag around it. He, too, felt deeply moved when she didn't withdraw his touch. Leticia was crying softly now, holding on to the solicitous arms once more cradling her. Her sister knew the pain didn't cause the tears. It came from an instant disquieting recognition that both of them were drawn to these men who after this evening would be gone out of their lives. Forever?

Tio Mauring grew impatient. He wanted to know what was keeping the supper from being served. He noted with chagrin how the young men hovered around his daughters like sheep dogs. Uncomfortable with the observation, he was beginning to see something as ridiculous as the romantic Filipino tales of "love at first sight," played in his movie houses before the war. His wife chose the titles and would cry over the ridiculously silly and sentimental plots that now seemed to be played out under his nose, in his own house!

Outrage yielded to a sense of protectiveness. He did not dare express his disapproval while he, Almanzur, and the older of the three Americans, the gunner, the one called Robert, were engaged in animated conversation that he only half-listened to. Though he plied them for necessary information, neither Almanzur nor Robert could at the moment tell him where they would be taken next. He was only assured that they had not been so generously taken cared of anywhere else before his hospitality.

Everything seemed to move in slow motion at dinnertime. *Tio* Mauring was certain the young men were famished but they hardly touched the food. They were hanging on to every word his daughters spoke, paying no attention to anything else. Their eyes were riveted to his two older daughters and they were most reluctant to get up from the dinner table to be ushered to their sleeping quarters. When the house was settling down for the evening rest, his oldest daughter pleaded while the younger sister listened in dumb dismay.

"Papa," she began. "We have always tried to be good, obedient daughters. We have never asked you for anything you were unable to give."

The voice betrayed the weight of the need that staggered the old man. He managed to answer brusquely,

"What is it *hija* (What is it, child?)"

"Papa, could you please ask *Kapitan* Almanzur if we could feed his friends one more day before they leave? They look like they could use food and rest before they move on."

He couldn't answer, but he didn't have to ask young Almanzur who certainly also took in the swollen foot, red rimmed eyes, and the sheepish, lovelorn look of the young men. However, there was an urgency that couldn't be postponed. They had to move on or risk being found by the Japanese. If they stayed, they would jeopardize the safety of others waiting to be transported beyond harm's way.

"*Hija* (daughter), surely you don't realize what you're asking. Even Almanzur doesn't have the authority to grant your request. He's only following orders from his superiors."

"Ask him, anyhow. Papa, please."

Kapitan Almanzur was eavesdropping at the doorway and was already wrestling with the issue in his own mind. He knew the danger of the delay but his heart warmed up to the anguish in the young woman's voice. He thought of his own wife when she would plead for him to stay for another day or even just a few hours more before he would leave for a mission. His heart yielded to the force of love.

"Listen, *Nanay* Sidra is also hiding six others in her house in the swamps. *Manong* Alvaro is still hatching up a plan to get everyone together, including these three, and perhaps run them by night in a *Batel* and take them under cover of darkness to several points till they get to where they could be picked up by a submarine. Not far from here, the river forks directly toward its mouth in the sea. It'll take us only a day on foot to join them but it may take more than a day to go in an outrigger *banca* because we couldn't be paddled in daylight. We'll make up for lost time by going on foot instead. Just prepare them as though they're leaving early tomorrow so the tenants cannot spread the news of a longer stay. I'll take them after the sun goes down tomorrow. Girls, not a minute more, okay?"

Leticia motioned to *Kapitan* Almanzur; she tried to get up to give him a grateful hug and a kiss. He bent down and whispered in her ear.

"They need good food for a day more, and the best of care you can give. After, they have to rough it up again. Who knows when they can get the next good meal? Already, I see unspoken gratitude. But hide them from anyone's notice. Though we think they're safe, the Japanese aren't far from here. We can never guess what they'll do if they're aware of what we're hiding."

She pressed her gratitude into his hands and nodded her assent. Her sister, too, bade goodbye with tears in her eyes. The old man sent *Kapitan* Almanzur away with a promise that if he ever needed help, or food, anything, it would be extended without hesitation.

* * *

The next day intruded with a premonition of gloom. A strong westerly wind, the *Amihan*, announced a change in the season. Disturbed, the old man sensed the danger ahead. The Americans must leave for as the wind gets stronger, travel by sea in a *batel* with six others plus a native crew would be hazardous once they get to the open sea at the southern tip of the island. Time to leave was imperative, yet time was what they couldn't do without. Helplessly they grasped at the heart's exchange, beating a warm tenderness that completely blotted out all awareness of danger.

Tio Mauring also sensed his daughters' helplessness. The look of despair in Leticia's eyes he had long ago seen in her mother's when her father forbade her to entertain his courtship. Nora had to choose between love of him and loyalty to her family. Opting to be with him, she was disowned as a daughter, and though her father was a tenant serving in his employ, she couldn't see her family ever again. She knew she broke her mother's heart, but she couldn't deny her need, for when he offered his name and everything that went with it, she couldn't refuse him. He was as protective as her father and his solicitude and tenderness drained her resistance.

Time stopped when she died. He lived only for the joy of raising three girls as lovely as she. Now for the two older ones, he had to acknowledge the need for what he had deeply felt: complete attachment to someone who filled his consciousness beyond anyone else's understanding. How could he deny them what had been the fabric of his existence? Had Nora been alive still, she would have understood her daughters' plight. For her, he would have given up anything, even that which now sustained him. The old man realized demand for this sacrifice was inevitable. Deep in his heart he knew it had to come one day, but with foreigners who can't even stay, who had to go back to a demanding war? What irony!

His love for Nora spilled to her daughters. Despite the danger, he had to give them one more day. The awareness of what he had to risk to extend what they needed seared his heart. This sacrifice made him see clearly what Nora had to give up for him. He missed her generosity, affection, selfless devotion, and surrender to his will without a trace of humiliation. In the household, in the entire *hacienda*, anyone who whispered about his origin was summarily, though kindly, dismissed. She disarmed those who were doubtful of his stature. She detected the hypocritical. She kept a close eye on his decisions about his tenants and with the utmost subtlety persuaded him to keep this one or let that one go. She was so unerring in her observations that he depended on her judgment without being conscious that he deferred to it. She was so close to him; he couldn't distinguish her breath from his own. Now she lives only through these lovely incarnations of her spirit, her equally lovely daughters. Must he lose them too?

Thank God for the war! If they survive, these men would be taken back to it. Would they come back to claim his daughters when it is over? He felt like the Old Testament king who knowingly sent a husband to the thick of battle, so he could possess a wife who, branded as sinful, nevertheless would spend her life in his arms and keep him content.

"Ah, David, David, you, too, lost the gift of human kindness because you coveted the breath of love; but God forgave you. Will he forgive me if deep in my heart I don't want these men back? I don't have Nora's sense of self-sacrifice. She would want them back for her daughters' sake. Oh, God! How I miss her."

The old man retired to his room bereft of the exhilaration he felt earlier in the day. He extended himself to these strangers. He didn't anticipate a loss because of them. He rejected the thought that they could take away what was left of her.

"Nora, Nora," he moaned in pain. Please, please, don't let me lose you a second time.

Chapter 37—The Unintended Betrayal

Tio Basilio's son, Cresencio, ran all night. Unerringly, his feet felt their way, knew where to lead the body without the brain's consent. He had walked this way in daylight so many times but more deliberately, careful to seek out the same guards he bribed with stolen chickens stewed by his mother and sealed into preserving jars with the precious wax from the honey bees in the lot next to the *bodega,* the storehouse for grain. He came home with a fat lip or loose teeth, or half-closed eyes after the guards roughed him up when the stew was devoured. Sometimes, he also carried a flask of *tuba* he offered with the chicken meal. The drink made the guards tipsy enough to ignore him as he stole into the prison square and out of there before they could lay hands on him.

The corrugated tin roof and walls raised the temperature so hot it baked the earth floor. The corners were damp with urine and were lined with holes covered with coconut leaves to hide what little the prisoners disposed of. The smell always half-suffocated him. He had to quickly do what he came for or the guards would drag him out of there and hit him on the stomach or on the head with the butt of their rifles. Wherever the rifle hit, blood would ooze; it always infuriated the guards even more. He would roll on the ground as if he, too, were drunk, but he managed to roll under the barbed wire fence which tore into his skin but saved him from more hits from the rifle butts. The guards would double over with laughter, amazed at the desperate feat. They would wave him off and yell in broken English.

"Come back—bring more chicken. You no come back, maybe you no see your papa san no more."

A few times, lizard meat or dog or cat's meat skillfully sautéed with garlic and ginger before boiling could pass for chicken. A couple of times, the guards would sniff suspiciously and pull him by the ear or press his mouth into a hollow before they smashed it with a rifle butt. At times he was only half conscious when they would let him be close to his father. He would whisper for the old man to hug him and reach into his pocket for steamed rice in young coconut leaves woven into balls. His father would toss the green toys to another prisoner who would throw them under the wooden bench that passed for a bunk. There they would lie, out of sight of the guards who avoided getting near the offending smell of the prisoners' quarters. Later, the rice would be meticulously, grain by grain, divided among all the men who were just skin and bones.

Whenever the guerrilla bands attempted to harass the Japanese forces at the garrison in *Binalbagan*, ten prisoners were eliminated for every Japanese soldier shot dead or wounded. Since the B-29 crash, more soldiers were dispatched to *Binalbagan* from central *Murcia*, about eighty kilometers away. Every day a large contingent scoured the hills, captured more hostages or killed them at will to frighten their families into informing against their own people. After they killed too many hostages, people knew better than to trade information. Though desperate, they realized the Japanese couldn't be trusted to bargain straight, so they either joined the guerrilla units or supported them with their silence.

Cresencio had not been anywhere near the prison cell for weeks. He didn't even know if his father was shot or had somehow survived. He knew enough to stay away. No bribe would work after the successful hiding of the Americans raked the Japanese pride. Gosh, he knew about the Americans at the *hacienda*. He cut the banana trunk for his sister, Lina, who told him about the golden haired one who held the senorita Leticia in his arms while the dark-haired one held her sister, Laura's hand and bandaged Leticia's sprained ankle. Lina also found out the Americans would stay longer, perhaps another day. She had been ordered to cut more lemon grass and gather achuete fruit to season pork into appetizing dishes. Melon rind had to be candied into dessert overnight. Why all this fuss if the guests weren't staying? She made her brother swear not to tell anyone what she knew, but it took him no longer than sunset to make up his mind. He calculated the risk. He had seen the legendary *Kapitan* Almanzur with *Tio* Mauring.

He would push a tough bargain: information for the release of his father. They could take him in exchange for his father because he knew where to lead them and if he took them to the *hacienda*, surely the *Kapitan* Almanzur had enough men and guns to ambush the Japanese. It would be an even fight.

At dusk, he told his sister he would be gone for a day. If his services were needed, she should say he went to barrio *Andulawan*, to visit his cousin Manuel to ask him if they could, with *Tio* Mauring's permission, join the guerrilla band *Kapitan* Almanzur commanded.

The next day was quiet at the *hacienda*. True to their word, the girls kept the men in and plied them with food and coconut drink. Robert cut the *Camote*, delicious yellow yam, into thin strips and the girls and their young men fried them in high heat into the desired crispness. The girls were full of questions. Before the war, where did they come from? Why were they flying in this part of the world when no other planes like the one they crashed in had come so far?

George was first to oblige with an explanation. He told them he was born in Lodi, California and he went to the local high school. After high school, he was admitted to Loyola University for a degree in Law but shifted to Engineering at his father's urging. He was conscripted into the air force at the start of the war and was sent to Davis Monthan Air Force base in Tucson, Arizona for training a year before his first mission.

Why were they shot down in this part of the world? That's a long story that has to do with the history of the entire B-29 program. George was not at liberty to discuss why and how they crash-landed in Negros but Leticia was partly right. The Philippines was never considered a route for the B-29s. But while these super-fortresses were used to hit targets in Japan, a far more important event was taking place some 1500 miles away—the invasion of Saipan in the Marianas. B-29s carried out the first attack from the Marianas, hitting Japanese sub pens in the Truk Atoll. Some one hundred eleven B-29s left the Marianas to bomb a target—the Musashimo aircraft factory in Tokyo.

George continued to describe his background.

"Ludi is farming county. It's not unlike this *hacienda*, except that my parents have fruit orchards and vegetable farms instead of rice or sugar cane fields. I have two brothers. My older brother died during the attack at Pearl Harbor. His ship, the USS Arizona, was sunk at the harbor in Hawaii. My younger brother is in Australia; I don't know exactly where. My only sister is older than both of us. Her husband would have enlisted too, but the army rejected him because he limps from rheumatoid arthritis. Mom keeps lighting candles in church for my younger brother and me. My older brother's death had nearly devastated her and my dad."

"Are you catholic?" Leticia asked. Thank God, we may have something important in common.

"Oh, Yes, I was an altar boy in Ludi and Loyola University is a catholic school. I don't know if my mother's candles have kept me alive so far, or if I am just lucky, or if I was spared because God meant for me to meet you."

"All of the above," Robert interrupted. "And to those also add because he means for you to be out of here, back to base in Australia into another B-29 to win the war. I'm not so sure we could have survived if you hadn't been quick witted to maneuver us to safety. Thank God for young brains like yours. I mean it, George; I'm glad to be alive."

"Amen," said Frank. "My mother does not light candles, but I'm sure she prays as hard for my safety in a Lutheran church in St Joseph, Missouri. My dad's a minister there. I have two younger sisters two or three years older than you are. My mother wrote me once that all three of them work in a munitions factory making torpedoes for submarines. It would be a splendid coincidence if we were picked up by a sub carrying torpedoes they have helped to make. You may be wondering how an Italian can be a Lutheran minister. My father is a minister but not Italian. He adopted me when I was just a baby. Later, he allowed me to use my birth parents' name.

Tio Mauring rushed into the room half dragging Lina by the arm. Tears of protest made her inarticulate when she was made to answer questions. The old man told them what he had uncovered.

Cresencio had disappeared. No doubt he had gone to bargain for his father's life and put the lives of the guests in jeopardy. All of them, even his girls, must leave before the Japanese arrive. Central Palma is further than they attempt to go under ordinary circumstances, but with the Americans there, it's likely, in fact really certain, they would come to the *hacienda* and engage the guerrilla forces.

Chapter 38—From the *Hacienda* to the Swamps

The distant drone of an airplane confirmed *Tio* Mauring's suspicions. Travel by foot would be unimaginable with the girls along. He had asked for expert rowers on *bancas* without outriggers. Outriggers would be clumsy. If it would be necessary to hide into a narrow waterway to avoid bring spotted from the air, *Bancas* without outriggers would be more manageable. *Tio* Mauring had already anticipated the girls' needs.

"I made Lina wrap a change of clothes in a bundle for the three of you and she threw in the Americans' uniforms already washed and ironed the night before."

"Who'll paddle us, Papa?"

"I'm paying the paddlers double rations of *bugas* or *mais* (rice or corn). Don't worry about anything. There's no time to change. You need to run to the river. A *banca* is waiting. I sent yesterday's leftover food and water and the paddlers will pile bundles of *nipa* palm leaves over everyone for cover."

Two men at each end of the *banca* and two more at the middle paddled in silence. They understood that the lives of their cargo as well as theirs were at stake. Movement in the *banca* was tricky; a delicate balance had to be maintained. Twice within the hour, the paddlers had to shift their own weight, careful not to tip over. Stopping to rest was out of the question; even shifting positions wasn't wise. The girls were tucked into the men's arms and Robert's eyes filled up as he cradled the youngest, Maria Elena. Except for hair color and slightly darker skin, she looked and felt like his daughter.

"Please, God," the girl breathed into his face, "Please keep my father safe."

"I'm almost certain my own daughter back home is praying for the same thing," Robert said under his breath. I was about to add that information to Frank's statement before your father rushed in. My wife, daughter, and two sons live in Royal oak, Michigan, a suburb of Detroit. My wife's parents live two blocks away and often baby-sit for my kids while she teaches for a Community College. You remind me so much of my daughter."

"*Inday*, (honey)," one of the paddlers interrupted in *Ilongo*. "You have to keep your conversation very low. Perhaps it would even be better to keep quiet altogether. We can't risk being heard, especially since you speak in English. Also, it takes away from our concentration."

Maria Elena translated for Robert. He apologized. All communication ended, except for the quiet exchange of their hearts beating the joy of being together and in each other's arms. They ached from the pressure of lying on the same side for what seemed forever until the girls pleaded for the paddlers to get into the nearest waterway alongside the riverbank so they could shift positions without tipping the *banca* over.

The paddlers shifted direction and the *banca* barely hugged the riverbank when the drone of airplanes got louder and nearer. The *banca* didn't have the chance to get into the cover of the waterway so the paddlers went straight for the *nipa* palms along the bank. Not much protection, but at least they would not be visible from the air. The plane swooped down low and strafed all the other small *bancas* desperately trying to get to some protection. One of the paddlers jumped to one side of the *banca* and pushed as hard as he could into a ticket of *nipa* palms. There was no question of tipping now; the *banca* was supported on each side by low-lying *nipa* fronds.

As the plane swished by, bullets hit the shore and tore into the vegetation that clogged the riverbank. *Nipa* trunks inches away fell with the spray of bullets, completely blanketing the *banca* and burying it from view with the debris. An airplane circled over them a second time, but seeing nothing, it went on to spew its burden of death elsewhere. Call it luck or the answer to prayers; surely, believers would say, the act of a benevolent and watchful God. How else could the situation be explained? War is insane. Within its context, life was cheap. At any time it could be snuffed. Existence was a fragile thread that tangled into inexplicable incidents without rational connection. Religious faith provided the only comfortable rationalization; it demanded a complete trust in the power of God. At a time of extreme danger over which no one had the ability to control, to doubt God's omniscience was to face a blank, bleak wall of despair. The girls clung to the men even more, hoping that God in his wisdom would decree that together they would outlive this danger.

After the airplanes disappeared, the men surveyed the damage. The *banca* had been spared, but the water was red with blood. The paddler who pushed the *banca* into the *nipa* grove was hit. Thank God only a flesh wound on the arm, but bad enough to need a tourniquet. Laura acted promptly. She pulled a cotton petticoat underneath her long skirt and tore the fringes into long strips. Frank took a *bolo* lying at his feet, hacked at *nipa* trunks, cut strips a foot in length, pressed them tightly around the arm, took the strips Laura had prepared and tied them around the arm to stop the bleeding. George put the paddler's hat on his head and pulled it far down to hide his face and give-away blond hair. He took command. Once more the rest had to lie down inside the *banca* to maintain balance. George took the long paddle, stuck it into the mud and pushed the *banca* off the bank. The wounded paddler sat at George's feet telling him what to do. He shut his eyes in pain and George, in awe of the man's silent determination to endure pain, paddled in his stead. He automatically responded to the rhythm of the rest of the paddlers. He paddled to get to the point where the river forked and meet the people who would take them to the guerrilla hideout where the rest of his crew were waiting.

On the main river, the *bancas* that had been strafed drifted with the current. The lifeless bodies of those hit during the strafing hung on the sides or on the outriggers. No one in these *bancas* was spared. Men, women, and children on their way somewhere would never get there. The men paddled close to the riverbank not only to avoid the horrendous sight, but also to get into the *nipa* grove lining the banks in case the airplanes returned.

Kapitan Almanzur knew of the flight of the girls and the Americans. The progress of the *banca* was monitored by two of Procopio's men. The two appeared on the riverbank. They had been ready to relieve the paddlers, but the airplanes kept them from advancing to their aid. They chased the *banca* on land and when they caught up with it, they dove from the shore and came up just as George lifted the paddle with weary arms. Their heads bobbed out of the water; one man held on to George's paddle and pointed the *banca* toward the bank. George was too exhausted to offer any resistance. What now? He wondered. Surely, these are not informers.

The injured paddler recognized the intruders and identified them as guerrilla soldiers. "*Kapitan* Almanzur assigned us to track you and help you. Just give us time to take off our wet clothes. We'll take over the paddling."

Without further delay the *banca* moved fast and finally arrived at the spot where the river forked. Though it was only five o'clock, it was already dark. There was no more need to hide inside the *banca*. After half an hour of complete silence, they heard with alarm the lapping of more paddles. A large outrigger *banca* came alongside the one they paddled. With a sigh of relief, *Kapitan* Almanzur's men recognized the paddlers of the approaching *banca*. They were Colonel Alvaro Gomez's men looking for the Americans. *Kapitan* Almanzur sent a radio message that they were being delivered in a *banca* without outriggers. The girls had to board the larger *banca* so the Americans lifted them quickly into the hull.

Shortly after, everybody, including Colonel Alvaro's men, got hungry. Leticia opened the two tin pails her dad provided. Even men in the smaller *banca* shared all the food and water. Energized, the men paddled in synchronized motion. Eight men wielded paddles expertly to the rhythm of a tune one of them was softly humming. Soon the girls were almost asleep in the arms of the weary Americans. The paddlers joked around in a language the Americans didn't understand. Though they spoke in undertones, the girls heard and understood the jabber. Curious, Frank asked what the banter was all about. Laura translated. This time it was the natives who didn't understand what was whispered back.

"They're saying we have to be part foreigners ourselves to want to have anything to do with men who're as white as ghosts, or fairies perhaps. They speculate maybe starvation has drained the color out of you."

"They also say Clark Gable never looked as pale as any of the three of you, so you must be weaklings. No muscles; only lots of brains. Anyone who knows how to fly the monster planes you crashed in must have incredible brains. Yet, no Filipino women would prefer you to husky Filipino men like the *Kapitan* Almanzur, who, unfortunately, is already married," Leticia added, laughing softly.

The mention of the name of the guerrilla leader raised all sorts of speculation about what happened to the home they left. What would happen to their Papa and the people in the compound? Would the *Kapitan* really be able to defend them against the Japanese?

Chapter 39—Conflict at the *Hacienda*: The New Command

At noon, *Kapitan* Almanzur's men surrounded the Luzuriaga compound. In command, the *Kapitan*, with studied care, put every man in a specific position. He addressed Lt. Balinas.

"Poping, a lot depends on discipline and determination. Man your . 50 caliber machine gun and defend the area to the left of the gate. Put as many men with automatic rifles behind the acacia trunks about fifty meters inside the gate. Put your best grenade throwers on huge branches above the rifles and position the submachine guns between the rifles."

"Sir," Lt. Verzosa spoke. "Ten of my best shots will cover the right side of the lane to the main house and five of my best grenade throwers will support them from the acacia trees directly above. I will use my sub machine gun and Ricardo will use his. We'll cover the main house with three others using rifles and are good shots."

"Excellent. Caesar and Rafael mounted a machine gun behind the concrete walls of the *bodega*, a few meters beside the main house. Keep absolute silence and hide under the best cover. Let the Japs move in. Make them think we're not aware they're coming. Open fire only when you hear Caesar's machine gun. I have a Garand and a bazooka I'll use only against a cannon or an airplane."

The Japanese advanced cautiously through the gate. Everything was quiet. Unsuspecting, they came within a hundred feet of the concrete walls of the *bodega*. Caesar's machine gun, mounted on a platform tied to bicycle wheels, opened fire. It took its toll of Japanese soldiers caught by surprise. Simultaneously, a chorus of rifle fire erupted. Grenades hit advancing motorcycles. Procopio's machine gun and all the sub machine guns were busy with their targets.

Realizing how vulnerable soldiers on foot were, Colonel Takamatsu rushed three Japanese trucks with machine guns mounted within to surround the remaining Japanese soldiers. Caesar's machine gun had to be rolled away from the concrete walls of the *bodega* when a cannon was fired behind the trucks though it immediately turned around and retreated.

Lt. Verzosa's men on acacia branches threw hand grenades and kept the cannon inoperative, but motorcycles ran close to the trees and

Japanese sharp shooters hit three of his men. They fell to the ground like over ripe fruit.

Procopio's men behind the gate opened fire and threw more hand grenades at the trucks. The trucks retreated some distance away from the gate. However, familiar with the terrain they had earlier occupied, the Japanese rallied and steadily advanced. To *Kapitan* Almanzur's surprise, the fieldhands were prepared to help. They threw lighted torches like javelins and temporarily halted the advance. Again, Japanese rifles took out most of the unarmed fieldhands. Seeing the fieldhands' plight, an enraged *Kapitan* Almanzur got out of cover and used his Garand. When his Garand was silent, he pitched hand grenades left and right. Bodies flew in the air like rag dolls discarded by children at play. A machine gun fired by Procopio's men from behind the gate threatened to block retreat. Fearing an unexpected rout, the Japanese withdrew as fast as they could.

The shout of victory was loud and joyous. As Crecensio anticipated, it looked as though it could be an even fight. But when they regrouped to assess their loss, the guerrilla contingent mourned nearly a dozen men and many fieldhands lay dead or dying. This was the fieldhands' first experience in combat. Overcome with grief, they rushed to gather the fallen bodies of their co-workers, though they excitedly retrieved some of the weapons from the fallen Japanese soldiers.

The drone of low flying small airplanes sent men scattering for cover. The Japanese planes flew as low as they could and strafed the entire area with machine gun bullets. Guerrilla soldiers scrambled for adequate cover, but *Tio* Mauring's tenants and fieldhands were not as disciplined. Again, bodies fell and covered the area with blood. *Tio* Mauring was among those caught by surprise. Unable to find adequate cover, he lay helplessly on the ground as immobile as a picture frame hung on a wall. Lina, the servant girl, lay a few feet beside him. The planes circled a second time and strafed the area again. Seeing *Tio* Mauring's danger, Lina, without regard for her own safety, rolled over him and shielded him from machine gun fire with her own body. Warm blood soaked the helpless *Tio* Mauring. Lina's self-sacrifice astounded him and he cried tears of gratitude. Her selfless loyalty touched him to the core. She more than made up for her brother's treachery.

As the planes turned to circle over the area one more time, a very angry *Kapitan* Almanzur grabbed his bazooka, waited underneath the broad trunk of an acacia tree and aimed it at the lowest flying airplane. He anticipated the curving angle of the plane and fired. The plane whizzed by swiftly but it fell down in flames not long after. More shouts from *Kapitan* Almanzur's men. The two other planes flew higher but managed to spray machine gun fire and scared the fieldhands immobile but otherwise did little damage to life. Finally, the planes left, but they left the *bodega* thoroughly burning. The men in the area formed a fire fighting line to douse the flames, but it continued to burn.

The women gathered the wounded and tended to their injuries with native remedies. Some survived, but many would die the very next day. Desperate, the men tried to salvage as much of the grain stored in the *bodega* before it burned down completely but the loss was staggering. The loss meant very little food before the next harvest season. If what was left would be used to feed the hungry, there would be less seed to sow. God is in His heaven, but nothing's right with the world. Mourning their dead, the fieldhands whispered amongst themselves. This calamity, they acknowledged, happened only because of the coming of three white strangers.

* * *

The new Japanese commandant was relentless. He came determined to apprehend the three Americans harbored at the *hacienda*. Unfamiliar with the terrain, he ordered Captain Akagi to draw a map detailing entrances to the *hacienda*. He wanted to know exactly where the exits were and where they led. Colonel Takamatsu, in many ways as cruel as Colonel Asaki, was less sadistic but extremely more methodical about his tactical maneuvers and his ways of torture. The impulsive *Kapitan* Almanzur would find him a more formidable challenge.

His officers respected this new command; while they regarded him with awe, they also began to fear him. They were almost sorry they had Major Takasaki replaced by this meticulous, demanding, self-righteous and overbearing high command. Now they all had to tread on tiptoe and make absolutely certain they discharged their responsibilities in the light of this superior's expectations.

Captain Akagi wracked his memory for the exact details of the terrain surrounding the *Hacienda Luzuriaga*. He drew a map indicating (1) entry and exit from the river, from a trail at the back of the compound; 2) Entry from Central Palma, using a road that forks from the main thoroughfare from *Kabankalan* and continues to *Ilog* proper; 3) entry from the *Malabong* bridge, the trail *Kapitan* Almanzur, Caesar and Rafael took the day they drove into the *hacienda*. Captain Akagi didn't know that Caesar, Rafael and the *Kapitan* had destroyed the bridge on their way to the *hacienda*.

Colonel Takamatsu studied Captain Akagi's map and expected all other officers to look at it and speculate on the whereabouts of the Americans. They could still be hiding in the *hacienda*. That guerrilla men are still defending it certainly does not rule out the possibility. If they are still here, surely, the guerrillas do not expect to hold out against superior arms? They may have paddled the Americans out by night and hid them by day, but where are they most likely to take them?

Lt. Sadaaki Iwanaka raised his hand. Before the garrison at Central Palma was abandoned, he had taken a *banca* downriver and crossed to a place called *Embarcadero*. They walked on foot to barrio *Manalad* and rode on carts pulled by carabaos to *Vista Allegre*, where the road forked then went all the way to *Enclaro* to the mouth of the river emptying to the sea. A road also went straight from *Vista Allegre* to barrio *Dancalan* to the mountains in *Candoni* behind *Kabankalan* and to other barrios farther along. So far, Japanese patrols had never ventured there because those may be the strongholds, perhaps the headquarters of guerrilla units. Under Captain Akagi's command a search column had been to *Enclaro* looking for the missing commandant, Colonel Asaki. It's likely the guerrillas can take that route again and transport the Americans by sea to the southern towns of this island. Perhaps that's where they will eventually take the Americans.

Captain Akagi concurred. He suggested a contingent should speed with trucks to *Enclaro* to block that exit. Another platoon should stay at *Vista Allegre* to block access to barrio *Dancalan* and farther on.

Lt. Urabi Konishi offered another possibility. He speculated guerrilla men might have taken the Americans on foot to the swamps. An earlier search column led by Major Takasaki went deep into the swamps to look for their missing commandant. Very likely, there's a guerrilla hideout in the swamps, though it's a bad risk to go in because the mangrove jungle is dense and guerrillas have the advantage of natural cover. The Americans may be taken there until they can be transported elsewhere. If the Americans have left on foot to get to the swamps, there's a chance they've not left too long ago. On foot they can't go faster than trucks can. Their escape could still be cut off if pursuit is organized quickly.

"Hmmm, Hmmm." Colonel Takamatsu said nothing more as he paced deliberately.

"Sir," Captain Akagi remarked, "Whether the Americans are on their way to *Enclaro*, or are being taken to the swamps on the bank of the *Ilog* River, they still have to get to a final destination. A week ago, I suggested to Major Takasaki we need gunboats to outrun *batels*. These hardly have any motor power. Our gunboats must patrol the exits from the mouths of the river into the sea. It must patrol the sea route to the southern tip of this island."

When Colonel Takamatsu was still silent, Captain Akagi offered this last suggestion:

"It's obvious the gunboats wouldn't be available until a week later, at the soonest. There's a great possibility the Americans will shortly be taken somewhere by sea. There's nothing we can do about that now but maybe we can delay that possibility. We can do two things:

Dispatch trucks to *Vista Allegre* and *Enclaro*, to block those possible exits. Take a truck across the *Malabong* Bridge and catch up with the Americans if they're fleeing on foot. If they're fleeing by outrigger *bancas,* we must stop them with air power. Let's hope we're not too late."

Colonel Takamatsu dismissed the meeting, and ordered Captain Akagi to take charge of the entire mission. The Colonel will continue engaging the guerrillas at the *hacienda* till they surrender to his superior force.

"Mind you, I'll not tolerate failure."

With this remark, he threatened to exact performance from his officers. Colonel Takamatsu looked at his watch. It read a few minutes past 2:30 p.m. In thirty minutes, the trucks were ready and he prepared to move into the *hacienda* once more.

Chapter 40—Guerrilla Counter Plans: Route of Escape

Though the Japanese trucks withdrew, *Kapitan* Almanzur saw that the cannons, though inoperative, were still in place. He anticipated the Japanese would attack again.

"The Japanese have retreated, but they'll attack again soon. We can't defend this compound much longer. They have airplanes, cannons, trucks, motorcycles and inexhaustible ammunition. It's not good common sense to expect to hold out against that for very long. After a while, we'll be nothing but sitting ducks. Our successful encounters have always been hit and run. This is no different. What do you guys think we should do now?" He asked the younger lieutenants.

Serafin had lost three men and had only seventeen left, including himself. Procopio sustained the heaviest loss. Seven of his men died and four more were seriously wounded. Earlier, two of his men had gone to track and help the Americans and the Luzuriaga girls in a *banca*.

"There are more than a dozen volunteer fieldhands, but they're not much to depend on. They're useless in fierce combat. Many of them have already died. The rest are really terrified." Procopio calculated their chances.

"*Nong* Manzur, altogether there are less than thirty-five of us left. Against half of the garrison from *Kabankalan*, we don't stand a chance."

The *Kapitan* agreed. "My problem is the old man. I have to tell him we have to flee."

"I also have to tell the fieldhands to cross the river at once and run for their lives. If they stay, their prospect is sadistic torture or death. We have to stay long enough to cover their escape," Serafin added.

"The odds are against us." The *Kapitan* leveled with his lieutenants.

"You must design your own plans of escape, but if I may make a suggestion, think of three different routes and use them all. Don't all exit the same way or they'll cut you to pieces."

"What are we going to do now? I think the Japanese are going to attempt another attack in less than thirty minutes," Lt. Verzosa anticipated.

"When they come again, ask men deployed in excellent cover to use their guns. Meantime, let some of Procopio's men, two at a time, swim across the river and escape to *Embarcadero* or *Manalad.* Find a small *banca* to get the wounded across the river. More important, you need to agree to meet again at an appointed place and regroup because in one large group you'll have more chance to survive," *Kapitan* Almanzur suggested.

Lt. Balinas agreed. "We'll go by way of the abandoned *Central Viaren*, or even farther to barrio *Salong,*" he told his men. "Ultimately, we must regroup at the hills of *Candoni.*"

Sisong promised they would run hard on the other side of *Mapa-it*; they would hide well, and then meet with the rest to re-group soon.

"Avoid the wide road," *Kapitan* Almanzur cautioned. "Seek cover under trees and where there's water to drink. When tired, you can easily get dehydrated. Then you'll be too exhausted to run when it's necessary to fly."

Procopio listened intently though he was busy mounting the machine gun. He checked on those who had hand grenades. "Don't throw unless you have a definite target. You mustn't waste ammunition. You need to save everything, including your energy for self-defense. I'll use this machine gun and cover those who only have automatic rifles. Those deployed in good cover must stay while the others slip away. Let's use every route of escape *Manong* Almanzur outlined."

He spoke encouragingly. "We've done this before; we can do it again. We know the terrain better than the Japs do. Just keep your cool and be good guerrilla soldiers. We'll fight in the open when the odds are even. Meantime, we hit and run. Okay? Give me each your hand and God be with you till I see you again in *Candoni*, in no more than three days. Okay?"

"I'll ask you to do me a big favor. I need you to cover me for I'm going to try something almost foolhardy," the *Kapitan* pleaded.

"Here he goes again, the man with the unusual solutions. What is it this time?" Procopio was excited to know.

"If you cover me well, the Japanese will think we're fighting to the bitter end; but we have a Japanese truck we salvaged at *Mang* Kari's. Caesar hid it in a banana grove three hundred meters from the gate. I hope that's well beyond the last line of Japanese soldiers. Caesar and I will get to the truck quickly through the thick *kogon* grass. Rafael and five fieldhands (Rafael is right now picking them out) will carry the old man to the truck before the Japs are aware of what we're doing. When we get there, Caesar would have the motor running and humming low."

"Most of the fieldhands have already disappeared. Some want to go with me but I told them they would have a better chance if they run now. Poor people. They have no choice. If they stay they'll be massacred. The women had all gone earlier today. They went looking for relatives or friends wherever they think they'd find them. After the airplanes appeared, they helped take care of the wounded but they knew better than to stay around. Honestly, sometimes I think women have more sense than men," Serafin said.

One last time the *Kapitan* tried to bid goodbye to Procopio and Serafin.

"Please cover us well; keep the Japs busy. That's our only chance. Driving fast, we will zoom to T*alubangui*, cross the bridge, and get to *Dancalan* still in one piece. How's that? Hopefully, the Japs will not figure that out. That's the only way I can get the old man out of here. He can't walk a darn."

Lt. Serafin Verzosa, known to his men as *Manong Apin,* had seventeen men to think about.

"My men came from barrio *Andulawan* three days before. They plan to go back there through barrio *Malabong* and we'll re-group at barrio *Binicuil* in another swamp setting close to the sea."

"Do you know that we destroyed the bridge at *Malabong* on our way here?' Caesar asked Serafin.

"Well, I bet the Japanese think the Americans are trying to cross the bridge to get to the swamps. They must think they can catch up with them because they have trucks. Since they don't know *Tio* Mauring's daughters are with the Americans, their logical conclusion would be they're escaping on foot."

"Their truck can't cross at *Malabong* now," Caesar repeated.

"I hear. I know what to do," Serafin replied. "My men and I will run to barrio *Malabong* fast and cross the river upstream. The huge cottonwood trees on the riverbank would be excellent cover. If the Japanese are stupid enough to swim across, we'll pick them off easily."

"The river there is not too wide, but the current is swift because the water flows down stream from *Andulawan*. Farther down, it empties straight into the big trunk of the river," Procopio informed Serafin. "Those cottonwood trees line the riverbank clear to *Andulawan*. There, the trees give way to *nipa* groves running into the swampy mangrove area toward barrio *Binicuil*. From there your men should know the terrain by heart. Right?"

"Certainly. It's the best route of escape for us," Serafin concurred.

"Men, we have to move now. Let's run fast without resting until we get to the bridge. We need to get there before the Japs do."

* * *

Lt. Konishi realized it would be dark before he could get to that clearing they reached on their way to the swamps to look for Colonel Asaki. To his dismay, when he got to *Malabong*, the bridge was gone. He needed a way to cross the river. He decided to get only as far as *Ilog* proper and turn back for his own good. There was no evidence that the Americans traveled on foot and had crossed the river here. He concluded they were taken by *banca.* He knew this was a useless task. How was he to locate them if he ordered his men to go on foot? He was tempted to turn back, but he heard Colonel Takamatsu's voice clearly.

"Mind you, I will not tolerate failure."

He hated to save face at the suggestion of failure. He only had sixteen men with him, a small squad really. Anticipating no resistance from the *hacienda* side of the river, he left only two men with a machine gun to guard the truck. He ordered the rest to swim across or look for lumber or something to lean on while they tried to cross.

Serafin and his men arrived at the *Malabong* Bridge twenty minutes after Lt. Konishi did. He didn't have time to cross to the cottonwood grove. The Japanese were already wading in the water, their rifles raised above their shoulders. They put their rifles on remnants of burnt lumber they found, intending to push it to the other bank.

Serafin saw the truck with the two men left to guard it. His problem was the sub machine gun. If he fired at them, they would fire back and the other Japanese soldiers in the river would be alerted. Two Japanese soldiers were sitting at the back of the truck smoking cigarettes and talking. Federico threw a small pebble at the dashboard to create a diversion. The soldiers got out to see about the noise up front. Two of Serafin's men crawled fast underneath the bed of the truck. One Japanese soldier put his hands on the front fender and lifted himself on the hood. He continued to smoke. The other soldier walked to the back and sat at the edge of the truck's bed; his legs dangled over. Federico crawled under the dangling legs, pulled them down hard and as the soldier fell on the grass, he sat on top of him and stuffed his shirt in his mouth so he couldn't cry out. He pulled him quickly underneath the truck. The smoking soldier flipped his cigarette butt, wanting to know what was going on.

"Hey, what are you doing down there? Anything wrong?"

When he turned his head around to look at the back of the truck, a rope closed around his neck; he made a gurgling sound when the rope tightened. Two men took him down and wrung his neck. Losing no time, Serafin and Ricardo took off the soldiers' clothes, put them on top of their own, wore their caps low, and strode a few meters close to the riverbank. All fifteen men had very quietly crept through the *kogon* grass and spread out in good range of the Japanese. The ones farthest out had telescopic rifles; the ones closest to the Japanese crossing the river had sub machine guns. Serafin had two hand grenades, just in case. Each guerrilla soldier kept a man in sight, ready for Serafin's order to fire. There were only fourteen Japanese in the river, including Lt. Konishi; the two left to guard the truck were already dead.

Serafin sauntered closer to the river's edge, careful not to be in the line of fire of his own men. He shouted and waved his hands way over his head. Believing he was one of the two left to guard the truck, the men in the water turned their heads in his direction wondering why he was waving his hands at them. The minute their heads turned, Serafin and all of his men fired at their targets. Lt. Knonishi, closest to the other bank, fell first. Some men missed their targets. The Thompson M1 Sub Machine gun behind tall *kogon* grass toward the left side of the riverbank took care of them as they thrashed vigorously to get to the other side.

Serafin didn't even have to throw a grenade. He hoped the sound of all the shooting wouldn't carry back to the *hacienda*. Now a Japanese truck with a machine gun in it came part of the booty. Serafin's unit had an M1 Garand Sub Machine Gun, the better, lighter version known as the M1 1903, a .30 caliber gun that had a high volume fire capacity. It could fire 600 rounds per minute. Lighter than the M3 45 caliber sub machine gun known as the "grease gun," it had a good spraying effect and was excellent for close combat. They had two M 1903 magazine fed Springfield rifles good for precision shooting and a 1093 04 sniper weapon. These weapons were taken from the submarine from Australia that surfaced at *Maricalum* a month before. Serafin had just received them a few days ago when he volunteered to distract a unit of thirty-six Japanese soldiers on the trail of six Americans rescued by *Kapitan* Almanzur. These were the best guns ever given to a guerrilla unit north of *Kabankalan*. It was really a tribute to all of Lt. Verzosa's men for their self-sacrifice, bravery and proven steadiness in combat.

From Crossing *Aguisan* where they ambushed Lt. Ishda's platoon, his unit raced to *Binicuil* and then to *Andulawan* and to the *Hacienda Luzuriaga* where he lost three of his men. Remembering how the three fell, the rest of his unit wanted to get back to the *hacienda* to avenge them.

"Let's go back and help Lt. Balinas. He's still holding out there so his men could escape," Ricardo said.

"Besides." Serafin reminded them, "We're indebted to *Kapitan* Almanzur for recommending we receive the weapons we now have. We could at least show our appreciation."

"Now we have more," the men shouted. Exhilarated with the thrill of victory and shouting jubilantly, all of them slid down the riverbank, each trying to retrieve a rifle from a dead Japanese. A sub machine gun on floating lumber was also *salvaged*. Guerrilla men use this term to refer to firearms or equipment retrieved from the Japanese.

Serafin assessed the situation. They now had fifteen more rifles and two more sub machine guns. "Lt. Balinas doesn't have an even chance of surviving without our help. Let's use this truck and speed back to the *hacienda*. We have to help reduce the odds against him," he told his men.

"Perhaps," Ricardo said, "the Japanese would assume one of their trucks came back from its mission. We can get close enough to do real damage."

"That's right. Strip as many Japanese uniforms and put them over your clothes as I did earlier. Then let's zoom back to the *hacienda* and surprise the bastards," Serafin gloated.

Now Lt. Konishi didn't have any explaining to do; if the wild hogs don't find him, perhaps the crocodiles would.

* * *

Back at the *hacienda* before Serafin and his men left for *Malabong*, *Kapitan* Almanzur carefully explained to *Tio* Mauring why he had to take him somewhere else. He apologized for not sending him with his daughters earlier. It wouldn't be wise to stay within reach of the vengeful Japanese. He outlined what they needed to do.

"Hidden in a banana grove not far from the gate is a Japanese truck we *salvaged* at *Mang* Kari's place. Some of your most loyal fieldhands will quietly carry you there. I'm sorry you can't bring anything but your life. I can't assure you the Japanese won't discover what we're trying to do and stop us on our tracks, but we'll try our best. I think we might make it because they won't expect something like this to happen right under their nose. I'm risking my life to do this because I'm not willing to let them capture us; they will, if we stay. I don't plan to be savagely tortured. Are you willing to risk your life and come with us? If you do, I know God will take care of the rest."

"Do what you have to do, son. I'll go with you only if I may be permitted to take just one very small bag with me. It'll not be on your way. I'll carry it always."

Tio Mauring hurried to his bedroom, took a small picture frame with pictures of his wife and children and put it in a black bag with a pouch of jewelry and all the money he had.

"Now, I'm ready."

The *Kapitan* helped the old man down the back stairs where five fieldhands were waiting. Caesar and Rafael had gone ahead; they crept through the thick *kogon* grass under *talisay* trees and circled behind the gate to the banana grove where the truck was hidden. *Kapitan* Almanzur devised a *duyan* a hammock-like contraption made of fine hemp ropes, and wrapped *Tio* Mauring in it. Fieldhands lifted the precious burden running closely behind *Kapitan* Almanzur who had several grenades around his belt and an M1 30 caliber sub machine gun slung on his shoulders. Another fieldhand cut a path through the grass with a long knife used to cut cane. The *Kapitan* threw a red rag in the air as he run past a side gate to the left of the still burning *bodega*.

Waiting for this signal, Procopio's men immediately opened fire at the Japanese advancing for another attack. Colonel Takamatsu had repaired a cannon and his men were pushing it close to the gate. Deployed about a hundred meters inside and to the right of the gate, Procopio manned an M 1919 A4 machine gun. Though easy to set up, gun and tripod weighed 45 lbs. Three men could move it around; at least it had a low profile making it easy to conceal. Japanese soldiers on motorcycles tried to race inside the gate advancing toward the front of the main house. Procopio opened fire; the gun spat twenty rounds of ammo. Though running at high speed, three of the Japanese on motorcycles were hit. The other three raced back outside the gate where the main unit was deployed, but one managed to throw a torch onto the porch of the main house. The house started to burn. Busy attempting to get inside the gate, the Japanese didn't hear the soft humming of the truck Caesar had quietly inched to the road, way beyond the gate. As soon as *Tio* Mauring was safely laid on the seat behind Caesar, *Kapitan* Almanzur opened the back door for fieldhands to file into the bed of the truck.

"Lie down flat on the truck bed and hold on to anything you can grab." Rafael told them.

Caesar revved the engine and put the pedal down. As he drove out to the main road, he spied another Japanese truck flying down from the direction of barrio *Malabong*. He hoped the truck wouldn't chase him; he drove over a hundred kilometers per hour. The *Kapitan* rested his M1 Garand on the side window ready to answer any gunfire directed at them. The fieldhand sitting beside *Tio* Mauring, now sitting up and out of the duyan, swore he saw, not Japanese, but Filipinos in the truck.

The truck didn't chase them but swerved on the trail to the compound toward the banana grove they had just left. Rafael, too, thought he saw Serafin waving a sub machine gun, but he wasn't sure. Though it looked like him, the figure was dressed in a Japanese uniform.

"Don't let that fool you. Remember the *Kapitan* did the same thing near *Mang* Kari's place. It could be Serafin. He must have taken that truck from the Japanese at *Malabong* and came back to help Procopio. Viva Serafin! " Caesar was jubilant.

The cannon blasted the house. Debris flew all over. Confusion reigned. The Japanese sprayed the acacia trees in front of the house with machine gun fire. Serafin's truck moved close to the gate. Procopio, by now pitifully outnumbered, desperately needed help. Serafin threw grenades and silenced two of the Japanese machine gun positions. He used the machine gun *salvaged* with the truck and sprayed around the soldiers manning the cannon. All his men fired at the Japanese close to the gate, but the cannon had turned around ready to blast his truck out of the way. Procopio's sergeant, Raul, fired a bazooka at the cannon. Still perched on a huge acacia tree branch, Sisong threw a series of hand grenades. Both bazooka and hand grenades hit the cannon. Japanese soldiers manning the cannon lay dead or wounded on the ground. While soldiers were busy trying to help the wounded, Serafin backed the truck out to the main road, flew at top speed and raced on the road to *Andulawan.*

Colonel Takamatsu held his ground; at dusk, the only light came from the still burning house. By nightfall, the area was strangely quiet.

As soon as the first light of dawn came, Colonel Takamatsu scoured the whole compound. Bodies of Japanese soldiers and of Procopio's men who died in the conflict still lay where they fell. Evidently, those who lived carried the wounded, crossed the river in small *bancas* and fled. The trail of blood led clearly to the riverbank. Sensing he had much less men than he started with, Colonel Takamatsu decided not to pursue.

Some farm animals were running loose. Japanese soldiers helped themselves to pigs and goats. The chickens were difficult to catch, but the farm boys in the Colonel's command knew fowls would roost in the evening. They took those too. For two days, the *hacienda* burned. Since the Americans and the guerrilla band keeping them were nowhere to be found, the Colonel expected they fled where Captain Akagi had gone. Or they could be going on foot with Lt. Konishi chasing after them. After three days, he decided to return to *Kabankalan* very much perturbed.

He neither heard from Lt. Iwanaka or Captain Akagi. Lt. Konishi had not returned.

Chapter 41—Expectations Set against Performance

Colonel Takamatsu sent radio messages to three junior officers, but only one of them answered. Captain Akagi reported.

"I arrived here yesterday before dusk. I haven't found any clue that the Americans have been taken here. I've tried to contact Lt. Iwanaka and Lt. Konishi but can't seem to get through. I'm on my way to *Vista Allegre* and will soon know what the problem is. Lt. Iwanaka and I request permission to go together to barrio *Dancalan* before we go back to the garrison. We want to make sure the guerrillas haven't gone in that direction before we got here."

Response from Colonel Takamatsu was hot and irate.

"Why are those idiots not answering my messages? If those Americans are not captured by next week, I have a good mind to Court Martial both of them."

"Give them time to respond, Sir. I'm sure they'll answer soon."

"I have already burned the *Hacienda Luzuriaga* to the ground. I'm waiting for all of you to return to the garrison. You may join Lt. Iwanaka tomorrow, but you had better get an answer from him."

Colonel Takamatsu didn't mention that he returned to the garrison with an inoperative cannon, was missing two machine guns, and had far less soldiers than he had with him when he first launched the attack at the *hacienda*. But he expected better performance from his officers.

When Captain Akagi arrived in *Vista Allegre*, he found a dying Lt. Iwanaka and several wounded men. Unable to accept the situation, he demanded a full report. Sergeant Tanaka gave the following report for the unconscious lieutenant.

"We tried to send a message but the radio equipment we carried in both trucks were blown off. There are only eight of us left, excluding the dying lieutenant. We thought of sending some of us to *Enclaro* but we were afraid of being ambushed on the way. We were also concerned to leave the lieutenant here with just a few men. We've been waiting for you to pass here on your return to the garrison so we could flag you and join you," the sergeant informed Captain Akagi.

"Let me detail the rest of what happened, Sir. Traveling from the *hacienda Luzuriaga*, the truck I was in had a flat tire. We couldn't keep up with the lieutenant. We were taking time to fix the flat tire. Tired from the skirmishes at the *hacienda*, we were glad to be out of danger. We saw one of our trucks approaching. We assumed the truck was a reinforcement from the garrison, but ten meters before it came alongside, it opened fire on us."

"We were taken by complete surprise." Private Watanabe interrupted the sergeant.

"We had our rifles on the ground and had no chance to shoot back. Sub machine gun fire killed most of our men instantly. We were tightening the last bolts on the tire replacement so Sergeant Tanaka and I dove under our truck and were not hit. The other truck passed us; a few meters past us, the driver swiftly turned around. Before it came close, an officer threw a grenade and finished the job. The sergeant and I rolled away from the road into the ditch and played dead. There was not much left of the truck we were in. Eight of the twelve of us in the truck died even before the grenade hit it." The private was clearly shaken so the sergeant continued once more.

"We hid in the ditch till dark. The truck had sped on. After dark, we slowly walked this way hoping to find Lt. Iwanaka and the rest of the platoon in his truck. We found them beyond a ditch under the cover of a clump of trees. The truck was blown up like the one we were in. As we approached, we saw parts of the bodies of our men blown to bits. Four privates were gathered around the dying lieutenant. Two of them were wounded though not seriously. They were unable to do anything for him. It was impossible to move him any farther than they did because he was bleeding profusely. They told us later that anytime they tried moving him, he bled even more. When we got close, they blinded us with their flashlights. Three had their guns trained on us, ready to shoot."

"What have you done since you got here?" Captain Akagi demanded, livid with anger.

"We removed the lieutenant away from the road and laid him behind some cover but that was all we could do. Two of our men, deployed behind a clump of bamboo trees, tried to fix the half burned radio. We all took off our shirts and used them to quench the flames on the truck to no avail. I sent four men to cut down small trees along the road to push the burning truck into a banana grove beyond the ditch. The incline was too steep; we couldn't do it. Half the bed of the long truck had blown off; the glass had shattered, and the metal behind the exposed driver's seat was too hot. We cut banana trunks and dumped them on the burning truck. That did the trick; the flames subsided to a trickle. A few hours after dark, the truck cooled off enough for us to pry off the radio from it. We were still trying to fix the radio when you came, Sir."

The rest of the men all nodded to confirm what the sergeant reported, but Captain Akagi took another private and dragged him to his truck.

"Give me no excuses. Report the plain truth. Tell me exactly what happened here." Captain Akagi raged in disbelief.

The private gave almost the same report Sergeant Tanaka did:

"The lieutenant thought that the sergeant had fixed the problem the other truck had and was finally catching up to us. It was slowing down considerably. Suddenly, it picked up speed and opened fire on us with a sub machine gun. It took the lieutenant one quick look to realize the truck had guerrilla men in it."

"Quick, overtake it," the lieutenant yelled. "

We gave chase and the lieutenant himself used the machine gun and put holes on the speeding truck. I know he did a lot of damage because the truck was leaking both gasoline and blood. We were all using our rifles as well. Unexpectedly, the truck ahead swerved, slowed down, and almost stopped. A grenade hit our truck. It blew almost the left side off. We jumped out of the truck as the bodies of four of our men were blown to bits. Private Mikuma, who was also wounded, hugged the lieutenant as they jumped off. Together, they fell on the road as the other truck sped by and threw another grenade. It blew off the back of our truck entirely and we careened off the road and stopped at the shoulder. Our machine gun was blown to bits and so were all the equipment we had, including our radio and four other men. From the ground where we fell, we fired at the truck for several minutes, but it was speeding fast on this road and disappeared from view. That is the truth, Captain; I swear it is."

Captain Akagi determined the private's account supported sergeant Tanaka's report. Sergeant Tanaka, hanging his head in shame, asked him for help.

"We have not eaten since late yesterday, Captain. We don't have anything except the bayonets attached to our rifles, a flashlight fortunately hanging on private Mikuma's belt, and a water canteen I had on mine. The water is almost gone. We gave most of it to the lieutenant. We shared the rest among us and were hoping you'd come by soon."

Captain Akagi ordered his men to load lieutenant Iwanaka's body in his truck. He gave the sergeant and his men food and water. They ate as the trucks drove back to *Kabankalan.*

* * *

From Rafael's point of view, this is what happened: When Caesar caught up with the second Japanese truck, *Kapitan* Almanzur opened fire with his sub machine gun. Though the Japanese were again taken by surprise, they were holding their weapons and were ready to answer fire as soon as Caesar passed them. A Japanese officer was manning a machine gun, but he was at the right side of the truck; his bullets didn't hit *Kapitan* Almanzur since Caesar passed the truck on the left. Because the aim was slightly deflected, the machine gun bullets hit the back of the truck, passed straight to the front, missed the glass on the dashboard by inches, but damaged some part of the engine. If Caesar had not ducked low involuntarily, he would have been hit on the head. I sat on the seat behind the *Kapitan*; both of us were a foot to the right of the line of fire. Bullets hit two of the fieldhands sitting at the left, instantly killing them. Because Caesar involuntarily ducked, the truck jolted, shifted to the right and altered the path of the bullets.

As the truck shifted, *Tio* Mauring, sitting on the left side, was thrown against the fieldhand at his right. The movement saved him from instant death. The bullets missed his back but went through the left side of his body and hit his left arm. He bled instantly. Our truck slowed down almost to a halt. The Japanese truck had to pass to avoid colliding with us. As it passed by, I threw a hand grenade and hit it. The truck didn't stop; its speed and momentum held it on a straight course, but the grenade blew off almost the entire left side of the truck bed. The driver must have been stunned. Caesar picked up speed and desperately passed it a second time; the *Kapitan* threw another grenade that demolished the rear and sent the truck careening to the ditch. That was the last we saw of the truck as we sped by. Caesar was flying. We just managed to turn at a curve about fifteen kilometers farther; the engine sputtered and the truck slowed down a few more meters before it completely stopped. Evidently, Japanese gunfire hit the gas tank and the truck leaked gas. The tank was empty when the truck stopped. *Tio* Mauring slumped on the seat seriously wounded."

The *Kapitan* was horrified. He went over and cradled the old man in his arms. For the first time in a very long time that I've known him he didn't know what to do.

"Why did they have to hit you instead of me?" he sobbed. "You have been like a second father to me. I don't want to lose you. Please, God, don't take him away. Please."

I, too, began to cry. I asked Caesar to do something right away. Caesar didn't know what to do either, but he told me to run toward the houses and ask for immediate help. Caesar tried to console the *Kapitan*.

"What happened isn't your fault, Sir. Maybe we should try and get some help somewhere. I'll blow the horn to get some attention. I'm sure people still live here."

Caesar blew the horn, but nobody came out. Losing hope, he got out of the truck, ran to the houses by the roadside about a hundred meters away. People recognized the Japanese truck so they all hid to avoid capture, but when no Japanese soldiers came out, heads started to peep out of windows. They saw Caesar desperately crying for help. After a long while, an old man came out to ask what was wrong. Caesar shook him gently and explained our desperate need for help. The old man tried to think. He said, he knew of a woman who lived about ten minutes away. She used to be a nurse at the Health Center before he war; maybe she could help. He brought his grandson out of hiding and told him to run and try to get the nurse to come and help. By this time a crowd of onlookers had gathered around the truck. They marveled that it was a Japanese truck now at the hands of guerrilla men.

"What's wrong with it? Is it running or not?" A man in his thirties wanted to know. Caesar told him what happened and opened the hood. The hood was filled with holes where the bullets hit; it was smoking. Someone brought some water to cool off the radiator

The old man told Caesar no one there could help. What he needed was a mechanic.

"I'm a mechanic. I can fix what's wrong, but the truck's out of gas and the gas tank needs to be soldered. Japanese bullets have riddled it with holes."

The old man's grandson came back, bringing a lady in her fifties. He shouted at the onlookers to clear the way so the nurse could see what was wrong with the old man in the truck. *Tio* Mauring bled profusely. The *Kapitan* had taken his shirt off and pressed it on the wound, desperately trying to stop the blood from flowing from the old man's side. *Tio* Mauring was unconscious from the pain and the loss of blood. The nurse examined him. More onlookers, people curious to know what the throng was all about, crowded around. It was getting dark; the sun was going down. The *duyan* used to carry *Tio* Mauring to the truck when we left his *hacienda* was still at the back.

The *Kapitan* had calmed down considerably; apparently, he thought more clearly. He ordered two of the fieldhands still with us and two other men from barrio *Dancalan* to carry *Tio* Mauring in the *duyan* to the nurse's house where he could be taken care of. The other fieldhands were asking around for a cemetery to bury those who had died in the truck. The *Kapitan* ordered Caesar to contact the local priest to give the fieldhands a decent burial.

"This old man," the nurse announced, "needs a doctor to set the injury right. Besides, the wound on his side needs to be cauterized and sutured. It's still bleeding. I have heard Dr. Carbonel, who practiced in *Ilog* before the war, has evacuated to *Cawayan*, thirty-five kilometers away. Now and then he works for the army hospital in *Caliling* whenever there's an emergency and the medical staff there don't know what to do. *Kapitan,* you could go to *Cawayan* on horseback and bring the doctor here. Minong, a kilometer away, has a good horse you could borrow."

The *Kapitan* did just that. On horseback most of the night, he brought the doctor before daybreak to determine what could be done for *Tio* Mauring who hovered between life and death. *Kapitan* Almanzur would not leave his bedside for fear he would not be around if the old man regained consciousness. He felt guilty and responsible for putting the old man through the danger we went through. He had disobeyed his cousin's order to get to the hideout in the swamp in *Ilog.* He wondered what was happening at that end, but he refused to leave without being assured that *Tio* Mauring would live.

The next day, Caesar found a man who could solder the gas tank. I rode the same horse back to *Cawayan* and brought gas back. After *Tio* Mauring regained consciousness, Dr. Carbonel instructed the nurse to force feed her patient and make sure he gets enough water to prevent dehydration.

"He needs half a glass of water every ten minutes. Force him to drink even if he gags."

"We will cook some rich *arroz caldo* (rice soup with onions and chicken cut up in small pieces), and constantly spoon feed him with it," *Kapitan* Almanzur told the nurse.

After two more days, *Tio* Mauring could say *yes* or *no* by nodding or shaking his head. He was awake for a few minutes during the day but slept most of the time. He later gained enough strength to sit up with the *Kapitan's* support.

As soon as the truck could run again, Caesar, the *Kapitan* and I slowly drove *Tio* Mauring to the army hospital in *Caliling* where the *Kapitan*'s sister, *Manang* Norma, is chief nurse. The *Kapitan* made her solemnly promise to nurse *Tio* Mauring back to good health.

* * *

In retrospect, had Captain Akagi gone beyond *Vista Allegre* to barrio *Dancalan* as he wanted to do with Lt. Iwanaki, he would have caught up with Caesar, Rafael, the *Kapitan*, and a couple of fieldhands. Outnumbered and outgunned, *Kapitan* Almanzur could have been killed. Who could explain why Captain Akagi decided to go back to the garrison and brave the commandant's displeasure instead? Maybe he was unnerved after seeing Lt. Iwanaka near death?

Kapitan Almanzur's aunt and uncle, *Manong* Alvaro's parents, would explain the whole thing as God's will. God designs the course of events. He spares whom he decides to spare and takes away those ready to take away. Indeed this very much covered what happened everywhere, even the shape of things in the swamps. Lt. Verzosa was around when his help was needed and he certainly helped Lt. Balinas to survive. Lt. Balinas made it possible for the *Kapitan* to escape from the *hacienda* with *Tio* Mauring. Though wounded and very sick, *Tio* Mauring was brought to *Caliling* where his daughters could join him when it was possible to take them there. Who could quarrel with such providence?

Without doubt, the shape of things was uncertain. Though Colonel Gomez and *Kapitan* Almanzur had planned to deliver the Americans to the south of Negros for a rendezvous with an American submarine, events didn't turn out in straightforward simplicity. It seemed that God had arranged a journey through a timeless landscape toward an end that was specific though not fully known. *Kapitan* Almanzur was at this point dimly realizing this truth: There are some things you know inside yourself to start with, and there are other things someone needs to teach you.

Creating a legend around himself, he made his men believe he was invincible. He had an answer for every problem. He could get untangled from any knot devised by the Japanese to dispose of him. He overcame every obstacle on his path, but this last escape and *Tio* Mauring's near death taught him what he had never acknowledged before. He failed to acknowledge that he and his men were mutable. Had not Procopio,

Serafin, Caesar, Rafael, Nonoy, Ponsing, Pedring, Badong, Sauro, Crispin, Rudi, Sisong, Miguel, Rolando, Ricardo, Lt. Palacious, Sergeant Padriga, Sergeant Peralta, Paul Lindsey, and dozens more of his men not given of themselves to get him out of the dangers he put them and himself through, he would have been dead long ago.

He could hardly wait to go home and see *Manang* Pilar and his children. He had not seen his family in over a year. His father had died a year ago in the swamps, but he was too wrapped up in his missions to see him buried. He had not seen his mother or his younger sisters in a while. He promised himself as soon as the Americans were safely delivered, he would bring all his family out of the swamps into the safety of the army camp in *Caliling*.

Chapter 42—Anticipating the *Batel* Ride

Letiicia heard the lapping of paddles in the water. The *banca* moved at a steady pace gliding past *nipa* groves and staying close to the riverbank. She heard the *banca* paddled by her father's fieldhands trailing behind. Both *bancas* made steady progress. Early evening descended; it was getting pitch dark. She could hardly see the outline of trees as they circled bend after bend; all she was conscious of was the quiet movement of the *banca* gliding with the current. The paddlers seemed to know every bend of the river. How could they see in the dark? She tried to concentrate on the darkness. She began to realize that one did not see in the dark unless one accepted it. Bit by bit of acquaintance with darkness brought light. Finally, she understood that movement in the dark was possible only if the eye adjusted its light to the lack of light, to darkness as it were. Much later, Delia gave her this explanation: The fact is a paradox, an oxymoron really. Perhaps this was what John Milton meant by the phrase *darkness visible* in his epic poem *Paradise Lost*. Leticia wanted to share her thoughts with George who was clutching her tightly as though afraid he would lose her if he relaxed his hold.

It had been a while since they all ate. She heard George's stomach grumbling. She was sure he had not eaten much. She saw how he shared most of the food with the paddlers. She shifted her thought to food and the body's need for it. Her mind went back to the lavish banquets her father put on the table at the *hacienda* before the war. Funny, but it seemed, too, that eating a little at a time allowed one to eat more. If one ate all one could at any given time, he gets glutted. Excessive food doesn't benefit the body. When anyone identifies food with instant gratification, he, ironically, never gets satisfied at all. He merely gets satiated. Unable to savor what he gluts himself with, he simply gets bloated. Seems to be what happens when people heap food on top of food on their plates. The need to have all turns all to nothing.

Maybe this is true not just of the need for food, but for all kinds of need. Now she has this overwhelming need to be with George. Perhaps he needs her just as much. What happens when they get to where his crew is waiting and they finally have to leave? She could not let herself think of that moment. In the past two days, events had changed her life beyond her understanding. She had to steel herself to accept anything that could happen. *In times that are changing fast*, she told herself, *we need something that would preserve the moment*.

She pressed herself softly into George's arms, laid her cheek gently against his and kissed him in the dark. She could feel George searching for her mouth instead of her cheek. He kissed her back, long, and tenderly. She knew they had to move away from danger into the safety of the hideout in the swamp, but she wished this moment could last forever.

She wasn't aware that Frank felt the same way about her sister, Laura. To give more space to the others, Laura sat on his lap while he cradled her in his arms and put her head on his breast. He knew she was crying very softly as she, too, acknowledged a deep connection between them. He wiped the tears gently with his fingers. He, too, wished the moment could stay and not pass with the night.

Maria Elena, anxious about their father whom they had left behind at the *hacienda*, felt a premonition that made her very restless, for at that moment her father almost died from a bullet that shattered his left arm and left him unconscious from pain and loss of blood. Indeed, life was infinitely more complex and more unpredictable than any of them anticipated. Without their assent, the equilibrium of their lives had been disrupted. They couldn't tell what was going to happen next and as they moved through unfamiliar ground, they were filled with anxiety and unease against which they had no adequate defense. For the moment, they felt protected because they were loved, but beyond this temporary stay against confusion there was not much they could do to ease the unpredictability that threatened with what had yet to come.

Spencer was experiencing the same uncertainty, but he could not believe the happiness welling within when he thought of Milka and her love for him. Yesterday he was half dead; now he wanted to live forever. He saw everything around her pale in her radiance. Within her lived a gift; her sincere empathy with others was a wellspring within. She gave of it freely every time she catered to his welfare. How could he give her up? When? Tomorrow? Day after? He couldn't imagine how. Time was so elastic it stretched to any limit. The mind simply blocked off the need to stop the stretching. When he could bask in her love, he ignored the presence of danger; but every minute they were together, luxury run wild for there wasn't much time to spare. He was dimly aware that the time they spent together spun events so fast nothing seemed real. He, too, was conscious of the same prevailing thought common to all lovers: in these times that were changing fast, they needed to preserve the moment.

Yes, tomorrow, or the day after, Colonel Gomez's *batel* will take them to a submarine rendezvous. If he were taken away, what would happen to her? If the Japanese decide to go on an all out campaign, these people in the swamps hardly had any defense. He couldn't think of leaving her. This happiness they shared was too brief, like a flash of brilliant lightning soon to be obscured by a blast of thunder shattering the quiet sky, ushering tempestuous winds that churn and roll with more lightning and thunder and ending in a blinding downpour of heavy rain. Nature completed this wartime drama.

Spencer had no awareness of the fact that in the drama of life, nothing was riskier than acts of love. But at the moment both he and Milka belonged to an aristocracy of the spirit. Their mutual tenderness and regard for each other's safety lifted them beyond the limits of ordinary relationship. The past two days forced them to recognize that, *alongside pain and suffering, love and courage are also constants in the human condition.* They know that a commitment to love, regardless of the circumstances in which it happens, is the key to a happiness that overshadows any suffering.

Manang Aning was alarmed at the advance of infection in Spencer's wound. She told her husband Spencer needed more medication than he was getting. He should be taken to the army hospital in *Caliling* before the wound became gangrenous. Milka was always at his side putting on more herb juices to reduce pain, hoping to arrest infection. She didn't want Spencer to leave but she prayed the three other Americans *Manong* Alvaro was waiting for would arrive so Spencer could have adequate medical care. Yet as long as she was with him, Spencer didn't mind the pain; in fact, he hardly felt it at all. He was resting, basking in her presence, and he was content.

Milka is one of those people who have some correct intuition of fineness in themselves. She knew the danger of Spencer's condition but she carried the burden of knowing it quietly within. Without warning, Spencer's path had crossed hers like an unexpected rainfall, drenching her thoroughly with its refreshing wetness. He kept the hot, humid air of loneliness at bay. He loomed in her horizon like a friend from the past whose friendship she had outworn. Now he was so much more than just a friend. She could not imagine what she would do without him. She enjoyed the luxury of his warmth when he put his arms around her and laid her head on his breast. His intimate nearness threatened to suffocate her. She held her breath to bear the weight of his closeness.

When he first arrived, she remembered the warmth she shared with him when he was lying shaking and helpless from sheer exhaustion and bankrupt energy. Her heart went to that almost lifeless figure before she was aware of his human stature. When he expressed his feelings for her she was moved but afraid to open herself to the weight of his emotion. Now she realized that time waits for no one. The urgency in the events these past two days made it clear that those who go forward discover the selves they can't deny and those who turn back find themselves in a barren country without the comfort of love. She chose to go forward, risking her brother's disapproval and her family's displeasure. She gave herself up to Spencer's stirring passion.

When the compound had settled down to a disquieting waiting time for the three other Americans, five of the six in Mama Sid's care realized the danger they still faced and the danger they imposed on their hosts. Trying to compensate, they worked hard to restore the compound to its former state of comfort. They worked with Rodney to level the gaping holes left by the 75mm shells, but *Manong* Alvaro suggested they construct bigger huts farther in the heart of the swamps where Victor had built the tiny hut that stored rice. So the five others went to the *barasbaras* trail with Rodney. They cut *barasbaras* saplings to construct floors and sturdy walls. They cut *nipa* fronds and learned to use rattan vines to thatch roofing. They extended the dikes Victor built for protection and trailed underbrush on *barasbaras* saplings to camouflage the new compound from view. All this had to be accomplished urgently in case the Japanese patrol returned to look for the old, about to be abandoned hideout and even go beyond. BB, Joe, Scott, Valdez, excused Marco and Spenser from the work they were doing. Marco with his blistered feet sat in the makeshift kitchen talking to the guerrilla men making sure provisions for the *batel* trip was adequate.

Spencer rested and Milka tended to his wound. In the privacy of the *batel*, Spencer, though suffering intense pain wanted to make love to her. Unable to deny him, she yielded to his need. She asked *Manong* Alvaro's men who guarded the *batel* to go and help the men working at the *barasbaras* trail. With trembling hands, she led Spencer down the hull to the small cabin and closed the door.

Hardly aware of what she was doing, she made a bed and bolted out the boundaries of the world. They shielded themselves from interruption.

With a calm unknown to her, her fingers worked slowly to remove their clothes. When she was done, he stared at her naked body with blazing eyes. He asked if she knew what she was doing. Nodding her assent, she stirred a fire he had never known before. Overcome with desire, Spencer drew her close. With trembling arms he reached out to enfold her. He kissed her hands, her fingertips, moved his lips to her throat, down to her breasts and buried his head in their softness. She couldn't control her own response. She lay on his side trying to avoid pressure on his wounds. She lifted his head and laid it on the pillow. Then she kissed both his eyes softly and found his lips. His tongue devoured her mouth in a long, wet encounter. With great urgency, he sat up and lifted her on his lap all the while kissing her breast with a passion that stirred her loins. She felt his hardness, closed her eyes and arched her body backward. Her trembling legs parted to let him in. Time stopped with the flow of a lingering ecstasy; all danger was pushed aside, all fears swept away. They lay in each other's arms for a long time and like all lovers surrendered their solitary selves in exchange for the riches of a new found union.

As the need to fumble returned, Spencer tried to find her again, but pain and caution asked for restraint. She promised they would come together another time before he would leave, and she closed his eyes tenderly to usher sleep and rest. She busied herself with unlocking the hatch, walking around softly while he slept. She boiled a fragrant rice soup to feed him when he waked. When he stirred, she moved back to give him a kiss to reassure him of her presence.

When *Manong* Alvaro came to check on them, she was feeding Spencer the soup. Then Spencer did what she thought was unthinkable. He told M*anong* Alvaro he loved her and needed her. He asked if he could arrange their marriage. They were already wed in God's eyes. He only needed to provide official sanction to the union. Deeply embarrassed by this revelation, *Manong* Alvaro was at a loss; he didn't know what to say, but Milka's eyes were bright with longing and pleaded for his help. He decided Spencer needed sufficient and continued care. He told her to get ready to travel with them to the guerrilla hospital in *Caliling* as soon as the three others would arrive. Then he would arrange for an official wedding ceremony there.

Manong Alvaro would have occasion to doubt the wisdom of this decision, but he never regretted it. Spencer was ecstatic and Milka, grateful. The time they had together trying to elude the Japanese gunboats and finally arriving at *Maricalum* where Spencer and the rest of the crew of the Flying Fortress were picked up by a submarine would be for her a lifetime of remembering.

Chapter 43—Out of the Swamps and into the Open Sea

At midnight, the three Americans, the Luzuriaga girls, four of their father's fieldhands, two of *Kapitan* Almanzur's men, and Colonel Gomez's rescue team arrived at the compound.

"Oh my, we didn't expect you to arrive this late." Mama Sid was apologetic. "We don't have much to serve but rice soup boiled with ginger root and clams."

Panching and Milka woke up to welcome Leticia, Laura, and Maria Elena. They prepared food and their sleeping quarters to share with the Luzuriaga girls.

"Please don't bother too much about food." Laura said. We brought some from the *hacienda* and had eaten early this evening."

"Has anyone heard any news from the *hacienda*? We're afraid for Papa." Maria Elena asked timidly.

"We're certain Cresencio would lead the Japanese there because Papa was hosting George, Frank and Robert. That's why Papa sent us here with them. *Manong* Alvaro, Thank you for sending your men to help us get here safely," Leticia added.

"You're most welcome, girls. I'm glad you got here without any problem. Almanzur sent a message. He said he, Caesar, and Rafael went to the *hacienda* in a *salvaged* Japanese truck to help his cousin, Lt. Procopio Balinas, protect your Papa. Fortunately for Almanzur twenty more men led by Lt. Serafin Verzosa arrived to help them."

"We're glad to hear that," Laura said thankfully. We hope *Kapitan* Almanzur could use the truck to come here with Papa."

"I don't know if that's possible. It may be, but I can't wait for him to get here. I have to take these boys as soon as possible to *Maricalum*.

The six Americans welcomed their pilot, navigator, and tail gunner. Grateful to be together at last, they hugged each other. They mourned two who would not return. That nine of them survived and were now together was a miracle. Colonel Gomez told them to be ready within the hour to go south in a *batel*. There was room only for the nine Americans, Milka, *Manong* Alvaro, and eight of his unit to man the *batel* and defend it in case of Japanese attack. Nineteen people and the needed guns, ammunition, and provisions for five days were almost too much for the journey. If *Manong* Alvaro had a choice, he would not be so overloaded, but this was the best he could do.

"Munding, make sure you load everything we need. Take a few minutes to get ready," *Manong* Alvaro said.

The inevitable goodbyes hung in the air. Marco looked for Delia. Almost in tears, he hugged her as he bid goodbye to her, to Victor, Papa, Mama Sid, Panching, *Manang* Aning and her boys and *Inday* Choling, who had given birth to another son, and to her family as well. BB, Scott, Joe, Valdez and Spencer also went through the same routine.

Manong Alvaro embraced his wife and his two young boys.

"*Tatay* (Father)," they cried as they embraced him, "get back as soon as you can, okay? Please."

George, Frank, and Robert also said goodbye to *Manong* Alvaro's family. George and Frank asked for fifteen minutes of privacy to bid Leticia and Laura farewell. Faithfully, they promised to come back to them after the war.

Finally, *Manong* Alvaro embraced his family once more, took his father's hand, kissed it and put it on his forehead. He asked him to say a prayer and ask for God's protection and blessing on all. As soon as all nineteen boarded, everybody in the compound walked close to the *batel* and waved. *Kapitan* Almanzur's men pushed it from the riverbank.

It was 1:30 a.m. A light breeze was flipping the sails. It would be dawn before they could clear the other mouth of the *Ilog* River beyond *Enclaro*.

A strong wing flapped the sails noisily and moved the *batel* at a good speed. It stayed close to shore to avoid high waves in open sea. The wind steadily got stronger. The Americans snooped around and surveyed the arms carried on board. Mounted on the prow was a Browning machine gun the guerrillas had been using in fixed defensive positions. Gun and tripod weighed in excess of 88 pounds. Chambered for 50caliber ammo, it could fire 450 to 600 rounds per minute. There was an M2 machine gun that shot something short of cannon fire. The B17s carried as much as twelve of these guns to arm it against Japanese fighter planes.

Two of *Manong* Alvaro's crew had semi automatic rifles, the 1903 A4 .30 caliber M1 Garand rifle good for precision shooting. The six others had M 1903 Springfield automatic rifles. *Manong* Alvaro had a Thompson sub machine gun. It had high volume of fire with the mobility of a rifle for close combat. Equipped with a 50 round magazine, the gun could fire 600 rounds per minute. This sub machine gun had a good compensator and could deliver a spraying effect. *Manong* Alvaro said these were the best combat weapons ever delivered to the guerrillas. Several two-way radio systems came with the weapons a month before, when the submarine surfaced at *Maricalum*. The *batel* had to be armed with the best weapons available, especially if the Japanese used gunboats to chase them and in case some airplanes were to spot them and open fire on them. It would never be a fair fight but, armed with the best, they had a small chance to survive. The guerrillas had been doing exercises with these weapons and were prepared to use them, but since the American gunners were more familiar with them, *Manong* Alvaro asked if they could take over.

"Sir, we've followed your instructions carefully," Venancio said. "We camouflaged the weapons and made the deck look as if we're just transporting grain and fruit to trade for fish and salt."

"Good. Give each American a .38 caliber Smith and Wesson pistol to use in case the Japanese ever board the *batel*. Six wore the clothes Mama Sid gave them and the three others were in clothes given them at the *Hacienda Luzuriaga*. All had broad palm hats that farmers use. If the *batel* was spotted and they couldn't hide in time, at some distance they'd look as though they're Filipinos.

As *Manong* Alvaro anticipated, the *batel* skirted the other mouth of the *Ilog* River when dawn came.

"Munding," he spoke to the helmsman, "it looks like we're good for another hour or two before we decide whether to go on or go ashore for cover. We can't risk being spotted by aircraft."

Since there was no sign of airplanes, they took advantage of the wind to sail at their former speed. Towards noon, *Manong* Alvaro thought he heard the sound of a distant airplane. They sailed close to the *nipa*-covered shore a few kilometers from *Galicia*, close to the next town of *Cawayan*. They took the sails down and looked for cover in the thick *nipa* grove. Minutes later, two airplanes came, circled, moved away, and came back again, evidently looking for something. Seeing nothing except very small fishing boats, the planes moved out of sight. *Manong* Alvaro waited another hour before he felt safe enough to venture with sails again. When the sun finally sank in the horizon, he set full sail once more. But wind had died down. The *batel* moved very slowly.

After a while, there was no wind at all, not even a slight breeze. The guerrilla crew rowed for hours in the heat and humidity. Finally, they gave up. The *batel* came to a standstill. Shortly after, thunder and lightning filled the sky. Dawn came but no light filtered through the dark clouds. Signs of a typhoon wind rose at the horizon. Rain poured relentlessly. The crew bailed water as fast as they could; the *batel* was getting water logged. It bobbed up and down in the water helplessly as the waves pounded it. The typhoon struck. A heavy wind roared. The sails had to be taken down or the wind buffeting the *batel* would have sank it.

Bailing continued desperately, the Americans helping as much as they could. Every pail, every tin can was in use. Milka was exhausted from vomiting and a concerned Spencer had his turn to serve and comfort her. They had lost the cover of darkness as night yielded to day but another kind of darkness took over. The sky turned pitch black and looked as though it couldn't rid itself of water, pouring unceasing on the now top heavy *batel*. Effort for rowing was used for bailing. The *batel* stayed at the same spot for hours, bobbing in and out of waves that dragged it down. At times, it seemed as though it would never come up. A day and a half passed but it had not moved far from the same spot. It was still some distance to *Cawayan.*

Wind and water lashed. Everything was soaked; no fire could be lighted, no food cooked. All fruit was gone. A few coconuts were all that was left. The crew doubly secured the guns so they couldn't be washed overboard. The sails floated on deck and some of the oars were broken. Their spirit was almost broken as well. They tied the oars with ropes and hung on to them for dear life. Then as suddenly as it came, the typhoon lifted. The sun shone and they were in the middle of an empty sea. This was the fifth day since they left the swamps.

The water was as smooth as glass. *Manong* Alvaro's men untied the oars and tried to row. Exhausted and hungry, they made little progress. There still was no whip of wind. The Americans took over the rowing, but they, too, got exhausted. The sack of rice was soaking wet. With little success, Milka tried to build a fire to cook rice. It took an hour before she could get a fire going. She cooked the wet rice, put some dried fish on top of the steaming rice and covered it. It made a good meal and gave them enough strength to row with some vigor. It picked up their spirits.

After the meal, they put on the clothes left drying in the sun and wiped all the guns and equipment that had gotten wet. As Ponsing was rubbing the radio dry, it came alive with static. *Manong* Alvaro tried to get it to work but couldn't get anything except a loud buzzing.

"Here. Let me do it." Valdez took over. He brought the radio close to Milka's burning embers and rubbed it thoroughly dry. It worked and the Colonel deciphered a message. Lt. Procopio Balinas reported what happened:

"Lost so many good men: twelve dead and five seriously wounded. Re-grouped at *Candoni*. Lost two machine guns. Have few hand grenades, one sub machine gun and ten rifles. Down to eleven men, including me. Tried contacting *Manong* Almanzur. Silence. Heard from Lt. Verzosa at *Binicuil*. He lost three men but *salvaged* a Japanese truck, two sub machine guns, several automatic rifles, and a radio. He hooked up with *Kapitan* Efraim Jalandoni in *Himamaylan*. They're planning a raid at *Binalbagan*. The Japs are concentrated in *Kabankalan* and are busy with civilian reprisal. Verzosa and Jalandoni seek permission and help with plans for the raid. They'll radio you directly. My men are tired and discouraged. Don't know what to do next. Please advise, pronto."

Manong Alvaro tried to answer Procopio's message, but was interrupted by another.

"Urgent. Danger ahead. Two Japanese gunboats are speeding from *Binalbagan*. Heavily armed. Looking for you. Seek cover or fly."

A slight breeze was flapping the sails. Rowing for more speed, *Manong* Alvaro's men tried to get to shore as fast as the *batel* could go. They would never be able to outrun the gunboats and if the Japanese radio for aircraft assistance, they would have no chance in the world to survive.

Lt. Verzosa sent another urgent radio message to the headquarters in *Cawayan* and the hospital in *Caliling* asking for *Kapitan* Almanzur Villalva to make radio contact.

* * *

Caesar was very careful not to speed and overheat the engine; they had just arrived an hour before *Kapitan* Almanzur got Lt. Verzosa's message. *Tio* Mauring was delivered to the hospital; Rafael and Caesar were at the mess hall, but *Manong* Almanzur lingered at the old man's side. When his sister, Norma, came to tend to the old man, *Kapitan* Almanzur exacted an oath.

"You have to personally promise he'll get well. I don't care what your other duties are. Your primary task is to see he doesn't die. If he dies, you'll answer to me."

He was going to the mess hall when a soldier informed him he had a message. For days he had not eaten much; he was going to ignore the message for a while, but something told him he had better answer it first. He went to the CO's office. Colonel Celso Rosales sat with the familiar cigar in his mouth. He boomed at the *Kapitan* with urgent concern.

"Your cousin's in big trouble. You need to get together men you need and leave at once. Alvaro is trying to get ashore before the gunboats from *Binalbagan* catch up with him. He's well armed, but they just got through a typhoon. He's out of food; that's the least of his worries. Damn it," he continued talking, "he radioed saying their guns had been soaked by the typhoon. It better work for him or he can be slightly helpless. The Americans, Alvaro says, are experienced gunners and that should help him. Let's hope they're rowing fast and can get far enough toward shore where gunboats can't follow. You need to cover him from the beach."

Kapitan Almanzur was about to answer, but the colonel waved him out.

"Go, go, go. You don't have a minute to spare. "

Kapitan Almanzur found his voice. "Sir, I need help. I came with only two trusted men. The rest of my platoon is at my *Nanay* Sidra's compound where my cousin left them. Please use your microphone and order a platoon to assemble in front of the mess hall. I'll take whoever you can get ready at once."

Without waiting to be dismissed, he grabbed his Garand and ran to get Rafael and Caesar and the platoon ordered to assemble. Caesar asked for two trucks and one driver. Rafael asked for an M2 sub machine gun so they could spray the gunboats if they came close enough to shore. He also asked for as many Garands and for automatic rifles, grenades, a radio and two bazookas. In less than thirty minutes they were ready. Caesar drove the lead truck and flew out of the hospital grounds like a bear with a head full of hornets.

Chapter 44–The Commandant Wants to Save Face

Captain Akagi arrived at the garrison bearing a dead lieutenant and several dead and wounded soldiers, remnants of a platoon.

"How the hell did the guerrillas slip through your hands? How did they escape through Lt. Iwanaka's well-armed platoon? I don't understand this. Don't you know how to fight anymore? Colonel Takamatsu waited for an answer.

"Sir, they slipped through Lt. Iwanaka's platoon the same way they slipped through yours. They drove out of the *Hacienda Luzuriaga* with one of our trucks when you were in command there," the shame-faced Captain Akagi retorted.

"They did not kill my men the same way they slaughtered yours. Bury them with your sentimental fanfare if you choose. As far as I am concerned, they have dishonored my command." The commandant was hoarse with anger he tried hard to control.

Yes, they did kill some of your men. You didn't come back with the same number of men either, Captain Akagi wanted to yell back. Red in the face with the weight of the insult, he held his tongue. With some hesitation he said in an even tone. "Sir, they took Lt. Iwanaka's men by surprise. Since they were driving one of our trucks, our men thought you had sent some reinforcements from the garrison. They were wearing our uniform when they approached. Some of your men say that another truck came the very same way from somewhere to the *hacienda* and blasted two of our machine gun positions. Apparently, the first truck was one Colonel Asaki drove to the fringes of the swamps, and the other is one Lt. Konishi drove to chase the Americans. They must have taken him by surprise too."

Arrogant fool, the commandant thought, you better fight as sharply as your tongue lashes.

"We know that now," he said instead. "I sent two platoons to that bridge to pick up the dead bodies. We have to bury them all. I prefer you do it quietly and quickly. I don't want the native population to know any of our loses."

"They have their way of knowing, Sir. They observe our mood closely. They use it like a barometer; the angrier we get, the more likely that they know why. But I'm so furious over the death of both my lieutenants I could kill every last Filipino who crosses my path."

"That, I have already taken care of. I hanged every last one that showed the shadow of a smirk on his face. I killed some of their wives and children too, even the grandfathers and grandmothers. I just want to teach them some respect for power. We need to let them know we are the masters."

We can hang as many as we can, many more will spit on our faces if they can. That is not what we came here for, thought Major Takasaki who was in hearing distance. He simply swallowed his disagreement. Experience told him violence begets violence. Fair and humane treatment goes farther than weapons and killing. He wondered if these men, his own countrymen, don't have families to go home to. What would they do if their own people were treated the same way these people were treated?

Meekly, he addressed the commandant. "Can I do anything more for you, sir? I followed up on all your requests for arms and ammunition, for radio, uniforms, and food supply."

"Good, but remember, I need two gunboats ready. Have them filled with adequate fuel and stacked with the best machine guns, radios, and 75 mm guns. I'm going to get those Americans if it costs me my life. Radio *Bacolod* and let them know I need more gunboats to use when I get back from this mission. I'll root out those people from the swamps if I blast every single mangrove tree there is."

Captain Akagi heard the same words from the former commandant before he disappeared mysteriously.

The swamps, thought Major Takasaki, are eternal. No one can get them out of the way except the creator who put them there. Their darkness is a refuge for many of God's creatures, including those who're trying to escape our cruelty. When are we ever going to learn that life is precious, not just our lives, even those of the conquered ones. Conquered? They show us more than ever that we cannot conquer them entirely. Colonel Asaki was liquidated. Tyrants do not last long.

A radio message from *Binalbagan* said two light gunboats were ready; each can carry twelve to fifteen men. With good guns and ammunition, twelve men would allow better mobility. Colonel Takamatsu picked out his twelve men. He ordered Captain Akagi to do the same.

Now, we'll see what kind of fighting you can do, big mouth, he heard himself say to Captain Akagi silently. He wasted no more time in talk but went directly to the truck that will take them to the pier in *Binalbagan*. The gunboats arrived there from *Bacolod.* They, too, suffered the same buffeting as the *batel* did from the storm for two whole days. The privates were still churning the water out with small pumps when the colonel and the captain got there.

"Damn it, couldn't headquarters have sent me fresher boats? Turn the engines on. I want to hear them hum. We must move immediately to catch those bastards. I hope we'll still find them at sea," Colonel Takamatsu grumbled.

Fortunately for Colonel Alvaro Gomez, there were several small *batels* in the sea between *Binalbagan* and *Cawayan*. Both gunboats spent good time stopping and boarding them, checking if the fleeing Americans were in any of them. Colonel Takamatsu had the same penchant for cruelty as the late Colonel Asaki. He spent precious time torturing for information or simply for the pleasure of inflicting pain. Captain Akagi was a good twenty minutes ahead as his gunboat chugged farther toward *Cawayan*. He spotted Colonel Alvaro's *batel* halfway between him and Colonel Takamatsu's gunboat; it was close to the shore.

Maybe he just left the shore, he thought, but the prow is pointed in the wrong direction. Is he trying to get to shore? Why is he going past the open beach into that *nipa*-covered shore?

This is it. We have found them!

He shifted direction, turned around, and moved close to the *batel*; looking down on the shallow water, he discovered in alarm that he was moving too fast toward a reef. That's why the *batel* inched slowly; it picked its way toward shore carefully, trying to avoid the reef. The gunboat engine groaned as it slowed down too quickly. Captain Akagi used the foghorn.

"Hey you, come around and be boarded or risk being blasted."

He used both English and *Ilongo* so he could be understood. He brought along a Filipino *kempetai*, just in case. The gunboat was now parallel the *batel*.

"What's the fool trying to do? Why is he too close to shore? Doesn't he know enough not to be grounded?" Colonel Takamatsu grumbled to himself as he observed Captain Akagi on his binoculars.

All at once, the *Batel* opened fire. Alfonso used the M2 .30 caliber Thompson sub machine gun at the same time that Robert used the stationery .50 caliber machine gun. It took the Japanese gunner off guard; he fell with the machine gun from the prow of the gunboat. Bullets sprayed the deck as Alfonso intended. Captain Akagi got hit on the shoulder. Meantime, Colonel Alvaro's native crew rowed with all their strength toward shore, more than two hundred meters away. On the sandy beach to their left, *Kapitan* Almanzur had mounted the heavy Browning machine gun, turned it over to Caesar, and aimed a bazooka at Colonel Takamatsu's gunboat steaming fast to Captain Akagi's aid. *Kapitan* Almanzur missed it by a few feet.

"Damn it, we need to reload," the *Kapitan* swore.

Robert Coleman manned the machine gun at the *batel*'s prow and sprayed Captain Akagi's gunboat with .50 caliber bullets. As the bullets sprayed the deck, the 75 mm gun was silenced. The Japanese soldiers used their automatic rifles to little effect.

Unimpeded, Colonel Takamatsu used his 75 mm gun on the fleeing *batel,* almost missed it, but hit it close to the prow. Colonel Gomez was hit on the right shoulder with flying shrapnel and Robert got scraped on the temple. Milka and Spencer climbed from below onto the deck when the *batel* got hit. Three of the native crew got blasted away and Spencer and Milka were thrown on deck, just below Robert's gun. When Spencer came to, he saw Robert lying unconscious and Milka sat several feet away on top of an oar that Scott Rankin was using before he, too, got knocked unconscious. A bullet grazed Scott's scalp, injuring the brain and blinding him. Colonel Gomez was on his knees still using his Garand, aiming it at the on-coming gunboat. Marco was at the opposite end blasting away at Captain Akagi's crew. He picked up Alfonso's gun as he fell, but Marco, too, slumped on the gun as a shell fragment hit his right cheek.

Milka desperately held on to an oar as the *batel* tilted on the side that was hit. BB, Romero, and Frank Defacio and three of the remaining native crew were rowing as hard as they could to get the *batel* on shore before it would sink; George was sending an S.O.S. on radio to any one nearby asking for a rope so they could be pulled on shore.

"Hang on honey, please hang on for dear life," Spencer yelled at Milka. He pulled himself up and grabbed the machine gun Robert was using before he was knocked unconscious. He swung it around and let go of 600 rounds of .50 Caliber bullets at the approaching gunboat and slowed it down but not enough to prevent it from running straight into the reef. The *batel* had just scraped the reef and was inching to the shore.

Munding, (Raymundo), the helmsman, was zigzagging to avoid the sharpest corals and was shouting at the Americans to row with everything they've got. Milka pulled herself beside the unconscious Scott Rankin. She took his hands off the oar and used it herself.

"*Sige, Inday*, Go on, honey, *bugsay todo todo guid*, row with all you've got.," Munding rasped with fear.

"Yes, my love, we'll still get out of this alive, if I can help it. Send it directly to the shore this time," Spencer screamed at Munding. "If it's not the reef, it would be the guns that would sink us anyhow. Get as close as possible to the shore so we can all jump off."

He swung the gun left and right, spraying the gunboat deck with bullets.

A protracted scraping sound told the bleeding Captain Akagi that the boat was grounded. Water rushed in at both sides as the engine came to a halt.

Meanwhile, guerrilla men followed the flight of the *batel*, running with ropes and guns through the *nipa* grove bordering the shore. They looked like huge ants moving on the fringes of the shore. *Kapitan* Almanzur stayed on the sandy shore to the left once more aiming the bazooka at Colonel Takamatsu's speeding gunboat now getting close to the grounded Captain Akagi. Colonel Tamakatsu ran from one end of the gunboat to the other screaming his orders when a bazooka shell hit his gunboat in the middle of the deck. The shell stopped him dead on his tracks; bodies around him were blown to bits. The explosion blew his right arm off. Luckily, he was several feet away from where the bazooka hit. Four men shielded him before they were blown to bits.

Getting weak from loss of blood, Captain Akagi forced himself to stand and take command. He threw a jacket on the bleeding shoulder and shouted his orders. Colonel Takamatsu's gunboat was burning. Using the foghorn again, Captain Akagi shouted,

"Put out the fire, you morons. Throw us an inflated rubber boat and tow us in."

Captain Akagi cleared the debris from the deck and took the colonel's body to his cabin while two men tried vainly to stop the wound from bleeding. What was left of the arm was a stub that they put in a rubber vise to stop the bleeding. Captain Akagi was distracted from chasing the *batel*. His attention was divided between taking care of the unconscious Colonel Takamatsu and giving orders to the crew on how to proceed. As he was thus occupied, the 75mm gun remained silent.

Small outrigger *bancas* paddled to the *batel* and threw ropes the men tied on what was left of the prow and on the remains of the blasted masts. Guerrilla soldiers lowered the wounded and the unconscious on the side of the *batel* away from machine gun bullets still raining close but slightly out of range, for as new hands manned the machine guns both on the *batel* and on shore, the gunboat dared not get too near. George, BB, Valdez, Joe West, and Frank Defacio, were lowered to a separate *banca* and paddled to shore. The bodies of Marco, Scott, Robert, Alfonso, were in another *banca* with *Manong* Alvaro, Spencer and Milka. Only three of the eight men with *Manong* Alvaro, including Munding, the helmsman, jumped off the *batel*. The remains of the rest lay there till the *batel* could be towed on shore.

As soon as Colonel Takamatsu was taken care of, Captain Akagi maneuvered the surviving gunboat, speeding back and forth and strafing the shore with his machine guns; he could not get close enough. The reef became a formidable barrier; he could not get any nearer because of it. Also, he had to stay out of range of the guerrilla machine guns and *Kapitan* Almanzur's bazooka. Captain Akagi realized that if he could not keep the guerrillas covered with the heavy 75mm gun, they would be able to arrange for the Americans to escape. Quickly, he radioed for air support.

Colonel Gomez anticipated the move. Despite his bleeding arm, he worked the radio and talked to Caesar.

"Guard the wounded Americans, and Spencer and Milka, put them in a truck, and speed them to *Caliling* for medical attention as soon as possible. Take Rafael with you and you both guard these charges with your lives. Have them attended to immediately and keep them alive, if at all possible. Rouse all the medical personnel at the hospital even if you have to shake their quarters down."

In the *banca*, Milka laid Marco's bleeding head on her lap and Spencer had Scott's head on his. The colonel removed his soft, white undershirt and bandaged it around Robert's temple. Though still bleeding, Robert regained consciousness. He took off his shirt as well and put it over his bandaged head and pressed it on all the way to *Caliling*. Alfonso was still unconscious; his head was on the colonel's lap. All the while, the colonel's right shoulder was bleeding though he stuffed the wound with soft *kapok* from a pillow he grabbed and tied his shirt tightly around it underneath his armpit.

Spencer was crying openly now. Trying to rouse Marco and Scott, he cried passionately.

"You can't die on us now; not after all we've been through. Please hang in there. You can't die. You just can't die." Tears flowed freely down his face. "If there's a God in heaven, he can't let these brothers die. Please, *Manong* Alvaro, ask your doctors to save them."

The Colonel was also moved to tears. "We'll all do what we can to survive, God willing. We're not out of danger yet. We have to get on shore and get to the cover of trees before Japanese aircraft arrive."

"Oh, God," Milka moaned through her tears, "when will these savages stop hounding these harmless men."

The *banca* reached the shore. Rafael and Caesar and two other guerrilla soldiers ran to meet the Colonel, Spencer, and Milka and carried Marco, Scott, Robert and Alfonso to the cover of trees a hundred meters from the shore. Caesar ran to get his truck, came as close as he could, and laid the wounded men gently on the seat of the truck.

"Be careful with them. They're badly wounded." Milka warned Caesar. "I think they need something more to cushion them from the jarring movement of the truck. They'll bleed more without something soft to lie on. I'll hold Marco and Spencer will hold Scott. Robert and Alfonso will need cushions or someone to hold them."

The Colonel impatiently waved them into the truck.

"Do what you have to do but move on now. Drop me where there's better cover. I need to talk to Almanzur."

"You have to come with us, *Nong* Varo, please," Milka pleaded. "You'll bleed to death here. "

Rafael jumped in the truck.

"We have to go right now. If you drive close to the other truck, I'll rip off the backs of the seat cushions, but we need to move now before the airplanes come."

Just as he spoke, a 75 mm shell landed no more than twenty feet away. Caesar immediately put on the gas and zigzagged on the sand till he got to where a path took him under some trees. He yelled to Colonel Gomez.

"I'm sorry, Sir, but I think *Kapitan* Almanzur would know what to do. He ordered the other truck driver to take the other Americans and follow us, but I heard them refuse to go. They insisted on manning the machine guns in case the Japanese come on shore or their airplanes come, as you warned earlier by radio. They said something about giving the Japanese 'a run for their money.' None of us understood what they meant."

Colonel Gomez understood the American idiom. He looked pleased but seemed angry at the same time. For the first time Caesar and Rafael heard him swear.

"Those sons of bitches," the Colonel gave vent to his frustration. "They don't give a damn if they get themselves killed. I've worked so hard to deliver them for a submarine rendezvous but they'll let all my efforts go for nothing."

"Easy there, *Manong* Alvaro," Spencer spoke for his friends. "As long as the odds are 50/50 those guys wouldn't get themselves killed. They'd surely give the Japs *a run for their money*. I wish I weren't needed here. I'll join them to fight those devils, but I want to make sure these friends get taken care of. I can't let them die."

Caesar drove fast but carefully. Under the trees he was no longer visible to the gunboat; it took him forty minutes to cover the twenty kilometers distance to the hospital. He blasted the silence at the hospital compound with his horn. He blared loudly to declare the emergency he was carrying. Hospital orderlies ran out of bamboo buildings. Sirens started blaring and nurses and doctors putting on their white uniforms darted here and there. Alerted, the medical staff immediately began the long process of taking care of the wounded

* * *

When Captain Akagi was being transferred by rubber boat to the other gunboat, the 75 mm gun was silent. For a while, it was inoperative. Captain Akagi took time to fix it, but as soon as it could be fired he shifted his range and started pounding the shore. Careful to be out of range of the bazooka and the machine guns, he impatiently waited for the arrival of the airplanes from *Bacolod*. He took care of the severely bleeding Colonel Takamatsu, but he couldn't leave before the airplanes came to finish what the gunboats were unable to accomplish. The guerrillas demolished his grounded gunboat with a bazooka blast. He could not let them get away with that. He tried to spot where the shell came from but the shore was covered by dense *nipa* groves; nevertheless, he directed the 75mm shells twenty meters apart and started pounding the shore.

Kapitan Almanzur knew Captain Akagi's gunboat was out of range, so he changed his operational tactic. The fixed machine gun must be moved under better cover farther on the shore.

"We can't move farther up the shore, guys. We would be easy targets for the blasting 75mm cannon," he warned his men. "Load the machine gun in a small *banca* and push it very slowly along the *nipa*-covered grove. Take extreme care that the movement would not be visible through Captain Akagi's binoculars."

The guerrillas cut tall and broad *nipa* fronds to shade men, gun, and *banca*; they moved deliberately a foot at a time along the shore until the shoreline came to a sharp bend and traded vegetation for rock cover. At that point, the men on shore lifted the gun by rope and pulled it on top of rocks shaded by mangrove trees. The shore was now solid rock.

The easily movable submachine guns (the one that the B-17 flying fortress carried to defend itself from smaller aircraft) moved in the opposite direction. These moved through the *nipa* groves. The shore was swampy, but the lighter load moved faster. As soon as *nipa* grove gave way to mangrove trees, the men started the climb up shore. Four of the Americans, BB, Romero Valdez, and Joe, familiar with the M2 sub-machine guns, moved under excellent cover prepared to take on the expected Japanese airplanes.

The 75mm gun was slowly running out of shells but soon three small airplanes were buzzing in the air. The gunboat had been out of range of the guerrilla machine guns for sometime so Almanzur's guns were quiet. Not knowing exactly where the guerrilla guns were, Captain Akagi radioed the pilots to strafe an area covering 50 square meters on the shore. The pilots heard no counter fire at all; they began to feel this was futile exercise and a waste of ammunition. But to make sure they had not missed their target, they started to fly lower and lower, diving and darting up like hawks hunting for prey. When the airplanes flew almost to the level of the mangrove trees, Joe west let them have it. As soon as he sighted the wings of one of the planes tilting to make a slow turn, he swung the M2 sub machine gun following the motion of the wings and sprayed 20 rounds of bullets that had power and penetration ability. The bullets hit the belly of the airplane as it dived low into the mangrove trees trying to locate men and guns. It made its only mistake of the day. The bullets put fifty odd holes in the body of the aircraft; the fuel tank busted into flames. As the airplane lurched to clear the trees, it blew up in mid air.

"That was for Scott," Joe cried passionately with tears threatening to flow.

The second plane tried to strafe the area where the bullets came from, but it was flying much higher now, afraid another round of bullets would hit it too. The men had good cover and the strafing did no harm.

"Come back here you cowards. Fly as low as you did before so you can be in my range," Valdez blurted with disgust. "Strafing from up there will do you no good."

Captain Akagi was preparing to send another 75mm shell in the direction of the strafing, but the planes were flying so low he was afraid he might accidentally hit them. Besides, he was concerned about the still bleeding Colonel Takamastsu. He needed to return to *Bacolod* so Colonel Takamatsu would be attended or he might die. He sent a radio message to the pilots to carry on while he sped back to Bacolod. The damaged gunboat's engine ran at full speed.

"Damn these bastards," Captain Akagi fumed in frustration. "It must be the Americans using the weapons. These stupid guerrillas don't know any better."

The pilots also decided to leave, but as they swung around to leave the shore, one of the planes went on an arc that brought it within *Kapitan* Almanzur's bazooka range. This was their second mistake. Unable to use the machine gun, *Kapitan* Almanzur had been itching to hit the airplane with the bazooka. Taking careful aim under the mangrove trees, the *Kapitan* sent a bazooka shell that ripped the air and hit the tail of the airplane. The pilot tried to eject but was unable to. Losing altitude, he barely avoided the mangrove-shaded area. Coming down fast, he glided over the white beach and scraped it for half a kilometer before he hit a rock jutting out near the bend. The instant halt flipped his head backward; it came right back on the wheel. At impact, he passed out.

Following closely behind the damaged plane, the other pilot saw the glint of the bazooka under the cover of the trees. He strafed the area but had to climb up fast as Frank DeFacio swung the fixed machine gun around and answered with several rounds of 50 caliber bullets. The airplane circled above the hill around the bend and flew back to the airport in *Bacolod*. Captain Akagi wondered why only one plane came back. How could those untrained, ignorant peasants shoot down well-schooled pilots? And how could he explain the loss in this last maneuver? After all, he was the one who requested the gunboats and the air support. Again, the Americans were his excuse. It must surely be them, not the guerrillas, who used the weapons.

Arriving in *Bacolod*, Captain Akagi ignored the killing pain on his right shoulder, put Colonel Takamatsu on a stretcher, and asked for orderlies to take the unconscious colonel to the infirmary. With head bowed in utter embarrassment, he entered the office of the commandant. He had serious explaining to do before asking for treatment for himself.

* * *

Now that the imminent danger was over, the guerrilla men and the five Americans re-grouped above the beach where the other driver parked his truck. Some of *Kapitan* Almanzur's men slid down the rocks to the beach to get to the Japanese airplane. The pilot was still unconscious. The airplane sat at an angle with the cockpit high up on top of the rock. Guerrilla soldiers climbed up and kicked the body out of the airplane. The pilot lay face down on the sand when *Kapitan* Almanzur, limping from a bullet wound on the left leg, dragged himself toward the airplane. Miguel lifted his *bolo* to chop off the pilot's head. Carding stopped him.

"No, No, No. You want blood to splutter all over you? Use a pistol instead."

Kapitan Almanzur saw what was about to happen and yelled in anger.

"When they die in a gun fight, that's one thing, but to kill them when they're defenseless, that's nothing short of murder."

"Oy, *Kapitan*," Carding objected, "when they're up there in their airplanes shooting at us down here, we're defenseless too, except for the cover of the trees. They don't give a damn how we die; why should we?"

"Because we're not as inhuman as they are. You have more conscience, Carding; your wife wouldn't want you to die like that if you're defenseless. Besides, it would be interesting when he comes to, to question him about the garrison in *Murcia.*"

Carding yielded to this logic. He picked up the body like a sack of corn and marched with it in the direction of the truck uphill from the beach. He dumped the still unconscious pilot not so gently on the bed of the truck.

"He has a big bump on his forehead; he probably had a concussion. Let's get going so the medical staff can take a look at him at the army hospital. Isn't that where we are headed?" BB asked with some concern.

The guerrilla men looked at each other with apparent disinterest. The Japanese pilot could die for all they cared. Valdez thought he understood how they felt, but he looked at them intently and interceded.

"BB cares what happens to him. He's also a pilot, and if he bailed out in enemy territory, he would expect to be treated humanely."

Kapitan Almanzur finally exploded; he felt compelled to explain a difference. He met BB's glance.

"Look, we rescued you from the site of the plane crash. If we had left you there, and the Japanese found you, what do you suppose would have happened to you? All these past four weeks or so, we've been running with you, taking you here and there away from the Japanese patrols because we believe if they had found you, they would've tortured you beyond recognition and eventually killed you. We have witnessed what happens to people who have gone through Japanese torture. We can dump this pilot right here in the ditch for the wild dogs to tear up, but we're taking him to a hospital instead. That should be humanitarian enough for you."

Frank DeFacio intervened. He addressed the Captain and all the guerrilla soldiers present.

"We're grateful for what you've done. Of course we would not have survived if it weren't for all of you. We know many of your men have died because you hid us, and defended us when you didn't have to. What BB is asking is also a human question. In the end, isn't all human life precious? It doesn't matter if it is American, Filipino, or Japanese. Life is precious."

"Hell, who does he think he's talking to," Miguel was really angry. "Tell that to the Japanese. You think they should know that?"

"I know it's difficult to be fair to a cruel enemy like the Japanese," Frank persisted, "but in the same way you and I are fighting for our country, they're also fighting for theirs. They may not even have wanted to fight in the first place, but they couldn't refuse when their country called. It's the same thing with us. We're here to serve our country but war is a very inhuman thing and makes it necessary for us to kill each other whether we like to or not."

"This is bullshit. Do I have to listen to this absolute rubbish? Carding was furious.

Frank looked at the blank faces that stared at him squarely in the eye and he knew what he said made no difference to them.

He turned to the Captain and continued.

"My father is a Lutheran minister in St. Joseph, Missouri, and when he preached about human love and forgiveness, I turned my ear away. I didn't want to listen. But after what we have gone through in the mountains, after what people have done for us in the farms, at the *hacienda*, in the swamps, and now here, I thank God for human love and forgiveness." His voice quavered with emotion. But he spoke clearly and slowly so Captain Vilalva's men would understand.

That was a moving earful. *Kapitan* Almanzur talked to his men who listened to him.

"Compadres," (comrades) this is what we have trained for, to fight with valor and honor, but don't ever forget that to turn the other cheek to the Japanese whom we hate and despise is a lot harder than it is to kill them. I know what you want to do with this body, but I'm going to take it to the hospital and see what they can do for him."

"Oy, *Kapitan*, Carding tried to catch his attention. You don't have to do that. I think he just died."

The *Kapitan* stayed quiet for sometime. Then he addressed Frank, George, BB, Valdez, and Joe.

"From here on, we'll not encounter any more opposition. We'll get to *Caliling* in less than half an hour. Spencer took Robert, Marco, and Scott, to the hospital there. We'll soon know what happened to them. If they're too sick and can't be moved, they may have to stay behind; if they can receive better care in an American hospital somewhere, or perhaps in the sick bay of the submarine, we'll take them to *Maricalum* where a sub will pick up all of you."

"But how will they be taken from *Caliling* to *Maricalum?*" Carding asked the *Kapitan.*

"They can be driven by truck from *Caliling* to *Sipalay.*"

"But, Sir, the road ends there. How would we take them from *Sipalay* to *Maricalum?* That's still a distance of about fifteen kilometers or even more," Sergeant Peralta said. "They would have to be taken by *batel* again, wouldn't they? We could take them on foot, but what about the others who are wounded? How could we manage to take them on foot?"

"There may be no other alternative but to take them by *batel* again. I know you're all thinking about the Japanese gunboats that patrol that area, or the airplanes that support them. We'll decide what to do when we know better about the condition of those who're wounded.

In *Caliling* when things settled down, *Kapitan* Almanzur looked into his cousin Alvaro. He lay on the bamboo bed, his head on the soft *kapok*-filled pillow. He was so still Almanzur extended his hand over his face to see if he was breathing.

"It's bad. But I'll live. How's your leg?"

"It's fine. I'll probably limp for a while. I'm glad it's almost over."

"So am I," the Colonel agreed. "How are the three who were wounded?"

"It's touch and go, but they're still alive. All the hospital personnel and even my men, believe it or not, are on their knees praying. Do you believe in prayer?"

"Of course I do; all the time you had been away at the *hacienda*, and on the beach helping us, I was praying for God to spare not just the Americans, but especially you. You may not think much of this, but I think a lot of you."

The *Kapitan* bent down on the resting figure and gave it a tight hug.

They looked back at the events of the day thankful their lives had been spared. Both remembered with gratitude those who traveled the same road with them, had smoothed their way, but would not be back on it again. Worried about the wounded Americans, they wondered if they could be delivered to the rendezvous with the submarine.

After his cousin left the room, the colonel lay deep in thought. Intensely, he felt the suffering of those who had been critically wounded and had barely survived the recent ordeal. In the quiet of the bare hospital room he decided no matter what happens, this sadness that hung over him was simply part of the burden of life as it moved on. He smiled through his tears, not with irony, but in fervent faith.

Chapter 45—Wartime Dislocations

The typhoon struck four days after Colonel Gomez left the swamps in a *batel*. Concerned for the safety of Milka and *Manong* Alvaro, and of the guerrilla crew and the Americans, Delia's family and the Luzuriaga girls prayed earnestly. They didn't have much protection against the force of the weather so they huddled close to one another for warmth and shelter as strong wind and heavy downpour shook the small huts at the end of the *barasbaras* trail.

The Luzuriaga girls worried their hosts would be inconvenienced by their unexpected stay, but Papa and Mama Sid made them feel loved as their own children and asked them to feel part of the family. Papa knew they were worried about their father. He asked them to trust in God's care. Surely Almanzur would take good care of his compadre Mauring and assure him that his children were in good hands in the swamps. After Papa's counsel and his comforting words, the girls began to feel at home and learned to be part of the family. The girls talked, bathed, washed clothes, prepared food, ate together, and shared intimate thoughts with each other. Leticia and Laura were closer to Esperanza's age. They unburdened themselves to her about their incredible connection with George and Frank. Panching told them Milka felt the same way about Spencer. God works in mysterious ways. Perhaps the best way to understand how things happen is simply to trust in His wisdom, she assured them. Maria Elena was a couple of years older than Delia, but being the youngest she had been babied so much Delia could hardly stand her total lack of independence and her mental and emotional reliance on her older sisters. It seemed to her that Maria Elana couldn't make judgments on her own; yet she was a very sweet person who cared much for others. She wasn't self-centered, just softhearted and fragile, too fragile for her own good. Delia made up her mind to school her little by little into being her own person and be a strong individual. Maria Elena followed Delia around like a pet dog follows a child devoted to its care.

The war, Delia decided, uprooted people from their homes and their accustomed lives. Like any other calamity as earthquakes or typhoons and all sorts of difficult conditions, wartime incidents separated people from one another and deprived them of daily comforts as warm beds, adequate clothes, hot, nourishing food, and, in life and death instances, even the luxury of water. The Luzuriaga girls had to get used to the fact that drinking water at the end of the *barasbaras* trail was strictly limited and when water supply was low, it had to be rationed. But they easily adjusted to life in the swamps. In the three years of Japanese occupation they had come a long way to adjust to loss of property, including a beautiful ancestral home, exquisite clothes, stunning gardens, extensive orchards, bountiful vegetable nurseries, poultry houses, horse stables, a dairy, a piggery, and a network of life-time service structure that assured the maintenance and convenience of everything they needed or asked for.

So it turned out that Prudencio, a loyal field hand, heard his wife and two sons had fled to barrio *Manalad*. *Tio* Mauring gave him permission to go back and look for them. *Kapitan* Almanzur made him promise to go to the swamps to tell the girls that their father is okay and is well taken cared of. Prodencio did as he promised.

Chapter 46—On Foot to *Caliling*

A week after Colonel Alvaro left with the Americans, Prudencio arrived in the swamps. He asked Leticia's permission to go to the *hacienda* to raise food for his family.

"Yes, Prudencio. My father would have given you money for seed, but who has seed to sell these days? You have to be quiet about working there. If you are able to raise something, people won't hesitate to rob or kill you for what you have. You certainly can work there. The land belongs as much to those who work on it to produce something as it does to those who own it."

"Thank you, *Inday*. I'll be careful; I have no choice. I don't want my wife and children to starve. My son and I will go back to *Manalad* tomorrow. I left my wife alone with my younger son."

In turn, Leticia asked Prudencio for a favor. "May I and my sisters go with you and rest at your house before we proceed to *Caliling* to be with Papa?"

"*Inday,* (honey), you have to walk a very long way, about forty-five kilometers or even more. Are you sure you can make it?"

"We have no choice either, Prudencio," Laura answered determinedly. "Papa needs all of us. We'll make it."

The men who paddled them from the *hacienda* to the swamps volunteered to go with the girls. Thinking these men volunteered too readily for nothing in return, Victor asked to go with them.

"I'll go with you as far as *Galicia*. I'll find out if my father's tenant is still working on our land there."

Concerned for their safety, Victor had to invent a reason for going with them. He didn't want them to feel obligated, but he didn't trust their going with men regardless that they worked for their father. Mama Sid said she would prepare two *gantas*, a measure of a foot square, roughly two kilograms, of shrimp paste and two small bags of salt to trade for rice. It would be good to have more rice for the days to come.

Victor showed Prudencio and his son how to gather shells at the riverbanks and fish with safety pins at the end of a short line with worms for bait. They cooked the fish and wrapped them in *nipa* leaves. Mama Sid gave them salt she could spare and two scoops of *guinamos* (shrimp paste) to take home to his wife. She told Prudencio she would gladly exchange more for *camote*, *cassava*, and rice, as soon as he can harvest anything. She didn't want this loyal tenant to starve.

Panching suggested the girls should wear men's pants. They borrowed a couple from Victor for comfort and convenience. It would make them less conspicuous. The pants were too big for Maria Elena so she used the clothes she wore when they came to the swamps. Panching and Delia parted the girls' long hair and braided them and put them up neatly into men's *buri* hats. Mama Sid made ready all food provisions, labeled them into daily packets, enough for a week, and put them into a basket for Federico to carry. She asked Almanzur's men for two of their leather water canteens for Ismael, the other field hand, to carry. Each of the girls carried a bundle, with change of clothes, *patadiongs,* and hair clips. Delia made Maria Elena promise to hold her own and even help care for her older sisters.

Victor took the rifle he had *salvaged* from a dead Japanese, the same one he used to kill the intruders on that fateful day not so long ago. He wrapped it in a *buri* (woven palm) bag he slung at his back with the *guinamos*, the salt, and his change of clothes.

Barefoot, with only *bakias* (wooden clogs), to put on when the way got too rough, the girls followed Victor's lead. The group arrived at barrio *Manalad* late in the evening. They covered barely fifteen kilometers this first day so Victor told the girls he would wake them really early to have a good start the next day.

Dawn came too fast. Maria Elena woke up before her sisters stirred. Maring was apologetic; she had nothing to give them for breakfast but a single cooking banana.

"Feed it to your kids," Maria Elena told her. "We'll eat what *Tia* Sid prepared for us."

"Girls," Victor called their attention, "today we can't stop, not even to eat. You have to eat as you walk. You stop only for personal comfort. Just select a shaded spot under some trees and plenty of brush to hide you from view."

The girls tried valiantly to keep up with the men, stopping only once or twice for comfort. Victor didn't like the way the men looked at the girls when they asked to stop for personal need so he took the automatic rifle out of his backpack and carried it in plain view. The men kept their distance after that.

Asking questions from people around, Victor found out how to get to his father's tenant's house; they walked six more kilometers to get there. His Papa's tenant had a hut with two bedrooms, and an outhouse. An old house built before the war, it provided better accommodations. The girls had time for a cold bath in a four by four, bamboo and *nipa* enclosure next to a well. Victor filled earthen jars from which they scooped water with a coconut dipper and enjoyed a cold, refreshing bath. What a joy to be able to wash their hair and undo the tight braids now dirty from dust and perspiration. Victor sat down with his gun not too far from the bathing enclosure. They covered twenty-six kilometers this day. They couldn't turn down the hot supper of boiled chicken and papaya soup and steamed rice offered by their host. Their feet hurt and were swollen and blistered so they asked to be excused.

When they left the next day, Victor gave the tenant's wife a small package of *guinamos*, wrapped in banana leaves and two handfuls of salt. She was delighted and very grateful for the gift, something extremely rare and difficult to get in this inland town at the foot of the mountains. The girls helped themselves to star apples and *langka* and wrapped some in their *patadiongs* to take to *Caliling*. Victor also took some star apple, peanuts, *camote,* and *cassava* to bring to *Caliling*, and informed the tenant in case his *Manong* Almanzur needed food, he would come and take his Papa's share of the produce.

The next day, they covered twenty kilometers to arrive in *Cawayan.* The girls were grateful that Victor offered to go with them all the way to *Caliling.* It was market day in *Cawayan.* People with bananas, papayas, and all sorts of fruits and vegetables came to sell or trade. First, Victor asked around for information about the Agustins, some friends of his family; his mother is Mrs. Agustin's contemporary. Mrs. Agustin had a stall in the market place. When Victor introduced himself and the Luzuriaga girls, Mrs. Agustin would not hear of their leaving. They had to come home with her and meet her own daughters and her entire family. They had a big seven-bedroom house made of *Narra* and *kamagong* (oak and mahogany). It had corrugated tin roof, and indoor plumbing. Water was pumped into the house in lead pipes. Knowing how weary the girls were, Victor did not have the heart to refuse Mrs. Agustin's hospitality. If they leave before noon the next day, they would be in *Caliling* before four o'clock in the afternoon.

That evening, they met seven Agustin girls, their only brother, and their father. They were treated to a sumptuous dinner, with chicken, pork, rice, and candied desserts. They had coffee after dinner and after an enjoyable conversation, they were sent to a bedroom with rattan beds.

What luxury! The hospitality was extended for as long as they wanted to stay, but explaining that they were anxious to see their father in *Caliling*, they were regretfully excused.

Chapter 47—Reunion in *Caliling*

They arrived in *Caliling* by noon next day. Sweaty and tired, they ran to the hospital looking for their father. Overjoyed, the old man turned to the wall crying with joy.

"It's all right, Papa. We're all together again," Leticia put her arms gently around her father. The girls cried at seeing a very frail old man who couldn't get out of bed. *Tio* Mauring recovered very slowly from his ordeal. Maria Elena wouldn't leave his bedside, not even when supper was served elsewhere. She ate star apple and *camote* and insisted on sleeping on a cot beside her father's bed. The older girls went for supper at the mess hall. They looked like they had seen ghosts when George and Frank walked in with *Kapitan* Almanzur, Joe West, Valdez, BB, and *Manang* Norma.

"We thought by now, you had all been taken to Australia or back to the United States," Leticia said.

"Captain Al, that's what we call him, and his cousin, the Colonel, are not sure it's safe to move Marco, Scott and Robert. They suffered critical injuries last week, but if they don't improve quickly, they may have to send them with us to meet the sub. Spencer is still trying to recover from his wounds too, but at least he's happy with his new bride who takes very good care of him."

"Yes," George nodded seeing the unmistakable pleasure in Leticia's eyes, "they were married as soon as we got here. The Colonel simply ignored Captain Al's objection with a firm 'I promised them I would arrange it. That's all there is to it.' I guess Captain Al couldn't object too long when he saw the look of love on his sister's face. We're all very happy for them."

"We have a lot to tell you about how we got here; but you must be exhausted. When you have freshened up after supper, can we take you to the brook at the foot of the hill behind the hospital?" Frank asked. "It's beautiful there."

"Right now, we want to see how Scott, Marco, and Robert are doing. Scott was still unconscious early this afternoon; Marco has been sleeping a lot. He has lost so much blood; he isn't much aware where he is. Robert still feels a lot of pain, especially when the morphine wears off, but he can at least talk to us."

"Do you mind very much if we go with you to see Robert?" Laura asked. "We'll take Maria Elena with us. I think he might like that."

"When we go to the brook afterwards, we'll wash our feet and freshen up there. We don't have to take too much time away from each other. It may be the only chance to say goodbye another time," Leticia said tearfully. "Tomorrow, we have to spend time with our father too. He needs us just as much."

"We understand."

George took her hand, led her away from the dining area, and all four of them went to the hospital hut to see *Tio* Mauring and Maria Elena. She stroked her Papa's forehead and wiped it gently with the square piece of *patadiong* material dipped in warm water. The old man was contentedly resting. His daughter held his hand as if it were precious coin suspended on a magnet. Maria Elena wanted to see Robert too, but she didn't want to leave her father alone. Fortunately, *Manang* Norma and *Manong* Almanzur walked into the room. The old man greeted them with a broad smile.

"I brought your favorite meal for tonight, *Tio,* (uncle). I know your daughters are here, but let me feed you for the last time, okay? I'm afraid after this, your daughters will take over my job and I won't be able to feed my favorite patient anymore. May I have the privilege this one last time, girls?" *Manang* Norma went over to give each of them a hug.

George took the opportunity to talk to *Tio* Mauring

"It's a pleasure to see you doing well, Sir. We know you're going to feel much better with the girls taking good care of you. It's a joy to see them here. How are you feeling tonight? Much better, I hope?"

"I feel a lot better, thank you," the old man answered listlessly.

Maria Elena bent down to whisper something in his ear. He held his hand out to shake George's, but George took the old man's hand and put his forehead on it as a greeting of respect he had seen Colonel Gomez do a number of times to his Papa in the swamps. The old man was taken aback. He didn't expect the gesture and he was both pleased and a little shaken. Frank also came near the bed and did the same gesture of respect. The old man was secretly pleased.

"My daughter tells me she wants to go with you to see how Robert is doing. I hope he's doing better, too. Tell him for me, I wish him good health. Go with my blessing. Norma and Almanzur will keep me company until you return."

He addressed George and Frank one more time. "Maybe you can do me the favor of showing my older daughters around. They need to know everything about this place if they expect to be of help to the people here."

The girls were delighted with their father's attitude. They weren't so sure how he would react to the young men's presence. Leticia came around, bent down, and gratefully embraced the old man. So did Laura They thanked their father fervently and promised not to be too late. Norma told them the orderlies had readied the room they were taken to earlier and had prepared beds for the three of them, but Maria Elena asked her if it would be okay for her to sleep on the cot next to her Papa.

"Of course, it would be," *Manang* Norma told her. They all thanked her and *Kapitan* Almanzur once again. Then they left to see about Robert and Scott and Marco.

Robert couldn't hold back the tears as Maria Elena rushed into his arms and gave him a kiss on the cheek. He felt genuine affection for him as all three asked how he was feeling and told him their Papa wishes he'd feel better soon. He showed them the patch on his temple and assured them he would be okay, especially now that he can look forward to seeing them each day until they were ready to leave. Maria Elena promised to keep him company next day and she tucked him in bed before George and Frank took them to see Scott and Marco.

Scott was still unconscious. A nurse sat by his bed taking his blood pressure and vital signs every hour on the hour. The girls held his hand and pressed it to greet him. They stayed to talk for a while and as they were leaving, they saw the hand move from his side to his chest; it fluttered for several seconds and then went limp. The nurse got excited. She told them it was the very first sign that convinced her he might get his senses to work again.

Marco was a different story. The bump on his head was slowly subsiding. The nurse said he hears everything but he doesn't yet have the energy to reply. A deep gash on his right arm was bandaged, so was his head. It hid a swollen blood vessel that was black and blue. The older girls pressed his hand to announce their presence, but Maria Elena, moved to tears by the quiet figure, came close and gave him a hug and a kiss.

His head moved and he raised his hand to feel where the hug came from. He traced Maria Elena's shoulders with his hands. The shadow of a scowl darkened his face.

"De—Del—ia?" A tear rolled down his cheek. "Is that you?" He asked again in a very soft whisper that was hardly audible. The eyes squinted but didn't open.

"No, Marco. It's Maria Elena Luzuriaga. My sisters and I met you briefly in the swamps at *Tia* Sid's place. We brought Robert, George and Frank there from our *hacienda* and we bade you goodbye before you left in a *batel,* remember?"

Marco nodded and answered in a soft whisper. "I thought you were Delia. You're almost the same size. Please don't tell her I'm not well." He turned his head to the wall to hide his tears.

"No, I won't; by the way, she sent you this." Deeply touched by his show of emotion, Maria Elena lied. From her skirt pocket, she took out the square piece of *patadiong* Delia had given her; it was still damp. She knew Delia would not mind. It was a very impulsive gesture.

"What is it?" Marco asked.

"It's a square piece Delia cut from her favorite *patadiong.* She said you would need it to wipe the perspiration when it gets too hot and humid."

That was what Delia said to Maria Elena when she gave it to her.

Marco extended a trembling hand to take it. Maria Elena put it in the palm of his hand.

"Make sure you don't lose it. Delia sends it with her love."

"Thank you so much. Do you mind if I see you again tomorrow? I'm rather tired tonight, but I appreciate your visit very much. "He turned his head toward the wall and put the square piece of cloth over his eyes.

"Bye for now" Maria Elena said. "I'll see you again tomorrow."

Marco didn't say anything more. The girls saw the slightest nod of the head. All this time he had spoken he didn't open his eyes.

The nurse drew the group aside and whispered.

"Under the bandage, the hematoma extends over the eyes that remain closed all the time."

As they moved toward the door, the nurse told them something that Marco was not supposed to hear.

"This is the first time he has spoken since he arrived at the hospital. He has never answered when he was spoken to."

"That's true," George said. " Frank and I come to see him everyday since we arrived. BB, Valdez and Joe have also tried to get him to talk but he has never spoken."

The two were greatly moved. They wondered what made Marco so visibly shaken. They went out of the room on tiptoe; they didn't want Marco to know they had witnessed a near miracle.

Much later, when Maria Elena related this event to Delia, she sobbed as she remembered the tall stranger who stole a part of her heart. She felt he was the most sensitive person in the batch. He listened to their stories with attention and responded to their situation with genuine interest and appreciation. Something he had said stuck in her mind. Marco said it one evening while they looked up at the sky.

"This same moon that shines over these swamps is shining on my home in Chicago. I know my parents are hoping I'm still alive."

The next day, Marco looked forward to the visit of the girl he mistook for Delia but whose prattle was nothing like the enlightened conversations he had with her. She reminded him so much of the other girl. She told him she was two years older than Delia but Marco thought she talked like someone much younger. He was interested to hear about the arrival of the three other airmen at the *hacienda* and their narrow escape to the swamps. He missed the swamps and Delia's family and this girl's conversation stirred his memory. Though harrowing, his experience there crowned the long list of things that happened to him after their rescue, a pleasant change from the suffering on the rugged trail. The thought of suffering triggered the agony of the *batel* ride and the bitterness hit him hard. He was no longer with the girl. He held his bandaged head in his hand and sought the oblivion of sleep.

The girls established a daily routine that included visits to Robert, Marco, and Scott after they attended to their father's needs. Scott was still fed intravenously from the tubes that hung by his bed. The same nurse sat quietly by his bed. She noticed that a new color crept on his face and, every now and then, the hand moved from his side to his chest; it stayed there for a few minutes before it slid back to the side. He seemed aware of their presence for when they came to see him, the hand moved from the side to the chest. When Laura and Leticia held both hands at each side, they felt or perhaps imagined a feeble tightening in response. When they left, the hand that was free of the tubes moved to the chest and stayed there for a while before it dropped to the side.

After Maria Elena spent time with her Papa and Robert, she spent a half hour with Scott and stole back to Robert's hut again. She told him about the long walk to *Caliling* and the time spent with Delia in the swamps, about her childhood, her Mama, her *yaya*, (nanny), Carlito, about school, and the lavish life style at the *hacienda* before the war. She missed her mother; she was the center of all activities at the *hacienda*. Talk about her mother drew tears from Robert. He listened attentively until the heat of the day put him to sleep.

The girls helped with food preparation. Laura was an excellent cook. She seasoned vegetable in delicious, nourishing soups. She made delicacies from sweet rice and corn flour. She fried yams and *cassava,* boiled bananas and mixed them with other vegetables into casseroles the medical staff enjoyed immensely. She cooked dishes from the very limited ration of meat garnished with the magic proportion of shrimp and crab paste instead of plain salt.

Leticia prepared drinks from mint leaves growing around the hospital. Their smell drifted in the air. She took the mint stalks she had rooted for a few days in tin cans filled with water and transplanted them underneath bamboo windows so the smell of the leaves would permeate the air and drift through the huts. They made their presence felt in a way that was inconspicuous but invaluable. They made the hospital in *Caliling* a haven of rest.

George and Frank fell more deeply in love with the older Luzuriaga girls but time was running out. *Manong* Almanzur had to decide when to take them for the submarine rendezvous and what to do when the time came. Should Scott be moved? Now completely conscious, are Marco and Robert up to what could possibly happen next?

Chapter 48—A Time to Part

Understandably, George and Frank were in no particular hurry to leave; neither were Spencer and Robert. Marco and Scott could not speak for themselves, but already a couple of messages have been received from Australia asking when it would be feasible for the submarine to pick them up. BB, Joe and Valdez had to request a conference with the Colonel and Captain Al. The night before the scheduled meeting, Marco asked Maria Elena a favor; he asked her to please take him by the hand and lead him to Scott's room. When they got there, Maria Elena asked if she could wait outside. Again, Marco marveled at how sensitive these people are even when they're so young. It seemed almost as if it were an inbred quality. He told her he would ask for her to open the door when he was ready to leave.

Groping in the dark, he became aware of the nurse at the table by the bed. He dragged his leather slippers over the dirt floor that shone like a mirror from being polished with coconut scrubs by dozens of young orderlies everyday. He had to be careful to maintain his balance. The dirt floor was so sleek he slid on it without much effort.

"Sir, I can't leave the room, but I'll be very quiet and will be careful not to interfere."

The nurse pushed a chair by the bed and led Marco to it. He dismissed her with a nod, sat in the chair, reached for Scott's hand, and held it for a long time. He wept in silence and his tears dropped on the hand he held. He thought he felt a feeble tightening as he spoke.

"Scott, we've been taken here so we could have medical attention and a sorely needed rest, but we've been here more than a week already. I don't know how you feel but I don't think they have what we need to get better. They say we may have to be moved in a truck to *Sipalay*, a town some forty kilometers away, but that's where the road ends. We need to go about fifteen kilometers farther to where the sub can pick us up. We could take a short *batel* ride, but that could risk another gunboat chase and another air attack. The alternative is to be taken on foot by guerrilla carriers for fifteen long kilometers. Because of our physical condition, it's difficult for the Colonel to decide what to do. We can't risk staying here much longer. We need to get to a more equipped hospital somewhere. What do you think we should do, Scott?"

Marco felt the futility of asking; nevertheless, he continued to seek an answer.

"A decision must be made tomorrow. We must help them make that. If you think we can risk a *batel* ride, tell me. I know you can't speak, but I know you can hear me. I just know you can. Please tell me in some way. I don't know how. There must be a way."

Marco rested his head on the bed and began to sob. The nurse said she would not interfere, but she couldn't help herself.

"I beg your pardon, Sir," she spoke to Marco. "You know, in the movies they always ask them to blink their eyes. Maybe the Lieutenant could do that?"

Marco stopped sobbing. He got very quiet. Finally, he spoke softly.

"Did you hear that Scott? If you think we should go by *batel,* blink once. If you prefer to be taken on foot, blink twice. Remember that these tubes go with you and you have to be carried by men who would go on foot all the way. We don't know what the terrain is like or how difficult it would be to do that, but these people would spare nothing to deliver us to where we need to go. I wish we could decide to stay, but wouldn't that be just as dangerous as going as soon as we decide what to do?"

Marco continued to sob softly; tears fell freely on the hand he held.

"What do you think we should do, Scott? By *Batel* or on foot*?*"

The eyes did not blink. Marco asked again. When he didn't get an answer, he put his head on the hand he held and cried more.

I wish they could help you here," he whispered softly. But you know medical care here is rather primitive."

The nurse bristled with hurt pride when she heard this. She interrupted Marco despite her promise. "We do the best we can do here, Sir. Our doctors are excellent. Even though we don't have adequate medical supplies, lab, and surgical equipment, we do quite well." The nurse said this with passion.

"I know you do." Marco matched her feeling. "I wouldn't be sitting here if you didn't. Your surgeons do an exceptional job. I know that when I look at young Ponsing, the Captain's aide. When we were fighting for our lives last week, he spent all that time in agony in the hull of the *batel.* He had peritonitis; he, too, was fighting for his life down there. He sorely needed medical attention."

"And he got it promptly," the nurse insisted. "Dr. Carbonel operated on him immediately."

"I heard. But Robert told me how. They tied his hands and got him drunk with *tuba*. That was the anesthesia they used to numb the pain, and the doctor used a sharp Gillette blade to cut into his belly. Poor boy, I really don't know how he survived it," Marco talked to himself more than to the nurse.

"I know, but look at him now. He survived and has recovered quickly. That's testimony to our surgeons' skill, despite the lack of medical supplies and medication."

"I don't understand why they could give us morphine and why Scott here could have this ivy apparatus, but Ponsing could not get the anesthesia he needed." Marco registered his dismay.

"The natives, Sir, are given local anesthesia. We reserve our more sophisticated medicines for officers like you and Lt. Rankin here. We're glad we have something to give him, though we fear that our supply may not last." She was ready to drop the matter.

At her mention of Scott Rankin, Marco raised his head to look at Scott's face; he was shocked to see the eyes blink once every minute or so.

"Nurse, please let the girl in;" he was shaking. "Honey," he sought Maria Elena's hand, "look for George, Frank, BB, Joe, Valdez, Captain Al, everybody. Bring them here. Please hurry."

He held Scott's hand tightly and began kissing it. The nurse got agitated too. She came and gave him a pat on the shoulders.

"Take it easy, Sir. Please try to remember the lieutenant is not well."

Marco took the square piece of *patadiong* from his pocket and dabbed at his eyes; he turned to the nurse, pleading for her to confirm him.

"He blinked. Did you see that? He blinked. Not just once but several times."

He was still sobbing softly when Captain Al, George, Frank, BB, Joe, and Valdez came running in the room. Without explaining anything, he asked again.

"Scott, once if by *batel* and twice if on foot. Look at his eyes; look at his eyes."

They all looked at Scott's eyes; in minutes, it started blinking once several times.

"My God," the Americans said in a chorus, "he can hear you. He can hear us. This is a miracle. Thank God."

The nurse was getting angry; she addressed *Manong* Almanzur loudly.

"Sir, this is outrageous; you have to get out of here before you drain my patient's energy."

She held the door open, frantically gesturing for them to leave. They all trooped out, some crying, some laughing with joy. Marco was last to leave. He pressed Scott's hand.

"Thank you for the answer. We love you. Hang in there until we can make arrangements for leaving."

Kapitan Almanzur rushed to see his *Manong* Alvaro and told him about Scott. Together, they sent a radio message for the submarine to pick the Americans at *Maricalum* immediately.

"Explain the situation carefully, Almanzur," his *Manong* Alvaro said from his bed. "Tell them about the danger still remaining. Ask them what to do about the Japanese gunboats that still patrol the shoreline from *Sipalay* to *Maricalum*. How would you defend yourself from an air attack?"

The Colonel was obviously not too happy about the situation. But within a few hours a message was sent back specifying the location for the pick up saying the submarine would be ready to assist the *batel* against gunboats and airplanes. The submarine was ready and anxious for the pick up.

It wasn't easy to say goodbye to the Colonel. How can they find the words to thank someone who almost lost his life so that they would live? To be sure the entire episode was not easy on any of them, but for all who risked their lives when they did not have to, how could words ever be adequate? To say less was clearly the only way to say more.

On this day of their departure, all of them, except for Marco and Scott, crowded into the small hospital room, shook the Colonel's hand, crying their farewells, singing "glory, glory, hallelujah." They marched to the mess hall, rang the gongs that announced meals, continued to the kitchen, grabbed pots and pans, banged these with wooden spoons, and trooped everywhere in the compound, singing till they were hoarse, their eyes unashamedly filled with tears.

The medical staff was too stunned to say anything. They, too, joined the marching and took up the tune the Americans were singing. They were better with the words and sang three whole stanzas of the hymn. Everyone in the entire compound came out of doors, wondered what's happening, joined in the laughing, crying, and hugging at the same time.

When the marching ended back at the mess hall, BB, Valdez, Joe, Marco, Robert, and Captain Al were seated on the front table and the chief of staff, Colonel Rosales, convened a more or less informal gathering to say goodbye to the Americans. True to the Filipino sense of exaggeration in occasions of importance, the chief delivered a stirring impromptu speech in English, wishing the B-29 crew the best of health and good luck on the way home. When asked to give a similar speech that would be relayed by a public address system from his hospital bed, Colonel Gomez declined and said he would deliver his message by radio as soon as the Americans were safe in the submarine that would pick them up.

George and Frank were conspicuously absent and orders were issued to find them and get them to this final conference. The orderlies found them in the hospital beside *Tio* Mauring's bed. The girls were trying to muffle the sobs caught in their throats as both George and Frank tried to formally ask the old man for permission to come back after the war, if they were still alive, God willing, to ask for the girls' hand in marriage.

"Sir," George began rather tentatively, "we know you are aware that both Frank and I are deeply in love with your daughters. At his point, we have very little to offer except our word that nothing would keep us from coming back. We're leaving because we have to, but our hearts are going to remain here with you and the girls."

"Please, Sir," Frank continued, "we'll pray that God would spare all of us from harm until we see each other again. There isn't much to assure us that we'll survive this war, but if we do, we would like to ask your permission to return."

"We know we have to go, but if we have your permission to come back, leaving wouldn't be so difficult," George pleaded.

"Papa, would you please say yes, and give them your blessing?" Leticia sought her father's eyes and took his hand in a gesture that told him she had completely given her heart away. Laura couldn't say anything; she quietly went to Frank's side, held him in her arms, put her head on his shoulder and cried her farewell. The old man knew she braved his displeasure in doing this, but he felt no disrespect from her at all. All of a sudden, the past came flooding in. He remembered the same desperation his Nora felt when she went against her father's wishes. But he had already anticipated this scene. He knew it would all come to this. His resistance drained. He turned his head from the wall and held out his hands.

"Come here, both of you," he said in a shaky voice. "I hope you realize what it costs me to trust your word, but if you love my daughters, as much as I love them, keep your word. Come back with my blessing."

George and Frank came close to the bed and the old man laid his hands on their heads. Again, both young men took each hand and put their foreheads on it both as a gesture of deep respect and gratitude. The old man cried openly.

"Go, go somewhere and say goodbye to my daughters. Remember to keep your word. You know you'll break their hearts if you don't. Go now. Alvaro and Almanzur, bless their hearts, will be expecting you soon."

There wasn't much time to waste. Orderlies told them where they were expected, but they ignored them and hurried with the girls down the hill to the brook behind the hospital. The magnificent trees and the running brook couldn't be any more beautiful than it was this time. Wild flowers dotted the hillside beyond. A few days after their arrival in *Caliling,* the girls had to face the fact that the nightly walk under the trees and the time spent together by the brook at the bottom of the hill behind the army hospital would come to an end. Now time was trickling out in minutes. No longer could they wish that time could be extended, for the necessity of departure was a heavy door that would slam close and crush their feeble hope to be together. They held each other close and kissed with a tender longing and a passion that gripped their hearts. They had to believe in something that could bridge the chasm of parting.

"We'll be back," George promised. "As God is my witness, I'll do everything in my power to survive this war."

Leticia clung to that promise, but she acknowledged to herself no matter what took place after this moment she had already lived a full life in the certainty of George's love. She and her sister grabbed at life when they could and had in so short a time lived so completely. What did it matter if, somehow, continuity was only a faint glimpse. Some people live a lifetime in a few minutes. That's all the certainty this war allowed.

Spencer did not share in all the preparations for departure. In his own private world, he had room only for Milka and himself. He had long ago rejected the idea of departure from her. Though he wasn't well, he shoved his physical discomfort from his awareness. He had no thought for the next day. He only lived to be with his beloved. He was desolate to hear they were leaving within the hour.

Milka was always just a whisper away. Spencer sought her comfort at the thought of parting. Her lips were trembling with unacknowledged dread.

"Time to go? So soon? Do you think *Manong* Almanzur would let me go with you as far as *Sipalay?* Or even to *Maricalum?* Oh, sweetheart, I can't leave you until I see you safely in the submarine."

There was no hiding the pain in her eyes. He closed them with his lips before the tears could fall. Seeing her so broken up with the thought of his leaving gave him a calm he thought he would never have when the time came for him to go. He caught her in his arms and held her with all the tender assurance of his love.

"Don't cry, my love. Distance can't rob us of the wealth of deep exchange. We'll write to each other. I think there'll be much to give and more to share than we can imagine. We'll write and touch each other in a way we can't, even when we're together."

He seemed so sure of their future Milka could not let the tears fall. She bit her lip and nodded her assent. "Come, I will help put your things together. After, we'll go and find *Manong* Almanzur and I'll ask him if he'll permit me to accompany you to *Maricalum.* I'm almost certain he'll let me come with you."

They walked hand in hand into the hospital to get ready to leave. They met her *Manong* Almanzur around the corner, coming out of *Manong* Alvaro's room. Before she could speak to him, he spoke.

"Don't take too much luggage with you. We'll be gone less than a week, if all goes well. You can take care of your husband until he gets better care in the sub. He needs your help."

Spencer's fingers tightened around hers.

"Thank you very much for thinking of us, Sir." He stepped aside as Milka moved forward to thank *Manong* Almanzur

"Don't thank me," he said turning away from her. "Thank your *Manong* Alvaro. He insisted on it."

Overjoyed, she did not see his pain. She asked to be excused so they could go in and thank *Manong* Alvaro. Her steps were light again. On her way into *Manong* Alvaro's room, she let go of Spencer's hand, quickly turned around, and ran into her brother's arms. Her grateful hug was returned and though he frowned, his heart lightened as he felt her gratitude.

"Don't take too much time now; we have to be moving soon."

"We just need to say goodbye to *Manong* Alvaro. Spencer must see him before we go."

Her eyes were brilliant pools of tears about to fall. *Manong* Alvaro was waiting for them. He felt strangely responsible for this stranger who had shared his confidence and asked him to approve of his connection with his beautiful, young cousin. Together, they had braved the danger in the swamps and in the sea and avoided capture by the Japanese. Somehow, he thought it made his sacrifice worth twice as much, knowing he was doing it not only for Spencer who was part of the B-29 crew he was obligated to rescue, but also for her who loved him enough to risk her own life for him. His voice quavered.

"Well, Spencer, it's almost over. Tomorrow, the sub will be ready for you."

"No, Sir, it won't be over until I come back to take Milka home with me. I'm grateful for what you have done for us, but, please, do me another big favor, Sir. Please take care of her for me. Until this war is over, all of you will not be safe, but, with you looking out for her, I'll feel less worried about her safety."

Spencer looked down on the figure on the bed. He seemed so much smaller now than days ago when he took command in the *batel*.

"*Manong* Almanzur told us to hurry, Sir. I can't find the words to thank you, but they lie deep in the heart. God bless you and guard you from more harm till I see you again."

He bent down, took *Manong* Alvaro's hand, put his forehead on it. He, too, learned to value this gesture of respect, of love, really, and especially of unspoken gratitude.

Milka bent down and embraced her *Manong* Alvaro. Between them, there was no need for words. Minutes after they had left, *Manong* Alvaro turned his head toward the *nipa* wall crying softly not in grief, but in gratitude for love and life.

Chapter 49—To *Sipalay*

The trucks eased out of the hospital compound. Hospital personnel, guerrilla soldiers, officers, and civilians who worked in the compound lined the lane leading to the gate. The Luzuriaga girls were perched on benches at the end of the line. This day, thankfulness for their successful rescue outweighed the sadness of departure, but all the hearts that shared a connection felt like lead. George, Frank, and Robert waved their silent farewell to the Luzuriaga girls. They stretched their heads out of the truck to watch the girls until they lost sight of them in the distance. Belief in a Providence that had showered him with a rare gift shook Frank especially. He didn't expect to believe in the God his father always preached as the force that designed events in life. But how else was he to explain this experience? Now he had more reason to trust in the omniscient power that would design the shape of things to come. His old resistance to faith in his father's omnipotent God just about broken, he bowed his head in silent prayer.

"Please, protect her from harm."

Marco could not believe they were leaving. In the truck, he fudged about Scott's comfort. He ignored the throbbing in his own forehead. The nurse and an orderly were trying valiantly to steady the pole that held the tubes feeding Scott with intravenous medicine that was almost gone. Only one more bottle was handy. Marco held Scott's hand tightly. The truck shook so much the nurse begged Caesar to drive slowly. She was afraid the tubes would get unhooked. But driving slowly didn't make the truck shake less. Calmly assessing the situation, Spencer suggested a change in the seating arrangement.

"Sir, let Joe, BB and Valdez move in with Scott and Marco; Milka and I could move into the second truck. The three can support with steady hands the poles that hold the tubes and make sure they don't come unhinged," he said.

"Later, George and Frank can relieve the three. That way we can make better progress." Milka added.

Captain Al ordered a halt; the exchange in seats was done quickly and the trucks rumbled on. Joe and BB relieved the orderlies and steadied the contraption supporting the tubes, but their six foot frames were too tall for the truck and bending the head down to avoid hitting the roof when the truck lurched as the road increasingly got worse was hard on both. Only Valdez was the comfortable height for the job. When Joe rested, Valdez and BB did the job, and when BB got too tired of bending his head, Joe took over once more. Poor Valdez bore more of the burden of the task, but he was too devoted to Scott's welfare to mind.

"How are you doing back there," Captain Al from time to time would ask from the front seat of the truck.

"Valdez here must be exhausted," Joe remarked, the first time Captain Al asked.

"Don't you think I would ask you to relieve me if I got tired?" Valdez got irritated.

"We need to get to the *batel* as soon as we can. Right, Captain Al?"

"That's true, but remember you have to be prepared for the unexpected. You never know when those Japanese gunboats would turn up. You can't be too tired when that happens," Captain Al reminded them.

They had to stop two more times to arrange further exchange of places so George and Frank could take over, but they had the same problem with height so Valdez insisted on staying on the job till they got to *Sipalay*. He cautioned that though immobile, Scott could hear what was said. They should cut further reference to his special sacrifice for his friend.

Other than concern for Scott's comfort and stops for lunch and a late afternoon meal, the journey proceeded without incident though it was tedious. Everyone worried about Scott's condition, but the immobile body couldn't tell much. They arrived in *Sipalay* just before the tropical sun sank below the horizon.

Milka periodically wrung the towel she used on Spencer, making sure his wound stayed dry. Heat and humidity sapped his strength. Marco and Robert didn't do so well either. Both laid their heads on the back of the seats in front of them and slept most of the way; but they sagged when they got to *Sipalay*. They were barely able to walk up the bamboo steps to the huts prepared for their night's rest.

The beaches in *Sipalay* gleamed in the moonlight. The white sand stretched far into the sea. Tall coconut trees lined the edge of the beach. Filipinos slept on the beach to catch the night breeze. Some dipped into the ocean to get away from the heat and the humidity. Small *bancas* carrying lighted coconut lanterns to attract the fish dotted the shallow shoreline. Fishermen fished at night to deal with the heat as much as to catch fish. The white beaches ended where the land curved on the heel of the island. Beyond the bend, the steep hills took over and the white shore disappeared. The steep hills marked a radical change in the depth of the ocean. From this point toward *Maricalum* an abyss seemed to appear. Here the ocean depths allowed the submarine easy access.

After the Americans finished eating and were resting in the *nipa* huts, the guerrillas gathered to discuss the *batel* ride to *Maricalum*.

"Sir," Caesar broke the silence with a question. "Is there any way for us to anchor the *batel* so we can move these guys into the sub?"

"I remember the last time the sub surfaced we had difficulty unloading the weapons given us because the hills are so steep from here to *Maricalum*," Rafael answered Caesar's question and then asked another one.

"How are we going to manage getting them into the sub? We're going to have trouble especially with Scott and all the tubes and medical equipment he needs."

"They do have rubber tubes that they hoist to the top of the hill, remember? Anyway, that is not our problem anymore. We'll deliver them at the designated location. The rest is up to them. They have engineers who must have thought about that problem already," the *Kapitan* assured his men.

"I sure hope we have no more problems from here on," Pedring got into the discussion too.

"Don't forget we have more than fifteen kilometers to go. If there's no wind tomorrow, we may have to row again," Munding warned. "Somehow, the hills worry me," he added.

"Yes, and the water runs deep. I'm sure there are no reefs here. I hope there are no sharks. Whoever falls into the water would be food for those creatures," Ponsing said, half in jest, half in fear.

"You boys worry about the sea too much," the *Kapitan* said. "I worry about the gunboats and the airplanes. I think the Japanese Colonel who replaced Colonel Asaki has not quite given up on the idea of capturing our friends. He may turn up when we least expect him. That worries me a lot," he repeated.

"But didn't the message from Australia say the sub will take care of that problem?" Ponsing asked and wanted confirmation.

"It said it would, didn't it? Munding wanted to confirm but he had his doubts too.

"What if the gunboats turn up sooner than they expect? What if the sub is still too far away to help? What are we going to do?"

Valdez and Joe West had stepped out of their huts quietly and walked right into the discussion.

"That is a real possibility. We'll just have to fight our way till we get to the proximity of the sub." Joe tried to assure them.

"This time we'll not be outgunned." Valdez was as determined.

"That sub can move faster than any Japanese gunboat and when it surfaces, the guns it has on deck are awesome. They'll take care of any problem. I'd love to see any airplane dodge those guns." He bristled with confidence tinged with some anger. He was remembering his own desperation during the last *batel* episode.

Captain Al was quiet. Though he liked the enthusiasm of the Americans, he knew what was expected seldom prevailed. Sometimes, enthusiasm could cloud careful preparedness. He distanced himself from the group. A little doubt and anxiety can go a long way to reinforce caution, he thought to himself. Once more, when he was unusually quiet, he was wary and non-committal. In his mind, he was assessing the situation with great care.

"Sir, I can feel a strong breeze. Maybe we should take advantage of it and go sooner than we planned?" Again, the helmsman spilled his concern. "Shouldn't we ask the nurse to get Scott ready? I'm afraid it takes time to make sure Scott has all he needs in the *batel*."

"We'll give them more time to rest. The truck ride wasn't easy. You were cramped in that second truck. I think the heat has affected them more than they care to admit. Let's give them at least two hours more of sleep," the *Kapitan* answered Munding.

Still worried, Munding mumbled his anxiety. "I sure hope the wind holds. We need a good breeze to use the sails and not have to row."

"You could use some sleep too," the *Kapitan* noted. "Get to one of the huts and sleep. Go in quietly; don't disturb those who are already asleep."

Munding went in quietly. In a few minutes, the *Kapitan* heard him snoring. He didn't go into the hut; he thought he saw an *abaca* (hemp material) hammock underneath one hut. He lay without a sound and, half asleep, he mentally made plans for positioning men carrying particular weapons in specific areas of the *batel*.

Chapter 50—A Second Chance at Saving Face

Captain Akagi keenly felt the brunt of disgrace. True, he had rescued Colonel Takamatsu, now at the army hospital in *Bacolod* but he had to answer for the loss of a gunboat and two airplanes. Still smarting from the loss of face over the incident two weeks ago, Captain Akagi knew he had to reverse failure and make one last attempt to capture the Americans. His fellow officers asked about his shoulder wound, but he ignored the pain and only came twice a week to have it dressed. Some of the officers in the garrison thought he had been heroic to risk his life to save Colonel Takamatsu, but the others snickered behind his back, saying he had miscalculated the risks and made an unspeakable error in judgment.

He sensed that they censured him for his failure to capture a small band of guerrillas How could a small *batel* outrun a Japanese gunboat and sink another? That's an unthinkable turn of events. But of course only those who have not been in an engagement with the crafty band, regardless how small, cannot imagine how such a loss was possible. But he felt cheated. If they had not wasted their time boarding all those other small craft, torturing them for an answer that could have been theirs if they sped directly to catch the one they were looking for, they could have easily outrun it and captured their quarry. But who was to blame for what took place? He knew Colonel Takamatsu's penchant for torture. Why didn't he ignore him and speed away by himself? He would have risked insubordination to a senior officer then.

On his own, what can he do to reverse his error? He spent several sleepless nights reviewing what happened. Mentally, he went over every detail of the gun battle. Obviously, the guerrillas now had superior arms. Where did they get them? How could they have bazookas and .50 caliber machine guns? Before this engagement, they only had what they were able to recover from units they ambushed. As far as he knew, they had not lost any bazookas, perhaps a couple of machine guns, but no bazookas; none he was aware of.

He was embarrassed to admit the guerrillas had stolen more than two of their trucks in the past month. Why couldn't they have driven the Americans to their headquarters in the unoccupied territory in the south in those trucks? Why did they take them in a *batel* at sea instead? Is it possible that the same agency that had delivered the superior arms they now have had arranged to pick up the Americans as well? If so, there had to be a meeting place somewhere. Where? He worried himself sick trying to figure out why and where. Where were the guerrillas taking the Americans?

On his way to get his dressing changed, he passed by the Commandant's office and asked if he could barrow a map of the island. He studied it intently and put his finger on the town of *Sipalay*. Their gunboats had patrolled that part of the sea. He knew that farther around the bend, the beaches turned to sheer cliffs where the water ran deep. The more he pondered it, the more convinced he was that a submarine could hug that coast line and submerge at will. But if it intended to deliver something, it had to do it when the tide was high so that it could run level with the high cliffs. That's it. The guerrillas will have to deliver the Americans somewhere beyond the beaches of *Sipalay* on the high cliffs at high tide. He anxiously studied the tides. He was certain high tide came when the moon was full. That would be about a week from today. A surge of certainty raised his blood pressure. His chest ached with the surety of his conclusions. But whom could he share it with? No one; especially not the Commandant. He wouldn't listen to him now. He would think he's full of it and simply wants to reverse his loss of face. More tomfoolery from such a moron, he could hear all the other officers say. He could steal a gunboat, but he would need a crew to man it for him. What idiot would volunteer to do that under the circumstances? If only he could convince some top officer that he's right. God, what could he do? Who could he turn to?

Unknown to Captain Akagi, he wasn't the only one who felt a compulsion to make a last ditch attempt to save face. Lying helpless on his hospital bed, Colonel Takamatsu burned with a consuming anger at having lost a sea fight with the guerrillas. This loss to a small band of ill-equipped guerrillas was unforgivable. Somehow, he had to even the score, or he could never outlive the disgrace. If he died, he would be remembered only for his incompetence. He had come so close to capturing the Americans and he let them slip through his fingers. What a damn shame! In the proximity of his hospital bed, his unfortunate maneuver was the topic of discussion. He could hear the comments of those who came in and out of his room curious to see how he fared. He always pretended to be unaware of the officers who wanted to speak to him. He feigned loss of consciousness for another week. He wanted desperately to talk to Captain Akagi who came to visit him everyday, but he was always in the company of superior officers who wanted to interview him and the Colonel together. The colonel feigned inability to recover from his ordeal.

To his chagrin, he observed that Captain Akagi came only twice a week now to have the dressing for his wound changed. The fortunate bastard! At least he had not lost an arm. Colonel Takamatsu had lost so much blood that he hardly weighed anything. He was just skin and bones; the hospital gown clung to the sharp bones, but he did not feel like eating. He consistently refused food, so his recovery was minimal. At one point he wished he had died. That would have been more glorious. Surviving was an ignominy. Damn this young upstart for saving his worthless life. Now, the Colonel, too, replayed the images of the sea battle in his mind. They were so close to capturing them! He should have known more about the character of the coastline. He blamed himself for that, but he was no coward; neither was Captain Akagi. How he had misjudged the young man! He ached to speak to him. He must speak to him; he didn't care who was with him anymore. He waited for half an hour and was elated to see the Captain walk into his room alone. His eyes glared with an energy that was absent from his physique.

As soon as the captain was in, Colonel Takamatsu motioned for him to close the door. Captain Akagi was taken by surprise.

"Sir," he blurted as he saluted instinctively. "I'm so glad you have regained consciousness. Everyone had been afraid you would not get well enough."

"Fiddlesticks." The Colonel was extremely agitated. "I have been conscious all along. I was in no mood to talk to anyone, that's all."

Alarmed that his agitation would cause a stroke, Captain Akagi was about to call for help, but the Colonel shook a finger at him. "Don't you dare call for anyone. I've waited for this chance to talk to you alone. Close the damn door."

Captain Akagi complied instantly. Now the Colonel's voice diminished to a whisper. His energy obviously running out, he pulled Captain Akagi down and gestured his frustration.

"Let me close my eyes for a few minutes before I run out of energy completely. We have to talk," he repeated.

A few minutes later, he was in control again. He tried to sit up. Captain Akagi propped him on the pillows.

"Where do you think the guerrillas were taking those Americans?"

Captain Akagi could not believe what he heard; he could no longer contain his amazement. Their thoughts ran parallel! Though his emotion threatened to run away with him, Captain Akagi revealed all the thinking he had done in all the sleepless nights, all the details he had studied, and the conclusion he arrived at.

"So the full moon would be in about a week, you say? That does not give us too much time to plan our next move, but that should give me time to get more energy to revive. Without this chance to do something to intercept the pick up of the Americans, I would much rather die."

There was clear determination in the Colonel's voice. "Order me some food," he commanded.

There was conspiracy in the air when the Commandant of the garrison walked in.

"What are you two plotting to do now," he said rather casually, his eyes twinkling with merriment.

Did he hear what they had been saying? Or was he just kidding with them?

Colonel Takamatsu decided right then that without the approval of the Commandant, they would never get anywhere with what they knew was the key to an urgent situation.

"We planned to keep this to ourselves. Somehow we were hoping we could steal a couple of your gunboats again. But there's no reason why you shouldn't hear about our plan because we are dead certain that your approval is crucial to its success."

He challenged the Commandant. "Everything depends on how open-minded you are, and how willing you are to hear the truth of the matter. Do not prejudge us without hearing us this time. You can decide not to do anything about it, but you must at least be willing to hear what we were planning to do and why."

He grabbed the Commandant's arm and would not let go.

"We're turning this matter over to you, and if we finally capture the Americans, the credit should go to you alone," Captain Akagi pleaded.

"That's right. You should command this mission." Colonel Takamatsu blurted.

The Commandant sat down and released his arm from Colonel Takamatsu's grip.

Captain Akagi continued, with urgency. "If you leave immediately, you can capture the small boat the Americans are taken in long before it gets anywhere near the submarine that would pick them up. That would eliminate any risk of danger. As you all say about our last engagement, the guerrillas should have had very little chance against our superior gunboats. There should be no room for error this time."

The Commandant could not ignore the urgency in Captain Akagi's voice. He weighed the matter very carefully. Shaking his head, he stood, walked briskly to the telephone by the side of the Colonel's bed and rang for his aide.

"Issue an order for all the high ranking officers in the garrison to meet in the conference room immediately," he commanded. "Wait," he corrected himself. "Ask them to report to this room in ten minutes." Turning to Colonel Takamatsu, he said. "This is your idea. You should have the honor to present the mission to the officers. Let us see what they think about it."

If these bastards are wrong again and we do not catch the boat delivering the Americans to a destination, there really would be no great loss except for time and fuel. But he could not resist the idea he might really bag the Americans after all the trouble the southern garrisons had with trying to capture them.

The officers crowded into Colonel Takamatsu's room. Officers who had patrolled the area around *Sipalay* confirmed the truth about the coastline beyond that point. The idea caught fire and challenged them to volunteer for the mission. They decided to use six of the best gunboats in the harbor in *Bacolod*. Aware that some danger could arise if they could not catch the *batel* before the submarine arrived to pick up the Americans, they insisted on air support. Again, six of the best airmen volunteered to be part of the mission.

Feeling vindicated, Colonel Takamatsu expected to be part of the mission despite his physical condition. He felt intensely slighted when the commandant pointed out that in his condition he couldn't possibly contribute anything significant. On the contrary, he could be a possible hazard. No, he was told in no uncertain terms to stay and recover his health. The fire in his eye sockets subsided into a scowl. The Commandant assigned the officers to take command of each of the five gunboats. He would take the lead with Captain Akagi as second in command.

Sulking, the colonel congratulated Captain Akagi.

"You lucky bastard. Make sure you do not fail a second time. Crush those impudent guerrillas and capture the Americans for me."

This time he was sure the guerrillas will be mercilessly crushed. His eyes were blazing pockets of hate.

Chapter 51—A Few Hours to Rendezvous

Munding turned in his light sleep restlessly. He dreamt about the frustration of rowing hard because they were caught in a dead calm at sea. He woke instantly. Careful not to disturb the others, he went downstairs and sat on the last bamboo step. He felt the cool breeze.

The wind is still holding, thank God! Relieved, he slowly walked toward the *batel* bobbing gently with the breeze.

"*Oy, Kapitan*, I didn't know you're awake. What are you doing here?" Munding asked.

"Just doing some last minute check up. Would you find out if we have enough rope to use for disembarking? I noticed the boys had cleaned the cabin and made it ready for Scott and the nurse. They must have taken away the ropes stored underneath it. What are you doing here, yourself?" The *Kapitan* countered.

"I wanted to make sure the strong breeze I felt yesterday is still blowing. Sir, I think we better start soon so we can take advantage of the wind on the sails.

"Right, Munding. You stay here and get ready. I'll go and get the others."

"Sir, could you ask Caesar or Rafael to bring the coils of rope I left under the hut. I meant to bring those but I worried more about leaving I forgot about the things we need."

"Ah, so that's what you did with the ropes. No wonder I couldn't find them,"

"I figure we need the ropes in case we have to get to shore in a hurry. We did the last time. Remember?" Munding was hard at remembering the horror of their last experience.

"Yes, but you were higher than the shore the last time. We would be riding the waters below the shore this time. The shoreline ahead is steep. The rope would be useless unless you throw it at someone above who would catch it." The *Kapitan* was in deep thought again.

"Never mind, Sir. I will think of something, " Munding said. "Just please get everyone ready to leave. We need to leave while the wind blows steadily."

"Okay, worry wart. I'm going."

The *Kapitan* did not bother to use a *banca*. He jumped into the shallow water to determine if they needed to push the *batel* farther from the shore before the weight of equipment and people could get it grounded. The water came up to his shoulders.

"Push the *batel* farther, Munding, or we would be grounded before we leave. "Wait, here's more company." The *Kapitan* waded to the shoreline.

Munding craned to see who were coming. "Caesar," he yelled, "ask Rafael to go back and get the coils of rope I left behind. Come and help me move farther off shore."

The *Kapitan* was about to order Caesar to go back with Rafael so they could carry Scott to the *batel,* but by now a sense of urgency created great excitement. Everyone discovered his absence. Some apprehension spread. Joe West activated the group into motion. BB and Valdez lifted Scott's bed; the nurse supervised the orderlies, directed them how to carry the intravenous equipment and moved alongside the bed. Marco was not far behind. George and Frank joined the guerrilla contingent. They stayed to make sure guns and ammunition not loaded the night before were carried into the *batel*. Spencer and Milka helped Robert. Joe West kept running to see how Scott was attended to. When he saw that everything was handled right, he ran back to see how George and Frank dealt with loading the weapons.

BB and Valdez loaded Scott, the nurse, Marco and Robert into a *banca*. Marco turned to the orderlies. "Help load what Scott needs, but you have to stay behind. Sorry, you're not needed anymore."

The boys meekly obeyed. Rafael whistled for sergeant Peralta who came running and they paddled the *banca* to the *batel.*

Marco supervised the arrangement of Scott's bed into the small cabin. The top of the cabin rose three feet above the deck. The floor was recessed below but not far enough to extend to the bottom of the hull. Underneath the cabin was a crawlspace where miscellaneous cargo was stored. Munding cleared this space the day before to get it dry and rid of any mildew odor so Scott could breathe clean air.

Guerrilla men considered Scott's survival the center of this mission. Noting this meticulous concern, Marco was deeply moved. Horizontal poles crisscrossed the ceiling of the cabin. The intravenous tubes were attached securely on these poles. The bed barely fitted the room. The nurse and Marco sat on both sides of the bed. Marco held Scott's hand tightly. Robert crouched on a stool at the foot of the bed holding his head with both hands. The gentle motion of the *batel* gave him a headache; he was slightly nauseated.

"Turn around and lay your head on the bed, Robert," Marco ordered. "Nurse, could you please give Robert some pill to help with motion sickness?"

He asked though he was certain the nurse had nothing of the kind.

The excitement abated as everyone sat or stood at their appointed spaces. Joe West secured the .50 caliber stationary machine gun with a coil of rope. He handed the rope to Valdez while he steadied the gun. Valdez tied it to the railing on the prow twice around with another coil of hemp rope.

"This should give prowlers plenty of problems," Valdez declared.

"Just make sure, though the rope holds, it provides flexibility to turn around fast," Joe warned Valdez.

"I have an extra coil here to catch it if turning the *batel* around makes the gun list." Valdez bristled with certainty. "This time, I'll not be as unprepared as I was two weeks ago."

"Well, if I'm not needed here for a while, I'll go over to help George and Frank secure the .30 caliber machine gun. They have plenty of rounds to support us if we have trouble."

Joe sauntered toward the mid section of the *batel* where George and Frank were mounting a smaller machine gun. Sergeant Peralta sat on top of the cabin roof with his feet dangling on the side. He was cleaning an automatic Garand, the small, easy to handle sub machine gun. Below his feet, halfway between the .30 caliber machine gun and Munding, the *Kapitan* mounted his bazooka. Caesar helped him ground the bazooka firmly on a stand on the *batel* floor. Sitting two feet beside Munding, Rafael was ready with another automatic Garand. Pedring and Rudi perched lightly on each outrigger. They had rapidfire automatic rifles with telescopes for greater accuracy.

Munding gripped the rudder firmly; he told Rafael how proud he was he had set the sails up with Caesar's help before everyone crowded into the *batel*. The sails were flapping noisily. It pushed the *batel* as easily as if it were a chair with wheels on the polished hospital floor. They left the shallow waters of *Sipalay* and covered three kilometers before forty minutes were up.

"Where are *Inday* Milka and her husband?" Munding asked Rafael.

"They're down in the hull where they belong," Rafael answered. "She's taking care of her husband. I'm sure his wounds are still hurting. They hadn't given him much for relief at the hospital. She'll miss him terribly, but she'll be glad he's going where there's better chance to get well. Poor girl. The nurse told me she suspects Milka is pregnant. She hasn't been feeling too good lately," Rafael whispered to Munding.

The *batel* rounded the heel of the island. They were now beyond *Sipalay*. The Americans noted that the topography of the coastline changed radically.

"Munding, steer her where she can hug the shoreline. We can never be sure if we need to get to shore if the Japanese gunboats come too quickly for us to outrun them," the *Kapitan* warned the helmsman.

Munding did as the *Kapitan* asked. The *batel* ran parallel the cliffs. Though the early morning sunrise ushered some light, the giant *talisay* trees on steep cliffs shaded the waters and dwarfed the small sailboat. Sitting on deck near the outriggers, Rudi handled a coil of rope by his feet.

"The cliffs are too high for these ropes to work if we need to go on shore. They're practically useless," Rudi said, alarmed at what he discovered.

"Not if you use these metal prongs I borrowed from the fishermen in *Sipalay*. They use these as anchors. Tie the end of the rope to these and throw them on the roots of trees shooting out of the cliffs if it is necessary to pull ourselves on shore," the *Kapitan* said.

"The cliffs are still high. How do we get on shore? We can climb on ropes, but what about the wounded Americans," Rudi asked again.

"If you and I are up there, Rudi, we can find a way to hoist them up," Joe West answered his question.

"That won't be so easy to do, Sir." Rudi persisted. In an emergency, we'll have a difficult time doing that. It may be next to the impossible."

"Hey, do not be too pessimistic," Munding said. "I have been observing the shoreline very sharply since we left *Sipalay*. Don't you notice some crevices here and there? Wow, there's one right there not too far away. It cuts right into the cliff. Shall we move in just for practice," Munding challenged Rudi.

"It's not a question of 'shall we' anymore." Ponsing emerged from the hull below. "Do it, Munding. At once! Listen to this message from Colonel Gomez."

"What does he say, for Pete's sake. We can't hear way out here," Valdez yelled.

"Six Japanese gunboats are looking for us. They have been patrolling the sea from *Maricalum* back to *Sipalay* since dawn. Six airplanes are also looking for us. The Colonel says we need to stop right where we are and somehow hide from view. "What are we going to do, Sir?" Extremely agitated, Ponsing turned to the *Kapitan.*

Without waiting for an answer, Munding wedged the *batel* between the rocky sides of a crevice.

"Caesar, Rafael, Pedring, anybody with strong hands, hoist down the sails. Without them, we may not be visible. These big trees not only shade us from view, they'd help to protect us. Right?" Munding also turned to the *Kapitan* for assurance.

The crevice did not provide too much space. They were barely wedged in.

"Get out at once and turn her around, Munding, We need the big machine gun facing the sea. Here, Rafael," the *Kapitan* threw the pronged fisherman's anchor to Rafael. "Throw this high enough at that huge tree over there. That would help pull us in when Munding turns her around."

Joe West left the prow and raced toward Rafael. "Let me do it for you, Rafael. I did Discus Throw in college. Get back to my place with Valdez while I do this."

"Don't any one panic now. We don't have too much time, but we can still do what we need to do," the *Kapitan* deliberately calmed everyone.

"Munding barely had time to turn the *batel* around. The sails were still sprawled on deck. Pedring and Sergeant Peralta rolled the sails from the tallest mast and dropped it into the hull. Rudi and Caesar on one end and Sergeant Peralta and Rafael on the other end got the two smaller sails down and kicked them into the hull moments before an airplane flew past the *batel.*

Joe West raced back to the prow beside Valdez.

"Captain Al," Frank whispered. "You think he saw us?"

"Hard to say," the Captain answered. "Get your guns ready, in case he did."

"He flew low enough, but it's too dark in here to see easily. He might have missed us," George mumbled.

Once more, Ponsing popped on deck from the hull below. "Guys, very good news," he yelled once more. "Colonel Gomez says we should expect a message from the sub that would pick you up. It's speeding toward us."

Another airplane flew by.

"This one definitely saw us," BB said. "I saw the pilot's head. That's how low he was. Watch out now. He's going to turn around to get us soon."

Instead of an airplane, a gunboat was speeding toward the *batel*. Obviously, the airplane radioed their position. Not more than two hundred meters away, everyone heard machine gun fire from the gunboat, then, a thunderous explosion.

"The sub must have scored a direct hit with a torpedo," Joe West yelled. A spontaneous cheer rose from the Americans. But the yell of joy fizzled to deathly quiet as an airplane approached them. No one heard Spencer emerge from the hull and grab the .30 caliber machine gun from George and Frank and released a few hundred rounds at the airplane. The Japanese plane, taken by surprise by Spencer's turret gunner's instinctual maneuver, got slightly deflected from his course and dropped his bomb fifteen meters away. Water sprayed the *batel*. They hardly had time to shake the water from their faces when another airplane came into view. The *Kapitan* was ready for this one. He waited till the airplane was within his range and scored a direct hit with his bazooka. Joe West who sent a few rounds from the .50 caliber machine gun knew he didn't do the damage. Caesar and Sergeant Peralta cheered the *Kapitan*.

"Where the hell did he learn to use that weapon with deadly accuracy?" Joe yelled at Valdez.

"Wherever, Joe. I'm just grateful. Wow! What a hit!" Valdez shook his head in amazement.

Once more the cheers got quiet; another gunboat was approaching them. Everyone was just waiting for the big guns or machine gun fire to hit. It was too late for a bazooka hit now. The gunboat opened fire; Munding shoved the big oars at Caesar and Rafael. Row guys. We need to get out of this crevice. Hearing Munding give the order, Sergeant Peralta raced toward the two others and used a pole to push the *batel* out of the crevice where it was wedged tightly. He dropped another pole on the floor. Understanding Munding's problem, BB raced to the spot beside Sergeant Peralta, picked up the pole where the sergeant had dropped it. Together, they pushed on the rock as hard as they could. The *batel* barely moved out of the crevice. This motion must have taken only one or two minutes. The gunboat used a 70 mm cannon, hit the crevice and pulverized the rocks at the same instant that the gunboat exploded into a thousand pieces.

"The sub is at it again, BB screamed as he fell flat on the *batel* floor. Sergeant Peralta managed to duck behind a water barrel. He tried to pull Munding away from BB; thank God Munding had pinned BB on the floor with his weight. They were a foot below the path of sharp bits of rock from the crevice. These hit Caesar and Rafael. It looked like someone had stabbed them with sharp knives in half a dozen places at the back. Blood squirted everywhere around. The gunboat was racing toward them before it exploded. It was almost on them when it did. Flames from the explosion fell into the *batel* and a fire immediately spread. BB and Munding and Sergeant Peralta were helping Caesar and Rafael who were screaming with pain. The *Kapitan* dropped his bazooka and ran to cradle Caesar in his arms. Munding was holding Rafael in his arms too.

"BB, get the nurse, my sister, anyone. We have to stop the bleeding," the *Kapitan* sobbed.

"Sergeant, do what Captain Al asked. Captain Al, remove your shirt; we have to do this gently now. You may have to use a knife to make a slit around the rocks. They have to be removed fast; let's hope that no particles remain in the wounds. BB was taking charge.

The fire was spreading fast toward the cabin. The other men were too stunned to react. This time Milka emerged from the hull with tin buckets. Realizing that it would take too much time to get the men to use the buckets, she turned around, spotted the sails in the hull, threw the buckets on the floor, and screamed.

"Someone help me."

George and Frank heard her. So did Spencer. All three ran to her side. They thought she had been wounded too. Milka was desperately pulling the sail out of the hull onto the *batel* floor. Sergeant Peralta, also thinking Milka was wounded, raced to her side. He pushed George and Frank out of his way. Realizing that she was okay, Spencer looked to see what she was screaming about. Without thinking, he helped her pull the sail and then almost instantly knew what she was trying to do.

"Sergeant, get to the hull and push the other end of the sail up," Spencer yelled.

Together, they spread the sails over the fire and stomped with their feet to smother the flames. George and Frank followed suit. They pulled the bigger sail lying on the floor near the prow and succeeded in putting out the fire that now almost reached the small cabin door. The fire was out, but smoke came out of the still smoldering mess.

"For God's sake, close the cabin door," Spencer yelled again.

Exhausted, he and Milka sat down on the *batel* floor, their faces black with soot. He put his arms around his wife.

"Oh, my darling, what would the world do without you? You think of everyone but yourself. I love you so much," he said, tightening his hold around her.

While all this was happening, those inside the cabin could hear but never saw what took place, but when the fire spread to the cabin door, the nurse threw a panic and let out a piercing scream. Marco stood up and slapped her to stop her screams.

"Someone, get this bitch out of here," he yelled. "She is getting her patient terrified.

Marco was sobbing because he could not quell the tremor his friend was experiencing. Marco was still holding on tightly to Scott's shaking hands when Joe West rushed into the cabin.

"Scott, hey Scott, this is Joe."

He held Scott's hand and ordered Marco to tend to Robert who buried his head on the bed, also shaking with fear.

"Everything is over now. We're safe now. Can't you feel the *batel* rise? We're rising beside the submarine. It's here. We're safe at last." Joe tried to smother the sob caught in his throat.

Scott held on to Joe and would not let go. Eventually, the tremor stopped. Scott could not see what was happening, but he could hear the sounds of battle. Only holding on to a special someone could quite down the fear of the unseen danger and quell the felt desperation. The sounds of battle came to haunt everyone but especially the one who could hear but not see what was happening.

Pedring, and Rudi finished pulling the sharp rocks from Caesar and Rafael's backs. Munding, BB, and the *Kapitan* were soaked in blood.

"Damn it," the *Kapitan* swore. "This was supposed to be a safe trip."

Several four-inch deep wounds had to be patched up quickly before the damage to the *batel* and its crew could be assessed.

"Thank God, we were far enough away from the crevice when the 70 mm guns hit. If we had not moved out of there, BB, sergeant Peralta and I would have been hit too. These flying rocks are like knives thrown at targets, and if we were closer, they could have penetrated deeper than just three to four inches. Caesar and Rafael would have died instantly."

Munding tried to console the *Kapitan* who was visibly shaken. He cried openly over his wounded men. "Ponsing, radio the sub for help."

The *Kapitan* was unconcerned about anything else but his men. The submarine had submerged. When it re-surfaced, the *batel* was lying across its width like a small utensil on a smooth kitchen counter. Medical service men boarded the tiny vessel and removed all of the wounded and took them to the infirmary, or sick bay, or whatever the care center was called.

"Sorry we could not come to your rescue soon enough," the commanding officer said as he saluted Captain Villava.

"We tried everything to keep the airplanes and the gunboats from getting to you."

"Thankfully, no one had died, but we have badly wounded soldiers, both Filipino guerrillas and American B-29 gunners," the *Kapitan* informed him.

"We know about the Americans," the officer said. They will be promptly taken care of.

"What are you going to do about my men?" The *Kapitan* worried that his men would be overlooked.

"Their wounds are serious, but they're in stable condition. As soon as they're attended to and are safe enough to be moved, you can take them back with you. We will wait as long as necessary before we return to base," the officer assured the Captain.

"Thank you for your consideration. We'll go back to *Sipalay* and take them to our army hospital in *Caliling*, about sixty kilometers from here. We'll need medicines to take care of them, though." The *Kapitan* was short but polite.

"That we can take care of, along with as much weapons and ammunition you may need. We have prepared a few other care packages," the officer offered.

"We'll be grateful for whatever you can share with us," was the *Kapitan's* curt reply.

The commanding officer told Captain Villalva that half an hour before approaching the *batel* his submarine chased the Japanese gunboats and demolished four of them. "We shot the last one that almost got you with our big guns on deck. I don't think you need to worry about them anymore. We chased all except two that escaped by running back from the steep cliffs toward the shallower waters and the beaches beyond the heel of the island. They knew we couldn't follow them there. The reefs are a greater danger to us than those gunboats are," the officer said.

"After we demolished the gunboats with torpedoes, we had to surface and shot four Japanese airplanes; the pilot of a fifth airplane decided to become a bomb and dived on us, but, once more, the guns on deck hit it in mid air and what remained of it fell a few meters away," another officer told Captain Villalva.

"We were looking for the sixth plane. A message from guerrilla headquarters said there were six," the commanding officer said.

George and all the other Americans who were not wounded were listening to all this. "Captain Al took care of that one. He scored a direct hit with a bazooka," George proudly reported.

"I can never understand why the Japanese gunboats would think they had a chance against a submarine. Why were they so desperate to get us when they knew you were around?" George asked.

"I guess they didn't think we were around yet. We were submerged and we kept very quiet. They thought they could get to you before we came," the commanding officer said. "Ironically," he continued, we were supposed to meet you at daylight today, but we were so fascinated with exploring the colorful shoreline, we actually arrived a day before. We spotted the gunboats late last night and sent a message to Colonel Gomez. We thought he's with you."

"Did he receive your message," Captain Al asked.

"Yes, he did. He told us you were on your way and would need our help. We didn't anticipate so many gunboats and airplanes. We're so sorry for all your trouble."

"I suppose you need to be told 'all is well that ends well.'" BB spat out his sarcasm.

"Unfortunately, though the end is well, all is not well." BB knew how Captain Al felt about his wounded men.

Much later, the guerrillas learned from *kempetai* reports the Commandant and Captain Akagi died in the first gunboat the submarine directly hit with a torpedo. When the last two gunboats got back to *Bacolod*, a change in command was imperative. Colonel Takamatsu was first in line for high command, but frustrated with his inability to participate in the mission and shocked by the report of an almost total loss, he committed suicide in his hospital bed. He could not forgive himself for the disaster he caused. The mission was supposed to have saved him from a loss of face. Once more the Americans eluded the capture he was so certain of. After this last defeat, how could he survive more loss of face?

Chapter 52—After the Rendezvous

The commanding officer kept his word. All wounded Americans and Caesar and Rafael were attended to with great care. The *batel* attracted the submarine's attention. It became everyone's favorite toy. Engineers and mechanics repaired the deck and fitted the small toy with a new engine. Privates repainted it and outfitted it with new sails. Everyone wanted to add a little something to the toy. To the delight of the guerrilla men, a new .50 caliber machine gun was installed on the deck and a metal attachment allowed it to swivel freely in every direction. The *Kapitan* and his men were given a complete tour of the submarine. Pedring and Rudi, fascinated with the modern gadgets in the kitchen, volunteered to cook Philippine cuisine. They served what Americans enjoyed as exotic dishes out of fresh fish and vegetables. They made *Lumpia* (egg rolls) and *Pancit molo (*an *Ilongo* soup dish with meat wrapped in flour squares)* to the delight of the submarine crew. In turn, they enjoyed brewed coffee, frozen cakes, and canned corn beef. Time passed quickly as everyone enjoyed a pleasant exchange.

Five days later, the *batel* was ready to go back to *Caliling.* BB, Joe, Valdez, George and Frank made doubly sure that the *batel* was loaded with all the weapons, the medical equipment and medicines it could carry. George and Frank thought of everything that would help *Tio* Mauring get well. They gathered presents they could think of for the Luzuriaga girls. All six Americans asked the nurse what the Colonel would need to recover from his wounds. Marco tore the piece of *patadiong* he supposedly got from Delia in half and wrapped several bars of soap for Mama Sid and her family in the other half he was sending back with Captain Al. He asked for enough anesthetic to supply the operating room in *Caliling.* Valdez asked Captain Al if he could spare half a dozen hand grenades for the Gatuslao family.

"Tell them it's from Scott, Joe and Valdez in gratitude for a native feast."

Spencer loaded Milka with medicines for Sondra and a box of canned meat for the entire Gomez family. BB sent a pair of boots and sharp disposable razors with Gillette blades for Victor. Joe West sent a hunting knife for Rodney and improvised fishing poles and fishing lines for Colonel Gomez's two small boys.

Anything and everything they could think of to send, they sent. They presented Captain Al with American cigarettes and chocolate bars. They gave him a pair of sophisticated binoculars and Ponsing received another two-way radio set. All returned to guerrilla headquarters with lots of stories to brag about. It seemed as though everything ended well; unfortunately, all was not well.

Chapter 53—All Is Not Well

The war in the Pacific was not yet over, but it was for Scott, Robert, Marco, and Spencer. The submarine that picked them up took them to a U.S. air base hospital in Australia for treatment before they could be sent back to the U.S.

George, BB, Frank, Joe, and Valdez were reassigned to active duty in the Pacific theater. As far as Colonel Gomez and *Kapitan* Villalva knew, these five airmen flew another B-29B plane. Much lighter, it flew low and fast and minimized the danger from anti-aircraft fire. A new variant, it was designed to meet new tactics and had new improvements. All upper and lower turret guns were removed, along with the central fire control system. Only the tail guns remained, but without the 20mm cannon. It was felt that the only fighter threat to this low flying, very fast B-29B would come from the rear. The weight savings and better aerodynamics of this new plane gave it a top speed in excess of 365 mph.

Scott, Robert, Marco, and Spencer spent plenty of convalescing time in the hospital together. Marco looked after Scott and hovered over him like a mother eagle protecting its young. Robert, whose wounds were not as serious as the rest of this group, was shipped back home to Michigan ahead of everyone. Marco asked to stay and be released with Scott, but because his injuries were not as critical as Scott's he was released with Spencer. They were first transferred to Isley Field, in Saipan. From there, Spencer would be flown to Davis Monthan airbase in Tucson, Arizona and sent for further treatment to the University Medical Center where there was a clinic specializing in the treatment of skin infections and burns. Marco would be sent directly to a hospital in Chicago and sent home from there.

* * *

When the rendezvous with the submarine took place, Milka was positive she carried Spencer's child, but she spared Spencer the knowledge lest he worry unnecessarily. They wrote to each other everyday, but were lucky to get letters once every two weeks. In his last letter, Spencer wrote to Milka about his transfer to Arizona and she wrote him that she was with child. Spencer's answer was warm and ecstatic, filled with the joy of knowing he was going to be a father, hopefully to a son, though it would not matter much if it turns out to be a girl as soft and pretty as her mother.

The American Colonel sent from Australia as senior officer to advise guerrilla units in southern Negros did not relish giving Spencer's widow the sad news, but he felt that in all fairness she needed to know the truth. He assured her brother, Captain Almanzur Villalva, Spencer went without pain. By the way, so did Marco Yablowski, the Polish descent gunner. They probably were not even aware what happened. Their plane was shot down over Pacific waters somewhere between Guadalcanal and Guam. They were on the way back to the U.S.

The war was waning to a close, of that Spencer was certain. His last letter came from some island in the Pacific. He found out about General McArthur's strategy of *benign Neglect.* The strategy, Spencer explained to Milka in this last letter, "involves by-passing Japanese held islands to let them wither and die, using the U.S. navy to cut off their waterborne, logistical support. For sure the Philippines would not be one of these areas because General McArthur promised he would return, but even in the retaking of the Philippine archipelago, the strategy of *Benign Neglect* could still operate."

It did. Landing on Leyte, General McArthur by-passed Mindanao entirely. He left the western part of the Visayan Islands alone. Negros was by-passed as the American liberators went straight to Lingayen Bay and then to Manila Bay in Luzon. Five letters kept coming after this last one. Spencer wrote there was a special procedure at St. Luke Airbase Hospital outside Phoenix, Arizona. A skilled surgeon, a specialist in deep burns, would operate. Convalescence would take two more months and then he would be sent home. Once more, Spencer was ecstatic. He had already sent letters asking permission to send for his wife. In less than a year, he figured, they would be reunited.

"Patience, and loving letters would make time fly by, my darling," he wrote.

When three more letters after this one kept coming, Milka doubted the information of his death. Sadly, after the fourth letter, communication ceased altogether.

Leticia and Laura still received letters. George and Frank survived another crash landing in Saipan, but they only had minor injuries. BB piloted another B-29B and was shot down, but he bailed out and was safely retrieved. Valdez was badly crippled and was sent home. He and Joe were both tail gunners in the new B-29B. They were awarded the

Medal of Honor for exceptional bravery in the line of duty. All returned home with different degrees of injuries. Some were slightly incapacitated. Others escaped with a bit more than a scratch. Two were maimed for life. Spencer and Marco were on their way home, too. Only, they never made it home.

Chapter 54—The Shadow of Death

"*Manong* Alvaro, why did God single out Spencer and Marco to die? He spared the rest of them. Why couldn't He have spared them too? What had they done to deserve this judgment?" Milka asked her cousin in anguish. "Surely, God isn't fair; He's too cruel," she cried bitterly.

Her *Manong* Alvaro wanted to comfort her, but he had no answer for her. A week before the refurbished *batel* left for the swamps, Caesar and Rafael also died in *Caliling* despite the medicine provided by the submarine. After a week in the hospital, the two took a turn for the worst. Some rock residue had drifted into the blood stream and filtered into the heart. A fatal infection developed. The fever rose too high despite medication. In delirium, they asked the same question of *Kapitan* Almanzur.

"Sir, Why were Munding and sergeant Peralta not hit when they were also in the same spot we were in the *batel*?" The *Kapitan* had no answer either. He only suspected that if Munding had not tripped BB, had both of them not fallen on the floor, they, too, would have been hit by sharp rocks flying past them and hitting the water barrel instead. If the water barrel had not been where it was, sergeant Peralta could also have been hit. He was spared because he ducked behind it. Who could explain why circumstances turn out the way they do? Why couldn't the submarine have taken Caesar and Rafael somewhere for treatment? Why did the medical personnel think they were okay? Why had an infection developed when they had already been declared safe? The hospital staff did everything possible, but couldn't save them. *Kapitan* Almanzur was inconsolable. These two had been with him in every mission they attempted. No doubt they helped to save his life again and again. Why weren't they spared?

"Truly," he told his sister, "sometimes, our anguish and our human suffering make us feel God is not fair; from our human perspective, God is cruel. I feel the same way you do." The *Kapitan* was very much diminished by this loss

Manong Alvaro tried to comfort his cousin. "Almanzur," he said, "It is not God who is cruel. It is this war and what we allow it to do to us. The winds of violence blow us in many directions. Your men fight and sustain the violence because you make them believe in the myth of war. They think war is an opportunity for heroic deeds. There's nothing heroic about killing the enemy. We kill only to protect ourselves. We kill before they can kill us. Don't you see? *Violence is as constant as the tireless crashing of the Pacific Ocean.* I have learned one thing from the experiences we've had in these past few weeks: we are born into new life through pain.*"

"What, exactly, does that mean?" *Kapitan* Almanzur was skeptical. He didn't understand the idea of being born into a new life. What is wrong with this one? If you're lucky, you may keep it. How long before his turn to die comes? In his bitterness over the loss of his friends and loved ones, Almanzur was more determined than ever to even the score. Now that he was supplied with more weapons and ammunition than he had ever had before, he can fight and stand his ground with as much chance to kill as to be killed. Now, they do not have to be frugal with their ammunition, for there was more where it came from. He had been assured that a shipment would come regularly. Every full moon on the same spot a submarine will surface with more weapons and ammunition. He'll be damned if he wouldn't avenge the death of Caesar and Rafael, let alone the death of Spencer, his sister's husband. His other sister, Sondra, was still hovering between life and death. Nothing changes. Death is always knocking at the door. How the heck could he be born into new life? No, there's only the pain to be borne in this one while he still had it.

Manong Alvaro tried to explain what he meant since the truth obviously escaped his cousin. "Almanzur, our suffering should teach us to live life on another plane. We have lived with danger close enough, and long enough to realize that life is only a gift. No matter what we do to direct the turn of events, life turns on its own predetermined wheels. We can only surrender to a greater force that shapes our destinies." *Manong* Alvaro tried to explain his point of view.

"I know you're no longer thinking of ambushes, now that you're well armed," he said. "What are you planning to do next? Surely, you are not planning to attack the Japanese garrisons, are you? God has spared your life so far. Why must you risk it again? Shedding more blood is not necessary."

"Not necessary! How can you say that? Caesar's and Rafael's deaths demand it!"

"I know how you feel about that," *Manong* Alvaro continued. "But haven't you heard the news? The Americans are coming to liberate the Philippines and the Japanese know this. What happened in *Maricalum* should convince them that you are no longer playing a hit and run game. American weaponry has changed the tides of combat. I'm sure the Japanese command will order a retreat before long and consolidate their forces in *Bacolod*."

"Exactly. That's why they need to be stopped before they do that. Don't you see?" Almanzur argued. "It would be more difficult to attack a larger garrison."

"The American high command must decide that, not you. Why do you have to preempt the overall plan with a reckless attack and sacrifice more lives, perhaps even your own? Almanzur, listen to reason, please," his *Manong* Alvaro pleaded.

Kapitan Villalva was beyond listening. He vowed revenge and he would have it. In the past, he followed his instinct; it rarely failed him. He'll train more men to take the place of those who died bravely. He has integrity, intuition, courage, and charisma. Now that he can assure them of an even chance against the enemy, more men would be willing to fight with him.

"Let me tell you what I'll do. I'll wait till the next shipment of arms, ammunition, and adequate medicine arrives so we can treat those who may get wounded," Almanzur said.

"Aha! So you expect to have some of your men wounded, maybe even killed? Haven't we lost enough lives already?" *Manong* Alvaro insisted. "Wouldn't any other option than bloodshed satisfy you?"

"What other option is there? The longer we wait, the more rapacious they get. I know how they treat people within their reach. You and I know they rape, torture, plunder and kill at will. How can we stand for that? Just take a look at my sister Sondra."

Almanzur had been in a Japanese garrison in disguise. He saw how Filipinos in Japanese garrisons were inhumanely treated. Those in occupied territories were not exempt from their cruelty either.

"But there is a new commandant at the garrison in *Kabankalan; Kempetai* say he is more humane. He has made a number of reforms. People working for the Japanese now receive adequate food rations, I hear." *Manong* Alvaro tried to press his point.

"How long is he going to stay in command?" Almanzur countered. "He must be a different breed altogether. The rest of them more bloodthirsty than ever will question his authority. Anyway, even if he remains in command, it's a question of doing too little, too late."

"They can surrender, you know," *Manong* Alvaro still persisted.

"Surrender? Surrender to whom? If they do, that'll be a heyday for all Filipinos. Can you imagine what will happen to them, if they do?" Almanzur could not believe what he heard.

"They will never surrender to Filipinos," *Manong* Alvaro corrected. "American high ranking officers are coming with adequate arms and all kinds of supplies. They'll take over and we'll have to take orders from them. Knowing there is no point in continuing a lost cause, the Japanese may surrender when that time comes, and it will come soon enough," *Manon*g Alvaro maintained.

"I don't believe that'll ever happen. They'll ship their men out to join fortifications in other islands, maybe to re-enforce units in Luzon. They'll defend Manila to the teeth. They won't get out of here unless they have to, let alone surrender. They're fanatics, willing to self-destruct for their Emperor, their country, and their religion."

"You're quite right about that, but we should wait till we know they can't crush us with superior arms and better trained soldiers. At least wait until adequate American aid comes. I don't like to see our men die because we can't fight on equal terms," Alvaro pleaded with his cousin.

Almanzur listened and for the time being yielded to his cousin's counsel. His heart was heavy with his loss but he knew he needed time to reorganize his unit. He was determined to meet with Lt. Procopio Balinas, with Lt. Serafin Verzosa, with Lt Palacious, with Sergeant Peralta and Sergeant Padriga, with Pedring, Munding, Rudi, Nonoy and his trusted aide, Ponsing, and many more. There was a Sergeant Raymundo Valderama and a Lt. Garcia who rescued the pilot, George Miller, and the navigator, Frank Defacio, and the gunner, Robert Coleman. These were brave men who eluded the Japanese and successfully brought the three airmen to the *Hacienda Luzuriaga*. He must contact these men again. He must also find out where Captain Fernando Paterno and Lt. Renato Tabligan are fighting. They had also eluded the Japanese who chased them to Mt. *Kanlaon*. He will trace everyone who has a commendable fighting record. If they get together in one valiant unit, he can convince the American adviser from Australia that he has the manpower to take on the Japanese garrison in *Kabankalan*. Then, perhaps his cousin will be persuaded to command their unit again.

"I'll not wait till the Japanese consolidate their forces in *Bacolod*. Attacking a larger force is even more foolhardy, don't you think? I don't care if the Americans take command, they still have to take on a larger, stronger contingent."

Almanzur never questioned that life is precious, but in his heart he knew that under Japanese rule, it could not be lived with dignity, or with integrity. Tyrants will not allow that of subjects. He had to go on fighting. How long before his turn to go came around, he wouldn't even ask. In this war, life must always be lived in the shadow of death.

Chapter 55—Born into New Life

Captain Almanzur Villalva had become better acquainted with Spencer on the way to *Maricalum.* He admired his fighting spirit and the way he handled the .30 caliber machine gun as though he were still in the B-29 turret. He also noted his soft side, especially his love and devotion for his sister, Milka. He was glad they found each other, but he was sad that she married him, knowing the great risk of losing him when he returned to active duty again. He felt the heavy irony that Spencer was killed, not in battle, but on the way home to recuperate from wounds received in battle. Now his sister is going to have a baby, his baby. What a cruel turn of events! How can she ever bear the heavy hand of destiny?

Poor Milka seemed to be caught in a time warp. She cried as though there was no end to longing. Her mourning couldn't find a shore. Every morning she woke early and walked back to the hideout where she and Spencer met, where they spent a short time of love and happiness. She looked up at the trees that stood very quiet, supporting a heavy network of leaves, dry and windless in the morning shadows, haunted by death and passing time. The weight of her hopelessness hung on her like the leaves on the huge mangrove giants. A hard, receding core of inarticulate longing washed over her as all hope of happiness drained from her. Her spirit felt like a towel wrung dry after it had been soaked in a deep basin of cool, refreshing water.

Aimlessly, she wandered to the narrow waterway. The *batel* was still sitting there. Spencer first made love to her here. A sob got caught in her throat like a splinter of bone from a salted fish. She felt so alone, so desolate, discarded and buried in the midst of nature's indifference to her pain. As time wore on and she got more depressed, she sensed that her cousin, Delia, was very much aware of her pain. Delia mourned her loss with her.

"*Manang* Milka, you still have a life to live no matter what the circumstances; you must find capacity to discover meaning in your life, or you might as well be dead, too, Delia reminded her.

"There's nothing to live for now," Milka lamented. "Sure, I might as well be dead. What do I care?"

Delia retorted. "*Manang* Milka, it is not the predicament you go through that is important as much as the stand you take against it. You're carrying Spencer's baby. Isn't it almost as if Spencer were still with you? If you live for the sake of the baby, you'd live for Spencer's sake, too.

Milka thought long and hard about Delia's statement, turning it round and round in her head, like music that got stuck at one point because the phonograph needle couldn't move. What stand was she taking against the circumstances pitted against her? Alone, sitting by herself in a *banca* in the narrow waterway where the *batel* stood like a sentinel, a silent reminder of her intimate time with Spencer, she brooded. She touched her belly swollen with child and felt comfort in the touch. Spencer's letters always charted the core of her sensitivities. She read them again and again. She always carried them close to her heart and sought the words that awakened her spirit. They made her remember his touch. He wrote to tell her she was important because though remote from him in time and distance, she was as near to the touch as a brilliant flash of memory that sprung from the heart, *for it is only with the heart that one can see clearly.* She felt a quick tug, remembering in sharp detail his constant tenderness. She saw clearly the softness in his tear-filled eyes as he wiped away her own tears at parting. There was no hiding the pain in them then, though that was somewhat obscured by the promise of a future together.

Now that future was cancelled. But what a treasury of feeling they had stored in their brief exchange! She heaved a deep sigh of longing. Starved for a connection, she dimly understood why she felt alone and abandoned. Why, he was with her all along! She was going to have his baby! When the baby comes, she'd hold him in her arms again. He'd never be gone from her. He'd be dearly treasured as long as she lived.

I know what I have to do, she told herself. I'll ask *Manong* Alvaro to write an official letter to Spencer's folks and tell them about me and I'll write and tell them about Spencer's baby, our baby. She couldn't wait. With the thought of their child, she lingered longer at the places where she and Spencer spent time together, and looking up, she no longer saw death in the leaves on the trees. The giant mangrove trees had been a comfort to Spencer. Now, they were to her too. Their greenness signaled new life. Spencer's parents and his sister, especially, were delighted to hear about her and the baby, so she wrote them a grateful letter. In part the letter read:

"It is April and that means BABY. As you read this letter I could already have our baby this late March, though the due date is April 12th. My sister, *Manang* Norma, a nurse at the army hospital in *Caliling* where Spencer and I spent time, says she is a girl. I have already chosen her name, and my cousin, *Manang* Panching, has stocked a small crib full of tiny pink outfits she made with her hands. But the doctor says the baby stays too low in my belly to be a girl. He thinks it's a boy. I lie awake at night in anticipation of what's to come. I think I'll leave everything to God. Sometimes, ignorance really is bliss. If it's a boy, he'll remind everyone of Spencer. If it's a girl, Spencer thought a lot about his sister especially at times when they were in great danger of being captured by the Japanese. She'll be named after her. How would you like that, my dear sister-in-law?"

She went on and on and kept Delia in tears when she read the rest of the letter. Thank God her *Manang* Milka now looks forward to a full life even without Spencer; yes, hopefully with a little Spencer.

"Delia," Milka said sadly, "the choice is not mine to make, but I pray to God the baby will be a boy; then, perhaps, I can learn a different kind of happiness."

Spencer Ridley, Jr., a bouncing 6 pounds 8 ounces healthy baby, was born on April 5th. Milka gave birth in *Caliling*. *Manong* Almanzor insisted that she return there in the refurbished *batel*. Spencer junior's coming was much awaited by the entire medical staff devoted to his father when he was a patient in *Caliling*.

Once more, everyone relived the excitement of welcoming all nine airmen whom everyone got attached to during their brief stay. The Luzuriaga family postponed going home to the *hacienda* in anticipation of this new birth. *Tio* Mauring asked the special favor of being Godfather to *Kapitan* Almanzur's nephew. This newcomer looked so much like his father he made all feel as though Spencer had returned not only in spirit but also in the flesh.

Chapter 56—The Last Days in Hiding

News that both Spencer and Marco were in a plane blasted in the pacific skies on their way home saddened everyone. Looking at the bars of soap wrapped in the piece of *patadiong* Marco sent back from the submarine, Delia sobbed in anguish. With it was a note of thanks to the entire Gomez clan with a special message for Delia.

"Little one," it said, "I shall never forget you and the *banca* ride in the large earthen jars. I loved our conversations in the swamp hideout before the Japanese demolished it. Remember, the note stressed, the moon that shines in the swamps shines on Chicago too. I look forward to taking you around Chicago someday.

"Oh. Marco," she whispered every time she looked at the moon and the stars through the tall mangrove trees, "the same moon shines here as it does on Chicago or wherever you are. I swear, someday I'll go to Chicago to meet your folks and tell them about the difficult time we had here together. Maybe I'll get a tour of the museums and hear an opera with your sister."

The leaves turned backward in the trees. This observation came with some local wisdom. At the sight, Delia was sure a welcome rain was coming at last. It had been a long, dry summer. The water level in the river was unusually low. By mid morning, a trickle of rain came and dusted the leaves off but it was not enough to spray the brush along the tributaries that coiled underneath the giant mangrove trees. Twigs along the banks got brown and brittle; they sagged into the waterways and clogged the narrow passage into the swamps. The shells buried in the mud above the receding waterline rotted. No longer edible, they festered and added to the smell of decay in the surrounding area.

Victor and Rodney walked shirtless and were in ragged shorts. The women removed their blouses and tied their *patadiongs* on their shoulders. Though they constantly dived and swam after they paddled out to the main river, Alvaro Jr. and Arturo turned dark from the sun but found little relief in the warm water. Delia had just paddled them in from the main river. They walked through the dry path on the *barasbaras* trail where the *bancas* used to push through flowing water. The afternoon turned dark and windy. The clouds lifted high and curled into thick circles like smoke from a smoldering chimney. The air got hotter and the humidity so heavy you could almost cut it with a blade. This was the rain the leaves had signaled.

"Run, boys, get home and help your *nanay* (mother) close the windows before the wind blows them away. Use the rope and tie them to the posts. When is your *tatay* (father) supposed to arrive home? Don't stop to answer. Run. The rain is going to pour any minute."

Delia rushed to the kitchen as she spoke. Mama Sid stood stoking coals on the earth stove.

"Ma, I better dowse the embers before this wind blows them into a fire we can't put out. We'll see how long this rain lasts. Where's everybody?"

"Your Papa was fetching water for me down by the waterway. Rodney and Victor ran to the storage hut to secure it from the rising wind. Your *Manang* Panching sat by the window sewing clothes for Milka's baby. I made her stop; it was getting too dark to see. She must be inside the house making sure the windows are bolted. Go down and help your Papa. Make sure he gets home before the rain pours."

Mama Sid got worried. Delia's father was nonchalant even about circumstances that threatened terror or death. Delia ran to look for him. They made it back to the hut before the rain poured. Mama Sid got all the cans ready to catch the rainwater. They wouldn't have to fetch water from *Man*g Kari's well any more after this rain. As was her custom whenever she faced some danger she was not sure how to avoid, Mama Sid softly sang a hymn.

"Rock of Ages, cleft for me. Let me hide myself in thee."

She hummed the music more than sang the words. They all huddled together in the middle of the hut holding each other close. Delia crouched in front of her Papa. He held her in his arms and bent his head on her shoulders. She held her mother's hands while her older sister wrapped her arms around her mother. They had been in rainstorms fiercer than this before. They shoved blankets into buckets and turned them upside down so they would stay dry and warm. After the rain, they would all be soaked and wet. They would need them to dry out.

Wind shook the *nipa* walls threatening to drive the water right through it. Victor had made sure the thatched roof was reinforced with thick *nipa* fronds so water didn't leak from above. Delia wondered how he and Rodney fared in the tiny storage hut. An hour after the wind rose and the heavy rain poured, Delia could hear the boys screaming. She wrapped herself in extra clothes and ran out to their hut to see what was wrong. Wind had blown part of the roof away and the boys were terrified. She took her *Manang* Aning's hand, instructed the boys to hold on to each other and to her. Quickly, she half dragged everyone to the house where they sat with the rest of the family. Mama Sid was still softly humming the hymn and her Papa closed his eyes in silent prayer. Shivering from the cold wind, they huddled closely into each other's arms to keep themselves from shaking. They knew that sharing each other's body heat was the only way to suffer the fierce wind that blew and soaked them and made them shake from the cold and damp air despite the dense humidity.

Two days later, after heavy rain ceased, the family assessed damage to huts. The tropical sun blazed as hot as ever. The girls hang every piece of clothing out to dry. Victor and Rodney patched the holes on the walls and repaired the roof on *Manang* Aning's hut. They restored and thatched it with as much *nipa* leaves as they could gather, knowing that the same heavy, blinding rain could pour again. They paid imperative attention to the remaining food supply. Rain had soaked the sacks of rice stored in the tiny hut. The rice had to be dried before it got moldy and unfit to eat.

Life in the swamps was not easy. Between the spells of drought and the heavy downpours in the typhoon season, Delia and her family suffered privations the war brought on. Threat of hunger always hung on, though, somehow, fishing in the sea or hard work making salt to trade for rice fed everyone. Following the narrow waterways which coiled into the swamps like endless, dark corridors that took them away from the danger of Japanese capture, the family survived the Japanese assaults in the past three and a half years of the war that started in 1941. In those years, as soon as they were able to make themselves comfortable in one spot, the threat of discovery and danger of a Japanese assault disrupted their lives, creating pain, anxiety, and terror. But they moved on, following the corridors, deeper and deeper into the heart of the swamps.

They thought they had moved far enough at the hideout the Japanese demolished. Victor and Delia made that hideout more comfortable than any they had lived in before. That was their safety zone, a haven of unbelievable beauty bordered by the ugly smell of mud. There, the unpredictability of constant moving stopped. That was the last refuge against the vagaries of war. So they thought. But Delia paddled the surviving crew of a B-29 into that paradise and the Japanese blasted it.

The shallow waterways were drying up, but so was the war. This was the end of almost four long, agonizing years of ceaseless use of the corridors of pain into the heart of darkness. This *barasbaras* trail was the end of the line.

A month later, late in 1944, everyone enjoyed a lazy day. The little boys were fishing by the riverbank. Papa was reading the Bible and Mama Sid was grilling fresh fish on coconut charcoal. *Manang* Panching was mending Victor and Rodney's torn shirts. Both were waiting, shirtless, in a *banca* with Delia at the prow, dangling her feet in the cool waterway.

The sound came loud and clear. It rose in an unbelievably deafening crescendo. The unmistakable sound of airplanes shattered the silence. Not one or two but dozens, no, hundreds! Never had there been so many Japanese airplanes before. But no bombs fell. No bullets from machine guns threatened. Curiosity got the better of everyone. No one even bothered to run or hide.

In utter disbelief, people looked up at the sky covered by dozens of huge B-29s, smaller B-24s, medium-sized B-17s, and the small, doublebodied Lockheeds, fighter planes used to protect the larger bombers. There was no doubt about it. These planes were different from any that had flown by before. These are American planes! Every *banca* paddled out to the main river. People were yelling and screaming; they came out of the woodwork, so to say. They banged pots and pans, tin water containers, anything that made loud noise. Surely, the planes must hear their jubilation!

The airplanes moved in a patterned parade. They clogged the sky above. No sight could be more welcomed! The airplanes droned for what seemed like hours. People tirelessly continued to pound on whatever they could bang on. They banged on *bancas* with paddles. They turned hoarse from shouting cheers and welcome. Tears of joy flowed freely. They had been waiting for this event for years!

This was the final proof of deliverance! General MacArthur had kept his promise. He had returned. American liberation was now a reality. The war was finally over. The Japanese would abandon their garrisons in the south and congregate in *Bacolod.* Now everyone could prepare to get out of the swamps. They could all go home, at last.

Delia waved wildly at the passing parade. She cheered, shouted, laughed, and cried her heart out. Instinctively, she raised her paddle up to the sky in some form of a salute. For all she knew, George Miller,

Bradley Baker, Frank Defacio, Robert Coleman, Joe West, Romero Valdez, and the spirit of Scott Rankin, Spencer Ridley, and Marco Yablowski could be flying in the lead planes.

Acknowledgments

I like to thank the members of a fiction writing class at the West Campus of Pima Community College in Tucson, Arizona for thoroughly enjoying my very first drafts for this book. All of the members of the class, including the professor, Meg Files, had very positive comments about the quality of the writing. They all encouraged me to go on and finish the manuscript and try to publish it. If I ever doubted my capacity to write, I never did after their endorsement.

I like to thank my niece, Carla P. Gomez, in *Bacolod* City, Negros Occidental, Philippines, for her interest in this book, for taking me to places I could use as part of the setting of the story and making available materials that I could incorporate in this book.

I also want to thank my nephew, Dr. Arturo A. Gomez, for reading the first draft of my manuscript and for saying he did not want to put it down before he finished reading it. It is a riveting story.

Thanks are also due to my neighbors Gail Knudsen, and Mary Elaine Deaton for helping to edit typing, spelling, and other errors in the first two hundred pages of the book.

The Northwest Arkansas Writers' Guild has been very helpful with editing and encouragement when I can submit four pages for their perusal at our weekly meetings.

I owe the most to my friend, Ryan Smith, for his invaluable help in formatting the entire manuscript and for making sure I can send it and all other requirements in acceptable form to my publisher on time. I am not proficient with computer use. Ryan has been really patient and most serviceable. I couldn't have done what I needed to do without his help.

I like to thank Hil Mallory of Writers Literary Group for suggesting that I look into the Internet and get in touch with EloquentBooks.Com.

I wish to thank Elizabeth Page, Acquisitions Editor for EB.Com and to Lynn Ellie, Director of Administration for EloquentBooks.Com for their encouragement and invaluable help in getting this book published.

Printed in the United States
130516LV00001B/200/P